The Boston Jazz Chronicles

Faces, Places, and Nightlife 1937–1962

Richard Vacca

TROY STREET PUBLISHING, LLC
Belmont, Massachusetts

Troy Street Publishing, LLC

www.troystreet.com

Copyright © 2012 by Richard Vacca

The Boston Jazz Chronicles: Faces, Places, and Nightlife 1937–1962

ISBN 978-0-9839910-0-7

ATTENTION CORPORATIONS, UNIVERSITIES, COLLEGES, AND PROFESSIONAL ORGANIZATIONS: Quantity discounts are available on bulk purchases of this book for educational or gift purposes, or as premiums for increasing magazine subscriptions or renewals. Special books or book excerpts can also be created to fit specific needs. For information, please contact Troy Street Publishing, LLC, P.O. Box 477, Belmont, Massachusetts, 02478, or info@troystreet.com.

For my brother
Robert A. Vacca
1940–2004

Contents

Preface

The Boston Jazz Chronicles started because I like to walk, and because I like history, and especially because I like jazz.

Back in 2004, my plan was to create a walking tour that would guide tourists and townies alike through Boston's jazz history, one of the better stories about this city that most don't know. Boston has a rich jazz history, and I wanted to uncover it and bring it to life. I had no intention of joining the tedious debate about what jazz is and who is entitled to play it, and not being a musician myself, I wasn't going to try to interpret the ambitions and motivations of those who played the music 60 years ago. I saw my role as that of reporter, not critic, and my intent was to leave it to others to intuit deeper meanings.

The first task was to find places to walk to, and I soon learned that most of the places of Boston jazz are gone, demolished to make way for apartments, office buildings, expressway ramps, and parking lots. Some burned down. The few sites that remain house enterprises far removed from jazz music—storefronts, sandwich shops, private residences. A few are still nightclubs, but there hasn't been a lick of jazz heard within them in years. This was not a promising start.

It seemed a better option was to collect stories, find pictures, and assemble a book—an armchair walking tour. That's the first book I wrote, but that's not the book you hold in your hands. This book, though still organized primarily around places, is ordered chronologically. It sets those places in context better than the armchair walking tour did.

The earlier emphasis on geography did, however, lead to the creation of the Boston jazz maps, which start on page 7. These maps are true to the years of these chronicles; Broadway still runs from Park Square all the way to South Boston, Warrenton Street hasn't been rerouted, and Westfield Street still exists. Much changed in the physical city in the years immediately following this story.

I had three audiences in mind for the *Boston Jazz Chronicles*. One was the jazz fan, the person who knows who Lester Young was and why Dizzy Gillespie was important, but might not know about Dean Earl, who played piano in Boston for 60 years, or where the Hi-Hat nightclub was and what happened to it. The second audience was people who just like to know about all things Boston. They're pleased to learn, for instance, that a ballroom where their grandmother jitterbugged was just up the block from Symphony Hall.

The third group was the people who were on the scene and lived this story, and who want to stroll again beneath the bright marquees of their own Memory Lanes.

These chronicles cover the years 1937 to 1962. I picked these mid-century years for two reasons. First, I couldn't do all 100 years of Boston jazz because the result would be as thick as the phone book, and the jazz created in the postwar years and the 1950s is some of my favorite music. Second, I always pick these years. The story of the American city at mid-century has long fascinated me. Cities were immigrant entryways, ethnic bastions, economic engines, artistic crucibles, and media centers. Then at mid-century came suburbanization, and the urban environment as people knew it came undone. This is not a book about the development of the New Boston, but that development is the backdrop before which all this jazz, a city sound, was played.

Starting in the late 1930s was a practical decision; I needed to go back just far enough to give a context to the years that form the bulk of the story. We can better understand the postwar scene if we can see how the swing era built its foundation. Swing was king in 1937, Prohibition was forgotten, and the big bands were packing the dance halls. Jazz was as close to being America's popular music as it would ever be.

The material itself told me when to stop. Much changed in the early 1960s in the world of Boston jazz. Key people moved on, important venues shut down, popular tastes changed. The years 1960 to 1962 were a time of transition for many in our cast of characters, and new beginnings, and new conflicts, too, were all around— in jazz, in the city, in the society. It was the time of the New Frontier, the civil rights movement, urban renewal, the space race, the arms race, and the generation gap. Boston—and America—was into the sixties. That's a whole different story.

What's In, What's Out

I'd like to say this book is about jazz and nothing but jazz, but that's not the case.

Jazz in these years borrowed much from popular music and gave much back in return, and the line separating the two is not so easily drawn. Nor was the line so easily drawn for the ones making the music. It was difficult to make a living as a full-time jazz musician in a place like Boston. There wasn't enough work even in the best of times. To keep body and soul together, the jazz musicians worked in society bands, floor show bands, dance bands, theater orchestras, and any number of general business situations. They brought their jazz sensibilities to their other musical work. A nightclub like the Latin

Quarter wasn't a "jazz club," but jazz musicians played there, and some of the house bands fairly bristled with jazz talent. The club mattered to their livelihoods, and if the Latin Quarter was a mainstream nightclub with jazz tendencies, there were jazz clubs with mainstream tendencies, too. From the Cotton Club-styled revues at Southland to doo-wop music at the Hi-Hat to folk music at Storyville, club owners always did what they needed to do to put paying customers in the seats. If this story sometimes strays from one that is strictly jazz-fueled, it's because the people and places in the story strayed first.

As a window open only to the middle of the century, numerous notable Bostonians are absent, such as Harry Carney, who was too early, and Terri Lyne Carrington, who is too late. Likewise, stories of the Lido Venice are too early, and those of Lulu White's are too late. Wonderful people and places all, but we save their stories for another day.

There are similar omissions with Boston born-and-bred musicians of the right age who left Boston when young. First in this group is the drummer Roy Haynes, but also singer Dave Lambert, violinist and concert master Gene Orloff, guitarist Turk Van Lake, pianist Steve Kuhn, and a whole raft of saxophonists, including Roz Cron, Hal McKusick, Boomie Richman, and Sonny Stitt. There are also musicians who should be part of this story but were omitted because I couldn't learn anything about them. Research revealed next to nothing about musicians such as Herbie Lee, Walter Sisco, and Eddie Watson, and I wasn't fortunate enough to encounter anyone who could tell me about them.

Whenever the topic is Boston nightlife, people want to know about Scollay Square and the Cocoanut Grove. Neither was a particularly jazzy place, and we drop by both but don't stay long. Both are amply documented elsewhere. I've also omitted the well-known Blinstrub's Village. Stanley Blinstrub was not interested in jazz, and it was a rare week indeed when he booked a jazz group at his South Boston nightclub.

Boston in the middle of the twentieth century differed from the present-day city in ways other than the people and places of its nightlife. The economy, demographics, media, laws governing nightlife, and the cost of a night out were quite different from today. A short primer on those topics can be found in the Appendix starting on page 286.

It was the fashion of reporters and editors in these years to overlook the foibles and shortcomings of the news makers to concentrate on reporting the news, and I've done that here. You'll have to look elsewhere for stories about adultery, alcoholism, or addiction. Yes, some people slept around. Yes, some musicians drank away their careers and ruined their lives. Yes, many musicians were pot smokers and some used hard drugs. That, too, ruined careers and lives, and in a few cases, ended them. We can't avoid the facts, but we can skip the salacious details. If you have a taste for vice and headlines of the "Love Den Gal in Slip; Raiding Squad Catches Brunette in Scanties" type, you'll find them in the *Mid-Town Journal*, published weekly in Boston between 1938 and 1966.

There have always been questions about the role of "the criminal element" in the nightclub business. Not just in the speakeasies—those were illegal operations from the moment the doors opened—but in clubs operating in the years after Repeal and throughout these two decades. There are some well-documented cases of criminal association or official corruption, and then there is a sea of speculation. I have no proof that mobsters ran nightclubs or public officials were on the take. "Everybody knows that" doesn't constitute a green light to publish. No matter how well you label speculation as just that, somebody else will put it in a blog next month and call it gospel truth. I've heard the stories about bribery and protection rackets and late-night fires of suspicious origin—but if I can't prove it, I didn't write it. I'll tell you about the fires, and you can draw your own conclusions.

Sources

The public record is "old school," tattered city directories and reels of microfilm of varying quality at the Boston Public Library. Boston's newspapers from this era are not digitized and not likely to be, and almost nothing prior to 1980 is online and easily searched. The media sources themselves are gone; the *Post*, the *Chronicle*, and the *Daily Record* are already 50 years gone. When the witnesses to those years pass, that microfilm will be all that stands between us and forgetting. That is a scary thought.

Even if the tape proves to be indestructible, its content is sometimes barren. For years the papers paid scant attention to the people and places of popular music, especially in the African-American community, which the mainstream media pretended did not exist. Other than the column written by George Frazier in the *Herald* in 1942, Vin Haynes through the fifties in the *Chronicle*, and John McLellan in the *Traveler* between 1957 and 1961, there is little in the papers, and what you do find is often determined by who bought advertising. Of great help in documenting the scene of years ago were two newspapermen who weren't writing about jazz directly, but it found its way into their work. Bill Buchanan wrote about radio and television for the *Daily Record* in the late fifties and early sixties and often commented on musical matters, and George C. Clarke, the observer of all things nightlife, wrote his widely read daily column "Around Boston" for the *Daily Record* through this entire period.

Boston was covered by the national music press in these years, primarily in *The Billboard*, *Down Beat* and *Metronome*, and like the papers, these were available only on film (in the past few years, *Billboard's* back issues have been digitized.) Since *Metronome* ceased publication in 1961, it's doubtful we'll see it online any time soon.

Long story short: I spent a lot of time reading microfilm, for both the Boston papers and the national jazz press, and then more time looking at hard copies of anything people were willing to share: program notes, newsletters, direct mail pieces, scrapbooks, liner notes. The result was a reasonably good picture of what was happening in the Boston clubs and halls during this time. If my Boston-centric thumbnail histories of musicians herein vary from those in the established sources, such as the various editions of Leonard Feather's *Encyclopedia of Jazz* or the invaluable *New Grove Dictionary of Jazz*, it's because my research disagrees with those sources. If I've made mistakes, I take responsibility for them.

Photographs add immeasurably to a book such as this, but determining copyright ownership proved to be especially challenging. No one knows who took some of these photographs 60 or 70 years ago. I attempted to find and contact the copyright holders of all images, and I've provided such credit as I can in the accompanying captions. I invite you to contact Troy Street Publishing if your image was used without identification or acknowledgment. Images appearing with no credits whatsoever are from my own collection.

Some fine books written over the past decade or so shine quite a bit of light on the local scene. Autobiographies of Nat Hentoff (*Boston Boy*) and George Wein (*Myself Among Others*) are required reading. Biographies of Serge Chaloff (*Serge Chaloff*, by Vladimir Simosko) and Dick Twardzik (*Bouncin' with Bartok*, by Jack Chambers) offer insights into bebop-era Boston. The Berklee School of Music (it wasn't yet a college) and its forerunner, Schillinger House, are well documented in Ed Hazell's *Berklee: The First Fifty Years*. Information on these and other resources of local interest are listed in the Bibliography.

I relied on many interviews, my own and others in published sources. But memory is imperfect and subject to the tricks of time, and it was a long time ago. Two people often remember the same event differently. Not only did these events happen decades ago, they were often not the stuff of memories. Some of the musicians with stories to tell had long careers, and Boston was often just a stop along the way. Their greatest triumphs and disappointments happened elsewhere. Boston memories are thin, even for some musicians born and raised in the city. A musician who remained in Boston might recall with relish the week he substituted with the Duke Ellington Orchestra, and well he should, for it was a crowning moment. Forgotten are the hundred nights on a corner-bar bandstand with a drummer who couldn't keep time, which is bad luck for someone like me, trying to learn about those corner-bar bandstands.

Many of my interviews took place when I was working on the armchair walking tour, and the set of questions I asked then was different from the set I asked later in the process—I was asking questions about places, not about the people themselves, and missed a golden opportunity to add to what we know about some of the mid-century musicians. Unfortunately, in some cases there was no chance for a second interview. Time does march on.

There are many books on jazz in print. There are general histories, collections of essays and columns, analyses of particular styles of music or periods of time, biographies and autobiographies, and histories of events and record labels. There are books about cities, but most are about New Orleans and New York. A small number of titles look at other places. Among them are *Before Motown: A History of Jazz in Detroit 1920–1960* by Lars Bjorn with Jim Gallert; *Kansas City Jazz: From Ragtime to Bebop—A History* by Frank Driggs and Chuck Haddix; *Central Avenue Sounds: Jazz in Los Angeles* by a group of writers working as the Central Avenue Sounds Editorial Committee; William Howland Kenney's *Chicago Jazz: A Cultural History, 1904–1930*; and Barbara J. Kukla's *Swing City: Newark Nightlife, 1926–50*. This is the company which the present work aspires to keep, and to all of the authors I owe a debt of gratitude for showing me the way.[1]

That's the what, when, and why of it. The rest is in the reading. I set out to make *The Boston Jazz Chronicles* both informative and entertaining, and I hope that is how you find it.

Boston was covered by the national music press in these years, primarily in *The Billboard*, *Down Beat* and *Metronome*, and like the papers, these were available only on film (in the past few years, *Billboard's* back issues have been digitized.) Since *Metronome* ceased publication in 1961, it's doubtful we'll see it online any time soon.

Long story short: I spent a lot of time reading microfilm, for both the Boston papers and the national jazz press, and then more time looking at hard copies of anything people were willing to share: program notes, newsletters, direct mail pieces, scrapbooks, liner notes. The result was a reasonably good picture of what was happening in the Boston clubs and halls during this time. If my Boston-centric thumbnail histories of musicians herein vary from those in the established sources, such as the various editions of Leonard Feather's *Encyclopedia of Jazz* or the invaluable *New Grove Dictionary of Jazz*, it's because my research disagrees with those sources. If I've made mistakes, I take responsibility for them.

Photographs add immeasurably to a book such as this, but determining copyright ownership proved to be especially challenging. No one knows who took some of these photographs 60 or 70 years ago. I attempted to find and contact the copyright holders of all images, and I've provided such credit as I can in the accompanying captions. I invite you to contact Troy Street Publishing if your image was used without identification or acknowledgment. Images appearing with no credits whatsoever are from my own collection.

Some fine books written over the past decade or so shine quite a bit of light on the local scene. Autobiographies of Nat Hentoff (*Boston Boy*) and George Wein (*Myself Among Others*) are required reading. Biographies of Serge Chaloff (*Serge Chaloff*, by Vladimir Simosko) and Dick Twardzik (*Bouncin' with Bartok*, by Jack Chambers) offer insights into bebop-era Boston. The Berklee School of Music (it wasn't yet a college) and its forerunner, Schillinger House, are well documented in Ed Hazell's *Berklee: The First Fifty Years*. Information on these and other resources of local interest are listed in the Bibliography.

I relied on many interviews, my own and others in published sources. But memory is imperfect and subject to the tricks of time, and it was a long time ago. Two people often remember the same event differently. Not only did these events happen decades ago, they were often not the stuff of memories. Some of the musicians with stories to tell had long careers, and Boston was often just a stop along the way. Their greatest triumphs and disappointments happened elsewhere. Boston memories are thin, even for some musicians born and raised in the city. A musician who remained in Boston might recall with relish the week he substituted with the Duke Ellington Orchestra, and well he should, for it was a crowning moment. Forgotten are the hundred nights on a corner-bar bandstand with a drummer who couldn't keep time, which is bad luck for someone like me, trying to learn about those corner-bar bandstands.

Many of my interviews took place when I was working on the armchair walking tour, and the set of questions I asked then was different from the set I asked later in the process—I was asking questions about places, not about the people themselves, and missed a golden opportunity to add to what we know about some of the mid-century musicians. Unfortunately, in some cases there was no chance for a second interview. Time does march on.

There are many books on jazz in print. There are general histories, collections of essays and columns, analyses of particular styles of music or periods of time, biographies and autobiographies, and histories of events and record labels. There are books about cities, but most are about New Orleans and New York. A small number of titles look at other places. Among them are *Before Motown: A History of Jazz in Detroit 1920–1960* by Lars Bjorn with Jim Gallert; *Kansas City Jazz: From Ragtime to Bebop—A History* by Frank Driggs and Chuck Haddix; *Central Avenue Sounds: Jazz in Los Angeles* by a group of writers working as the Central Avenue Sounds Editorial Committee; William Howland Kenney's *Chicago Jazz: A Cultural History, 1904–1930*; and Barbara J. Kukla's *Swing City: Newark Nightlife, 1926–50*. This is the company which the present work aspires to keep, and to all of the authors I owe a debt of gratitude for showing me the way.[1]

That's the what, when, and why of it. The rest is in the reading. I set out to make *The Boston Jazz Chronicles* both informative and entertaining, and I hope that is how you find it.

Acknowledgments

I had a lot of help.

Genevieve Niessen provided the excellent maps of Huntington Avenue, Copley Square, the South End, and the Theatre District. Ms. Niessen's maps are based on a 1940 map of the city, and they show Boston as it was during these 25 years, before decades of urban renewal removed landmarks and rerouted streets.

Al Ehrenfried, Janet Murphy, Frank Newcomb, Steve Provizer, Don Stratton, and Bob Young read the manuscript and offered comments and suggestions at various points in its development.

Research materials specific to Boston jazz proved elusive, and in particular I thank Jack Bradley and Dan Kochakian for their ongoing assistance in finding source materials, recordings, and photographs.

I am grateful to Dan Kochakian, the Berklee College of Music, the *Boston Herald, Jazz Journal,* and *DownBeat* magazine for granting permission to reprint previously published materials.

DownBeat presents a special case. Throughout the text, I used the magazine's name as it was through these 25 years—*Down Beat*, with a space. For at least the past 20 years, however, its name has been *DownBeat*, no space. It is the same magazine, and my hope is that this note will allay any confusion that might arise from seeing *Down Beat* quoted on the same page as the *DownBeat* Archives are credited for use of a previously published image.

The staffs of many archives and libraries provided worthy assistance. In particular I wish to thank Anne Vosikas and Nancy Richard of the Bostonian Society, who taught me much about getting it right, and a sizable crew at the Boston Public Library, in the Print Department, Microtext Department, and the Music Library.

I visited numerous other institutions, including the Boston Athenaeum, the Boston City Archives, the *Boston Herald* library, Boston Symphony Hall Archives, Historic New England, the Massachusetts Department of Vital Records, New England Conservatory of Music's Spaulding Library, Northeastern University's Snell Library, the Stan Getz Library at the Berklee College of Music, the Rotch Library of Architecture & Planning at the Massachusetts Institute of Technology, the Simmons College Archives, the Institute of Jazz Studies at Rutgers University, and the New Hampshire

Library of Traditional Jazz at the University of New Hampshire in Durham. My thanks to all.

Thanks also to my editor, Sue Collier, and to Juanita Dix, whose evocative cover design integrates the photograph of Nishan Bichajian.

Finally, my deepest thanks go to the men and women who were on the scene and generously shared their time and their memories with me. The list is long, and I omit it for fear of leaving someone out. Sadly, some have died since the time of our conversations, and their passing makes today's scene less bright. I hope this book honors their memories.

Introduction

The story of jazz is a story of cities. In the popular telling of that story, the first city is New Orleans, credited as the birthplace of jazz. It emerged from that city's rich musical stew, a bubbling mix of ragtime, minstrelsy, European concert music, spirituals, back-country blues, and brass bands. It was the birthplace of Louis Armstrong, the music's first superstar and the eminence from whom so much inspiration flowed.

Then jazz moved up the Mississippi River to its second city, Chicago, where it learned its big-city ways in the cabarets and speakeasies of the 1920s. It swept across the wide-open southwest and didn't stop until it got to Kansas City, the Paris of the Plains, where its bluesy, driving swing became synonymous with thirties jazz—and the sound of Count Basie's band.

It was New York, though, that became the jazz capitol of the world and the place that attracted talented musicians from all the other cities. From the early days of syncopation in the 1910s, to the Harlem Stride piano men, to the musically advanced orchestras of Fletcher Henderson and Duke Ellington in the 1920s, to the eruption of big band swing in the 1930s, New York was every bit the Big Apple. By the time the world went to war, there wasn't much room left for any other place in the popular story.

As fine as it was, though, New York had no monopoly on jazz. Perhaps New Orleans, Chicago, and Kansas City never reclaimed their prewar heights, but their musicians didn't stop making music. And what of other places? Jazz is a city sound, so what about Detroit, Philadelphia, St. Louis, or a dozen more? Musicians in those places weren't standing still, either. There were jazz scenes in all of them, smaller than New York's but vibrant nonetheless.

Let's add one more city to this list: Boston, Massachusetts. Boston not only had an active jazz scene, it had an important one, worthy of a prominent place on the jazz map. Of modest size before Pearl Harbor, the scene grew amidst the bustle of wartime activity in a busy port town. The late 1940s and 1950s were a time of tremendous energy and creativity both on stage and off. Boston was an incubator of musical talent, a training ground for jazz journalists, a magnet for music education, and a proving ground for new approaches in jazz presentation. Other cities made contributions as well, but Boston was unique in that it made major contributions to all of them. It wasn't only about playing notes. It was about building a scene.

Although our Boston story starts in the late 1930s, after the repeal of Prohibition and in the midst of the big band era, the city's full story starts years earlier, in the music's first decades. There were black musicians playing jazz in the 1910s, the same decade they formed their own local in the American Federation of Musicians (AFM). AFM Local 535 was chartered in August 1915.

Even back then Boston had trouble hanging on to talent. Jazzmen were leaving Boston for New York while people were still singing "Over There." By the early 1920s musicians from Boston or with strong Boston ties, such as Charlie Dixon, Kaiser Marshall, Phil Napoleon, and Tom Whaley were making an impact far beyond the city limits.

There were dark days in those early years, two in particular. On May 9, 1919, James Reese Europe, an important figure in the development of black music and arguably the country's best-known black bandleader, was stabbed backstage at Mechanics Hall by his drummer, and died later that day. His death was a serious loss for American music. Six years later, early in the morning on July 4, 1925, the Beach Street building housing the Pickwick Club collapsed. Some actually blamed the catastrophe on McGlennon's Jazz Orchestra, whose hot playing so inflamed the dancers that their vigorous Charleston shook the building to the point of its destruction. Forty-four people died, and in the popular imagination, it was a jazz band's fault.

The Pickwick Club was one venue among many that were part of a burgeoning dance scene in the 1920s. It was a period of feverish activity in Boston and all of New England, and at the center of it was Charlie Shribman, who controlled bookings for a ballroom network that stretched across the Northeast. Shribman was a kingmaker in the band business, and together with his brother Cy, made Mal Hallett a star, and played a significant role in the early career of Duke Ellington. They owned ballrooms, financed bands, and used radio and publicity as well as anyone in the business. It was Ellington who said, "There wouldn't be a band business if it wasn't for Charlie Shribman. He's kept the whole racket going and a lot of guys would be starving if he hadn't helped them."[1]

Shribman was abetted by the geography of New England. Physical distance was the enemy of the road band. Bands mostly rode busses, and across most of the country, the distance between one-night engagements could be 300 miles or more, a distance that had to be covered overnight. It was a dreadful way to live. But in the northeast, no such distance separated the population centers. The jumps were a much more manageable 50 or 75 miles, and Shribman arranged a booking in all of them. Musicians follow the work, and Shribman had the work. His circuit made the dance-crazy northeast the big band capital of the country in the 1920s and 1930s.

A deep talent pool emerged in Boston in the 1920s, a whole generation of jazz musicians we now associate with swing. They were born in the early years of the century and came of age before the stock market crashed. Most were African-Americans. They grew up together, played in schoolboy bands together, and became professional musicians together. Their careers were well underway before Congress repealed the Volstead Act in 1933. Some went on to long careers and a few achieved great fame. They flourished in New York and many lived out their lives as members of that city's jazz scene. Others made their way west to Los Angeles and the Hollywood studios. A few went to Europe. The reason for leaving Boston was simple: The opportunities were elsewhere, and the best opportunities were in New York.

New York has a prominent role in the Boston story; it isn't only in baseball that Boston has a troubled relationship with the Big Apple. Boston has both suffered and prospered from its proximity. On the one hand, it meant good New York players were frequent visitors to Boston, enriching the local scene in numerous ways. On the other, New York was constantly siphoning off Boston players. New York was where they went to grow as musicians and make a living. Boston was a town where a musician kept a bag packed…the call might come at any time.

An exhaustive list would be well beyond our scope, but a few names, a "best of Boston," can stand in, and we'll limit the list to saxophonists. Harry Carney, jazz's first great baritone saxophonist, joined the Duke Ellington Orchestra in 1927. As Duke's longest tenured musician, he anchored the saxophone section for 47 years, staying with Ellington until the very end. Johnny Hodges went with Chick Webb in 1927 and Ellington's Orchestra in 1928, and there he became one of the most influential alto saxophone players in the history of jazz. Charlie Holmes, a childhood friend of Hodges and like him an alto player, moved to New York in 1927 and over the years worked with Louis Armstrong, the Mills Blue Rhythm Band, and many others. Howard "Swan" Johnson, yet another alto player, was in New York with Benny Carter by 1928, and was one of the few swing musicians of his generation to make the jump to bebop, working in Dizzy Gillespie's late-forties big band. Still another alto saxophonist, Nuncio "Toots" Mondello, joined Mal Hallett's band in 1926 and Benny Goodman's in 1933. He became one of the most sought-after lead altos in the business and reigned for years as one of the princes of the New York studios.

The list of worthies quickly grows long. They were all Bostonians, a gang of glorious musicians who came and went before our story really starts—but without them, there wouldn't *be* a story. They were the teachers and mentors, the friendly faces in distant places, and the inspirations for the next generation.

The talent drain was significant, but Boston was fortunate in that it kept a core of veteran musicians who for reasons of family or lifestyle chose to stay, and we'll meet many in the following chapters. If saxophonists showed a tendency to leave Boston, the pianists showed a tendency to stay, and among them were Highland Diggs, Preston "Sandy" Sandiford, Mabel Robinson, and Sabby Lewis.

William Sebastian "Sabby" Lewis was the most important figure in Boston jazz in the 1940s; if we had a "Man of the Decade" award, he'd run away with it. He also represents the fortunes of his swing generation colleagues, from his rise in the late 1930s, through his 1940s successes, to his career's gradual decline in the 1950s as swing gave way to newer styles of jazz, and finally his exit from the music business (for a time) in the 1960s. His story not only represents the trajectories of the other swing musicians in Boston, but of many others across the country.

It took the presence of Lewis and the trumpeter Frankie Newton in the war years to establish the roots of something we'd now call a jazz scene, regularly covered by the music press. Boston had what it needed to sustain a small jazz scene, but it took the war for it to grow. With peace came the GI Bill, and that enabled musicians to come to Boston to study at the New England Conservatory of Music, the Boston Conservatory, and Schillinger House. These incoming students, coupled with the region's own musicians already in Boston, enabled the scene to reach the critical mass needed to grow. The student musicians, with their energy and new ideas, were an essential part of scene-building.

The swing era came to an end gradually, not all at once in 1946 when the big bands expired. It might have died during the war, when the music simply copied what had come before and the talent was diluted across too many bands—quite a few of them military bands in the employ of Uncle Sam. Or swing might have been eclipsed by other styles of jazz. In Boston, as elsewhere, the music of the late forties had to sort itself out. The swing generation did carry on. The new thing, bebop, which was itself a reaction to the tired swing formula, was expanding from its New York base. Another new style, jump blues, was small-band, get-up-and-dance music played by musicians formerly employed in the black big bands. It became the basis of rhythm and blues. Finally, there was a revival of the traditional jazz styles of the 1920s, all lumped together as Dixieland, a reaction not only to the tightly arranged charts of the big swing bands, but especially to the revolutionary harmonies and melodic liberties of the beboppers. All these sounds were happening at the same time in the late forties in Boston, and from the confusion emerged the musicians central to our story.

Born in the 1920s, these musicians grew up in the Depression years, and World War II shaped their lives. The older members of this group served in the armed forces, and many later studied music with help from the GI Bill. Those too young for wartime military service had ample opportunity to advance musically as they replaced those serving with Uncle Sam. High schoolers neglected their studies to sit in at the Ken Club and work as substitutes at the Roseland-State Ballroom or the RKO Boston Theatre.

Although members of this successor generation played all styles of music, the ones most important to our story are those who heard bebop and wanted to play it, and who gave birth to the modern jazz scene in Boston. Some were transitional players, with deep roots in swing but with eyes for the new music. Others missed swing completely, and though they learned its lessons and knew how to play it, they considered themselves bop players. The names of the key figures of this group come up time and again: Nat Pierce, Jaki Byard, Charlie Mariano, Herb Pomeroy, Sam Rivers. They starred as players, arrangers, and composers; led innovative bands; and acted as mentors. They weren't the only ones who stepped into leadership roles, but they were leaders at key moments. Around them were a talented cast of characters, and we'll meet them all in the following pages: Toshiko Akiyoshi, Serge Chaloff, Alan Dawson, Joe Gordon, Rollins Griffith, Gigi Gryce, Varty Haroutunian, Lennie Johnson, Teddi King, Boots Mussulli, John Neves, Ray Perry, Ray Santisi, Sonny Truitt, Dick Twardzik, Dick Wetmore, Jimmy Woode, and others.

It was a brilliant collection of talent, but the outstanding presence on the scene in the 1950s was an unapologetic swing piano player, George Wein. If Lewis was man of the decade for the 1940s, Wein has to be that man in the 1950s. Wein was a dynamo: a pianist, newspaper columnist, university instructor, disc jockey, personal manager, and record company owner. But all of these were sidelines to his two primary activities—running Storyville, the room that set the standard for how a *jazz* nightclub should be run, from 1950 to 1960; and producing the annual Newport Jazz Festival, beginning in 1954. At a time when nightclubs didn't have the best of reputations—nor did jazz itself, for that matter—Storyville presented the best in jazz, and showed respect to both the musicians and audience. And there were no jazz festivals prior to Newport. Wein set that whole scheme in motion.

Although we don't cover much of the sixties in this story, we can jump the gun and name Lawrence Berk the man of that decade. He started Schillinger House on a shoestring budget after the war and grew it all through the fifties. Renamed the Berklee School of Music in 1954, it became a world leader in music education. In the fifties Berk immersed his school in programs in music education and television production, launched ventures in music publishing, and made a commitment to jazz education by hiring a top-notch faculty and encouraging them to innovate. In the 1960s Berk expanded the school into new facilities, initiated the Bachelor of Music degree program, and encouraged activities that sent the faculty around the country and the world, extending the boundaries of the campus far beyond Boston. It is an overused term, but Lawrence Berk was a visionary.

There is a key difference between the swing players, who left Boston early in their careers, and the modern players in the late 1940s and 1950s. The latter stayed in town longer, or didn't leave at all, or left and came back. Boston was attracting more talent than it was losing to New York. They were finding in Boston what they would otherwise have found only in New York: like-minded players, working bands, contacts. They had frequent contact with established musicians passing through Storyville and the Hi-Hat. And they had Berklee.

Was there a "Boston sound"? Evidence suggests not, and none of the participants made a claim for one. It was good modern jazz, well arranged and well played, and in the spirit of the times. One writer in the mid-1950s called the Boston sound "warm," jazz at a midpoint between the West Coast cool school and the fiery hard bop then dominating New York.

It's a question you'll have to answer for yourself. The recordings are out there, some perhaps hard to find: The Transition Records sampler LP, *Jazz in Transition*; Toshiko Akiyoshi's *The Toshiko Trio*; the Herb Pomeroy Orchestra's *Life Is a Many Splendored Gig*; Serge Chaloff's *Boston Blow Up!*; and others listed in the Discography. You'll find the search worth your time, and hearing the sound of Boston jazz will make reading about it that much more enlightening.

The Jazz Maps of Boston

These four maps show the Boston entertainment districts where most of the jazz spots were located during these years. They are based on a Boston map originally distributed by the *Boston Transcript* newspaper, an institution that passed from the scene in 1941. A map of this vintage is faithful to the streets of Boston as they were before urban renewal changed the face of the city. Some of the streets and intersections shown no longer exist, but you could use the maps to find your way around in a pinch.

- Downtown and the Theatre District shows Lower Washington Street, the Theatre District, and Bay Village. The emphasis here is the 1940s, and here are Izzy Ort's, the Ken Club, the Tic Toc, and the Latin Quarter.

- Huntington Avenue and the Ballroom District shows the neighborhood around Symphony Hall where the dance halls were located—the "Ballroom District." Here are the Raymor and Play-Mor, the Roseland-State, and other sites from big-band Boston. Some sites popular with the Dixieland crowd are also on this map.

- The South End shows the clubs in the vicinity of Mass Ave and Columbus. This neighborhood was the constant home of jazz in Boston, and sites here were active through all the 25 years of this story. Here are the Hi-Hat, the Pioneer Social Club, the Savoy Cafe, Wally's Paradise, and others.

- Copley Square and Park Square became active in the 1950s, even as the Ballroom District and Bay Village went dark. Here are Storyville, the Stable, and other sites associated with the modern jazz years in Boston.

Follow the references listed with the sites for more information. Sites that do not have a reference are mentioned in the text but not described in any detail

Downtown and the Theatre District

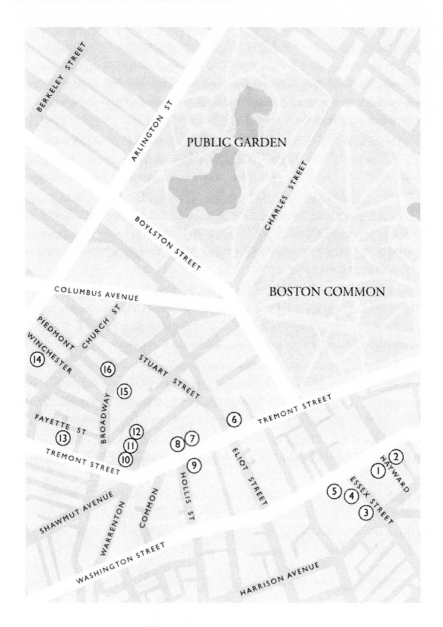

Guide to the Map: Downtown and the Theatre District

1. RKO-Boston Theatre, 614 Washington Street (Chapter 2, Big Band Boston)

2. Checker Cafe, 16 Hayward Place (Chapter 4, Swinging the Home Front)

3. Spotlite Cafe, 47 Essex Street (Chapter 8, Scuffling)

4. Izzy Ort's Bar and Grille, 25 Essex Street (Chapter 8, Scuffling)

5. Silver Dollar Bar, 644 Washington Street (Chapter 8, Scuffling)

6. Knickerbocker, Petty Lounge, 1-2-3 Lounge, and others, corner of Tremont and Stuart Streets (Chapter 17, Stories from the Fifties)

7. Tic Toc, 245 Tremont Street; later Down Beat Club (Chapter 4, Swinging the Home Front; Chapter 5, A Late Forties Interlude)

8. Bradford Hotel, 275 Tremont Street

9. Metropolitan Theatre, 268 Tremont Street

10. Theatrical Club, 58 Warrenton Street; later Ken Club (Chapter 1, Before the War; Chapter 4, Swinging the Home Front)

11. Showtime, 74 Warrenton Street; later the Jazz Box

12. Southland, 76 Warrenton Street; later Rio Casino, Jazz at 76 (Chapter 1, Before the War; Chapter 5, A Late Forties Interlude)

13. Kit Kat, 28 Fayette Street

14. Latin Quarter, 46 Winchester Street (Chapter 17, Stories from the Fifties)

15. Mayfair, 54 Broadway; later Sugar Hill

16. Cocoanut Grove, 17 Piedmont Street (Chapter 4, Swinging the Home Front)

Huntington Avenue and the Ballroom District

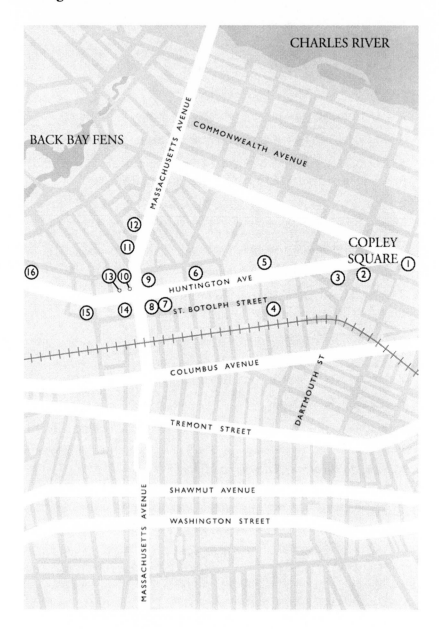

Guide to the Map: Huntington Avenue and the Ballroom District

1. Hotel Brunswick, 520 Boylston Street (Chapter 2, Big Band Boston)

2. Copley Plaza Hotel, 138 St. James Avenue

3. Copley Terrace, 36 Huntington Avenue (Chapter 6, Dixieland Revival)

4. Convention Hall and AFM Local 9, 52-56 St. Botolph Street

5. Mechanic's Building, 111 Huntington Avenue

6. Strand Ballroom, 177 Huntington Avenue

7. Ritz-Plaza Hall, 218 Huntington Avenue (Chapter 5, A Late Forties Interlude)

8. Maxie's, 220 Huntington Avenue (Chapter 6, Dixieland Revival)

9. Uptown Ballroom, 241 Huntington Avenue (Chapter 5, A Late Forties Interlude)

10. Symphony Hall, 311 Massachusetts Avenue (Chapter 2, Big Band Boston)

11. Roseland-State Ballroom, 217 Massachusetts Avenue (Chapter 3, Charlie Shribman and the Roseland-State Ballroom)

12. Flamingo Room, 199 Massachusetts Avenue (Chapter 2, Big Band Boston)

13. Raymor/Play-Mor Ballrooms, 253-263 Huntington Avenue (Chapter 2, Big Band Boston)

14. Arcadia Ballroom, 252-254 Huntington Avenue; later Zanzibar and the Show Boat (Chapter 5, A Late Forties Interlude)

15. New England Conservatory of Music, 290 Huntington Avenue (Chapter 7, Reading, Writing, and Rhythm Physics)

16. Boston Opera House, 343 Huntington Avenue (Chapter 5, A Late Forties Interlude)

The South End

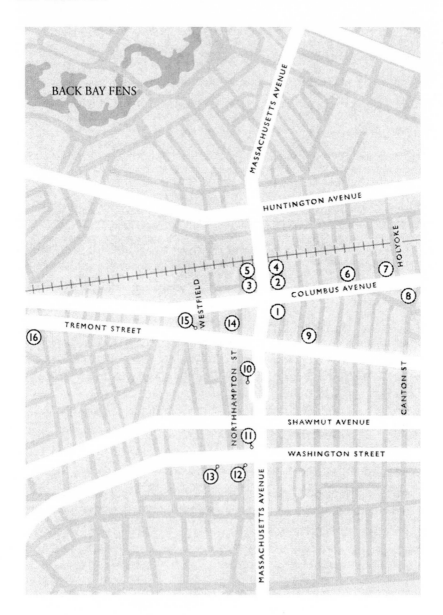

Guide to the Map: The South End

1. Hi-Hat, 572 Columbus Avenue. (Chapter 13, The Hi-Hat: America's Smartest Barbecue)

2. Wally's Paradise, 428 Massachusetts Avenue; previously Little Harlem, Little Dixie. (Chapter 10, Paradise; Chapter 1, Before the War)

3. Eddie's Cafe, 425 Massachusetts Avenue; later the Wigwam (Chapter 9, The Jazz Corner of Boston)

4. Savoy Cafe, 410 Massachusetts Avenue, second location (Chapter 6, Dixieland Revival); previously Royal Palms; later Big M

5. AFM Local 535, 409 Massachusetts Avenue (Chapter 9, The Jazz Corner of Boston)

6. 4-11 Lounge, 411 Columbus Avenue; previously Monterey Cafe, Golden Gate Cafe, Sunnyside Cafe (Chapter 9, The Jazz Corner of Boston)

7. Savoy Cafe, 461 Columbus Avenue, first location (Chapter 4, Swinging the Home Front)

8. Mother's Lunch, 510 Columbus Avenue (Chapter 9, The Jazz Corner of Boston)

9. Handy Cafe, 723 Tremont Street (Chapter 9, The Jazz Corner of Boston)

10. Professional & Business Men's Club, 543 Massachusetts Avenue (Chapter 9, The Jazz Corner of Boston)

11. Shanty Lounge, 1781 Washington Street (Chapter 20, Looking Forward, Looking Back)

12. Louie's Lounge, 1788 Washington Street (Chapter 20, Looking Forward, Looking Back)

13. Trinidad Lounge, 1844 Washington Street; later Basin Street South (Chapter 20, Looking Forward, Looking Back)

14. Johnny Wilson's Swanee Grill, 815 Tremont Street (Chapter 4, Swinging the Home Front)

15. Pioneer Social Club, 2 Westfield Street (Chapter 9, The Jazz Corner of Boston)

16. Connolly's Stardust Room, 1184 Tremont Street (Chapter 9, The Jazz Corner of Boston)

Copley Square and Park Square

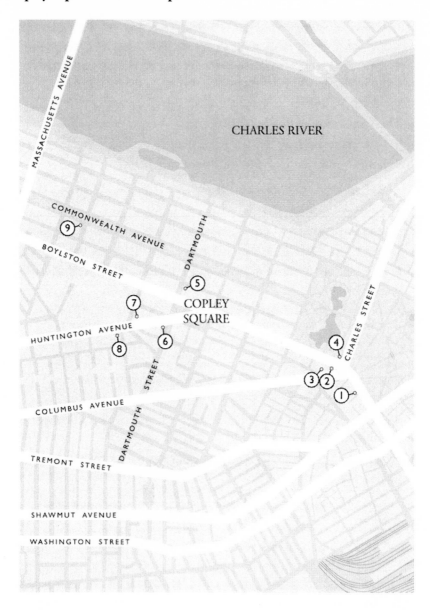

Guide to the Map: Copley Square and Park Square

1. Ace Recording Studio, 1 Boylston Place (Chapter 5, A Late Forties Interlude)

2. Downbeat, 54 Park Square (Chapter 17, Stories from the Fifties)

3. Saxony Lounge, 35 Providence Street

4. Boston Festival of the Arts, Public Garden (Chapter 19, Into the Great Outdoors)

5. Darbury Room, 271 Dartmouth Street (Chapter 17, Stories from the Fifties)

6. The Stable, 20 Huntington Avenue (Chapter 15, Stablemates)

7. Storyville, Mahogany Hall, and the Music Box, 49 Huntington Avenue in the Copley Square Hotel (Chapter 16, Dynamo; Chapter 6, Dixieland Revival)

8. 5 O'Clock Club, 78 Huntington Avenue (Chapter 5, A Late Forties Interlude; Chapter 17, Stories from the Fifties)

9. Schillinger House, later the Berklee School of Music, 284 Newbury Street (Chapter 7, Reading, Writing, and Rhythm Physics)

Chapter 1

Before the War

On January 1, 1937, the Boston papers declared that the New Year's Eve just celebrated was the first since the onset of the Depression when Boston's night-life was truly back in business. "Baby 1937 Gets Wild Welcome" proclaimed the *Post*:

> A good part of Boston's population burst loose last night and with an old-fashioned orgy of spending, noise-making and general hoopla, and served notice on the statisticians and economists that, as far as they are concerned, good times are back once more. It was the wildest and by far the most enthusiastic New Year's Eve celebration Boston has seen since the breakneck days of 1929.[1]

The night started slowly, said the reports, but as midnight neared, the clubs, theaters and restaurants were full and the streets were jammed. The spirit of celebration was back! People could stay out a little later, too. The Boston Licensing Board allowed clubs to serve food and offer entertainment until 4:00 a.m., provided they stopped serving liquor at the regular time of 1:00.

What of jazz music on this night? Good jazz was being played, mostly by black musicians, and most prominently at two clubs on Massachusetts Avenue just off Columbus. The headliners in the show at the Royal Palms were singers Eddie Deas and Evelyn White. The better bet was a few doors down at Little Harlem, where Dean Earl's eight-piece orchestra, with its fine rhythm section of pianist Earl, drummer Dave Chestnut, and bassist Leroy "Slam" Stewart played for the revelers.

One white band was playing small-group jazz that night, and attracting its usual crowd. Downstairs in the Metropolitan Hotel, in the Theatrical Club, Bobby Hackett's band with trombonist Brad Gowans was at work. Hackett, the sensational young cornetist from Providence, was building his reputation in that cellar room. In a few months he would leave it for New York.

Small-group jazz was one piece of the picture on that New Year's Eve. The other was the big band. Oddly enough, even though it had been well over a year since Benny Goodman's revolutionary appearance at the Palomar Ballroom in Los Angeles, Boston hadn't yet produced a big band capable of cashing in on the craze. Frankie Ward and His Rhythm of the Dawn

Orchestra, playing for dancers at the Bradford Hotel, might have been the strongest contender. At the Brunswick Hotel was the Roly Rogers Orchestra, whose crack arranger, Jerry Gray, had just joined Artie Shaw's group.

The rest of the town was, from the jazz fan's point of view, a bit of a bore. At the RKO-Boston Theater, Ken Murray's *Broadway Rhythm Review* featured a reconstituted Original Dixieland Jazz Band, the white New Orleans outfit whose leader claimed to have invented jazz, all evidence to the contrary.

The road bands that night weren't big jazz draws. Will Osborne's was at the Normandie Ballroom, Hank Biagini's at the Raymor, and Xavier Cugat's orchestra, with its commercial Latin music, played three shows at the Metropolitan Theatre. Charlie Shribman's Roseland-State featured a sweet band fronted by its vocalist, Don Mario.

That was the picture 'round midnight, and it represents rather well the state of things in the local jazz world. For the men playing the jazz, especially if they were young and single, they were like Bobby Hackett and Slam Stewart, and heard New York calling. Both had many musical friends there who had already made the move.

Dean Earl and Dave Chestnut had plenty of friends there, too. Earl was a New Yorker himself, who found Boston to his liking, and Chestnut was an able drummer who had substituted for Sonny Greer in Duke Ellington's Orchestra on occasion. That connection was probably made through the two Bostonians then anchoring Ellington's saxophone section, Harry Carney and Johnny Hodges. Ellington, through his association with Charlie Shribman, spent so much time in the area during his orchestra's early years that he practically qualified as a New Englander himself.

Even before swing took the country by storm, Shribman was committed to it, and he brought the best of the bands to town in the mid-1930s: Ellington, but also Cab Calloway, Fletcher Henderson, Jimmie Lunceford, Chick Webb, and Don Redman. Redman, one of the very best arrangers in jazz in 1937, had studied at the Boston Conservatory. Slam Stewart had also attended the Boston Conservatory for a year. Like Hackett, Stewart would move to New York in 1937 and form his famous duo with singer Slim Gaillard.

In 1937, we already see the outline of the pieces that would make the Boston jazz scene so noteworthy in later decades—the good local musicians, the conservatories, a promoter actively supporting the music, and the intermingling of the New York and Boston scenes. Boston had its first jazz journalist in 1937 as well, and he was already causing trouble in the world of jazz letters.

"Boston Remains as Dull and Stupid as Ever"

There weren't many people writing about jazz when George Frazier started with *Down Beat* in 1936, and there certainly wasn't anyone else writing about it in Boston. This brash young man listened to the music in his city, and he was not pleased. "Boston Remains as Dull and Stupid as Ever," thundered the headline over Frazier's column in the February 1937 *Down Beat*.[2] It was pure Frazier, colorful and controversial.

A South Boston boy, Frazier played clarinet while attending Boston Latin High School, and was writing for obscure European magazines like *La Revue Musicale* while still an undergraduate at Harvard (class of '33), an institution he mocked in the lyrics of "Harvard Blues," later recorded by Basie's band. He wrote record reviews for *Mademoiselle* commencing in 1936, in a column called "Let's Look at the Record," but he was best known as *Down Beat's* Boston correspondent from 1936 on and off to 1942.

Frazier immediately established a reputation as a bad boy, with a writing style that was highly personal and purposely provocative. No one was safe from Frazier's barbs. He held the Hub's musicians in especially low regard. He praised Frankie Ward's new big band in 1937 not for splendid musicianship, but because "any Boston band that plays in tune is a rarity." Other Boston bands? Ruby Newman was "amateurish," Sammy Izen "incompetent," Mickey Alpert "excruciating." Singers? "No one seems to know where they came from, but this town is certainly flooded with horrible girl singers."[3] The *Down Beat* editors were delighted. They called him "Acidmouth." Everybody read Frazier. His wit and wrath helped *Down Beat* survive its infancy. And he always had it in for his home town:

> This is still the biggest small town in the country and it is still a matter of knocking twice and asking for Joe if you hope to get a drink after one a.m. There is neither jazz nor excitement to be had in the wee hours and the haggard look on people's faces is not from lack of sleep. It's from frustration.[4]

The other side of Frazier was his relentless promotion of the music and musicians he favored. Frazier was the first to write about Bobby Hackett during his days as an unknown at the Theatrical Club, and after hearing Frankie Newton's recording of "Please Don't Talk About Me," Frazier wrote that with it "Newton reaffirms his right to be classed with the really top-notch trumpets of the day, for his swing, tone, taste, intonations, and inspirations are above reproach."[5] He liked other horn players too, such as Red Allen, Bunny Berigan, and Cootie Williams, but for the rest of his days he looked back fondly on Hackett and the Theatrical Club.

Late Nights at the Theatrical Club

The Boston of today is physically very different from the Boston of 1937, but that city was quite similar to the Boston of 1954, pictured here. The photographer is standing on the corner of Tremont Street and Broadway, looking northwest across Frank T. Foley Square, where Broadway, Tremont, and Shawmut converge. That's Tremont Street in the foreground, running northeast toward the looming Hotel Bradford. Broadway is on the left, heading north to Park Square, and if you can make out the first intersection, that's Carver Street, turning north.

Broadway Hotel, 315 Broadway at Tremont Street, ca. 1954. Courtesy of Historic New England.

The building is the Hotel Broadway, which operated for 30 years at 315 Tremont Street, and as the Metropolitan Hotel for at least a decade before that. On the far right side of the Hotel Broadway at the corner of Warrenton Street is the French Village restaurant. All of this today is part of a lost world.

Broadway is gone. Carver Street is gone. Foley Square is gone. Warrenton no longer crosses Tremont. And the Hotel Broadway? It's an area of concrete known as Elliot Norton Park, named after the *Boston Post*'s esteemed theater critic who wrote "Second Thoughts of a First Nighter" for many years.

But when there *was* a Hotel Broadway, there were jazz clubs, good ones, in the basement space marked by that French Village sign in 1954. The Ken Club was a prominent Boston jazz address all through the 1940s, and an after-hours haunt much loved by jazz fans, the Theatrical Club, preceded it.

The Theatrical Club was an after-hours place, and although it was by no means a secret, it didn't hang a sign over the sidewalk or advertise in the papers. People just knew about it. But the Theatrical became a local legend because the jazz was good at a time when jazz was in short supply, and because of the after-hours cachet, that sense of doing something naughty. The jazz was fine, the company congenial, and it was all happening after you were supposed to be home in bed. What could be better?

The Theatrical Club, through its political connections and supposed status as a private club, could ignore the 1 a.m. closing hour and stay open until 5 a.m., serving drinks and food and providing entertainment. And if people were enjoying themselves, why stop at 5? The key was to stay squeaky clean. That meant no hoodlums or hookers hanging around the place, no serving drinks to minors, no annoying the neighbors. Do nothing that might force the police to act. Thus there was a doorman (a gentleman known as Little Arthur) and his authority was undisputed. If you didn't look right, you didn't get in. If you caused trouble, Little Arthur threw you out. It was a good system.

The Theatrical's cast of characters was led by the manager, Al Taxier, but when he was actually hired and when the club actually commenced operation is unclear. Late 1935 is a reasonable guess. The suave Taxier was a savvy guy, he'd been on the Boston scene since the mid-twenties and he'd worked in more than one high-end speakeasy. It was nothing new for an old speakeasy boss to manage a room that needed to remain inconspicuous. He just needed a little push to get things rolling.

To provide that push, Taxier hired Herb Marsh (Herb Arntz) to supply the music. Marsh led a busy dance band in the mid-thirties, playing clubs like the Brown Derby and the Cocoanut Grove. Shortly before the Theatrical's planned opening, Taxier had Marsh bring the band in to play when the nearby theaters were letting out. Then he propped the doors open so the music was audible on the street. The people passing by heard the music and wanted to enter, but Taxier's doorman turned them away. "Private party, come back next week" he'd say. The curious people did come back, and word-of-mouth took care of the rest. The club was successful from the start.

Marsh departed the Theatrical early in 1936 and continued to work around town until 1941, the year he broke up his band and enlisted in the Navy. He returned to Boston after the war, but he never resumed his career as a bandleader, and today Marsh is only a footnote in the Boston jazz story. The man Taxier hired to replace him as the Theatrical's bandleader is still revered the world over.

Taxier asked one of Marsh's sidemen, a 22-year-old from Providence who played cornet, trumpet, and guitar to form a new band. His name was Bobby Hackett. He accepted. Hackett's first call went to pianist Teddy Roy, with whom he had worked extensively starting in 1932; in 1933 they formed a trio with clarinetist Pee Wee Russell to work a Boston speakeasy called the Crescent Club ("a hoodlum hangout," Hackett called it).

Hackett hired saxophonist Billy Wildes to play tenor and a "name" to play trombone. That was Brad Gowans, a veteran of a number of important bands in the twenties, including those of Joe Venuti, Mal Hallett, and Red Nichols. "I knew Brad Gowans only by reputation," Hackett told *Down Beat*, "so I went and dug him up. He was out of the music business at that time, but I talked him back into it."[6] Finally, Hackett recruited clarinetist Pat Barbara and drummer Russ Isaacs from the society band of Meyer Davis, then playing at the Copley Plaza Hotel.[7]

The joint was packed and people raved about Hackett, no one more than George Frazier, a regular at the Theatrical Club's horseshoe-shaped bar. Frazier loved Bobby Hackett and without question did more than anybody to bring him to the public's attention. As early as July 1936, Frazier wrote that Hackett "has taste, tone, swing, and interesting ideas. Nobody has ever caught Bix's eloquent tone quite so successfully…He plays with an amazing delicacy, avoiding meaningless technical displays and high notes."[8] That easy swinging style remained Hackett's hallmark until his death in June 1976. Frazier, in fact, liked everything about Hackett's band except the girl singer with them in 1936, Freda Gibbons from Worcester. Ms. Gibbons changed her name to Georgia Gibbs in 1942 and later became a successful pop singer. Despite a respectable big band pedigree, she is mostly remembered for her toned-down (some say "ripped off") cover versions of rhythm and blues numbers in the 1950s.

Though warmly remembered by such as Frazier and Hackett, the Theatrical club had its flaws. This was Boston in the thirties, and it is no surprise to learn that the club maintained a strict Jim Crow policy for both patrons and performers. Whites were free to sit in, and blacks were not. Frazier and Hackett convinced Taxier that opening to all would not only be the right thing to do, it would also attract a more sophisticated and free-spending crowd. Taxier agreed to a trial run, and Frazier and Hackett arranged for Fats Waller to make an appearance in November 1936.[9] On the chosen night, Waller breezed in, took Roy's spot at the piano, and kicked off his signature song, "The Joint Is Jumpin'." That was the end of Jim Crow at the Theatrical Club. When he finished, Fats proclaimed, "This joint is now *officially* jumpin'!"[10]

Not all the excitement at the Metropolitan Hotel was taking place in the Theatrical Club. The manager of the hotel was James Welansky, a gambler and character of dubious reputation, and the brother of Barney Welansky, the owner of the nearby Cocoanut Grove nightclub. Early in the morning of December 17, 1937, Welansky was in the hotel lobby, in earnest conversation with one David "Beano" Breen, a notorious gangster, who took his nickname from a variation of bingo popular at the time. Breen was shot and killed there in the lobby during or just after this conversation, and Welansky departed immediately for Florida, safely beyond the reach of the law. Breen and Welansky, as it turned out, were partners in a failed gambling operation in Nantasket, Massachusetts; Welansky was out $20,000 and wanted it back, presumably from Breen. Welansky was named as the shooter by prosecutors and eventually arrested, but a grand jury failed to indict him. The presiding judge, however, left no doubt that he thought the gambling debt played a part in Breen's demise. He didn't say "Welansky did it," but he did point out that Welansky had both opportunity and motive.

The Breen murder and surrounding events did the Metropolitan's reputation no good and probably pushed it into bankruptcy. Think of what it meant to the unfortunate Theatrical Club, a place that could only operate if things were quiet. Taxier's club sought no attention at all, but a flashy crook had been shot in the lobby and reporters from all the Boston papers were crawling all over the joint day after day. Any municipal largess the Theatrical enjoyed surely withered away with all the attention.

Hackett broke up his band and left for New York in early 1937. Gowans stayed, joining Frankie Ward's fledgling orchestra. Hackett was part of the magic, and Taxier couldn't find a band to replace him. The crowds got smaller, and eventually Taxier called it a day, closing the club in the spring of 1938. That's where things stood when Irving Saunders bought the Metropolitan out of bankruptcy in 1939 and renamed it the Broadway Hotel. A year later, he found a new tenant for the basement space. That was the Ken Club, and we'll visit that haunt presently.

It's Southland This Season!

There hasn't been an intersection of Tremont and Warrenton Streets for years. It once was possible to exit the Theatrical Club on the southeast corner of that intersection and walk a short block to the old church at 76 Warrenton Street, but that little leg of Warrenton Street from the corner to number 76 is now part of a block of apartments. Warrenton Street itself was diverted to follow an old service alley into what was Carver Street but is now Charles Street South. While many of its neighbors fell to the wrecking ball in the 1960s, the old Greek Revival building at 76 Warrenton survived, its sturdy pediment still watching over the street, saved by its historic significance if not its cultural one. Today it is the home of the Charles Street Playhouse, and oh, if only buildings could talk.

Seventy-six Warrenton is listed on the National Register of Historic Places. It dates back to 1839, when it was designed and built by the renowned early American architect Asher Benjamin as the Fifth Universalist Church. In 1864 it became the Hebrew Temple Ohabei Shalom, the first synagogue in Boston. Still later, it housed a Scotch Presbyterian congregation, and after that, the YWCA. During Prohibition, Benjamin's church housed a ritzy speakeasy called the Lido Venice, where the famous Casa Loma Orchestra played. This was a good place for a nightclub. The second-floor hall of worship provided a large, open space with a high ceiling, just right for live entertainment. Jack Levaggi owned the club and the building then, and he was clearing $16,000 a month on the operation in 1929. Albert Rosetti was the headwaiter, and he judged any night that he didn't walk out with $300 in his pocket to be a bust. That was how it was in 1929.[11]

Levaggi sold out and the club went legitimate after Repeal in 1933. It shortened its name to the Lido and operated through the mid-1930s.

In 1937, the place was named Southland, and it featured reviews of the type made famous at New York's Cotton Club: *Black Rhythm, Copper Colored Follies, Black Follies of 1937.* The fast-stepping dance numbers in all of them were choreographed by Hazel and "Ma" Green, and the 14-piece orchestra behind them was led by Blanche Calloway, Cab's older sister. The "Tan Typhoon" was already a show-business veteran when she arrived at Southland, having come to prominence as a singer and bandleader in Chicago in the mid-1920s, where she worked regularly in Al Capone's nightspots. Blanche was a pacesetter, a black woman leading a jazz orchestra, the Joy Boys (among them Vic Dickenson and Ben Webster) in the early and mid-1930s, and recording extensively.

Blanche Calloway was among the first established jazz stars to land a lengthy location job in Boston. She fronted the band at Southland for the entire 1937-1938 season, a fact generally overlooked in her biographies.

Southland was wildly successful right up until the wee hours of the morning on February 29, 1938, when a fire of unknown cause gutted the place. The owners claimed that they'd be back in business in four weeks. It took six months, but when they reopened they showed off a gleaming room

Boston Daily Record advertisement for Southland,
December 13, 1937.

rich in art-deco detail, with booths along each side and a dance floor up front
near the band. They needed that dance floor, because when Southland finally
reopened that fall, it was competing with the Ritz Roof and the Roseland-
State Ballroom for big-name swing bands. Compete it did: for fans of swing,
Southland was *the* place in Boston in 1938–1940, when a who's who of jazz
worked the club. There was Louis Armstrong, Charlie Barnet, Count Basie,
Bunny Berigan, Cab Calloway, Fletcher Henderson, Earl Hines, Gene Krupa,
Jimmie Lunceford, Jack Teagarden, Fats Waller, and on and on. This was a job
musicians welcomed because they were signed for multi-week engagements,
which provided a needed respite from the one-nighters.

Radio also figured into Southland's prominence. Southland aired radio
broadcasts, and Fred B. Cole hosted them over the NBC network for their
local affiliate, which was then WBZ. Some of those 1940 broadcasts found
their way on to recordings over the years, including dates by Count Basie,
Duke Ellington, Harry James, and Chick Webb. It's been more than 65 years,
but Southland lives on through those recordings.

It had the best jazz and dance music in town and a lively atmosphere, so
perhaps it was inevitable that the Boston Licensing Board did not like
Southland. It was…*decadent*. The girls on the kick line wore skimpy
costumes, and the club's matchbooks pictured a girl wearing less than that
lounging in a hot-tub sized cocktail glass. The advertising, the menus…it all
had that Cotton Club kind of decadence. And the audience was *mixed*.
Southland was just too rich for the stuffed shirts, and days before Christmas
1938, the club gave the BLB an excuse to act. On December 23,
commissioner Edward M. Richardson caught the show:

> While a member of the Boston Licensing Board watched in wide-eyed aston-
> ishment, scantily clad colored chorus girls danced onto the floor of the
> Southland, South End cafe, and sang a jazz version of the Christmas carol,

"Silent Night." The girl entertainers in the cafe at 76 Warrenton street, described by Licensing Board officials as "partially nude," sang the well-known carol not only to jazz time but with gestures, it was stated. The performance took place two nights before Christmas.[12]

Commissioner Richardson considered the carol singing "entirely irreverent."

We do not know how often Commissioner Richardson returned to Southland to observe the irreverence, or why he considered the dancers "partially nude" instead of "partially clothed," but because of it, Southland was ordered to close at midnight instead of its usual 2 a.m. for all of one week. As a measure of good citizenship, Southland agreed to remove the bathing beauty from its matchbooks. The incident typified the board's approach, though—make a big noise but impose a small fine; appease the prudish but don't impede business as usual.

Southland closed after its spring season in 1940, despite the fact that bands with star power were still packing the house and the radio wire was still in place. Whatever the financial or political reason, the club closed, even though Boston's appetite for bands was undiminished.

Southland may have been gone, but Blanche Calloway wasn't quite done with Boston. In between the Theatrical Club and Southland, at 74 Warrenton, was another spot that changed its name and its entertainment policy yearly. In 1938, Rose Chapman ran the Club Congo there, and when Blanche Calloway's job at Southland went up in smoke, she moved into Chapman' club. In 1939 she toured the northeast with Joe Nevils's Boston band, the Alabama Aces, serving as her orchestra, and whenever she lined up a job in the area in 1940–1941, she'd use the Alabama Aces similarly. All this Boston activity over a four-year period is more than enough to earn Calloway the status of honorary Bostonian.

Little Harlem, During and After Hours

It didn't take long for nightclubs to arrive on Massachusetts Avenue after Repeal. Two clubs opened near the busy corner of Massachusetts and Columbus Avenues in 1935, serving a mixed clientele with lively floor shows and good jazz bands. The Royal Palms opened at 410 Mass Ave, and its rival, Little Harlem, was just a few doors away at 428. There was even a family rivalry of sorts involved, as for a time the Royal Palms featured the band organized by vocalist Eddie Deas, while his son-in-law, pianist Sandy Sandiford, was bandleader at Little Harlem. Although the Royal Palms and Little Harlem were the first post-Repeal spots to open along Massachusetts Avenue, their lives were relatively short, and both were replaced by other more famous clubs, the Savoy Cafe at 410, and Little Dixie and then Wally's Paradise at 428.

Little Harlem opened in 1935 in a space previously occupied by a pool hall. It was a spot with a prominent owner, hot bands, and a short life. The owner, Eddie Levine, had the good sense to hire leaders who knew talent, and the top bandleaders in Boston led the Little Harlem Orchestra, including saxophonist Joe Nevils and a pair of pianists, Sandy Sandiford and then Dean Earl. *Metronome* reported that Dean Earl's Little Harlem Orchestra played "mostly hot numbers with a mercifully very small sprinkling of sweet." Its sax section of Jackie Fields, Amer Graves, and Thornton Avery was "one of the best in town," and "the absence of a reedy tone being very welcome to the long suffering listener." The rhythm section of Earl, Dave Chestnut, and Leroy Stuart (better known to us as Leroy "Slam" Stewart) gave the band "a solid lift," while the brass, Maceo Bryant and Buck Halstead gave the band "bite."[13] Others who passed through Earl's band included the multi-instrumentalist Ray Perry, drummer Joe Booker, and trumpeter Jabbo Jenkins, a high-note man who could play trumpet without a mouthpiece.

Levine regularly tussled with the city authorities over issues of closing time and after-hours liquor sales. Clubs were supposed to close at 1 a.m., but clubs like Levine's often stayed open much later and charged more for the booze after hours, claiming they couldn't make it as a business without the after-hours revenue. Nonetheless, the Boston Licensing Board was on the warpath in early 1937, repeatedly citing Levine for after-hours violations. The club was cited three times in one week in February 1937, for instance; when hauled before the BLB, Levine maintained that the persons seated in his club at 3:10 a.m. on February 9 were in fact employees listening to a lecture. It's doubtful Mrs. Driscoll was satisfied with this explanation, because the board cited the club in March for violations of liquor laws and the "conditions of the establishment," whatever that meant. Ongoing problems with the BLB led to Little Harlem's closing in spring 1937. Levine returned to Massachusetts Avenue with another club ten years later.[14]

Little Harlem, incidentally, wasn't Earl's first job in Boston, nor would it be his last (he was still playing professionally in the 1990s). His first job was at the Railway Club, at 13 Yarmouth Street, around the corner from the Back Bay Station. Earl, born in 1914 in Brooklyn, was working the RKO theater circuit, and he'd stay at the Railway when his travels brought him to Boston.

The Railway was initially a rooming house for black railroad men, but Prohibition presented an opportunity to branch out, so in came a piano and men to play it. One was Hi Diggs, who recalled the club itself as little more than a converted apartment with an upright piano and owner named Corbin, who "afforded Harvard students the opportunity to get loaded on bootleg booze and be entertained by the best local talent as well as many big name guests. It was here that Jabbo Jenkins lost his chance to join the Duke Ellington band because his extra-curricular activities were not quite what Duke was looking for!"[15]

After Repeal, the Railway continued as a rooming house and after-hours club, and Earl settled in as the house piano player when the RKO job ended in 1934. He remained until he became the bandleader at Little Harlem.[16]

The Railway was never a major club, but it was a busy one for a time. In 1938 longtime bandleader Herbert Pierce took over the Railway, changed its name to the Rhythm Club, and opened its doors to the public. His bandleader was another first-generation Boston jazz man, guitarist Jackie Jackson, who played banjo with George Tynes in the 1920s and led his own groups in the 1930s. The club was active until 1944.

Little Dixie, the Hottest Spot in Town

The space was not idle for long following Little Harlem's demise. Later in 1937 Albert Rothstein opened the Little Dixie at 428, and it remained a popular place through the war years, when the line sometimes snaked around the corner of Columbus Ave. As its advertisements said, it was the hottest spot in town.

Why "Little Dixie"? Who knows, but Little Dixie's primary downtown competition in the 1930s was the Southland, so it must have been the fashion for mixed-clientele urban establishments to evoke "sleepy time down south" with their naming choices. I'm sure the white clubowners never considered the racial overtones in such names.

Little Dixie worked hard to bring in customers. It advertised heavily starting in the fall of 1937, in the *Chronicle*, the *Record* and the *Afro American*, the Baltimore-based paper that for years ran a few pages of New England news and advertisements. Starting in 1937, a Boston writer, Elliott Freeman, penned the column "The Whirling Hub," in which he reliably plugged the bands playing in establishments like Little Dixie—if the clubs bought advertising.

With Joe Nevils and the Alabama Aces supplying the music, Little Dixie quickly established itself as a top jazz room and the place for late-night sessions. A series of bandleaders followed Nevils on the stand, including Burgess Brown, Bob Chestnut, Wilbur Pinckney, and Danny Potter. Trumpeter Phil Edmunds (Felix "Phil" Barboza) was a club favorite, and for a time in the mid-1940s, the young Roy Haynes was his drummer.

Finally, there was Jack Hill and His Jacks. Hi Diggs remembered this band:

Jack Hill and His Jacks. From left, Highland Diggs, piano; George Jones, bass; Frankie Gatewood, vocals; Dave Chestnut, drums; Walter Sisco, alto and clarinet; Bill Stanley, trumpet; Wilbur Pinckney, alto and tenor saxophones; Buster Daniels, trumpet; Amer Graves, tenor saxophone and clarinet. Courtesy of Dan Kochakian.

Undoubtedly, one of the most versatile bands Boston ever produced was the Jack Hill band, consisting of Bill Stanley, first trumpet, Buster Daniels, second trumpet, Wilbur Pinckney, first alto sax/clarinet, Walter Sisco, second alto sax/clarinet, Amer Graves, tenor sax, Dave Chestnut, drums, George Jones, bass, and myself on piano. Not widely known nor much publicized, it attracted the attention of many notables of show biz, one of whom was Blanche Calloway, the sister of the legendary Cab Calloway. Most bands of that period could do one or two things well, but this one could do so many things that we were in a class by ourselves. Blanche came to check and was captivated to the point where she wanted to take us on a national tour. Unfortunately, we were doing so well at home, this offer was rejected... Jack Hill and His Jacks was a "cooperative" band; there was no designated leader. In fact, "Jack Hill" was a fictitious name![17]

Chronicle columnist Rudy Williams called the Hill band "the best night club band that Boston ever has produced." Maybe so, but as Diggs wryly reported, they still got let go because they asked for a bonus for playing a long New Year's Eve night. They immediately went downtown to Rose Chapman's Club Congo.

There were a few stars on the Little Dixie stage as well. One name especially associated with the Dixie was Hazel Diaz, the "hip-twisting, blues-singing Queen of Torch," who went on to make movies in the late 1930s with black cinema pioneer Oscar Micheaux. Another was with the Will Mastin Trio, a teenager too young to be appearing on a nightclub stage. He was sometimes called "Sunshine Sammy" and clubs booked him as a midget. It was Sammy Davis, Jr., already singing and dancing and drumming with his father and Mastin, his uncle.[18]

Little Dixie became the site of such exuberance that at one point in 1943 manager Danny Galliano declared the place off limits to U.S. military personnel because they were scaring off his civilian customers. If fights broke out, Galliano and his bouncers were pretty much on their own, because the Shore Patrol and Military Police rarely battled their way out of Scollay Square and Washington Street to collect the rowdies at the uptown clubs. Galliano added to the notoriety that year by getting arrested for fencing furs and jewelry stolen in burglaries in the western suburbs. There was always some kind of action at the Little Dixie.

When the entertainment tax rose to 20 percent in 1944, the Dixie cut back, ending the floor shows and offering only a house band. Hillary Rose and Danny Potter were two of those bandleaders in the waning days of the war. The club's profile diminished in the war's aftermath. It didn't advertise and wasn't mentioned in the papers. Operations ceased in 1946, which was a bad year for nightlife all over town.

Diggs reflected on Little Dixie and its demise when he said "It was a world of party time, not only in the clubs, but on the streets. The whole city was wide open to everyone. I really hated to see it change."[19]

Chapter 2

Big Band Boston

If you wanted to go dancing when swing was king, you headed uptown to the corner of Massachusetts and Huntington Avenues. That's where the action was. Nobody at the time called it a "Ballroom District," but that's what it was and that's what I'll call it. The Roseland-State, the Raymor and Play-Mor, the Arcadia, the Uptown, the Strand, Convention Hall, the Ritz-Plaza—all were within a few blocks of Boston's musical *grand dame*, Symphony Hall. Add in a few nightclubs with big dance floors, rental halls that often out-swung their commercial cousins, and a room or two where you would never expect to find a dance floor, and you have the makings of a Ballroom District. Beneath the newer buildings of more recent times lie buried the heart and soul of Big Band Boston.

Dance hall culture extended far beyond any Ballroom District. The Boston area, and all of New England, was home to countless dance floors. A quick tour around the area in the dance-crazy years from the mid-thirties to the mid-forties would find Nutting's-on-the-Charles in Waltham, Wilbur's-on-the-Taunton in Somerset, and Moseley's-on-the-Charles in Dedham. There was the Bournehurst in Buzzards Bay and the Lyonhurst in Marlboro and the Charleshurst at Salem Willows. There was Sun Valley in Shrewsbury and the Coral Gables in Weymouth and Wrentham's King Philip Ballroom "on the shores of beautiful Lake Pearl." There was the Lakeside in Wakefield and the Starlight in Lynnfield and Fieldston's in Marshfield. On Revere Beach, the Moorish Castle and Spanish Gables competed for dancers. And the Totem Pole, at Norumbega Park in Newton, was strictly deluxe.

A few of these places, like the Raymor and the Roseland-State in Boston, and Nutting's and the Totem Pole in the suburbs, earned a place on the national map. Others had a more modest existence, rarely rising above the level of general dance music. After all, even during the swing era, there was plenty of dance music being played in the Ballroom District that wasn't swing music at all. "Swing era" conjures up a Hollywood-driven image of crowded rooms packed with wild jitterbuggers and wailing jazz bands, but that's not the way it was, in Boston or anywhere else. The truth is, many dance bands worked the Ballroom District, and some attracted the young dancers with swing and others appealed to an older and more sedate crowd with a blend of popular hits and old favorites. Some commercial dance halls wouldn't allow jitterbugging, in order to keep the crowd from becoming unruly.

High-octane, jazz-driven swing music wasn't ubiquitous, but the dance scene was, and all that music being played meant jobs. A good musician could always find work on Huntington Avenue.

Looking east on Huntington Avenue in 1941. The Play-Mor and Raymor Ballrooms are on the left, with Symphony Hall, Horticultural Hall, and the Uptown Ballroom (at the vertical marquee just past Horticultural Hall) beyond them. Across the street from the Raymor is the Arcadia Ballroom. Courtesy of Historic New England.

Activity in the Ballroom District peaked in the late 1930s and stayed near that peak until about 1944. There was a sharp decline in 1945–1946 as the big bands swooned and the appetite for social dancing diminished. The last dance hall on Huntington Avenue closed in 1952, and the Roseland-State, on Mass Ave, limped along until 1958. Today there is no trace of Boston's thriving dance scene.

Boston Big Bands

The Boston area contributed more than its share of musicians to the big bands, particularly those working the northeast circuit. It amounted to a second talent exodus, but unlike the migration of the 1920s that claimed many of the city's best African-American musicians, this one involved mostly whites. There weren't enough good bands to keep them in Boston.

Dan Murphy's Musical Skippers was cut from the same cloth as the Casa Loma, if the little information known about the Skippers is accurate. Active from at least 1930, the band ranged far from its Boston home in its barnstorming days, and in fact broke up in Kansas City in 1934. Murphy reformed the band in 1936 and played regularly around Boston until the band finally broke up for good in 1937. Among its distinguished alumni were two kids just out of Massachusetts high schools, singer Irene Daye (she later sang with Mal Hallett, and on Gene Krupa's 1941 hit, "Drum Boogie"), who had to take a night off from the band to attend graduation ceremonies at Lawrence High School, and trombonist Ray Conniff, who joined the band right out of Attleboro High. He went on to a long career playing and arranging for the big bands of Bob Crosby, Bunny Berigan, Artie Shaw, and Vaughn Monroe, and later arranged pop music for Columbia Records and led the Ray Conniff Singers, the popular easy-listening organization of the 1960s and 1970s.

Frankie Ward and his 12-piece Rhythm of the Dawn Orchestra held down the location job at the Penthouse in the Bradford Hotel for more than two years, ending in late 1938. It was a prized gig, with a regular spot on WMEX radio, and it entailed playing for floor shows as well as for dancing, but reed man Ward could swing when given the chance. His jazz resume was already lengthy by the late 1930s. He'd been on the speakeasy circuit in the 1920s with Phil Napoleon, was among the first of the Boston jazz men to record during that decade, and had organized one of Boston's first big bands in the wake of Benny Goodman's mid-1930s emergence. By the late 1930s he was playing clarinet in the Goodman style himself. Ward's key players at the Bradford were pianist Frank Bellizia; trombonist Brad Gowans, who signed on after Bobby Hackett broke up his Theatrical Club band; bassist Fred Whiting; and the well-regarded drummer Fred Moynahan, a longtime musical associate of Gowans. These formed the band-within-a-band that was responsible for most of the hard swinging at the Bradford.

Ward's outfit was a promising and prominent one on the Boston scene, a status recognized by reviews in *Metronome* and *Down Beat*. The bassist was absent the night George Simon dropped by for *Metronome*, and the band suffered because of it. He graded them with a B- in his "Simon Says" column. *Down Beat's* hard-to-please George Frazier wrote that Ward "has unquestionably formed what is far and away the best large band ever produced around town. Its musicianship is expert, but, as a unit, it still misses fire. The biggest fault is a lack of good arrangements. Too much of its book strikes one as second-rate Fletcher or second-rate somebody else." He also noted the band "does need soloists, and in the worst way. Only the trombonist is at all good." He ends his review by damning Ward with faint praise: "Boston has certainly never harbored half so good a large band, and everything considered, Ward deserves a world of praise. Any Boston band that plays in tune is a rarity."[1]

The Normandie Ballroom, on Washington Street near the corner of West Street, generally offered music on the sweeter side, as played by the likes of Al Donahue's Orchestra. Donahue, from Dorchester, was a violinist by trade and a graduate of both the New England Conservatory and the Boston University Law School. His prewar orchestras played posh places like the Rainbow Room and Waldorf-Astoria in New York and the Cocoanut Grove in Los Angeles; when he played Boston, he was in the hotels, like the Ritz and the Statler, as well as the Normandie. In 1938 he, too climbed aboard the swing bandwagon, using the tag line "Low Down Rhythm in a Top Hat," and over the next five years hired a number of good Boston jazz players: drummers Buzzy Drootin, Jimmy Felton (Falzone), and Joe MacDonald; saxophonists Al Anthony and Al Drootin; and trumpeter Ray Borden.

In 1938, Donahue hired a new vocalist, Paula Kelly, with whom he made more than 60 recordings. Kelly later went with Glenn Miller, as the girl singer in the Modernaires. When wartime travel restrictions limited band mobility, Donahue returned to Boston and played long engagements at the Ritz and the Totem Pole. He returned to sweet music at the war's end. An astute businessman, Donahue at one point owned the famous Meadowbrook Ballroom in New Jersey, and had more than 30 orchestras working under his name, with a virtual monopoly on bands entertaining aboard Bermuda-bound steamships.

Bobby Hackett, who had been so successful at the Theatrical Club a few years before, was off the Horace Heidt band and back in Boston in 1941, and it didn't take him long to reunite with old friends. Al Taxier from the Theatrical Club was managing the Versailles Restaurant, upstairs in the old church at 76 Warrenton Street, where Southland had been. It made sense for Taxier and Hackett to work together again, and the Theatrical Club connection didn't stop there. Hackett assembled a new 11-piece band, and it included Theatrical veterans Brad Gowans and saxophonist Billy Wildes. Taxier showcased this band at the Versailles and bought radio time on WMEX, and so it was that the Versailles recreated a little of that 1930s magic between January and May of 1941. It didn't last because Hackett didn't remain in Boston long, joining Glenn Miller in June 1941. His Versailles band was only a footnote in his long career, and isn't mentioned in his biographies.

The one commercial success coming out of Boston was Vaughn Monroe's Orchestra. Monroe studied voice at the New England Conservatory and played a fair trumpet, and he learned the band business working for Jack Marshard, Boston's top contractor, in the late 1930s. His own band debuted in 1940, a 14-piece swing band that mixed instrumental and vocal numbers and enjoyed great popularity on college campuses. He introduced his theme song, "Racing with the Moon," in 1941. As his commercial success grew, the show featured the vocals of Monroe and his girl singers exclusively, with the band relegated to the background. Nonetheless, plenty of talent passed through the band, and in the postwar years, when big band jobs were scarce, the steady work with Monroe lured men like Conniff, Don Alessi, and Ted Goddard into the fold.

Monroe was a bankable star, selling millions of records and hosting the *Camel Cavalcade* program on CBS Radio. In 1946 he opened the Meadows, a sprawling nightclub west of Boston on Route 9 in Framingham, where his band established its home base. He made forgettable films in Hollywood and had a weekly variety series on CBS television in 1950–1951. Monroe was still a commercial draw when he broke up the band in May of 1953. Noteworthy were saxophonist Andy Bagni and trombonist Joe Connie, two Boston musicians who were with Monroe for the whole 14-year odyssey. Maybe they didn't play as much jazz as they liked, but they made a good living.

All the bands to this point were white bands. There were prominent black bands as well, but they weren't covered by the local papers, much less *Down Beat* or *Metronome*. At 10 to 12 pieces, they were comparable to the Ward or Hackett bands in size, and larger than the Mass Ave nightclub bands. Those sextets or octets working the clubs cost less to hire, and simple economics might explain why there were only two prominent large bands made up of black musicians in the late 1930s and early 1940s. The better of these was the Alabama Aces, led by alto saxophonist Joe Nevils. The second was the band of Tasker Crosson.

Joe Nevils was a contemporary of the better-known Boston alto saxophonists, Johnny Hodges and Charlie Holmes. He led the Alabama Aces from as early as 1932, when the band included one of the best arrangers in the business, trumpeter John Nesbitt, who came to fame with McKinney's Cotton Pickers. Even though they left behind no recordings, it isn't hard to imagine that the Alabama Aces were the best large ensemble in Boston in the 1930s. Big bands start with the brass, and Nevils always had the town's top trumpeters: Howard Callender paired with Nesbitt, Jabbo Jenkins in the mid-1930s, John Cooke and Gene Caines from 1937 to 1940, and Charlie Hooks added when Nevils joined forces with Blanche Calloway in 1939 and 1940.

In 1937 and 1938, a 10-piece version of the Alabama Aces worked as the house band at the Little Dixie club. The stability certainly helped them develop their sound, as did some consistency in the group's personnel. Tenor man Danny Potter, trombonist Ralph Harding, and drummer Virgil Baker were constants in the band from 1936 to 1940.

Nevils broke up the Alabama Aces in 1941 to focus on nightclub work with his sextet, and he entered the army in 1942. His career resumed on a more modest scale after the war; he went to work for the post office but still had time to lead a small group, and from 1949 through 1953, that group worked at El Tropico, the upstairs room at Izzy Ort's on Essex Street. Nevils was also deeply involved in the affairs of Local 535, serving as vice president for about ten years.

For years Nevils listed his occupation in the Boston City Directory as musician. Starting in about 1960, he changed it to letter carrier, acknowledging the end of his musical career. Joe Nevils died in Boston in 1980 at the age of 75.

Tasker Crosson first played banjo, guitar, and bass, but he's remembered more as a bandleader than as an instrumentalist. He led bands in Boston from the late 1920s, and newspaper ads from 1932 have his Boston Troubadours engaged in battles of music at Ruggles Hall in Roxbury. By the mid-1930s his band, by then named Tasker Crosson and His Ten Statesmen (sometimes Twelve Statesmen), was busy all the time as a dance band for hire. There were sororities, social clubs, fraternal organizations, and church groups, and they all hired a band sooner or later, and it was Crosson who often got the call. In the late 1930s, Crosson's group added a Maine itinerary to its summer schedule, working fairs and dances in far-flung towns like Newport and Dover-Foxcroft. At the end of the decade, the Crosson unit was working some pretty respectable gigs, like playing at the King Philip Ballroom in Wrentham, a well-known spot that generally did not hire black bands, and ringing in the new year of 1939 in a battle of music with Wingy Manone's Orchestra at the Roseland-State Ballroom.

For all of that, the Crosson band is generally remembered as a "schoolin' band," where young musicians learned their craft and then moved on to a better band. The Roxbury bassist Lloyd Trotman recalled playing one of his first jobs with Tasker Crosson, as a teenage substitute.

> It was during the war when there were no bass players around, and they needed one. Tasker knew my father, that was the connection. My father used to hold dances and he'd hire all these bands so they knew him and knew his sons were musicians. Al Hines was Crosson's bass player, and he was a legitimate player. And Hines said you're going to get in the way up here, let me

help you... so he taped up my two fingers so fat I couldn't get them between the strings to play too many wrong notes![2]

Drummer Alan Dawson recalled his first experience with Crosson, too.

My first job was on New Year's Eve in 1943 with Tasker Crosson. And the reason I got the job was because I had a hi-hat. They wanted my hi-hat and I came with it. I wasn't going to let it out of my sight. Actually I only played one tune on the gig. Of course, I had been practicing lots of fast things and I couldn't wait. I was sitting up there just begging to play something fast. So what do you think they played—a ballad. I never had a pair of brushes in my hand and I didn't know what to do. I really stunk. But I guess Tasker saw some potential, because he hired me a couple of months later to work with him two nights a week at the USO on Ruggles Street in Boston.[3]

Perhaps those Statesmen lacked polish, but if Crosson ran a schoolin' band, he and his longtime collaborator, alto saxophonist Clifton "Smickles" Smith, turned out some fine pupils. Sabby Lewis started with Crosson, as did Joe Booker, Gene Caines, and Ricky Pratt from Sabby's 1940s band. Lloyd Trotman and his brother Ernie started with Crosson, and Ernie stayed for three years. Others putting in formative time as Statesmen included trumpeters Andy Kelton and Jabbo Jenkins, guitarist Tom Brown, and drummers Bobby Donaldson and Roy Haynes.

Crosson's band continued after the war, and some of the young modernists, like Sam Rivers and Gladstone Scott, worked jobs for Crosson. They played his stock charts to popular dance tunes, and it was a far cry from the bebop they loved. But it bought groceries, which was often more than the bebop did.

Crosson dissolved the Statesmen around 1950, the year he and Smickles Smith organized a quartet to play regularly on the *Boston Belle*, the Boston-Provincetown ferry. Various Crosson quartets, always with Smith alongside, continued into 1955. Tasker Crosson died in Boston in 1985 at the age of 81.

Home of the Big Bands: RKO Boston Theatre

One of the best singers to come out of Boston was Teddi (Theodora) King, from nearby Revere. When Teddi was a kid, she'd pack herself a lunch, arrive early at the RKO Boston Theatre to get a front-row seat, and then stay all day studying the big band singers. It is amusing to think of the diminutive Ms. King, barely five feet tall, elbowing her way down front in the 2,400-seat theater to get a good seat. Teddi, waiting through the comics and the sword swallowers and the dancing dogs, waiting for that other great Boston singer, Frances Wayne, to take the stage with Woody Herman's band. Teddi, big ears, right up front, with her sandwich and an apple and all that anticipation.

That's how one jazz singer was born. And it was at the RKO that Teddi recorded her first triumph, winning a Dinah Shore sing-alike contest in February 1945.

Actually, there were two RKO theaters on Washington Street, just blocks apart. The building at 539 Washington was one of the jewels of the chain, dedicated to Benjamin Franklin Keith himself, one of the princes of vaudeville. That was the Keith Memorial Theatre, or the RKO Keith, and after decades of neglect it was fully restored and reopened with great fanfare in July 2004 as the Opera House.

The RKO Boston was a few blocks south and across the street at 614 Washington, at the corner of Essex Street. Opened in 1925, the RKO was part of a massive building that filled (and still fills) the entire block bounded by Washington, Hayward Place, Harrison Street, and Essex Street. The main entrance was on Washington Street, leading into an elaborate mirrored lobby with crystal chandeliers. The theater itself was built on a pronounced back-to-front slope, with the stage actually below street level.

There was plenty of musical history at the RKO long before Ms. King ever lunched there. The theater programs mirrored popular taste, perhaps even helped define it, first with vaudeville shows, then with large-cast spectaculars like George White's *Scandals* and Earl Carroll's *Vanities*, then with lavish stage shows featuring glamor girls like Ann Corio and Sally Rand, and finally with the big bands.

A typical RKO big-band show featured a movie, two or more opening acts, and the headliner. The films were, for the most part, B-pictures: *Doughboys in Ireland, Honeymoon Ahead, That Brennan Girl.* Does anyone remember them? Doesn't matter. Teenagers weren't lining up at 8:00 in the morning for the movies.

There were comics, singers, and dancers aplenty in the opening acts, but there were also acrobats, roller skaters, psychics, magicians, contortionists, and numerous animals, including Pansy the Wonder Horse, which was actually two guys in a horse costume. And down in the pit, playing spooky sounds for psychics and waltzes for roller skaters, was the house band, and they had to be sharp, recalled trumpeter Al Natale:

> Ralph Fuccillo was the lead trumpet player in the RKO house band during the war. He got me on the band. I was a good reader, and that's what you needed to be to work all the different shows. Larry Flint was the conductor, and he'd recommend me as a substitute when visiting bands needed a trumpet player, so I worked with Bobby Sherwood, Freddie Slack, and Charlie Spivak in 1944, '45. That's how I came to join Bob Chester's band. I caught up to Chester in Philadelphia at the Earle Theater and hit the road. I'm all of

17 or 18. We worked at the Steel Pier in Atlantic City, opposite Harry James, and here I am, a kid from the North End never much farther from home than Scollay Square, and I'm working at the Steel Pier and meeting Harry James, who I admired... fabulous. And that started because of the RKO.[4]

Like Natale says, though, the best part was the bands. Bands for every taste, from the novelty bands of Spike Jones and Milt Britton to the sweet bands of Guy Lombardo and Sammy Kaye to the swing bands of Lucky Millinder and Bobby Sherwood to the very best bands in the land, the jazz bands. All the top bands played the RKO, and most played it often: Charlie Barnet, Count Basie, Cab Calloway, Duke Ellington, Ella Fitzgerald/Chick Webb, Benny Goodman, Lionel Hampton, Woody Herman, Stan Kenton, Gene Krupa, Jimmie Lunceford. It was *the* live performance venue in Boston in the swing years.

This was not easy work. A show opened on Thursday, played for seven days, and moved on to the next stop on the RKO circuit. Five shows a day was not uncommon, and between the morning shows on holidays and the midnight shows catering to wartime defense workers, a workday at the RKO might start before lunch and end in the small hours of the morning.

The big bands ran out of gas in 1946, about the same time the stage shows became too expensive to produce. In 1947 there were long stretches on the calendar with no live shows, just double-feature films. The few bands still touring (Basie, Hampton, Kenton, Ina Ray Hutton) created a lively spring season in 1948, but after that there were no more bands and fewer and fewer live shows of any kind. The last live show at the RKO Boston wasn't musical at all, but a week of legitimate theater in November 1952, when a cast including Charles Boyer, Cedric Hardwicke, Charles Laughton, and Agnes Moorehead performed G. B. Shaw's *Don Juan in Hell*. After that it was all celluloid.

In 1984, the *Boston Globe's* Bill Buchanan stood outside the then-shuttered theater, and recalled Glenn Miller's last Boston appearance 40 years before, two weeks before Miller broke up his band and entered the army:

> As I stood looking at that boarded-up entrance, it was hard to imagine lines extending around the corner to Essex street as fans waited to get into the theater to hear the Miller orchestra. But for those in the audience, there was nothing quite like that moment when the movie would end, the house lights would dim, the band's theme song, "Moonlight Serenade," would begin to play, the lights would come up, the curtains would part, and there before you would be Glenn Miller and his orchestra.[5]

The RKO was, he believed, the most exciting place in Boston in the big band era.

Although the building still stands at 600 Washington, there is no sign of the theater. The stage doors on Hayward Place are bricked over, the marquee is long gone, and the entrance leads to a subway station instead of a spacious lobby. The theater, dark now for many years and used only for storage, is still intact within.

"Rowdy After a Certain Polite Fashion"

The Brunswick Hotel, at 520 Boylston Street at the corner of Clarendon Street, earned its spot on the Boston jazz map during the Jazz Age when it hosted the orchestra led by Bostonian Leo Reisman, a spritzed-up society band if there ever was one. For a time, the hotel's Egyptian Room was the hottest spot in the Back Bay. Trumpeter Max Kaminsky worked for Reisman in those days.

> Leo, an institution as a society bandleader in Boston during Prohibition, was perfect for the twenties. John O'Hara once wrote about "that minor phenomenon called Leo Reisman," whom he dubbed "the Spirit of Expensive Fun," and though the band's style, he said, was mannered and affected, it had a great vitality and "was rowdy after a certain polite fashion." That last phrase brings to my mind the picture of Leo lying on his back on the bandstand and kicking up his legs to mark the beat of the band—a position he resorted to when he became tired of waving his baton.[6]

Leo's run at the Egyptian Room is a little early for us, and his jazz *was* mannered and affected. Yet he released dozens of records on Victor, and when he left Boston to take up residence at New York's Central Park Casino, he had the good sense to take along his piano player, a young pharmacist from Cambridge named Eddy Duchin, and later to hire Fred Astaire as a vocalist. Alas, the Egyptian Room lost its luster after the stock market crash and the Brunswick spent the 1930s trying to recapture it. The Egyptian Room gave way to the Brunswick Casino and then the Marionette Room, in which a marionette band battled with "real" musicians. How, I wonder, did *that* work? Reisman gave way to Ranny Weeks and then to the Rippling Rhythms of Roly Rogers, whose violinist and arranger was Jerry Gray (Graziano) from East Boston, who a few years later arranged "Begin the Beguine" for Artie Shaw and "String of Pearls" for Glenn Miller, among many others

Finally in 1940 the Brunswick created the Bermuda Terrace and called in the name bands to provide the music. They came—Charlie Barnet, Les Brown, Lionel Hampton, John Kirby, Will Osborne, Raymond Scott, and Jack Teagarden among them. The Terrace was popular from the day it opened its doors. Ella Fitzgerald, then leading Chick Webb's orchestra, played the room several times. Boston was good to the Webb/Fitzgerald band, first for their long engagement in 1939 at the Hotel Gardner's Flamingo Room, and then after Webb's death that year, at the Brunswick where they became Fitzgerald's band.

Bands settled in at the Brunswick for a month at a time, and the importance of month-long location jobs like this were critical to a band's success—the band could get off the road and out of the grind of one-nighters, learn some new music, catch up on sleep, and generally regroup.

It ended abruptly at the Brunswick just after Will Osborne played his last set on April 21, 1942, when the U.S. Coast Guard took over the hotel to provide quarters for its personnel for the duration. The Coast Guard quit the hotel in December 1945, and the Brunswick re-entered the hotel business but not the entertainment business. As it turned out, the property was more valuable than the hotel on it, and with an office building on the drawing board, developers demolished the Brunswick in 1957.

The Flamingo Room

Jack Levaggi[7] opened a nightclub downstairs in the Hotel Gardner, 199 Mass Ave at Norway Street, sometime in the mid-1930s. For two years, in 1938-1939, his room added sparkle to the Ballroom District doings.

Levaggi started in the nightclub business in Boston since the mid 1920s. He'd run the Ten Acres, a big club in suburban Wayland, then sold it and bought the old church at 76 Warrenton Street. There he opened the Lido Venice, which was one of Boston's premiere speakeasies, a place where his headwaiter made $300 per night in tips and he could hire the Casa Loma Orchestra for his dance band. Competition from newer clubs, like the Cocoanut Grove, put him out of business. Then he opened Levaggi's Downtown on Hayward Place, and Levaggi's Uptown in the Gardner. He was again doing well, so he plowed his money into a five-masted schooner, which he planned to use as a show boat. It flopped. He sold Downtown to concentrate on Uptown, which he renamed the Flamingo Room in 1938. The cover charge at the plush Flamingo was $2 (just over $32 in 2012 dollars), quite high for the time, but the entertainment was good, including the orchestras of both Jimmy and Tommy Dorsey, Woody Herman, and his old friends the Casa Loma.

The Flamingo Room's high point was a two-month engagement by the Chick Webb Orchestra in spring 1938. Webb's singer was the young Ella Fitzgerald, and she and songwriter Al Feldman were fooling around with a nursery rhyme, trying to put catchy music to it. They did, and Ella sang it for the first time at the Flamingo with the Webb band. "A-Tisket, A-Tasket" sold a million copies and spent ten weeks at number one on radio's *Your Hit Parade* in 1938. Over the years, critics have dismissed "A-Tisket, A-Tasket" as lightweight, but it could have been worse. Fitzgerald and Feldman were also working on something called "No Matter How Many Porkchops You Eat, You Gotta Leave the Bone." Be happy they went with that little yellow basket!

The black press took notice of the positive response to Webb's engagement at the hitherto white-bands-only Flamingo. The *Afro-American's* Lillian Johnson, reporting that the nightclub was extending its engagement of Chick Webb's Orchestra, drolly noted that "Chick and his band, and Ella, of course, will be held over four more weeks, and maybe longer, in Boston, where ordinarily, about the only thing that holds over is winter."[8]

Jack Levaggi presented good music and gave the club his best shot, but the Flamingo Room wasn't especially successful. By 1940 the name bands were gone and a Boston sextet led by singer Rudy Bauer provided the entertainment. Then a heart attack forced Levaggi out of the nightclub business and into a quieter life running a restaurant in the comparatively bucolic North Reading, where he died in 1951. The Flamingo itself was long gone when the Gardner Hotel was demolished in the 1960s to make way for the Church Park Apartments.

Broadcasting Jump Sessions from Coast to Coast

If you switched on WBZ radio in late July 1939, you might have heard this:

> The Duke is on the air! Good evening Ladies and Gentlemen, the National Broadcasting Company proudly presents Duke Ellington's internationally famous orchestra in a program of dance music from one of the Hub's smartest summer spots, the beautiful terrace on the roof of the Ritz Carlton Hotel in the City of Boston.[9]

The swank Roof at the Ritz Carlton Hotel, 18 floors above the intersection of Arlington and Newbury Streets, featured big bands and dancing under the stars from the mid-thirties until 1943. Sometimes it hired the very best, like Basie, Ellington, or Shaw. Generally, however, the dance bands were of a sweeter variety, quite often the high-caliber society bands fielded by Ruby Newman.

Jazz fans of a certain age remember the Ritz fondly even though it really wasn't much of a jazz place. Perhaps it was because dancers enjoyed being outdoors on the roof, beating the summer heat and admiring the views. The Roof was a May-to-September affair, and with nice weather even a so-so attraction could draw 2,000 paid admissions for the week. If you couldn't be there yourself, you could listen to WBZ and hear Fred B. Cole utter things like, "Any of you children from coast to coast like a jump session? If you do, keep right on listening because here's one that's going to rock Beacon Hill from Arlington Street right over to Bowdoin Square."[10]

Being outdoors on a pleasant summer night was one thing, but you can't always trust the New England weather. The Ritz Roof had to factor in hurricanes. Basie's was the last band to play before the big one hit on September 21, 1938. When Basie's men showed up for work, they found the bandstand blown into the street and the remainder of their engagement canceled. In fact, the remainder of the season was canceled.

During the war years, with travel restrictions in place, local bands like Newman's picked up more of the work, and some of Boston's long-absent bandleaders hunkered down for long stays at the home town Ritz during those wartime summers. In 1942, Leo Reisman played the Roof, his first Boston engagement since his fabled days at the Brunswick, and the following year Al Donahue, back after years in California, did the same.

After the war, the society work continued indoors, but the Ritz Roof and the name bands did not. In fact, about the only postwar event of jazz significance at the Ritz transpired when Benny Goodman collapsed in his suite in April 1953, at the very beginning of his national tour with Louis Armstrong, a portent of the dismal things to come on that ill-fated tour.

The Long Jazz Career of Symphony Hall

From the day it first opened in October 1900, Boston's Symphony Hall, at the intersection of Massachusetts and Huntington Avenues, has been one of the world's great concert halls. But it was as much a musical home to Armstrong and Ellington as it was to Heifitz and Serkin.

Paul Whiteman gained great fame with his "symphonic jazz" concerts of the 1920s. Leo Reisman followed soon after with more of the same. True jazz bands appeared more frequently as the swing era gained momentum in the 1930s. More fun, perhaps, were the nights when the seats down front were removed and Symphony Hall became a fancy dance hall. Many of these dances were held on Thursday night, traditionally the domestic servants' night off. Only the good bands played at Symphony Hall, such as those of Basie, Ellington, Goodman, and Lunceford. Some even staged battles of music on its storied stage.

Symphony Hall's finest hour in jazz came January 28, 1943. On that night, Duke Ellington's Orchestra presented the second complete performance of "Black, Brown, and Beige," Ellington's ambitious 43-minute "tone parallel to the history of the American Negro." It was one of only three complete performances of this landmark work. Although not critically acclaimed, the show was a smashing success at the box office. The performance was sold out, and 1,200 people were turned away, all on a wintry night after 12 inches of snow fell on Boston. One must believe that Harry Carney, whose baritone anchored the Ellington reed section, and alto saxophonist Johnny Hodges, the orchestra's star soloist, shined on this night, playing for the hometown crowd.

Two Ballrooms, Two Bands, One Admission

Ray Galvin owned both the Raymor Ballroom, at 253 Huntington, and the Play-Mor Ballroom, next door at 263 Huntington, and most people spoke of them in a single breath, as in "the Raymor-Play-Mor." Whatever they called it, this location, just off Massachusetts Avenue in the shadow of Symphony Hall, was a busy place for about 25 years.

The ballroom at 263 was the older of the two, operating from at least the late 1920s, first as the Tent Ballroom until 1935, then the Onyx for a year, then the Aragon Ballroom for two years. All of these places generally used local bands, with name bands from New York dropping in for one-nighters. Galvin took control of the property and opened the Play-Mor in December 1938. Thus did Galvin silence his neighborhood competitor—he had opened the Raymor Ballroom next door in 1936, and having the Aragon presenting Tommy Dorsey or Fats Waller couldn't have helped his own box office. So he bought them out.

Galvin's strategy for his two-room operation, revealed through month after month of advertising, was this. All things being equal, the name bands played the Raymor, while local outfits played the Play-Mor. And again all things being equal, swing bands played the Raymor while sweet bands played the Play-Mor. On any given night, one or both rooms might be in use; during the week it was common practice to open just the Raymor, while on the weekends both rooms opened. Regardless, one admission was good for both. It cost 55 cents, increasing to 75 cents on the weekend. A partition separated the two rooms, and patrons could pass freely back and forth. The advertising slogan was "2 Bands—2 Ballrooms—1 Admission."

Before Galvin opened the Play-Mor, though, he operated the Raymor on a different model, with bands coming in for a month and backed by Galvin's purchase of radio time. Two bands in particular took advantage of the Raymor in 1937–1938, using it as a place to work out the kinks musically before moving on to New York City. One was Woody Herman, who began his long association with Boston jazz at the Raymor in 1938. Booked for two one-month stints and on the radio every night, the Raymor was one of his last stops before the New York engagement at the Famous Door that put over

Symphony Hall and the Raymor/Play-Mor in 1941, with the tiny
Symphony Record Shop wedged in between, glimpsed over a construction
barricade. Courtesy of Historic New England.

"The Band That Plays the Blues." Woody liked Boston and Boston liked
Woody; Herman would return to Boston again and again, and he filled out
his bands with literally dozens of Boston musicians over the decades.

The other Raymor band was Glenn Miller's. George Simon, the long-time
editor of *Metronome* and chronicler of all things Miller, recounts the saga of
the early Miller band at the Raymor, where they played three lengthy
engagements (starting in June and November 1937, and April 1938) while
they struggled along the road to success. Said Simon about the Raymor:

> Once probably considered elegant, it had aged into a typical mid-city ball-
> room. Heavily draped and dimly lit, it offered about as much glamour as a
> men's locker room. But it had a loyal clientele and a very gentle and under-
> standing manager in Hughie Galvin, who liked Glenn and the band, and
> who took them back after they returned from their first road trip.[11]

Miller's first network broadcast over NBC originated from the Raymor on
December 15, 1937, more than a year before they clicked.[12] Fred B. Cole of
WBZ was at the microphone that night.

Artie Shaw played his first job as a leader in Boston at the Raymor, calling it
"a little beat-up joint."[13] (Les Brown and Stan Kenton also worked their first

jobs as bandleaders in Boston at the Raymor, but their opinions aren't on record.) It might have been beat up, but the Raymor featured a long list of name and local bands all through the war and in the years leading up to it. But study the names on that name-band list—Georgie Auld, Bobby Byrne, Bob Chester, Buddy Morrow, Red Nichols, Will Osborne, Teddy Powell, Tommy Reynolds, Bobby Sherwood, Jack Teagarden. Or study the names on the local band list—Johnny Alaura, Tony Brown, Allan Curtis, Larry Funk, Andy Jacobson, Jacques Renard—and what jumps out at you is, these were all white bands. In this the Raymor differed from its contemporaries. The RKO Boston Theater, the Ken, the Savoy, the Tic Toc, and their competitor right around the corner, the Roseland-State, all regularly presented black entertainers. Draw your own conclusions.

Even before the war ended, the ballroom operators saw attendance declining and noted that people weren't as interested in brass-heavy swing music as they once were. By V-J Day, the name bands were gone and Galvin was rotating a group of Boston dance bands: Andy Jacobson (the longtime leader of the Metropolitan Theatre orchestra, Jacobson got Saturday nights), Johnny Alaura, Syd Ross, Pete Cutler, Allan Curtis. Then came 1946, which was a murderously tough year for the band business. Nightlife in general went into a postwar decline, bands folded by the dozen, and ballrooms shuttered. Exactly when Galvin sold out is unclear, but sometime in fall 1946 both rooms closed and the decorators moved in. Boston was getting a new ballroom, to be called the Symphony Ballroom, next door to Symphony Hall on the site of the Play-Mor. Where for years there were two rooms, there was now just one, at 263 Huntington. The Raymor was replaced by a chain-store cafeteria.

The new Symphony Ballroom had its grand opening on Christmas night, 1946, with the music of Mal Hallett. Mal Hallett was a constant in those first years, appearing weekends throughout 1947 and 1948, although his band at that point was a high-turnover affair staffed by young musicians. Unlike its predecessors, though, the Symphony presented a varied program that went beyond standard dance band fare, eventually including jump and bop bands. For the big bands still on the road in the bleak postwar years, the Symphony was a frequent stop.

Based on the 1947–1949 schedule, one might get the impression that there was nothing wrong with the band business. These were good bands, surviving on the circuit playing one-nighters or weekends: Charlie Barnet, Jimmy Dorsey, Dizzy Gillespie, Lionel Hampton, Woody Herman, Stan Kenton, Hal McIntyre, Tommy Reynolds, Claude Thornhill. Artie Shaw debuted his new 20-piece orchestra at the Symphony in September 1949. Maybe it even seemed like the good old days for some of these bands, coming in on the weekends and engaging in a battle of music with Mal Hallett's orchestra.

With the new decade, though, the bands got smaller and the music got more modern. The Symphony, like other spots, cut expenses by hiring singles and matching them up with local musicians. Billie Holiday, Stan Getz, Dizzy Gillespie, and Charlie Parker worked this way. In April 1951, Charlie Parker worked with Joe Gordon for the first time, and Gordon made such a strong impression that he became Parker's first call trumpet player for his later Boston gigs. Don Stratton recalls:

> Joe Gordon played with Bird for the fist time at Symphony Ballroom because Red Rodney, who knew Joe's playing, convinced Bird to let him sit in that night. They played a blues and Joe acquitted himself well. Then Bird called "Cherokee" and Joe played the hell out of it![14]

George Shearing, who became one of the biggest box-office draws in jazz in the 1950s, made his first New England appearance at the Symphony in May 1950, working opposite Nat Pierce's Orchestra. Shearing liked Pierce's vocalist, Teddi King, so much that he hired her to sing with his Quintet.

The Symphony proved to be the Pierce band's steadiest gig; the often-idle unit worked weekends at the ballroom all through the spring of 1950.

The Symphony Ballroom closed in late spring 1952. It couldn't make money on dance bands, and the small-group attractions had migrated to the Hi-Hat. When the Symphony Ballroom closed, only the Roseland-State remained to mark the Ballroom District.

Chapter 3

Charlie Shribman and the Roseland-State Ballroom

If we were to follow only one place to tell the story of the Ballroom District, it would have to be the Roseland-State Ballroom. It was the right room, in the right neighborhood, with the right owners to push it along.

Those owners were Charlie and Cy (Simon)[1] Shribman, the kingmakers of the big band era, not only in Boston but throughout the northeast and beyond. Through their company, Charles Shribman Orchestras, they had a hand in every aspect of the band business, as booking agents, personal managers, ballroom owners and operators, venture capitalists, and promoters. They knew talent when they heard it, and they nurtured and managed a series of high-profile bands from the twenties through the forties. They actively advertised and promoted their bands and properties, and shrewdly saw the role of radio in the band business from the early days of both. In 1942, Duke Ellington said that there wouldn't have been a band business without Charlie Shribman, and people would have starved if he hadn't been around to help.[2]

The Shribmans started in the amusements business in the years following World War I, managing bowling alleys and the Social Hour pool hall in their home town of Salem, Massachusetts. In the early twenties they opened their first of many ballrooms, the Charleshurst in Salem Willows, and began booking a variety of bands to play it—dance bands, polka bands, hot bands. Then, as Ellington wrote in *Music Is My Mistress*, "The time came when Charlie Shribman heard a big band, and ever after that he dedicated himself to supporting, patronizing, and subsidizing—not one, but all of them." Charleshurst was where they first hired Duke Ellington in 1924, and Ellington used Salem as his New England base of operations through the twenties.

Building a Band: the Mal Hallett Orchestra

While the band and ballroom businesses percolated, Shribman met a Boston bandleader named Mal Hallett. Hallett was a tall, good-looking guy, likable and outgoing, a fiddler with Boston Conservatory training and an ear for talent. When Charlie Shribman talked about promotion, Hallett listened. What Shribman understood better than anyone else in the band business was the

power of "noise." Today we'd call it "buzz." Shribman was a relentless promoter. He saturated the papers with advertising and bought radio time to
showcase his bands. Charlie Shribman signed Hallett and made him a star,
one of the first bandleaders to be so recognized, and gave the band all the
work it could handle around the populous northeast, with side trips as far
away as Los Angeles.

Mal Hallett, 1938

As part of his promotion, Shribman set
up battles of music, with two or more
bands playing for an audience that by
acclamation would declare a winner.
Hallett did quite well battling the best
bands of the day, like Paul Whiteman
and Speed Webb and Coon-Sanders.
Duke Ellington recalled being blown
across the Charles River in a band
battle with Hallett,[3] and Count Basie
recalled a battle with Hallett a few
years later in Buffalo: "he chopped
heads…it was murder…he ran us out
of there…I'll never forget that
experience."[4]

Hallett's career was derailed by an
accident; in June 1930 he fell and
broke his arm, which ended his violin-
playing days for good. The long
convalescence forced Hallett to break
up his band and cancel his contracts, and he dropped from sight for two years.
He made his comeback with the 1933 band that featured Frankie Carle, Jack
Jenney, Gene Krupa, and Toots Mondello, and he continued to run a good
band all through the 1930s and the war years. George Simon, reviewing the
Hallett band in *Metronome* in October 1936, said Hallett's band was playing
"uninhibited swing." The next year he hired the sensational vocalist Teddy
Grace. And so it went; as late as 1943 the Don Fagerquist-led version of the
Hallett band was in residence at New York's Park Central Hotel.

Noise and showmanship and good music. That's how Shribman and
Hallett made it, or as one writer put it, through "honest management and
splash publicity."[5] The 1930s were more successful than the 1920s for
Shribman, despite the country's economic woes. By the early 1930s Charlie's
brother Cy was fully involved, and everything they learned in making Hallett

a success—about the ballroom network, radio, publicity, the battles of music—would be put to work in the coming decade for many more bands.

The Heart of the Ballroom District

The Shribmans quietly built a sprawling business. By the time our story commences in earnest in 1937, they had moved their company to Boston, to the tenth floor of the Little Building on Boylston Street, the headquarters of the New England music industry in the years before World War II. They opened an office in New York. They booked more bands and invested in more ballrooms, owning some and leasing others. One of those properties was the Roseland-State Ballroom in the State Theater Building.

The State stood on the west side of Massachusetts Avenue, stretching the entire block from Burbank to Norway Streets, intersections now erased from the Boston map. It was an early version of what we might call an "entertainment complex." Besides the ballroom, there was E. M. Loew's 3,500-seat State Theatre, the State Bowling Alleys in the basement (the Shribmans owned that, too, and nephew Joe managed it), and a small second-floor movie theater, the Fine Arts. Retail stores and offices filled out the building. In 1940, Charles Shribman Orchestras moved its offices there and stayed for about 20 years.

For a time in the 1930s, there were actually two ballrooms, the State and the Roseland. The entrance to the State was at 217 Mass Ave, while the entrance to the Roseland was around the corner at 15 Burbank. Advertisements indicate that the name attractions played the State, while the Roseland/Colonial featured local bands. At some point the Shribmans assumed control of the Roseland and removed the wall between the rooms. By 1937, the Roseland-State Ballroom was going six nights a week and only the Boston blue laws stopped it from going seven.

There were other ballrooms in the neighborhood, but the Roseland-State was the biggest and the most popular. *Down Beat* reported that an Ellington one-nighter in March 1943 set the box office record with 2,725 paid admissions.[6] The very best bands came here, including those of Count Basie, Charlie Barnet, and Jimmie Lunceford. Admission was 55 cents during the week, 75 cents on the weekends. Business was good.

The northeast, and especially New England, was the strongest band market in the country in the Shribman years, a result of its large population in a small geographic area. Hops between population centers were short, making the one-nighters easier to bear, and when the band got to where it was going, there was a Shribman booking waiting and a good crowd in attendance.

Working with the Shribmans, a band could base itself in Boston and make out fairly well.

Consider Artie Shaw. When Shaw was building his band in 1937—this was the band that included Billie Holiday—he sold a piece of it to the Shribmans, and they put their big-band conglomerate to work for him. They booked Shaw's band (then called Art Shaw and His Rhythm Makers) into the Roseland-State on Tuesday and Saturday nights, and gave him rehearsal space in the building's basement. They advertised every day in the *Boston Post*. The Roseland fed live pickups to the CBS radio network, so every Tuesday and Saturday the Shaw band was heard throughout New England and beyond, and Shaw surely played "Rockin' the State" and "Back Bay Shuffle," the tunes he wrote to commemorate his residency on Mass Ave. The rest of the week, Shaw worked in other Shribman properties throughout the northeast on "runouts"—one-nighters in communities within a day's range of the band's broadcast home. They'd play all the Shribman ballrooms, the Charleshurst, the Lyonhurst in Marlboro, the Roseland in Taunton, Nuttings-on-the-Charles in Waltham, the Starlight in Lynnfield, the Bournehurst in Buzzard's Bay. This regimen continued for three months, and when Shaw's band finally left Boston in spring 1938, the world knew all about it.

The Roseland-State, with its spacious waxed floor and colored neon was an exciting place, described by Malcolm Little, who recalled his time there (probably late 1940) when he was working the shoeshine stand:

> "*Showtime!*" people would start hollering about the last hour of the dance. Then a couple of dozen really wild couples would stay on the floor, the girls changing to low white sneakers. The band now would really be blasting, and all the other dancers would form a clapping, shouting circle to watch that wild competition as it began, covering only a quarter or so of the ballroom floor. The band, the spectators and the dancers would be making the Roseland Ballroom feel like a big, rocking ship. The spotlight would be turning, pink, yellow, green, and blue, picking up the couples lindy-hopping as if they had gone made. "*Wail, man, wail!*" people would be shouting at the band; and it *would* be wailing, until first one and then another couple just ran out of strength and stumbled off toward the crowd, exhausted and soaked with sweat.[7]

Little left the shoeshine concession, moved on to other jobs, turned to crime and went to prison, and emerged a changed man, eventually adopting the name Malcolm X. Malcolm also noted that during his time there, the Roseland-State was segregated, with one night for a white audience, the next night for a black one. Like other men of their time, the Shribmans worried about the backlash mixing might provoke.

Regardless of the audience, the room just rocked. Consider one two-week period during the Roseland's peak years, January 12–26, 1940. January, after the holidays, was typically a slow month in the entertainment business, but not at the Roseland-State. On the 12th, Cab Calloway. On the 13th, a black-and-white battle of music between the hometown orchestras of Joe Nevils and Gene Dennis. On the 16th, Mal Hallett. On the 19th, another battle, this time between the big bands of Harry James and Tony Pastor. Finally on the 26th, Duke Ellington. It was a who's who of the big band era, and the Shribmans presented talent like this month after month over a period of years. Of this group, the Shribmans were managing the Dennis and Hallett outfits, financially backing Pastor, and handling the New England bookings for Calloway and Ellington. Nowadays someone might accuse the Shribmans of running a monopoly.

Hotter Than Hot! Duke Ellington at the Roseland-State Ballroom. Ad ran in the *Boston Post*, January 26, 1940.

Duke Ellington wrote that Charlie Shribman didn't want to support just one big band, he wanted to support *all* of them. And it seems as though he did. Starting with Hallett, the Shribmans put over band after band, and among those they managed or partially owned were those of Van Alexander, Sam Donahue, Woody Herman, Gene Krupa, Hal McIntyre, Glenn Miller, Mel Powell, Artie Shaw, Charlie Spivak, Tony Pastor, Tommy Reynolds, and Claude Thornhill. It was no understatement to call the Shribmans kingmakers.

Don't get the idea, though, that it was exciting every night at the Roseland-State. Even during the most frenzied months of the swing years, more than half the nights were given over to dancing of a different type. It was "old timers" making the music. Saxophonist Paul Vignoli didn't play in an old timer band, but he knew how they operated:

> The old timers were playing all the old tunes, the old waltzes and polkas, and they could work seven nights a week if they wanted to on the circuit, all the ballrooms. They just worked constantly. They played all the tunes that every-body knew, I don't think they even had music, they just played harmony to

each other. They were playing the way dance bands played when they weren't playing jazz during the '20s and early '30s. That's what they played. Everybody would just play the melody, maybe take a solo occasionally. The solos made it more attractive to the audience, and they'd get used to it: "Is Charlie gonna play his solo tonight?" And if you didn't play the same tempo that they're used to, they'd complain: "You guys don't know how to play a waltz." You'd get that from the regulars.

They were good musicians, they had to know everything, and when they got on a job calling for that music, they nailed it. So it wasn't artistically wonderful stuff, but they were working almost every night, and they were making 50 or 60 bucks a week for it. And Joe Mack played every week at the Roseland-State for I don't know how many years.[8]

George T. Simon, the chronicler of the big band era, wrote that the Miller band would play the Roseland-State in 1938 for perhaps 300 people. The next night, Joe Mack's Old Timers would play for 1,000. Said Simon: "The corn was still hard to cut."[9] That was okay with the Shribmans, because they sold the tickets whether it was Mack or Miller.

The Shribmans were essential to the success of the Glenn Miller Orchestra, and both George Simon and bandleader Charlie Barnet (another recipient of Shribman largesse) were angered by the portrayal of Cy Shribman in the 1955 film, *The Glenn Miller Story*. Both thought the portrayal was grossly inaccurate and the movie badly flawed. Shribman and Miller were close friends in real life but antagonists in the film, and Shribman himself was a well-spoken, well-educated man—not the lout portrayed by Hollywood. But Glenn and Cy were both long dead by 1955 and unable to speak for themselves.

George Simon wrote of Cy Shribman 28 years after his death:

> Cy has emerged as a legendary character among ballroom operators. His business acumen, his courage and his memory all figured in his nightly transactions, when he would travel alone between the various bands and ballrooms with which he was involved, his pockets stuffed with thousands of dollars, some of which he would collect in one place, after which he'd ride to another to pay off one of his bands, collect more money from the box office and continue to another spot where he would repeat the process. How he managed it nobody ever really knew. All his pockets bulged with rolls of bills of apparently undetermined amounts. But Cy knew exactly how much there was in each, and when he'd arrive to pay off a band, he'd merely put his hand into a pocket, finger one of the rolls and out would come the precise number of dollars to which the band was entitled. Then, when he'd return to his office, he'd enter all his transactions in the daily ledger. It was all strictly from memory, and yet the Shribman books remained in perfect order.[10]

The Last Days of a Dance-Crazy Era

Cy Shribman knew the big band era would come to an end someday, but he didn't live to see it. He died in June 1946, at age 55, about the time the band business went into decline. Charlie kept at it, though some of his zest for the business clearly died with Cy. Facing a changing economic climate, Charlie brought in bands when he could and worked to promote some new ones, such as that of Clarence "Shorty" Sherock, but by 1952 only the old timers were making money. As of that year, there were no more advertisements in the *Post* or any other paper for name bands at the Roseland-State, although *Down Beat* would note the occasional appearance of a Herman or Kenton there. *Time* wrote the place up in 1954 because it was pulling in big crowds for mambo bands, the national dance craze of the time, noting that the ballroom "was jumping higher than Bostonians had seen in a long while."[11] And Joe Mack's Old Timers were still playing there in 1958! Count Basie drew 1,100 fans one night in August 1958, and if that wasn't the last hurrah for Charlie, it was close, as he sold the ballroom shortly thereafter. By November 1958 it was under new management and renamed the New State Ballroom, serving up a steady diet of Irish music and old timers.

By 1952, Shribman had shifted the focus of his operation to his Roseland-Taunton location. Always shrewd with the numbers, Shribman saw his audience diminishing and moved his main attractions to a location equally accessible to both the Boston area and New England's south coast. In Taunton he booked the surviving big bands, like Ellington, the Dorsey Brothers, and Buddy Morrow, as well as former big band musicians now touring with their own small groups, like Gene Ammons, Hal Singer and Charlie Ventura. By the late 1950s, the ballroom was presenting mainstream dance bands twice weekly. Attempts to book more modern groups with appeal to a younger crowd met with local resistance. The *Providence Journal* reported that the mayor of Taunton forced Shribman to cancel a September 1960 dance date featuring Bill Doggett "because the dance was expected to draw a large number of Negroes to Taunton" and the mayor "doesn't want any colored in Taunton or any colored dancers at the ballroom." Shribman was ordered to cancel the event or face revocation of his ballroom operating license. He canceled it.[12] At about the same time, whether by design or coincidence, Shribman began his exit from the music business.

In 1960 Charlie closed the Charles Shribman Orchestras office in the State Theatre Building, but he continued to dabble, booking one-nighters for old friends like Basie, Ellington, and Kenton. He sold his last holding, the Roseland-Taunton, in 1964. Then he retired to Florida, ending more than 40 years in the business. He died there in 1976, at age 84. Charlie Shribman was a titan in the music business, but his passing merited only a few short paragraphs in *Billboard*.

Charlie's death truly marked the end of the Ballroom District. The New State Ballroom was the last of the dance halls, and Charlie outlived even that by eight years; his old haunt, the State Theater Building, fell to the wrecker's ball in May 1968. There isn't a trace left of the Roseland-State Ballroom, the crown jewel of the Ballroom District, or of Boston's big-band past.

Chapter 4

Swinging the Home Front

The six months following Pearl Harbor swamped the nation in bad news: Singapore surrenders…Java overrun…Bataan falls…Corregidor surrenders. At home, the war meant blackouts and price controls and rationing on meat, sugar, coffee, shoes. Non-essential driving was virtually eliminated. There were no new cars, no tires for old cars, and gasoline was rationed at three gallons per week. Scrap steel became a prized commodity, kitchen fat was recycled into explosives, and record shops collected shellac by buying back 78s for two and a half cents each.

The war undeniably boosted Boston's economy. In April 1942 the army selected the port as a major embarkation point for men and material, and wartime employment at the Charlestown navy yard peaked at about 47,000. Moribund industries revived, and there were more jobs than people to work them. Everybody made money during the war. There were just fewer ways to spend it.

A ticket seller at downtown movie theater in July 1942 told a reporter: "The town is just mobbed with soldiers and sailors. Almost every other man you see is in uniform. And there are a great many officers, especially naval officers." The manager of an all-night restaurant on Scollay Square told the same reporter that "the square was ready to fold up before the war. Now no one knows what to do to quiet it down." Compared to the previous summer, his business was double, even triple, serving office workers by day and a swollen downtown population by night. Business boomed from seven in the evening until seven in the morning, with the nightlife crowd clearing out just in time to seat the early-shift defense workers.[1]

George Frazier's "Sweet and Low-Down"

The man who left a record of Boston jazz during the war years was George Frazier. If his work in *Down Beat* and *Mademoiselle* played to a national audience, Frazier made his jazz mark back home with his column in the *Boston Herald* that began January 27, 1942. "Sweet and Low-Down" was a full-time job, five columns a week, 300 words per column. It was the first regular jazz column to appear in an American big-city daily. Frazier was also on the radio in 1942, on WEEI on Saturday mornings, and occasionally hosting *Millions for Defense* on WORL, selling war bonds.

In "Sweet and Low-Down," Frazier had a daily column and nowhere near enough Boston news to fill it, but he did his best. He promoted the Sunday jam sessions, disk jockey Bill Ingalls on WCOP, and the comings and goings at the hot spots of the day, such as the Tic Toc, the RKO Boston, and especially the Savoy. That was where the best jazz in Boston could be found, and the best players at the Savoy in 1942 were in the bands of Frankie Newton and Sabby Lewis.

In "Sweet and Low-Down," Frazier praised his friends (Pee Wee Russell, Mildred Bailey, Eddie Condon) scorned his enemies (the Andrews Sisters, Buddy Rich, Bob Eberle), and regularly spanked the celebrities in the big band business. Here the recipient is Stan Kenton:

> My own reaction to Kenton's music is that it is neither fish nor flesh, but pretty foul. It seems to me pretentious, artistically phony, and without any attributes that might even charitably be called jazz... It plays too loud, it has no exciting soloists, its intonation is deficient, it lacks light and shade, and it never, never, relaxes. But it is only accurate reporting to state that it was a smash hit in Boston.[2]

And here, Benny Goodman:

> Somewhere along the road he became a charlatan. He became the worst sort of aesthetic phony... Goodman's supposed to be an artist. He's not supposed to have a singer as third-rate as Peggy Lee cluttering up the platform. He's supposed to be Benny the Magnificent. I'm afraid, though, that he is just about anything but.[3]

Every Sunday, George opened the mailbag. There were letters from servicemen overseas, from those nostalgic for the good old days of the 1920s, from readers branding him a hack. Frazier loved those. "Dear George Frazier: I hate you bitterly," wrote one. "You've got enough nerve to even dine with Hitler and enjoy it," wrote another. One told him to be more like "looked-up-to" writers such as Louella Parsons, the Hollywood gossip columnist in the Hearst papers, because "You're only a small time person and plenty naive." Small-time perhaps, but big enough to sue the Hearst chain in 1941 for copyright infringement—and win.[4]

Frazier's column hit its high point on June 3, 1942, with his homage to Bunny Berigan, who had died the previous day. The news came late and Frazier had to scramble to make his deadline. He was late, and they stopped the presses at the *Herald* until Frazier finished the column. Think about that! Despite war news that was unrelentingly grim, the editors chose to stop the presses for story about a dead trumpet player. The silver-tongued Frazier must have been at his sharpest in order to buy the few minutes he needed to finish. "He said we would always remain friends. I am proud to remember that on this, the day of his death."[5]

"Sweet and Low-Down" sputtered toward the end, as its author's attentions were elsewhere. The last column ran on October 16, 1942, but Frazier was already gone by then, having accepted the position of entertainment editor at *Life* magazine in New York.

The Ken Club's Sunday Matinees

The Ken first opened its doors in 1939 at 74 Warrenton, and moved into the vacant Theatrical Club space on October 1, 1940.

Mostly it was jazz at the Ken, although there were short interludes of "soft and gentle" dance music and oddball floor shows with singing acrobats and various trained animals. But jazz always found its way back.

In its ten years of operation, the Ken was the downtown home for small-group swing and Dixieland, and it was important to Boston jazz because it created playing opportunities for local musicians, from high schoolers on up. Teenagers played with jazz masters. You don't find a lot of that anymore.

During the war years, the biggest stars of small-group jazz, like Red Allen, Sidney Bechet, Pete Brown, Wild Bill Davison, J. C. Higginbotham, Max Kaminsky, Frankie Newton, and Pee Wee Russell were regulars. It's not like these guys didn't know from big bands. They all put in their time but preferred the freedom of the small-group setting, and the Ken was where they found it. And there was always a place for local musicians, although the club favored Boston bands with some 52nd Street experience, such as Ray Perry's or Nick Jerret's.

The Ken's claim to fame, though, was the Sunday afternoon jam session.

Musicians have gathered in informal settings to make improvised music as long as music's been played. The musicians played what they loved and played for themselves, usually after hours when their work was done. That's the way it's always been, and that's how young musicians learned and proved themselves—play, make mistakes, get better, be challenged, get "cut" by someone better, practice, play some more. It was the forum where reputations were earned and the local pecking order worked out. Sessions could and did happen anywhere; even a place like the Cocoanut Grove was known to swing after hours, when the jazzmen working the shows could stretch out at last.

In the mid 1930s, the idea of a public jam session took hold in New York, where a small group of musicians played for an invited audience. Over the course of the decade, the audience broadened and Sunday afternoon became a preferred time for the public sessions. In Boston, they were called "concerts," just to make sure nobody in city hall would get the idea that there was any dancing going on in violation of the blue laws. The admission fee was nominal, and the musicians were paid minimum scale to satisfy the union, which insisted members be paid if there was an audience present.

That was the state of the public jam session when the Ken Club brought them to Boston in 1942. The Ken didn't invent the jam session in Boston, but it surely established the Sunday afternoon tradition. The organizer and emcee was Bill Ingalls of WCOP radio's *Jazz Nocturne* program, and a clerk at Krey's Music on Washington Street. Ingalls always had good players on hand, drawing from the band in the club that week, the bands from Massachusetts Avenue, the road bands passing through, and the day-tripping New York musicians. Once the jam sessions caught on in spring 1942, paid admissions (50 cents and always less for servicemen in uniform) reached about 450 at the Ken, and the Ken wasn't the only club in town with a Sunday matinée.

The success of the Sunday jam session in Boston was due in part to the workings of the musicians union. The AFM did not mandate a uniform set of work rules nationwide. Each local determined what constituted a work week for its members. New York defined its work week as six days, and for many their day off was Sunday. In Boston, the work week was seven days. With the Sunday session added in, the musicians worked what they called an "eight-day week," a routine that visiting bands dreaded. However, there were more than a few New Yorkers willing to travel to Boston on their day off for a little more blowing. Even during wartime they could catch a train, most of the time anyway, and the one-way fare on the New Haven Railroad was only $3.85. So they came, Coleman Hawkins and Red Allen and Hot Lips Page and the rest. For the Bostonians, it was good exposure and good experience. It wasn't called networking then, but that's what it was, and that's how bassist Lloyd Trotman remembered it:

> The Ken Club had those Sunday afternoon jam sessions. Guys would come up from New York for them, Pete Brown, Coleman Hawkins. No Sunday afternoon jam sessions on 52nd Street! I might even have a picture of Louis Armstrong at the Ken. I met a lot of people that way.[6]

There was nothing like a little press to get the ball rolling, and in 1942 that meant George Frazier and his "Sweet and Low-Down" column in the *Herald*. Frazier suspended his usual jaundiced view of the Boston scene for the jam sessions. He happily promoted them, noting with satisfaction the paid attendance of about 250 per Sunday. With Frazier's help the sessions took off, and by May 24, the crowd numbered about 450.

Sunday session at the Ken, spring 1943. Lem Davis, alto saxophone; Roy Haynes, drums; Lloyd Trotman, bass; Vic Dickenson, trombone; Frankie Newton, trumpet.

At the end of May, the Hotel Buckminster debuted its own Sunday session, with Frankie Newton and James P. Johnson. Frazier was always an unabashed Newton fan, but on this day he thought Frankie outdid himself, effortlessly breaking off his solo in "Exactly Like You" to slip into the *Lohengrin* bridal theme without missing a beat when a wedding party entered the room. Frazier couldn't get over it. Frazier, the man who called Boston dull and stupid, was moved to wonder, "What is the name of this city, with jam sessions every Sunday afternoon?"[8]

That particular weekend the talent was abundant. Frankie Newton and James P. were at the Buckingham, but on the Ken's bandstand at one point were Red Allen and his drummer Kenny Clarke, bassist Al Morgan from the Sabby Lewis band, tenor saxophonist Sam Donahue, then leading his own big band, and three members of Fats Waller's band.

Thus began a competition with the Ken for both musicians and fans. In May Red Allen was featured at the Ken, and Buzzy and Al Drootin were at the Buckminster. One week the Ken featured pianist Joe Sullivan, and the Buckminster countered with James P. Johnson. And so it went. Buckminster,

Sandy Williams and Max Kaminsky. Ken, Al Morgan and Cecil Scott. (That particular week, Pee Wee Russell finished his engagement in New York at 8:00 a.m., caught the 10:00 train to Boston and arrived at the Ken before 4:00. When the session ended at 6:00, he cabbed over to the Buckminster and played the last half hour of *their* session. *That's* stamina.)[9]

On it went: Ken, Zutty Singleton; Buckminster, Eddie Condon. Ken, Pete Brown; Buckminster, Edmond Hall. All this was wonderful for the jazz fans of Boston, but the clubs were bidding up the price of the guest artists, and the Ken was winning the battle for hearts and minds. It all got to be too much for the Buckminster, which exited the jam session business that summer, blaming the lack of air conditioning, then exited the hotel business altogether in September as the U.S. Army put the hotel into War Department service for the duration.

The local musicians always showed up on Sundays, hoping for a chance to sit in with the stars. With the supply of musicians depleted by the draft, even a handful of high school musicians got their chance. Among them was pianist Al Vega:

> The first time I sat in at the Ken was with J. C. Higginbotham from Red Allen's band, and Jo Jones was on drums because Basie was across the street at the Metropolitan Theater. I look up and I see Jo Jones, and I look to one side and I see Red Allen, and I look the other way and I see J. C. Higginbotham, so I put my head down and played and hoped I'd make it. And I did pretty good, so every week I'd end up playing a few numbers. I'd hear "Body and Soul" one week and I'd go home and practice it. I'd get back there, and they'd ask "what do you want to play" and I'd say "Body and Soul."[10]

The jam session could be a beautiful thing, but Frazier pointed out the one problem that had to be overcome for the jam to succeed.

> A jam session is one of the most informal things imaginable, but it is never (if it is right) quite so informal as a lot of people seem to suspect. There has to be a certain pattern to proceedings and, above all, there must be a rather rigid regimentation of just who is to be permitted to take part. Practically anyone who wears a broad-brimmed hat, says "watcha know, man?" reads *Down Beat*, and has a nodding acquaintance with an instrument is allowed access to the bandstand at the Ken. That's a terrible mistake. Last Sunday, for example, there was a tenor player on hand whose performance was just about as utterly unzippy as anything I've ever heard (and I have heard some bad, bad tenor players in my lifetime). It would have been a better session if someone had locked him in a closet.[11]

Frazier perhaps was yearning for the more structured jazz scene of New York or Kansas City, where musicians were ranked, like tennis players, and only the top players could play with the other top players. Boston was not so fussy.

There were other wartime jam sessions. The Savoy started one after the Buckminster's closed down. Little Dixie had one. Frankie Newton was a bit of a pied piper during the war years; wherever he went, the Sunday sessions were sure to follow. He was featured at the Buckminster, as well as at all of the places he played extended engagements in 1942 and 1943, at the Savoy and Vanity Fair, as well as the Ken. Vic Dickenson was alongside the entire time, inexplicably identified as "Dickerson" in advertisements.

Between 1947 and 1955, the Sunday jam session proliferated in Boston. The floodgates opened with Ray Barron's Sunday sessions at the Down Beat Club, and shortly thereafter every place that called itself a jazz club (and a few that didn't) hosted one—the Hi-Hat, Izzy Ort's, the Knickerbocker, Louie's Lounge, the Mardi Gras, the Melody Lounge, the Stable, Storyville, Wally's. Eventually the Sunday jam sessions faded away, and among the various culprits blamed for their demise are rock music, complex jazz arrangements that don't accommodate the spirit of improvisation, the National Football League's Sunday telecasts, and the migration to the suburbs, where the former cats and kittens spent their Sundays doing yard work.

The Checker Cafe, and a Tale of Two Families

The RKO Theatre, at the corner of Washington and Essex Streets, was the dominant musical presence in downtown Boston in the war years, and its story is told in Home of the Big Bands: RKO Boston Theatre, page 36. There were other places in the neighborhood, smaller, where the jazz was better. The best one was at 22 Hayward Place, opposite the RKO's stage doors. Lou Baker's Checker Cafe was that jazz room, and the rising stars of Boston's jazz scene, the pride of Local 535, played there from 1941 until fire closed it in late 1943.

Boston was one of the many cities where the American Federation of Musicians had two locals, one for whites (Local 9) and one for blacks (Local 535). It was never a written rule, but by custom certain places contracted with Local 9, and others with Local 535. The Checker Cafe was the Local 535 stronghold in the neighborhood around the RKO.

The sextet at the Checker in 1942–1943 was Sherman Freeman's. It was a pared-down version of the well-known larger band, the Alabama Aces of Joe Nevils. Nevils played alto saxophone, but unlike his better-known contemporaries Johnny Hodges and Charlie Holmes, chose to remain in Boston. He was drafted in 1942, about the time the Checker gig started. That's when leadership passed to Sherman Freeman, leader of the house band at Johnny Wilson's on Tremont Street.

The Checker Cafe in 1943. Sherman Freeman, clarinet; George Perry, tenor; Andy Kelton, trumpet; Bey Perry, drums; Lloyd Trotman, bass; and Charlie Cox, piano. Courtesy of Dan Kochakian.

All the musicians in this sextet were well known in Boston in the 1940s, and groups led by Nevils and Freeman invariably included at least one Trotman and one Perry, both prominent Boston jazz families in those years. Each family contributed three sons to the Boston jazz scene, and bassist Lloyd Trotman and drummer Bey Perry made the jump to the national stage in the postwar years. The Perrys and Trotmans had grown up together and worked with Tasker Crosson, the Alabama Aces, Blanche Calloway, and Freeman. To replace Nevils, Freeman's first choice was Bey Perry's brother Joe, who was later replaced by saxophonist George Perry, shown in the 1943 picture. This made Freeman's a mixed combo—not an everyday occurrence in Boston then, but not a rare one either. By 1943, this group, with the tight arrangements of pianist Charlie Cox, was second only to the band of Sabby Lewis among the small bands in Boston, and when Lewis left the Savoy in 1943, Freeman took his place.

Let's back up a bit and meet the Trotmans. Lambert and Lillian Trotman of Shawmut Street had three sons: Ernie born in 1920, Stanley in 1921, and Lloyd in 1923. Lambert was himself a jazz musician, and he organized the Music Lover's Club, a social club that sponsored dances in the South End. Lambert's vocation, though, was teaching piano. He had a studio on Lenox

Street, and as Ernie later recalled, Lambert enjoyed teaching so much that if a student in those Depression years could not afford the price of a lesson, he taught it anyway. He taught all three sons how to read music and play the piano. All learned to play classical as well as popular music, and they all loved jazz. Ernie and Stanley stayed with the piano, but Lloyd switched to bass when he was given one to play in the high school band.

By 1937, Ernie and Lloyd were learning their craft with Tasker Crosson's orchestra, and both graduated to the more advanced Alabama Aces in time to tour with Blanche Calloway in 1940. When the tour ended, Nevils broke up his large band and took a sextet into the Tic Toc Club on Tremont Street. Ernie and Lloyd were in that band too. When it moved over to the Checker, the brothers split up, Lloyd staying with Nevils and Ernie joining Pete Brown at the Savoy. He accompanied Brown back to New York's 52nd Street, but that ended when he was drafted in 1943. He played in a band at Fort Devens with Joe Nevils before shipping out to the Philippine Islands.

Both Lloyd and Stanley Trotman failed their physicals. Stanley spent the war years in New York, while Lloyd worked in Boston with Freeman and the Perry brothers. He was a regular at the Ken Club jam sessions, where he made the musical contacts that enabled his move to New York in 1946.

Now let's turn our attention to that other musical family, the Perrys of Harrishof Street in Roxbury. Saxophonist and violinist Ray was born in 1915; drummer Bazeley, better known as "Bey," in 1920, and saxophonist Joe (the youngest, Joe's birth year is not known). Bey and Joe shared some of the same musical experiences as their friends the Trotmans; Joe played tenor on the Blanche Calloway tours, and both were members of Sherman Freeman's band at the Checker. Ray took a different path.[12]

Ray Perry played all the saxophones, most famously the alto, and also the clarinet, but he is remembered today for his violin playing. Early on, Perry had developed a technique of wordlessly singing the melody of a song as he bowed it on the violin, singing an octave below his playing. This inspired bassist Slam Stewart, who heard Perry nightly when they played together in the Little Harlem Orchestra, to adopt the same technique. Slam, however, sang an octave *above* his playing. He did this constantly, to the displeasure of many critics.

Ray Perry organized his first band, the Arabian Knights, in 1929, and through the early 1930s the underage Knights worked around the South End and Roxbury at dances and social functions. Perry joined Dean Earl's Little Harlem Orchestra in 1935, Chick Carter's Orchestra in 1938, and the Alabama Aces, as a member of Blanche Calloway's touring band, in 1940. In September 1940 he went with the Lionel Hampton Orchestra, joining Dexter

Gordon and Marshall Royal in the reed section, and played alongside Illinois Jacquet when Hampton recorded "Flying Home," one of the swing era's most popular anthems. The Hampton band's frequent visits to Boston (Egleston Square Gardens, Brunswick Hotel, Tic Toc Club) must have been welcome homecomings for Perry. Perry remained with Hampton until spring 1942, when ill health brought him back to Boston. He worked with his own group at the Ken Club, and on and off with Sabby Lewis 1944–1946. He made private recordings with the Lewis band that feature extended violin solos that were not subject to the three-minute time limit imposed by the 78 rpm disc.

Ray Perry had the chops to star in New York and perhaps he wanted to, but after Hampton he spent more of the 1940s in Boston than out of it. Perry's own band of 1943–1945, the Perry Brothers Orchestra, featured all three Perry brothers with three more musicians from that Checker Cafe picture— Lloyd Trotman, pianist Charlie Cox, and trumpeter Andy Kelton. The final member of the band was saxophonist Eddie Gregory, a former Boston Conservatory student better known to the jazz world by the name he took after his 1947 conversion to Islam, Sahib Shihab. The Perrys worked a long engagement at the Ken Club in 1945, which turned out to be one of Lloyd Trotman's last Boston gigs. "I felt I had to leave Boston if I wanted to make a living as a musician, so my wife Gertrude and I moved to New York for good in 1946. Four months after I got to New York, I was working with Duke."[13]

In 1946 Perry was back in New York, and that year he won the New Star award in *Esquire* magazine's Musician's Poll. He continued to work in Boston and New York in the late 1940s with his own groups and with those of Sabby Lewis. In 1949 he went on the road again with Illinois Jacquet, with whom he made his last recordings. Ray Perry's promising career ended in 1950 when he died in New York at the age of 35 of what was then called Bright's Disease.

Bey and Joe Perry were active in Boston during the war years as well, at the Savoy, Tic Toc, and Johnny Wilson's, as well as the Checker. We'll catch up to them and the Trotmans again when we visit Massachusetts Avenue and the postwar jazz scene.

All this takes us a long way from the Checker. When Sherman Freeman moved over to the Savoy in 1943, George Irish took his place, and the Irish band was working at the Checker when a fire shut it down in late 1943. That marked the end of this address as a jazz spot. When it reopened in 1945, it was as the Checker Chinese Restaurant.

Sabby Lewis, Frankie Newton, and Boston's Hot Spot of Rhythm

The Savoy was the center of Boston jazz in the 1940s, and Stevens Connolly was the man at the Savoy. He managed the room, bought the liquor, and booked the bands. During the war years, he made the Savoy the most important jazz club in Boston. Boston jazz grew up at the Savoy.

Malcolm Little describes the Savoy in his *Autobiography of Malcolm X*, and his close friend Malcolm "Shorty" Jarvis does likewise in his book, *The Other Malcolm*. It was in the Savoy where Nat Hentoff learned about the music that would form the core of his writing career, a time he describes in *Boston Boy*. George Wein, the man who revolutionized the presentation of jazz, tells in *Myself Among Others* how he worked there first as a piano player and later as music director. It was simply the place to be in Boston in the 1940s.

The Savoy Cafe opened in 1935 at 461 Columbus Avenue. It was a small room, not even big enough for a dance floor, but manager Connolly wanted music anyway, and apparently he didn't want the bland floor shows that often came with it. Together with his brother Jim, he was able to concentrate on the music and inaugurate the policy that established the Savoy as the jazz center of Boston in the early 1940s. Steve was a bluff, no-nonsense guy, rumored to carry a gun, but as a jazz promoter, he was the right guy with the right room at the right time.

Connolly started 1941 with the Jones Brothers, a trio of harmonizers who played their own instruments and were already attracting attention as an opening act for the Duke Ellington Orchestra. Max, Herb, and Clyde Jones were popular locally, smooth enough to star in shows at the Ritz. But Connolly wanted more jazz, and he got more of what he wanted when he hired pianist Sabby Lewis, who advertised his outfit as "the greatest band in New England."

William Sebastian Lewis was 22 when he organized his first band in 1936, after a short stay in Tasker Crosson's orchestra. Sabby's brand of swing—a little Earl Hines, a little Bill Basie—grew steadily in popularity as Lewis worked the Massachusetts Avenue clubs, dance halls like the Roseland-State Ballroom and Egleston Square Gardens, and every kind of social event and dinner dance imaginable. The Savoy job was a big prize and surely some of the other capable bandleaders in town must have sought it. But Connolly picked Lewis, who promoted his band for a time in 1941 as "Sabby Lewis and the Savoy Sultans."

Sabby's was the best band in Boston, and one of the reasons for that was the stable core of the band. The normal configuration was eight pieces—three saxophones, two brass, three rhythm. There was often a vocalist. His two brass men had been with him since 1938, trumpeter and writer Gene Caines, and Maceo Bryant, who doubled on trumpet and trombone. Both stayed with Lewis until 1949. Drummer Joe Booker also joined in 1938, and though he left for short stints with other bands, he too remained until 1949. Tenor saxophonist and chief arranger Jerry Heffron, who studied at Boston Conservatory, was in Lewis's first band in 1936 and remained until he was drafted in 1943. His other saxophonists in 1941–1942 were Elliott "Ricky" Pratt, a talented tenor who died quite young of tuberculosis, and journeyman altoist Jackie Fields, who had been with Coleman Hawkins at the time of the landmark "Body and Soul" recording.

William Sebastian "Sabby" Lewis in the 1940s. *Boston Traveler* photo, courtesy of the Boston Public Library, Print Department.

Finally, in 1941 Lewis hired bassist and sometimes vocalist Al Morgan, a veteran of the Cab Calloway and Les Hite orchestras, and certainly the best-known musician in Lewis's circle. He, too, stayed until 1949—then returned in 1952 for five more years. Morgan's walking bass stabilized the Lewis band and became a major contributor to its success. The hard-swinging rhythm section of Lewis, Morgan, and Booker could stand up to any in the east, and it was Count Basie himself who listened to the Lewis band at New York's Famous Door in 1941 and sent Sabby a telegram the next day, saying simply "Rock 'em, Pops."[14]

In the summer of 1942, the Lewis band won a listener contest sponsored by the F. W. Fitch Company, a maker of hair care products and a national sponsor of radio programming, to select a Boston-area band for its popular *Bandwagon* program on NBC. *Bandwagon* was then heard on more than 120 stations on the NBC network, so the contest winner would be playing for an audience numbered in the millions. The Fitch broadcast aired from the Statler Hotel's Terrace Room on Park Square, where, coincidentally, the resident orchestra was that of the contest runner-up, trumpeter and singer Jack Edwards. A few local bandleaders groused about a black band winning the contest, but that was not of interest to the Fitch people. The best band won their contest, and that's the band they wanted on their program. We can assume the Lewis band wailed at the Statler that night, but we don't know how they sounded. No air check or broadcast recording has ever surfaced.

Our man Frazier was a Lewis enthusiast and urged his readers to vote for Lewis in that Fitch contest. He liked the "little big band" aspect of the Lewis Orchestra; the previous April, he wrote in "Sweet and Low-Down:"

> The seven pieces—piano, bass, drums, two reeds, two brass—accomplish wonders. The voicings are so expert that there are moments when the seven men sound like 13 or 14. And by that I don't mean they're loud and blary, and strictly for the jazzers, but that they somehow manage to achieve the depth and resonance of a good small band.[15]

Lewis advertised his band as the Fitch Band Wagon Orchestra thereafter.

Sabby Lewis recalled the night when Steve Connolly's bartending brother Jim tried to silence Benny Goodman. Goodman dropped by twice to catch the band in July 1942 when he played the Metropolitan Theatre:

> We started playing some things that we knew he'd like, "One O'Clock Jump," things like that, and it got to be a little too much for him. He just took his coat off and sat in with us. He stopped all the action right away. Everybody's mouths dropped open, and they listened. It went on for about an hour, and I'll never forget, the bartender, Jim Connolly, who was the brother of the manager of the Savoy, Steve Connolly, said, "Get that bum down out of there. We're not selling any booze." At the time, he didn't know it was Goodman.[16]

Goodman was effusive in his praise of the Lewis band, telling George Frazier that he was deeply moved by what he heard. "Pretty good? It's more than that. It's a great band, one of the greatest bands I've heard in a long time." Will Roland, Goodman's manager, heard Lewis as well, and said of the Savoy that "it jumps every minute."[17]

Lewis was back in New York in 1944 for a lengthy engagement at the Club Zanzibar, which in addition garnered the group a regular spot on WOR radio.

Unfortunately, the recording ban of 1942–1944 cost Lewis a contract with Decca, and the sound of one of his finest bands is lost to time.

Sabby Lewis was a home-grown star, but the stature of the Savoy grew with the arrival of trumpeter Frankie Newton in January 1942. Both Newton and his trombonist, Vic Dickenson, became favorites in Boston.

Newton at the age of 36 was well-established in 1942. His career reached back into the late 1920s, with the bands of Cecil Scott and Charlie Johnson, and he played on Bessie Smith's final recording session. In the 1930s, he worked with Charlie Barnet, Teddy Hill, and John Kirby. He recorded with the Port of Harlem Jazzmen, and with Billie Holiday on her recording of "Strange Fruit." Newton was probably at his very best when he came to Boston in 1942, playing lost to us because of the recording ban. Nonetheless, his spare, expressive playing style—now fiery and exuberant, now muted and introspective—marked Newton as a star, and with his long residences at the Savoy, Vanity Fair, and Ken Club in 1942–1943, one of the first real stars to settle in Boston for an extended stay. Newton's presence added a legitimacy to the Boston scene that had been lacking. Good musicians *left* Boston. Newton reversed that trend.

Frankie Newton, 1943. Courtesy of Frank Newcomb.

As Newton continued at the Savoy into February, his band was boosted by George Frazier, who wrote in the *Herald*:

Frankie Newton's band at the Savoy on Columbus Avenue is far and away the most exciting small group to play Boston within at least the past ten years. Newton is one of the more distinguished trumpet players around today and his performance each night is in itself enough inducement for you to drop by the Savoy. He's not a powerhouse trumpeter... but a musician who plays subtly and exquisitely.

It's Jazz, Jazz, Jazz every minute they're on the stand. You're missing something authentic and heartfelt if you fail to hear them. It isn't arranged jazz, but collective improvisation. Collective improvisation can be described in a great many ways. It is gimme the ball and the h--- with the signals. It is the trumpet, the trombone, and the two saxes fooling around with the melodic line and building something lovely and moving while the rhythm section gives out with the good time. It is a lot of things but it is always Jazz.

Frazier added that in skill Newton was second only to Louis Armstrong among the active trumpet players.[18]

Lewis and Newton traded off at the Savoy for the rest of the year. Lewis was there when the bottom fell out of Boston nightlife in November 1942.

The Night the Cocoanut Grove Burned

The Cocoanut Grove at 17 Piedmont Street was the center of nightclubbing in Boston until the night of November 28, 1942. Not jazz nightclubbing, but the kind "modeled after some interior decorator's idea of a Hollywood night club set; plenty of garish gauze, girls, gin and prices that were very discouraging."[19] Much has been written about the club, the seedy back story, and its owner, Barnett "Barney" Welansky, former legal counsel to King Solomon and the man who gained control of the nightclub when the gangster Solomon was shot dead in 1933. At least four books have been written about the catastrophic fire and the 492 lives lost in it. The Grove-as-nightclub isn't really a part of our story, but the reaction to the fire, and the permanent scar the tragedy left on Boston, both are.

The Cocoanut Grove wasn't anybody's idea of a jazz club, and Mickey Alpert, the bandleader that night, ran a tuxedo-clad outfit that played for the floor shows. But there were good musicians in that band, attracted by the steady work. Union scale for the Grove musicians was $90 per week, but the musicians only saw $45 of it. The rest was kicked back—maybe some to the club, some to Albert, some to the union man who got you the job. Such an arrangement was not uncommon at the time, although the 50 percent kickback must have seemed very dear indeed, and some musicians refused the work for that reason. Nonetheless, the band played on, and despite the fact that the *Herald's* Frazier called the Alpert band "excruciating," it was an institution of sorts, and on its 180th consecutive week at the Grove at the time of the fire.

Mickey Alpert was a baton-waving front man. The real job of leading the band (ten pieces plus a singer) fell to the music director, violinist and songwriter Bernie Fazioli. As the first flames raced across the ceiling, he ordered the band off the stand, and seven of their number exited backstage and made their way out through the kitchen. The drummer, however, tried to remove some of his equipment, and the big bass drum got stuck in a doorway. The three men behind him—Fazioli, saxophonist Al Willett, and bassist Jack Lesberg—were felled by the fumes. Taken to Boston City Hospital, Fazioli succumbed to the effects of smoke inhalation sometime during the night. Willett and Lesberg fared better, and both went on to long careers in music.

If there was a real jazz man in the band it was Jack Lesberg, a Bostonian who had played with Max Kaminsky and Bobby Hackett, and was not long off the band of Muggsy Spanier. Family matters brought him back to Boston and the job with Alpert. Lesberg fully recovered from his fire-related injuries, and moved to New York in 1943 and quickly found work with Kaminsky. He went on to play both jazz and classical music for 50 more years.

The fire started a chain reaction on the Boston scene. The Boston Licensing Board suspended the entertainment licenses of 1,161 night clubs, hotels, taverns, and restaurants effective December 1, pending their passing a city fire inspection. Most establishments were allowed to remain open to serve food and liquor, but they could not offer entertainment. Fifty-two nightclubs, on the other hand, were padlocked outright until inspections could be completed, and these included every popular night spot in town, many to be visited in the pages of this book: the Checker, the Hi-Hat, Johnny Wilson's, the Ken Club, Izzy Ort's, the Pioneer Club, the Rio Casino, the Savoy Cafe, the Silver Dollar, the Tic Toc. *Down Beat* estimated that as many as 5,000 people were temporarily thrown out of work. Nobody felt like much like nightlife anyway.[20]

The human cost of the tragedy was incalculable, the pain of its aftermath immeasurable. The Boston Fire Commissioner's report listed the cause as "unknown." Boston has no sadder story in its long history.

A New Home for the Jazz Oasis

Word was already out in September 1942 that Steve Connolly was looking for a new spot for the Savoy. He was still looking when the fire at the Cocoanut Grove forced the immediate shutdown of his club. The city cleared the Savoy to reopen, but Connolly kept it shut and let his lease expire. He never did reopen on Columbus Avenue. No other club occupied the space, either. The room just went dark.

In April 1943, with the club closed and its future uncertain, *Down Beat* published an obituary of sorts for the old Savoy, with the author remarking, "I have never again seen the same atmosphere, the same willingness on the part of both musicians and audience to give out and enjoy swing music."[21] There was a particular night during the Lewis band's tenure in April 1942:

> Of course, there were special nights which seemed even better than others. One night, when the bands of Count Basie and Les Hite were in town, many of the guys from both bands came over to sit in. I can remember seeing eight trumpets blasting away at "One O'Clock Jump," while a yelling crowd tried to force its way into the Savoy when there wasn't enough room left to squeeze in Pee Wee Russell after he'd been on a long diet. The combined brass was so loud that it could be heard all the way up to the corner of Massachusetts Ave. and Columbus, almost a quarter of a mile away.

In spring 1943, Connolly was talking about a vacant space at 410 Massachusetts Avenue, the site of the shuttered Royal Palms. The Savoy Cafe reopened there in July 1943. Said *Down Beat*:

> The newly remodeled and modernistic Savoy, formerly the Royal Palms, had its opening July 8 with Pete Brown's fine crew doing the musical honors. Doing turn-away business, it looks as if Steve Connolly has hit the jackpot again and the Savoy should prove to be the most popular strictly jazz spot in the city. Pete Brown will probably be there indefinitely, but with Sabby

Lewis's return from Toronto's Top Hat, it is likely both aggregations will share the spotlight.[22]

Savoy Cafe, 1945: Sabby Lewis, piano; Al Morgan, bass; Ray Perry, alto; Joe Booker, drums. Courtesy of Dan Kochakian.

The move to the new home ushered in the Savoy Cafe's 52nd Street phase. Now just a few doors down from the Little Dixie, the competition and the wartime economy helped both clubs. The new Savoy was stylish, with red brick and glass block on the outside, mirrors and murals of jazz musicians on the walls inside. And it was air conditioned. The musical anchor was Sabby Lewis. He stayed at the Savoy through 1946, often for months on end. These were some of his greatest bands, and they featured some of his greatest stars: saxophonists Bill Dorsey, Paul Gonsalves, Big Nick Nicholas (who gave music lessons in a studio above the club), Sonny Stitt and Jimmy Tyler; trumpeters Cat Anderson, Freddie Webster, and Idrees Sulieman (Leonard Graham); and Ray Perry playing both alto and violin, all driven by that rhythm section of Lewis, Al Morgan, and Joe Booker. When Booker left for a time, his first replacement was an 18-year-old Boston drummer named Roy Haynes, himself later replaced by Osie Johnson. The vocalist was Evelyn White. The air-checks and private tapes that have found their way on to record make it clear the Lewis band was something special during the war years.

In 1944, the Savoy was advertising itself as "the maker of bands," listing Lewis and Newton among them. When Lewis departed for an extended engagement at New York's Club Zanzibar that January, the Savoy added another, that of George Irish, a Boston tenor player with a long resume. Irish didn't need "making," though. He came to the Savoy fully formed.

Irish was a late bloomer, a New England Conservatory graduate, but he did not come to prominence until the late 1930s when he was about 30 years of age. He played saxophone and arranged for Blanche Calloway in 1937–1938, then went with Teddy Wilson, Fletcher Henderson, Don Redman, and finally Benny Carter. In 1942 he returned to Boston and a job leading the house band at the Checker Cafe until it burned in 1943. When Irish came to the Savoy, his band included trumpeters Louis Douglas and Oscar Dunham, altoist Buddy Pearson, pianist and arranger Charlie Cox, bassist Bernie Griggs, Sr., and drummer Dave Hill. It was the last of the great Savoy war years bands.

Local bands were the mainstay at the Savoy, but Connolly began engaging name bands in 1945, when wartime travel restrictions eased. Between 1945 and 1948, he hired a succession of small swing bands, all led by big band veterans coming to terms with the end of that era. Among them were groups led by Coleman Hawkins, Lester Young, Roy Eldridge, Arnett Cobb, Earl Warren, and Hot Lips Page. But that's getting ahead of the story.

Johnny Wilson's Swanee Grill

Johnny Wilson (born Giovanni Panica) was a larger-than-life character who ran the Swanee Grill, a nightclub and sometimes jazz room, at 815 Tremont Street. He opened in March 1938 for what turned out to be an 18-year run. Most people just called it "Johnny Wilson's."

Wilson was a prizefighter, and a good one, before he became a saloon keeper, battling his way to the middleweight championship of the world from 1920 to 1923. Wilson fought 122 professional bouts before retiring in 1926 and opening the Silver Slipper on Broadway in New York, a renowned Prohibition-era haunt of gangsters and entertainers. Wilson moved to Boston and re-entered the nightclub business with the Swanee Grill, but he also operated dance marathons and other amusements, and managed tassel-twirler Sally Keith for a time.

Wilson may not have set out to run a jazz club, but because of the music's popularity, the Swanee Grill ended up becoming one. The house bands were good ones. Saxophonist Sherman Freeman led one, the Swanee Rhythm Boys with vocalist Novella Taylor, in 1940 and 1941, before his days at the

Checker. Mabel Robinson worked with her sister, singer Frances Brown, and sang with saxophonist Roscoe McCrae's house band, the Rhythm Aces, in 1942–1944. Jimmie Givens and His Harlem Swingaroos had a silly name but a gem of a piano player in Elmo Hope. The Swingaroos worked at Wilson's for much of 1944.

Johnny Wilson's was a good-times place, and Harvard *Crimson* writer Charles Miller urged his fellow Yardlings to venture down to Tremont Street to dig the band there, but to be on good behavior while doing so:

> The band is led by one Sherman Freeman, who plays alto and clarinet with a nice gutty tone, blending wonderfully with the completely undisciplined style of the rest of the band. It's pretty wild stuff, and you won't care for it if you expect to hear singing song titles and Tex Beneke whistling choruses, but if you feel like listening to five musicians who have the right idea about fighting out a tune together, then Johnny Wilson's is the place for you (and me). I might add that the clientele has never heard of Harvard, and unless you feel like getting your teeth knocked in, you'll do well not to remind anyone of your presence. Get it?[23]

Wilson's club faded as an entertainment spot at the end of the free-spending war years, but remained open until 1955. Wilson himself died in Boston in 1985 at the age of 92.

The Tic Toc: Always a Famous Band

For three years beginning in September of 1941, Ben and Jack Ford's Tic Toc was the spot for name bands downtown, featuring among others Louis Armstrong, Billy Eckstine, Coleman Hawkins, Jimmie Lunceford, and Fats Waller. There was, as the advertising claimed, "always a famous band."

Joe Nevils led the house band in 1941–1942, until it moved over to the Checker Cafe when he was drafted. In 1943 their place was taken by the band of drummer Art Blakey; Blakey left the Tic Toc to join the Eckstine big band.

The Fords ran an integrated club, but it was early in the day for integration, and the Fords walked a fine color line. Black Bostonians attended the shows, as did white soldiers and sailors who came from places where the races did not mix socially, and the Fords strove to pacify unhappy white servicemen at the expense of black city dwellers. Sometimes it got them into trouble. The singer Novella Taylor brought suit against the club in 1943 claiming discrimination. Ms. Taylor and her party wanted seats in the center of the floor for an Ella Fitzgerald show that April; they were told "for whites only" and were seated to the side. In June, Taylor, considering a civil lawsuit, was threatened by an alleged employee of the Tic Toc. Taylor not only took the Tic Toc to court, she appealed to the licensing board to suspend the club's liquor license. In the midst of this, Sabby Lewis turned down $1,000 a week to appear at the club in August, pointing to the murky segregation policy as the reason. The case was settled in November 1944 in Taylor's favor, but the club was already closed by then.[24]

Other incidents never reached such proportions; Earl Hines cooled one of them most cleverly on a busy Saturday night in August 1944, when two members of the Navy Shore Patrol attempted to remove a black sailor. The sailor's mates went to his aid, and the Shore Patrol called in reinforcements. Other club patrons objected to the show of force, and a near-riot was in the offing. Hines ordered his band to play the "Star Spangled Banner," which brought all hands to immediate attention. While the temperature cooled, the Shore Patrol walked its man out of the crowd and the clash was averted. All applauded Hines for his calming role.

Although the Tic Toc was important to Boston jazz, it had a short life, and the notoriety brought about by lawsuits and the Shore Patrol probably had something to do with it. In September 1944, the Fords were evicted, even though their business was profitable and they never had any trouble paying the bills. They shut down on October 4, announcing: "Last Time Tonight! The management of the Tic Toc thanks all its patrons for making our four years' stay at the Tic Toc a success. Watch newspaper ads in the future for our new location featuring big name bands."[25] The Roy Eldridge Orchestra closed the room. Ad-watching would have been in vain, however, because the Fords never reopened. Instead, they consolidated their operations at the Rio Casino, their other downtown club on Warrenton Street, a block away.

***

Jazz was heard in Boston from the music's first decades, and in earlier chapters we had a taste of what was being played in the years before Pearl Harbor. In 1942, though, the local scene showed a definite quickening of the pulse. That was the year the Sabby Lewis Orchestra had its guest spot on the Fitch Bandwagon radio program and let the nation know there was good jazz being played in Boston. It was the year George Frazier's "Sweet and Low-Down" column in the *Boston Herald* spread Boston news across New England five times each week. It's the year Frankie Newton brought his estimable presence to Boston for what stretched into a two-year stay. It was the year the Ken Club jam sessions attracted the New York players for weekly musical meetings with their Boston counterparts. And we haven't met Professor Quincy Porter yet, but 1942 was the year he started the Department of Popular Music at the New England Conservatory of Music.

Lewis and Newton were at the top of their games in the war years, and it is forever our loss that the recording ban of 1942–1944 prevented them from putting their sounds on wax. As those are silent years in jazz history, we'll have to take it on faith that they were the years when jazz grew up in Boston.

Chapter 5

A Late Forties Interlude

What goes up, they say, must come down, and in the postwar years, nightlife came down from its wartime high, and not just in Boston, but everywhere. The big bands collapsed and the swing era ended, a second recording ban was imposed in 1948, and the crooners ruled America's entertainment landscape. Jazz splintered into warring camps, with the advocates of bebop on one side and of traditional jazz on the other. It was the entertainment equivalent of Hatfield versus McCoy.

The latter half of the 1940s in Boston jazz saw the birth of Schillinger House and the arrival of the GI Bill students, Duke Ellington's only Broadway musical debut at the Opera House, some skirmishes in the battle for civil rights, the end of the Ballroom District, the Crystal-Tone and Motif record companies, Nat Hentoff in print and on the radio, and Boston's first jazz festival. The Boston scene was reshaping itself.

Rumbas—and Rumbles—at the Rio

In September 1941, the old church upstairs at 76 Warrenton opened with a new name and a new look. Called the Rio Casino, the upstairs room featured fake palm trees reaching to the ceiling and an elevated stage with a back-drop view of the harbor at Rio de Janeiro. The operator was Jimmy Welansky. We know him from the Theatrical Club. He was implicated in the Breen murder. Welansky was also indicted for his role in the Cocoanut Grove tragedy. He was managing the club the night of the fire, filling in for his hospitalized brother Barney, the owner of the Cocoanut Grove. Both brothers were charged with manslaughter. Barney went to jail but Jimmy was acquitted, and shortly thereafter he sold the Rio Casino to former vaudevillians Jack and Ben Ford, who with their brother Abe formed the Ford Theatrical Agency in 1936 and quickly rose to prominence as one of the top booking agencies in the east. They also bought nightclubs, first the Tic Toc on Tremont Street, which they turned into Boston's busiest name-band room in the war years, and then the Rio Casino.

The Fords closed the Tic Toc in September 1944, and the band action shifted over to the Rio. By 1946, the Rio was advertising itself as "the house of name bands," and again the Fords had the top downtown spot. In early 1946, the focus was on white bands (Ina Ray Hutton, Hal McIntyre, Shorty Sherock, Bob Strong, Jerry Wald), but after the summer shutdown, the Fords changed the program. On the schedule that fall were Tiny Bradshaw, Benny Carter, Mercer Ellington, Earl Hines, Andy Kirk, Sabby Lewis, and Jimmie Lunceford. All went well until a December 1946 appearance by the Billy Eckstine Orchestra.

Eckstine was booked for two weeks, and on the Saturday ending the first week there was trouble. It started when someone in the audience directed a racial epithet at Billy Eckstine as the show was ending on Saturday the 14th. Accounts differ. In one, a woman insulted Eckstine and the two had words, after which her companion kicked Eckstine, and Billy threw a punch. In a second account, the woman requested a tune which Eckstine said the band could not play because the show was almost over—it was midnight on Saturday and the music had to stop. This prompted her companion to do the insulting. The two had words, and Billy threw a punch.

There followed some pushing and shoving, and someone threw a chair, and the crowd headed for the exits without paying their tabs. The Fords were furious. They promptly fired Eckstine and refused to honor the remainder of the contract, claiming damage to the furniture and premises. Four patrons filed suit against the club claiming injuries. Eckstine filed a claim with the American Federation of Musicians for the pay the Fords withheld. The Fords, through their lawyer, told *Down Beat* that the Eckstine band was trouble from the start, in that "they refused to stop playing jive," and worse, the band members insisted on using the front entrance to the club. Even though the Fords claimed they'd never had this kind of trouble with any other band, they didn't want to take the chance it would happen again. The new policy: no more black bands as headliners at the Rio.

Quite a story, but apparently not enough of one to make the Boston newspapers. It is a comment on the times that they chose to ignore it. The black-owned *Chronicle* covered it. *Down Beat* covered it. Nat Hentoff covered it in his *Counterpoint* newsletter. But the mainstream press? Not a word.[1]

The Fords never got back into the name-band business at the Rio Casino, and in fact, there wasn't much of interest for the jazz-minded at the Rio after the Eckstine affair. The club itself declined in the postwar 1940s; the razzle-dazzle style of nightclubbing it represented was on the way out. Starting in 1948, the big room upstairs was used only on the weekends for dance bands, and nightly entertainment was in the smaller lounge on the first floor. The Fords closed the club in late 1952. They were using the space as a function hall when they sold the building in 1958.

Symphony Hall, 1947

The year 1947 was a slow year for jazz in Boston, but you'd never know it from the Symphony Hall schedule. On January 12, Lionel Hampton's Orchestra. On March 1, Mal Hallett, already 25 years in the band business. The next night, the bands of Jimmie Lunceford and Sy Oliver, who rose to prominence with Lunceford. On March 21, Jack Teagarden's group, which featured four jazzmen with deep Boston roots: Max Kaminsky, Bobby Hackett, Jack Lesberg, and Buzzy Drootin. On March 30, the piano genius of Art Tatum. On April 18, Louis Armstrong and Billie Holiday in a "Birth of the Blues" concert that coincided with the opening of *New Orleans*, the movie in which they both appeared.

Following the summer doldrums, Norman Granz's Jazz at the Philharmonic rolled in on September 28, anchored by saxophonists Coleman Hawkins, Illinois Jacquet, and Flip Phillips. Bebop arrived on October 19, with Dizzy Gillespie and Charlie Parker in a program called "The New Jazz." On November 30, Armstrong returned with his All-Stars. The year closed with the Duke Ellington Orchestra ringing in the New Year. *Everything* that happened in jazz in its first half-century was represented on the Symphony Hall stage in 1947.

From Arcadia to Zanzibar

The Arcadia Ballroom was a modest second-floor dance hall at 254 Huntington Avenue, across the street from the Raymor Ballroom. It operated through the heart of the swing years, from 1935 until 1942. It was a small place, even advertising itself as the "coziest ballroom in Boston." The Arcadia was open to the public for weekend dancing (for a time these dances featured the delightfully named Katz 'n' Jammers, of whom absolutely nothing is known), but it mainly survived as a rental hall. The Arcadia was a favorite of the South End and Roxbury social clubs that hired the popular bands of the day, including Tasker Crosson, Sabby Lewis, and Joe Nevils, to entertain at their functions. After the Arcadia closed, this Huntington Avenue address assumed numerous names, offering something for everyone and apparently not making money with any of it. By the time the last of the musical tenants closed up, this address had seen a little bit of everything, literally from A to Z.

In October 1946, the garish Show Boat opened, with lounge entertainment at street level, on the "lower deck," and floor shows in the old Arcadia, the "upper deck." Its name and decor were inspired by the Jerome Kern musical *Show Boat*, which had been revived in 1946. The Show Boat opened with a splash, luring the Tony Bruno band away from its home at the Latin Quarter, but it perhaps took the *Cotton Blossom* thing too seriously. A November 1946 show, *Claude West's Minstrel Show*, was followed by the melodrama *Cotton Pickin' Time*. Now, good musicians can play anything, that's what they do, but one can imagine the jazz men in the Bruno crew—and he always had several—cringing in the face of *Cotton Pickin' Time*. Bruno's crew lasted a month at the Show Boat.

The Show Boat's fortunes were not such that they could afford a two-deck operation, so in spring 1948 they rented the old Arcadia to a group of black businessmen, who opened the Club Zanzibar. They planned to operate the Zanzibar as a restaurant and nightclub with a name band policy. They opened April 16 with Andy Kirk and His Clouds of Joy. The place was packed.

The Show Boat, one of many establishments to occupy 252 Huntington Avenue over the years. Courtesy of the Bostonian Society/Old State House Museum.

But there were complaints from the club's neighbors (including perhaps the *Cotton Blossom* types downstairs), who were upset about the number of black patrons in attendance. Club management was pressured to admit fewer blacks. They refused, telling the *Chronicle* that "under no condition would the club close its doors, but would continue to welcome all patrons who wished to enter." They did change the name of the club to the Zircon, but it isn't clear why. Perhaps the neighbors thought a club named after a mineral would not connote jungle rhythms, while one named after an island off the coast of Africa would. Zircon opened with Coleman Hawkins and his orchestra on

April 23. "We Are Open And Will Stay Open!" blared the advertisement. On May 1, they were still open and advertising—and then nothing. No more advertisements, no more shows, no news about openings or closings, even in the *Chronicle*. It was just gone, and shortly thereafter a Chinese restaurant occupied the space. What happened to the Zanzibar, and why, is a story unfortunately lost to time.[2]

The bad luck clinging to this site extended to bands, too. In fall 1949, Zanzibar apparently forgotten, the managers downstairs at the Show Boat hired Frankie Newton's band (Alan Dawson was its drummer and George Wein its sometimes pianist) to start a new jazz policy. In December they went all out, bringing in the Sabby Lewis band to alternate with Newton's. It should have been a slam dunk, but the show failed. It was especially painful for Lewis, as his band quit *en masse* just before Christmas because he couldn't make the payroll. They elected Jimmy Tyler their new leader and went into the Hi-Hat. Sabby built a new band (Alan Dawson was its drummer, too) and went into Wally's. The Show Boat abandoned jazz, and in January 1950 hit a new low with its *Ringside Revue*, featuring women wrestlers and midget boxers. Jazz couldn't have been more dead at this address.

Time heals all wounds, though, and the Show Boat gave it one more try, in spring 1954. The Jazz Workshop crew sent over a band led by Serge Chaloff, but his band didn't click either.

That was the last musical blast heard from the Show Boat. It moved back to the upper deck before sinking quietly in 1957. In its last years, its downstairs neighbor was McLaughlin & Reilly, a seller of church music. At least *they* had a consistent music policy.

Hall for Rent: the Ritz Plaza

When Sam Furash announced the grand opening of the Ritz Plaza's Crystal Ballroom at 218 Huntington Avenue in November 1932, he promised "a modernistic atmosphere of refinement." What he had, however, was a four-story rental hall that stayed busy with dances, weddings, functions, band rehearsals, and occasional concerts, until he closed the place in 1958. No one remembers refinement as having much to do with it.

The Ritz Plaza rented to everybody in the mid-1940s, but later in that decade something changed. There was nothing wrong with the rental business, but Furash got cold feet when it came to the idea of racial mixing, something that had been quite commonplace in earlier years. The year 1949 was a dangerous time for progressives in America, what with the House Un-American Activities Committee, the Hiss trial, and the Hollywood Ten. That summer, when the Young Progressives of Massachusetts wanted to rent the hall for a dance, Furash refused. "The police don't like it," he said. "They would take my license away." The problem? The Young Progressives had a racially mixed, left-leaning membership. So that summer, the sidewalk in front of the Ritz Plaza was the site of one of the countless skirmishes in the fight for social justice in Boston. The Ritz Plaza drew heavily from Boston's black church and fraternal groups, and they joined the protest. Furash wouldn't budge, despite petitions, daily picketing, and a community boycott.

The police put Furash in a tough spot. He needed customers, not only for the rental business, but because he had started bringing bands to the Crystal Ballroom that spring. Illinois Jacquet had opened the series and Dinah Washington, Hal McIntyre, and Eddie Vinson were scheduled when the picketing began. The boycott picked up steam when white bandleader McIntyre cancelled a June booking rather than cross the picket line. Finally, on August 17, Furash relented, and announced the Young Progressives of Massachusetts, and anyone else, could rent the hall. They booked the hall, had their dance, and Furash kept his license.[3]

That's what it was like in the Ballroom District in the summer of 1949, when the Communists scared people even more than racial mixing.

Stripp Club: the Uptown Ballroom

The Boston City Directories for the 1930s and 1940s tell us that 241 Huntington Avenue, at the corner of Mass Ave, was the home of the Paramount Ballroom, but there is no evidence to suggest that there ever *was* a Paramount Ballroom. It was only a name in the directory, perhaps the name of a legal entity. As far back as 1932, though, there was a ballroom advertising its presence at that corner, called the Uptown Ballroom, upstairs in the Uptown Theatre building, at 239 Huntington Avenue. The site is now incorporated into the Christian Science World Headquarters complex.

Beginning in 1936, the Uptown was the domain of Bill Stripp and his orchestra of old timers, three nights per week, with their program of "glide dancing and sing-songs." I am not exactly sure what that was, but I doubt there was much jazz in it. Things were more lively on the non-Stripp evenings, but the most significant jazz event might have been the night Dizzy Gillespie showed up there by mistake. He didn't stay.

The Uptown wasn't a victim of the big bands' twilight time as much as it was of changing economics. In early 1947, the building's owner discovered that renting the big second floor as office space would be more lucrative than continuing its use as a part-time dance hall. The landlord at the Strand

Ballroom, another Huntington Avenue dance hall, had come to the same conclusion a few years before. The Uptown closed in late March 1947, in Stripp's eleventh year on the bandstand, and shortly thereafter the Christian Science Church rented the space to house its youth programs. Stripp opened a New Uptown Ballroom a week later at the Intercolonial Hall in Roxbury, but it didn't last. It was just another Ballroom District hall gone dark.

Going Modern at the Down Beat Club

In December 1947, Al Booras opened a new club upstairs at 245 Tremont Street, once the home of the Tic Toc. Booras's place, the Down Beat Club, opened with a show anchored by the Milt Britton Orchestra, a strange choice from a jazz point of view but not from a commercial one. Britton had a novelty orchestra noted for destroying instruments. During the act, Britton smashed specially made violins over the sidemen's heads. The Britton organization smashed thousands of violins during its 24-year tenure, and audiences loved it.

In late December the place started booking jazz. Booras booked trumpeter Roy Eldridge and matched him with saxophonist Ted Goddard's band of Bostonians, which included trombonist Gus Dixon, drummer Jimmy Felton, and pianist Jack Medoff. Frankie Newton and Sabby Lewis also had bands at the Down Beat Club that winter and spring.

Booras asked drummer and bandleader Ray Barron to recruit Boston musicians for Sunday jam sessions. Barron found musicians for his weekly All-Star Jazz Jam that reflected his decidedly modern taste in jazz, and a rich source of talent was the big band of Ray Borden. From that band came pianist Nat Pierce, saxophonist Charlie Mariano, trombonists Mert Goodspeed and Sonny Truitt, and drummer Joe MacDonald. Other Boston men included saxophonists Gigi Gryce, Boots Mussulli and Paul Vignoli. The Down Beat's jam sessions were one of the first homes for modern jazz in Boston, but swing players such as Dick LeFave, Gene Caines, Al Morgan, and Dixon were regulars, and even a few Dixielanders came by to see what it was all about.

In spring 1948, trumpeter Cootie Williams brought his horn to a Sunday session, and he wanted to put a charge into the proceedings. As Paul Vignoli remembered it, "what Cootie wanted to do was march the musicians off the stage, go down the stairs, parade down Tremont Street to the Ken Club, blow a little down there, and then march back." Vignoli and the other locals, more familiar with dowdy Boston than the exuberant Williams, had to talk him out of it. "It just wouldn't have been a good idea, parading on Tremont Street on a Sunday afternoon." It would have been something to see, though, at least until the police showed up.[4]

The Down Beat Club, upstairs at 245 Tremont Street, 1948. Courtesy of the Bostonian Society/Old State House Museum.

Sabby Lewis was to open the new season in September 1948, but the Down Beat did not reopen after the summer shutdown. The rumor at the time was that Booras had lease trouble, brought about by a neighboring restaurant that complained about the distraction caused by the jazz spot. It was the Tic Toc all over again.

Perhaps the Down Beat was doomed from the beginning. Booras told his tale of woe to the *Record's* George Clarke:

> To begin with, business is not nearly as torrid, as, say, the trumpet riffs of Mr. Roy Eldridge (the headliner at the time). Then there are a couple of partners much more interested in the tinkle of the cash register than in drum rolls. And to top it off, there are the musicians themselves, as temperamental a bunch of double forte prima donnas as ever hit a succession of high notes...

> "One night," says Mr. Booras, "the piano player tells me he's got to go, his house is burning down. Next day I learned that he got himself off so he could play the piano at a rally for Henry Wallace!

> "Another night Mr. Frankie Newton, the eminent trumpeter, who talks like a minister but plays a trumpet like Mephisto, just didn't show up at all. He was the star, so everybody walked out. So I ask him what happened. He got sick, he said. What time, I asked. At 8 o'clock, he said. But you were due here at 7:30, I said. Yeah, he answered, but at 7:30 I was getting ready to get sick.

"It's rugged," he says, "but the jam sessions Sunday make up for a lot. Do you know, we've had as many as 30 men up there, all jamming, and it was wonderful!—and his eyes shone like a true devotee.

"Did you make any money?" you ask.

"What," said Mr. Booras, "is money?"[5]

With the Down Beat closed, Barron moved his Sunday sessions uptown to the Hi-Hat, and Booras went to work as manager of the Mohawk Ranch, a Stuart Street saloon featuring what was then called "hillbilly" music.

Boston's Most Expensive and Intimate Rendezvous

The Satire Room at the Hotel Fensgate, at 534 Beacon Street, owed much of its lively spirit to the man who ran the nightclub in the 1940s, Arki-Yavensonne, who, said George Clarke,

> operated the strangest nightclub in Boston, the Satire Room at the Fensgate, where he had room for just twenty-nine customers, and where he advertised that he served "the most expensive drinks in the world." One New Year's Eve he charged $100-a-couple, filled the room, but surprised his patrons by returning to each a War Bond. And he was never allowed to forget that he once turned down Leonard Bernstein as a pianist at $50-a-week because Leonard, now one of the world's greatest musicians, insisted on Wednesday nights off to see his girl.[6]

War or no war, Arki-Yavensonne advertised his club as "Boston's most expensive and intimate rendezvous." In 1942 he told the *Herald's* George Frazier, "We always place the check face down...We wouldn't like to have anyone choke to death or have a heart attack on the premises." Frazier was there to review Brazilian singer Elsie Houston, of whom he wrote: "She is so good that you forget for the moment that the check will be a sum only slightly smaller than the national debt. That's being pretty good." Ludicrous as the big-bucks strategy seems, it worked.[7]

Given that the Satire Room was no bucket of blood, Yavensonne hired singers with a touch of class. The Jones Brothers were favorites in the postwar years. For the better part of two years, from late 1948 until May 1950, the featured singer was Pat Rainey, who sang with her backup group, the Rain-Beaus, with twice weekly broadcasts over WVOM. The glamorous Rainey was often compared to Lena Horne.

Rainey's had been a whirlwind career to this point, from singing at the Savoy in the mid-1940s to appearing in a film with Louis Jordan and working in New York with Cab Calloway. In 1947–1948, she worked alongside pianist Dean Earl at Eddie Levine's. Rainey worked the Satire Room almost continuously from March 1949 to May 1950. She released a record on Gold Medal in 1949, "Gotta Love You 'Til I Die," and scored a local hit with it. *Metronome* graded it a B in their June issue, saying Rainey impressed them as an assured singer, who sang "with little restraint and much emotion." There was more local work capped by a month at the Hi-Hat in September 1951. She left for New York later that year.

Things did not go well there. She was arrested on drug charges twice in 1952, and lost her New York cabaret card. Rainey launched an international strategy, spending two years in Europe, in Paris, London, and finally at the Kit Kat Club in Rome, where she was a favorite of the exiled King Farouk of Egypt. A second tour of Europe followed in 1957. In late 1958, Rainey returned to Boston and the clubs, but after a few years she drifted out of music. She eventually commenced a second career in social work.

While all the intimate and expensive fun was happening in the Satire Room, a Boston University student named George Wein tried his hand at running a jazz club in another corner of the hotel. Perhaps inspired by the nearby Darbury Room, George opened Le Jazz Doux, "the quiet jazz," in spring 1949. George played piano, Frankie Newton played muted trumpet, and guests like Rainey dropped by. Cushions on the floor, dim lighting, soft jazz…it was all very Bohemian. It was also open for only about one month. In that time, though, the fledgling club owner Wein must have had some interesting conversations with the old hand Arki-Yavensonne.

Frankie Newton, who made such an impact during the war years, was a constant presence in Boston in the late 1940s, with numerous long engagements at the Savoy and the Copley Terrace, as well as the Down Beat Club. His longtime companion Ethel (whom he married in 1951) was a Bostonian, and he established roots in the community, playing benefit concerts to support social and political causes. Newton pushed the young musicians around him to be better, and bassist Al Ehrenfried recalled a small but indicative story about learning how to be a jazz musician from Newton:

> It was at the Copley Terrace, and one night Frankie asked me to play with him, but I begged off, because I had not brought the adhesive tape I used to protect my fingers. Frankie reappeared five minutes later with a roll of tape he had purchased at the corner drug store, and said, "Come on, Al. No excuses."[8]

Newton cast a long shadow in Boston, and Nat Hentoff and George Wein readily acknowledge Newton's impact on their lives. Newton, though, seemed to lose interest in playing in the early 1950s; he moved to New York in 1952, and made his last Boston appearance at Storyville in 1953. Newton died of gastritis in 1954 at age 50.

Twilight Alley

The Boston Opera House stood for about 50 years at 343 Huntington Avenue, but the only reminder of it now is Opera Place, the city street that once ran along the building's east side. Known for its excellent sight lines and superior acoustics, over the years the Opera House witnessed performances by Enrico Caruso, Kirsten Flagstad, and every other star of opera in the first half of the twentieth century. There were non-operatic highlights, too, such as Bill "Bojangles" Robinson's *Hot Mikado*, and I'm truly sorry I missed a 1951 production of *Peter Pan* with Boris Karloff as Captain Hook.

Symphony Hall had its great Ellington moment in January 1943, and the Opera House had its own in December 1946. That was when *Twilight Alley*, the Broadway musical written by Duke and John LaTouche based on John Gay's *Beggar's Opera*, opened its Broadway tryout. Ellington sent his most trusted associate, Billy Strayhorn, to supervise the Boston production. It was tough going. While in Boston, director John Houseman quit and Nicholas Ray replaced him, Bernice Parks replaced leading lady Libby Holman, and the name was changed to *Beggar's Holiday*. Reviews were mixed for Ellington's music, but it fared better than the production itself, which took a pasting. Nonetheless, after its three weeks in Boston, the play moved on to New Haven and then Broadway, where it ran for 111 performances.

Twilight Alley didn't have any trouble in Boston, but in New York it was picketed by some who objected to the interracial couple at the center of the story. After 1947, the play dropped out of sight, and little of Ellington's music made its way into general circulation. Still, none of that was the fault of the Opera House, which could rightfully boast of its role in the premiere.

The Opera House hosted a homecoming of note in 1948, in the person of Jimmy McHugh, the Boston-born songwriter who first hired Duke's band at the Cotton Club in 1927. The son of a Jamaica Plain plumber and piano-loving mother, McHugh's life in music started at the Boston Opera House in about 1910, as an office boy in the promotions department. McHugh, a onetime Boylston Street song plugger for Irving Berlin and a Revere Beach piano man, chose the Opera House to debut his musical *As the Girls Go*, in which Bobby Clark played First Husband and Irene Rich played the first woman President of the United States. The play marked McHugh's return to the stage after a long Hollywood hiatus. Lyricist and frequent McHugh collaborator Hal Adamson was returning to Boston as well, having attended Harvard in the late 1920s.

The show opened on October 13, 1948, and did not do well. Heavily revised, it moved on to Broadway the next month, where it had greater success and ran for 414 performances. No McHugh blockbusters came out of *As the*

Girls Go that could compete with his earlier efforts, including "I Can't Believe That You're In Love With Me," "Exactly Like You," "Let's Get Lost," and "A Lovely Way to Spend an Evening."

The largest single jazz concert staged at the Opera House was the "Jiant Jazz Jamboree" of November 1947, billed as a battle of music between Art Hodes and Sidney Bechet leading the Dixieland contingent, and Frankie Newton and Ted Goddard leading a swing band. It was good music but a box office flop, with fewer than 1,000 people attending. Where, Nat Hentoff wondered in his newsletter, were all the jazz fans who skipped the event? "They're gone, man, gone asleep."[9]

Nat Hentoff's *Counterpoint*

Before Nat Hentoff joined *Down Beat* in 1951, he had been a busy character on the Boston jazz scene as a disk jockey, activist, and writer. In 1947, Hentoff wrote his *Counterpoint* newsletter, the title he later used for his column in *Down Beat*.

Hentoff, born in 1925, hailed from Roxbury. He attended Boston Latin High School and Northeastern University, where he was editor-in-chief of the *Northeastern News* in 1943—a position he was forced to resign. It seems Hentoff asked uncomfortable questions and printed controversial stories, and when the university's president told him to desist, he resigned instead. A civil libertarian was born. Hentoff survived the tumult and graduated in 1945.

When he wasn't rousing the undergraduate rabble, Hentoff was peppering the musicians at the Savoy with questions, listening and learning, laying the foundation for his later career. He was probably better known, though, as the voice of jazz on WMEX radio with his studio program, *The Jazz Album*, and live broadcasts from various venues. Hentoff was jack of all trades at WMEX, spinning records, interviewing personalities, reading the news, and hosting the nightly remotes from the Savoy. Hentoff worked for WMEX from 1945 until 1953. He was an active jazz fan, leading the fledgling Jazz Society of Boston, and hosting Sunday jam sessions at Storyville.

Hentoff started *Counterpoint* in 1947. It was a labor of love for Hentoff and his partner, Ed Myers, and it was not without its challenges. "I'm not going to subscribe to your newsletter, because I'm positive it won't succeed," wrote one reader.[10] It was printed on a mimeograph machine in purple ink, and probably looked more at home in the classrooms of the time than in publishing. The newsletter went out by mail once a month, more or less, and Hentoff did his writing at WMEX in three-minute increments while the records played.

Nat Hentoff at the microphone at WMEX. Photo by Red Wolf. It originally ran in *Band Leaders and Record Review* magazine, October 1946.

Each issue included the local news, of which there was never enough in 1947. He wrote stories that the dailies wouldn't touch; for example, he wrote about the racially charged fracas involving Billy Eckstine's band at the Rio Casino in December 1946 in *Counterpoint's* first issue. He bemoaned the low attendance at jazz events, and didn't hesitate to call out those fans who claimed there wasn't any jazz in Boston and then stayed home when something like the Opera House concert took place. He reviewed records, critiqued the jazz-worthiness of local record shops and radio stations, and kept track of everything happening at the Savoy, the name synonymous with serious jazz in 1947.

> And there's Steve Connolly, the only bistro manager in Boston who, over the years, has consistently tried to hire good jazz musicians. The fact that not all the bands he brings in are jazz outfits is your fault. If you came into the place when a jazz combo was there, jazz would be a steady policy at the Savoy and at a number of other places that would hasten to follow its example. Steve deserves much credit, more credit than he'll ever get for there being any jazz in Boston in the past few years.[11]

Counterpoint gave Hentoff a forum to start writing longer pieces, with multi-part articles on Bunny Berigan, Sidney Bechet, and the long-ago dances in Congo Square in New Orleans. And Hentoff wouldn't be Hentoff without voicing strong opinions, railing against the two-local system in the musicians union, and echoing the "dull and stupid" comments of ten years before (in reporting that Steve Connolly was trying to book Bechet: "Sidney is not too fond of Boston—an attitude, incidentally, which would make an excellent criterion of intelligence"). Hentoff was blazing when he excoriated a record reviewer who linked Dixieland music to white supremacy.[12]

Hentoff recognized early on that the ideological war between the traditionalists and the modernists was far from helpful:

> Too many of the jazz followers I've met, talked with or heard from are narrow cultists. There is more to jazz than Dixieland, than jump, than be-bop...
> There have been, miraculous to relate, hundreds of fine jazz records pressed

since the Olivers, Mortons, and Armstrongs of the twenties. There are men like Joe Thomas, Lester Young, Buck Clayton, Lucky Thompson, Dodo Marmarosa, Shelly Manne, Kenny Clark, J.J. Johnson and a hell of a lot more who could give some of you Dixielanders a lot of kicks if you'd let them. Similarly the jump and be-bop adherents would be surprised how much there is to N.O. and Dixieland Jazz if they'd just listen to the music rather than parrot the more-than-musical-taste induced views of the publicists of "modern, dynamic, progressive" jazz. In recent years jazz has come to resemble a theological war rather than the relaxed, comfortable field it once was.[13]

Counterpoint excerpted parts of an article written by trombonist J. C. Higginbotham and published in *New Masses*, "Some of My Best Friends Are Enemies," in which Higgy expressed his frustration with white liberals who wanted to party with black musicians but didn't want regular social contact with them. Hentoff sided with Higginbotham, accusing such liberals of treating black musicians as a guilt-free avenue for raising hell, and reinforcing the very stereotype of blacks as irresponsible that they as liberals claimed to decry.

A good many of the jazz hangers-on I've seen hereabouts in the last five years unconsciously fall into Higginbotham's classification of phony ofays, and it would do them good to realize it. While I'm still on a missionary kick, and since this is the last issue, I've noticed a repellent tendency among some (let me accentuate the SOME) jazz followers. All profess to be entirely equalitarian with regard to Negroes, and that's a good and necessary thing. But I've heard many of these chest-pounding democrats follow a tirade on the evils of Jim Crow with anti-semitic, anti-Catholic, and anti-any other minority you can think up remarks, equally vicious in their pseudo-genteel context as the less well-disguised dyspepsia of a Rankin or Ellender. It's not a quarter or a half way deal; you either believe that every individual regardless of antecedents or physiological externals deserves to be judged on his own merits, or you have no business sullying jazz with your unwelcome attention.

Then there's another thing. Places like the Savoy and Eddie Levine's and the saloons on Columbus Avenue can do without the condescending slumming expeditions of supercilious crew-cuts and bebanged lassies with their inevitable sketching pads. If you want to be entertained, go to the Old Howard or a brothel. The Negroes who go to the Savoy and other bistros where they know they won't be discriminated against come in to relax, not to pose or to look quaint.[14]

After a year, Hentoff and Myers shut down *Counterpoint*. There were too few subscribers to justify continuing, and far too few to undertake its transformation into a "real" jazz magazine. A few years later, Hentoff was writing for *Down Beat*. In the meantime, he stayed busy at WMEX. Bill Coss, writing in *Metronome*, said that although Hentoff leaned toward music of older styles, he was "too much of a listener to ignore the modern," and he "spins records on the most erudite disc show ever heard."[15]

Hentoff wasn't the only writer observing the scene in the late 1940s. In 1948 Ray Barron settled in for a three-year stay as Boston correspondent for *Down Beat*, at what was a critical juncture for Boston jazz. Barron knew many musicians and club owners from his time as a drummer, bandleader, and organizer of jam sessions at the Down Beat and Hi-Hat clubs. He'd started a column, "Melody and Harmony," in 1947 that ran in the weekly *East Boston Times*, and his *Down Beat* work was an extension of that. Barron regularly publicized the efforts of Boston musicians, especially those of fellow veterans and of his East Boston pals, and he did what he could to help them. He had little use for Dixieland and lamented the fact that there was so much of it around. His tastes ran toward the modern, and he covered the places where it was played—the Hi-Hat, Eddie Levine's, Wally's Paradise.

Barron had a talent for public relations, and he later made a career of it. He scored a major coup in late 1949 when clarinetist Buddy DeFranco won the annual *Down Beat* poll. DeFranco happened to be in Boston at the Hi-Hat that December, and Barron arranged with *Down Beat* to have the award presented at the Hi-Hat—and he arranged for Arthur Fiedler of the Boston Pops to make the presentation. Talk about a photo op! It ran in *Down Beat* in the February 10, 1950 issue. "This is the photo you should refer to the next time some symphony cat puts down jazz," read Barron's caption.

Barron's tenure at *Down Beat* ended in mid 1951. He passed the Boston correspondent's baton to Nat Hentoff, who upon inheriting the job wrote:

> Ray Barron, former *Down Beat* staffer for Boston, has left for New York to concentrate on his personal management activities. Restless Ray combined an awesome number of vocations while in Boston: disc-jockey, publicist, jam session promoter, music publisher, record company owner, drummer, and advisor to perplexed musicians on tax matters. Localites doubt that even New York will be able to exhaust Ray's fervor for multifaceted musical projects.[16]

Record Men

With the recording ban of 1942–1944 and the wartime materials shortages finally at an end, independent record companies formed overnight in cities from coast to coast. For them, the small jazz combos coming to prominence in the late 1940s presented an opportunity. For one thing, the major labels like Columbia weren't paying much attention to the jazz groups, and they were under-recorded. Second, these groups required neither a studio orchestra nor extensive rehearsal. They were a bargain. Basically, they showed up and played, making their sessions both uncomplicated and inexpensive. Some of these newcomers, such as Keynote and Savoy, seemed to be making money at it, but they were doing so at the expense of the musicians themselves. Stories of swindles are legion.

All kinds of short-lived Boston independents were pressing jazz and pop 78s in the late 1940s and early 1950s, among them Back Bay, Baron, Gold Medal, Popular, Stellar, and Sheraton. Money was short, and there was no red-carpet treatment for the artists. Not only was there no contract or advance money, in some cases the artists themselves paid to press the records, and then peddled the product to the radio stations. There was always the hope that a bigger company might pick up a locally popular record for wider release.

Boston had two labels making records of interest to the jazz listener, Crystal-Tone and Motif. Manny Koppelman's Crystal-Tone Record Company ("Clear as Crystal") focused on Boston artists, and recorded sides by at least five different groups in 1947–1948—Sabby Lewis, the Ray Borden Orchestra, the Nat Pierce Septet (all members of the Borden Orchestra), Clarence Jackson and His Four Notes of Rhythm, and the Paul Clement Trio. Koppelman also recorded a variety of vocal hokum after the recording ban of 1948 went into effect. These were not very good records and certainly couldn't take the place of Lewis or Borden in the catalog. Why Koppelman closed is not known, but Crystal-Tone did not make new records in 1949 or any time thereafter. That task fell to one of Koppelman's employees, Reuben F. Moulds.

The Mississippi-born Moulds was nothing if not an operator. Some have described him more colorfully. Artist David Young, who designed Motif's distinctive record label, wrote that Moulds was "made of dingy clothes, deep eyes, a squarish head, southern charm, quick mind, fat promises, glib tongue, a charlatan's bravado, a sense of surprise…and was very well tuned to the wavelength then in the air."[17] He came north to attend MIT, where he was, among other things, a member of the Debating Society, on the business staff of the newspaper, vice president of the sophomore class, and leader of an 11-piece dance band—all useful training for a budding record company executive.

After leaving Crystal-Tone, Moulds opened an office at 250 Huntington Avenue in March 1949 and started his own record company, Motif Records. He recorded some of Boston's top jazz artists on his new label, including Serge Chaloff, Charlie Mariano, Jimmie Martin, Nat Pierce, and Fat Man Robinson. Moulds made perhaps 13 records in 1949 and 1950, although I can verify the existence of only 11. One of those, by Bobby Hackett, was actually a reissue of a record made a few years before by the equally obscure Melrose Records. It is anybody's guess how Moulds got his hands on it. The Pierce and Mariano Motifs were pressed in sufficient quantity to still be circulating among collectors 60 years later, but some of the others are quite rare, including those by the vocalists Deborah Robinson and Mamie Thomas.

In the end, Moulds wasn't any more successful than his former boss Koppelman. Projects languished and distribution was spotty; Moulds was slow to release records and even slower to pay his artists, and in fact, for the most part he never did. (One story has it that pianist Roy Frazee, who played on the Deborah Robinson date, threatened to push Moulds out of the office window unless he was paid immediately. Moulds allegedly paid.) In early 1951 Moulds slipped out of town with the master copies of the music, whatever money there was, and rumors of debt collectors or worse on his trail. Motif was finished, and Mould's Boston creditors never did find him.

Of Ralph and Frances and Nick

The 5 O'Clock Club occupied a long and narrow room at 78 Huntington Avenue near the corner of Irvington Street from 1947 to 1959. When it opened in 1947, there wasn't much of an entertainment scene on Huntington Avenue. The Ballroom District was much diminished and nearly finished. The Dixieland clubs of the mid-forties, Maxie's and the Copley Terrace, were gone, and Storyville and the Jazz Workshop were still years in the future. Hulking Mechanics Hall still dominated Huntington Avenue between Copley Square and Mass Ave, while facing it across the street was a row of brownstones occupied by used bookstores, thrift shops, and small hotels of modest means. Into this scene came the 5 O'Clock, and to the 5 O'Clock came Nick Jerret leading his trio.

Clarinetist Jerret, born in 1921 as Nicholas Bertocci, had been a successful bandleader in Boston and on New York's 52nd Street both before and after his wartime army days. He was back on 52nd Street in 1945 after his service, but later in the decade Nick returned to Boston, where he went to work at the 5 O'Clock. By April 1949, Nick's nightly playing was featured prominently in the club's advertisements, with Tuesday nights given over to "progressive jazz." For a time, his Tuesday companions were another pair of Bostonians who had climbed the heights of jazz stardom: Frances Wayne and Ralph Burns.

Singer Frances Wayne (Chiarina Francesca Bertocci), who named both Billie Holiday and Kirsten Flagstad as influences, was Nick Jerret's older sister by two years. Pianist and arranger Ralph Burns, born in the Boston suburb of Newton in 1922, had roomed at the Bertocci family home in Somerville in his student days at the New England Conservatory in the late 1930s. The professional paths of this trio were tightly bound throughout the next decade.

When Jerret went to New York in 1940, Burns went with him, and the two worked together at the Onyx on 52nd Street. Before Burns left Boston, he wrote arrangements for the big band of Sam Donahue. Frances Wayne was Donahue's vocalist.

In 1941 Burns and Wayne went with Charlie Barnet, and Wayne attracted serious attention with the band's recording of "That Old Black Magic," arranged by Burns. Both left Barnet in 1942 to reunite briefly with Jerret. In 1943, Burns joined Red Norvo's band, and Jerret and Wayne returned to Boston. Late that year, Burns and Wayne joined Woody Herman's band and Jerret joined the army.

Those were heady days for the Herman band, and for Burns and Wayne. This was Woody Herman's powerhouse First Herd, and Burns composed or arranged some of their most enduring hits, including "Apple Honey," "Northwest Passage," and

Frances Wayne, 1948. Courtesy of the *DownBeat* archives.

"Bijou." He arranged what became Frances Wayne's signature song, "Happiness Is Just a Thing Called Joe" in 1945. She married her Herman bandmate, trumpeter Neal Hefti, in Boston in October 1945, after the band finished a week at the RKO Theatre.

The jazz world took notice. Ralph Burns was awarded *Esquire* magazine's New Star in 1946 for his work as an arranger, and Frances Wayne earned the New Star for female vocalist. (A third Bostonian, Ray Perry, won a New Star for his work on violin.) Out of the Herman band and working with Hefti, she was in Chicago in November 1947 when a *Down Beat* reviewer wrote, "Chicago—I give you two words—Frances Wayne. That's all…and whatever I might write here would be an injustice to the effect she creates when she sings."[18]

Jerret, meanwhile, was out of the service and back on 52nd Street, and there he stayed until 1948. Then he returned to Boston and the 5 O'Clock, and reunited with members of his 52nd Street band, pianist Shelly Soreff and bassist Bob Costa.

Quirks in scheduling brought Ralph Burns and Frances Wayne to Boston in 1949. Wayne often returned to Boston and family when Hefti was on the road for extended periods. Burns, too, was relaxing at home, but he found time to cut two sides with baritone saxophonist Serge Chaloff in April for the

Motif label. In fact, Burns and Chaloff were both from Newton and in high school at the same time, although they weren't making music together then.[19] On Tuesday nights in April and May, Burns and Wayne found their way to the 5 O'Clock to join Jerret, playing for fun in an out-of-the-way room on Huntington Avenue. It must have been sublime, but we'll never know because there were no recordings or airchecks. It was a fleeting pleasure, and by summer Wayne was back in California and Burns in New York.

Although Frances Wayne gave up the hectic life of the big band singer, she performed and recorded into the 1950s, mostly with Hefti in California. She continued her frequent treks back to Boston, one being for the birth of the couple's son Paul in 1953. Her final trip home came 25 years later, when she was already quite ill. Frances Wayne died of cancer in Boston on February 6, 1978. The local media missed the story. It was the day of the Blizzard of '78.

Ralph Burns continued to write gems for Herman's Second Herd, including "Early Autumn," "Summer Serenade," and "Lady McGowan's Dream," and he recorded numerous albums of his own as pianist and arranger in the 1950s. After 1955, Burns wrote and arranged mainly for the stage and screen, and in the 1960s for television as well. He played less and less, and if he wasn't firmly in the jazz camp as the years wore on, jazz sensibilities continued to permeate his work. Burns scored *Sweet Charity* and *Cabaret* for Bob Fosse and *New York, New York* for Martin Scorsese, among many others. He subsequently won two Oscars, in 1973 for *Cabaret* and in 1980 for *All That Jazz*, an Emmy in 1980 for *Baryshnikov on Broadway*, and a Tony in 1999 for *Fosse*. Although his enormously influential career came to an end with his death in 2001, he won a second Tony and a Drama Desk Award posthumously in 2002 for a revival of *Thoroughly Modern Millie.*

Although Wayne and Burns left Boston, Jerret remained a presence in the city. He and his trio left the 5 O'Clock in 1950, first settling in for a long residence at the Jewel Room in the Hotel Bostonian, and then playing in just about every room in Boston that needed a jazz trio—the Saxony on Park Square, the Moulin Rouge at the Hotel Vendome, Guys & Dolls and Stuart Manor in the Theatre District, the Sports Lounge on Huntington Avenue, the Sherry-Biltmore Lounge, the Show Bar, Storyville. As late as 1959 he was leading a trio at Cafe Society in the Fensgate Hotel. He was also a music teacher and band director in the Cambridge public schools, a post he held for 30 years. Nick Jerret died in Boston in 2009 at age 90.

The Mid-Century Boston Jubilee

In May 1950, the City of Boston held a four-day extravaganza, the Mid-Century Boston Jubilee. It was an effort by Mayor John Hynes and the leaders of the business community to talk up the city's prospects, which in 1950 were somewhere between dismal and poor. Indeed, Boston then was widely regarded as a has-been, but the Jubilee showed it could still throw a good party. Numerous captains of industry attended speeches and roundtables marking 50 years of industrial and social progress in Boston, all evidence to the contrary. In a speech to business leaders, William Tudor Gardiner asserted that government agencies should not interfere in business affairs. It is in retrospect a good thing that Hynes didn't pay too much attention to Mr. Gardiner.

Politics aside, during the four days of the festival, as well as during several days of pre-fest warmups, the citizens of the town enjoyed a bounty of cultural activities, many of them musical. There was music at the Hatch Shell and the Parkman Bandstand, everything from the Gillette Safety Razor Company Glee Club to the Boston English High School Band to a dance band led by Tommy DeCarlo, a former trumpeter in the Glenn Miller Orchestra. Student bands from New England Conservatory of Music's Department of Popular Music and Schillinger House presented concerts at the Parkman Bandstand. On May 19, the Louis Prima and Blue Barron orchestras entertained at the Boston Garden. And finally, on Saturday May 20 came the big outdoor jazz concert, which was actually Boston's first jazz festival.

The Saturday concert was not the event for which the Jubilee was best known. That was the baked bean supper, served with ham and brown bread on long banquet tables set up on the Common. "10,000 Sit Down to Baked Beans on Common; 30,000 Turned Away," said the *Globe's* headline. Al Bandera's Garden City Band played through dinner, and Burl Ives strolled through the crowd, reprising his popular hit, "Gimme Cracked Corn and I Don't Care" to great applause. That evening, Charles J. Bourgeois presented a Jazz Festival at the Parkman Bandstand, featuring five bands playing a history of American Jazz. They were Frankie Newton's All Star Orchestra, singer Alice Ross Groves with her trio, Nat Pierce's Orchestra, the Charlie Mariano Boptet, and Ruby Braff's Quintet. These were among the finest musicians Boston had to offer. The emcee was Lindy Miller of WBZ radio.

No one knew they were making history; they were too busy staying warm. It was an unseasonably cold night, and the bean eaters donned their winter coats, as did some of the performers. "It was cold," remembered Dave Chapman of the Pierce Orchestra. "I was the only one in the saxophone section not wearing a topcoat." Alice Ross Groves remembered little of the event save for the cold wind whipping through the bandstand.[20]

Boston's newspapers collectively yawned. There were no reviews. There were barely one-sentence mentions. The reporters ate supper, filed their stories, and went out on the town. Perhaps they heard Sabby Lewis at Wally's Paradise, or

The Nat Pierce Orchestra at the Boston Jubilee, May 20, 1950. From left: Nat Pierce, Dave Gallagher, Dick Zubak, Dave Figg, Dave Chapman, Charlie Mariano, Randy Henderson. Courtesy of the Frank Driggs Collection.

Rex Stewart at the Hi-Hat, or Pat Rainey at the Fensgate. Metropolitan Opera soprano Inge Manski was singing pop music at the Copley Plaza, where she noted that she had sung the national anthem at five different Jubilee events already that weekend. Perhaps they saw John Forsythe in *Mister Roberts* at the Colonial, or Mae West in *Diamond Lil* at the Shubert, or the Ballet Russe de Monte Carlo at the Opera House. Maybe they admired Rose La Rose on stage at the Old Howard. Anything indoors on that chilly night!

The Jubilee ended on May 21, with an impossibly large crowd of 300,000 gathering on the Esplanade for band concerts and fireworks. Jazz went back indoors for another four years. And Boston was into the fifties.

Chapter 6

Dixieland Revival

Much has been written about the popular revival of the style of small-group jazz variously called "New Orleans," "Chicago," "hot," or "traditional," all of which can be mislabeled together under the heading of "Dixieland." Whatever it was called, it was popular, and nowhere more so than Boston. Numerous reasons have been advanced to explain this popularity. It was joyful, let-your-hair-down music. It wasn't read from charts, like big-band music; improvisation, the cornerstone of jazz, was at Dixieland's heart. It went well with beer, and collegians liked that. It was "authentic," and close to the way the music was played in the 1920s. It had a good beat and you could stomp your foot or get up and dance to it. Finally, it was an uncomplicated, two-beats-to-the-bar style, the antithesis of bebop, which the traditionalists abhorred. Whatever it was, it was undeniably popular, but over time the music changed from something joyful and exuberant to something pale and imitative.

The late 1940s and early 1950s witnessed ferocious internecine warfare in the jazz community, with the advocates of modern jazz on one side and the fans of traditional jazz on the other, each side calling into question the tastes, motives, and mothers' characters of the other. There was much talk during the revival years about the "true" jazz—what it was, and why that was so, and who was qualified to play it. There were endless battles in the jazz press. On one side were the traditionalists—derisively called "moldy figs"—who claimed that jazz died before 1930 and only strict adherents to those bygone days could resurrect it. The beboppers stood on the other side, claiming that Dixieland was backward-facing music with no bearing on the current scene, and no place in the future. The moldy figs said the revival music was good because it was old, and the modernists said it was bad because it was old. Those who stood up to say, "they're just different" were shouted down. This went on for years.

To complicate things a bit further, there were many tents in the Dixieland camp. One belonged to the aging black musicians of the New Orleans school who invented the style and were still playing it. *They* weren't reviving anything; they hadn't stopped yet. Another housed their young white imitators. Then there were white musicians with their roots in 1920s Chicago who had learned their hot jazz from the New Orleans musicians who moved north during that decade, and never ventured far from it. And there was a growing number of swing musicians playing the Dixieland style not by choice, but by necessity—that's where the work was.

With a few exceptions, the musicians avoided labels and litmus tests. They had the good sense to steer clear of the noise and concentrate on making a living. Sometimes they played Dixieland music, just as sometimes they played the smothering "businessman's beat" dance music, or numbingly repetitive show music. That's what the musicians had to do, and their kids never asked what kind of music paid for the corn flakes on the breakfast table.

Dixieland revival music was made mostly by white musicians and played for white audiences. This music of yesteryear had no black audience, and young black musicians disdained it. They drew no inspiration from the music itself, and felt the "Negro-as-entertainer" stereotype it represented ran counter to their emerging sense of black pride. In fact, some critics maintained that the Dixieland revival was not only musically reactionary, but also racist at heart—points hotly contested at the time.

Charlie Vinal and the Rhythm Kings

If Boston boys were playing Dixieland music in the mid-forties, chances are they were members of the Vinal Rhythm Kings. "Vinal" was clarinetist Charlie Vinal, and playing clarinet was only one of Charlie's many interests, all of which somehow involved jazz. He had a huge record collection and a home taping system (some of his Ellington acetates were good enough to release on record). He was a prolific letter-writer and on a first-name basis with many in the music business. He used to talk clarinet with Benny Goodman and Woody Herman. He did all this despite persistent health problems (he spent eight months in an iron lung after being stricken with polio at age 17) and being confined to a wheelchair.

Swing had lost its appeal for Vinal by 1943, by which time he was playing locally with Bobby Hackett and Brad Gowans. He formed his own group that year to play Dixieland music exclusively, in particular the book of the venerable Original Dixieland Jazz Band, the group credited with making the first jazz recording in 1917. He organized the Rhythm Kings with pianist Ev Schwarz, teenaged trumpeter Johnny Windhurst, a second clarinetist Jim Moynahan, drummer Jim Hart, and bassist John Field. All became well-known faces on the local Dixieland circuit, and Windhurst's fame went farther than that.

In 1944, Vinal and his cohorts, calling themselves the Jazz Club of Boston, organized a series of Sunday concerts, which featured established musicians like Hackett and Gowans playing with the Rhythm Kings. Vinal also turned author, writing the first in a series of planned articles for *Down Beat*, a controversial piece about saxophonist Coleman Hawkins that appeared in the May 1, 1944 issue.

Charlie Vinal and Bobby Hackett at the Hopscotch Room in the Copley Square Hotel, 1944. Behind Vinal is Brad Gowans. Behind Hackett is John Field.

He didn't live to see it in print. Vinal's health, never robust, failed on April 26, 1944. The Rhythm Kings pressed on with their Sunday concerts, and his friends kept the band together under his name. The Vinal Rhythm Kings, with Schwarz and Field, were gigging in Boston as late as 1950.

The Jazz Society

The *Record's* George Clarke labeled the group that was first called the Boston Jazz Society, and later simply the Jazz Society, "an esoteric organization of sufferers from a mild form of jazz mania."[1] In their own newsletter a few months earlier, they said of themselves: "We're only a bunch of jazz enthusiasts like yourselves, although perhaps slightly more so."[2] Their claim to fame was their sponsorship of about 40 Sunday concerts between May 1944 and April 1946.

The group owed its start to Charlie Vinal. After his death a group came together in May of 1944 to stage a memorial concert in his name, featuring the Rhythm Kings and various guests. Among the original board of directors were Richard Schmidt, who had been staging concerts at the Copley Square Hotel; Charlie Kallman, student and *Harvard Crimson* jazz columnist; Bill Whitmore and Jim Weaver, MIT students; John Bergen, a friend of the Vinal family and resident artist; and pianist Ev Schwarz and bassist John Field, original members of the Rhythm Kings. By October they'd found the Huntington Chambers Hall, which they could rent on Sunday afternoons for a modest $20. Here they staged biweekly concerts until the end of the year— and lost money on all of them.

On October 23, 1944, the Jazz Society held the first of a planned series of Sunday concerts at the Huntington Chambers Hall, featuring the reliable Frankie Newton with pianist Sandy Sandiford and the ex-Goodman tenor man Artie Karle. They broke even. Two weeks later they brought in the stride piano man Willie "The Lion" Smith and paired him with Chicago clarinetist Mezz Mezzrow—and lost $100, serious money for the volunteer organization. Undaunted, they staged ten more concerts through April 1945, and lost money on most of them. But the worthies in the Jazz Society decided that if they were going to lose money promoting concerts, they may as well promote the kind of music they wanted to hear themselves, so starting in January 1945 and continuing until May, the Jazz Society switched to a diet of strictly Dixie; as they ironically stated in their newsletter, they "took a definite stand for the future."[3] On came Danny Alvin, Sidney Bechet, Sidney DeParis, Johnny Windhurst—and the Jazz Society lost money on nine of ten concerts. They had fun doing it, though, and they paid for the privilege. For the year, they lost a total of about $558, a sum having the purchasing power of about $7,000 in 2012 dollars.

That was quite a chunk of change for college students and jazz musicians to absorb, but they somehow did. When they returned for their second concert season, they got help from some professionals, first from Steve Connolly at the Savoy, then Al Booras at the Copley Terrace. They left Huntington Chambers Hall in September, and held a few events at a Huntington Avenue club called Lindy's, but it shut down. By November they were at the Savoy, where Connolly absorbed most of the expenses, including the cost of the guest performer, which allowed the Society to make a little money. In January 1946 they moved again, this time to the Copley Terrace, the venue that took over the Lindy's location. Here they stayed through the end of their season in May.

The group stayed together through the concert season, but disbanded at the end of it, probably from sheer exhaustion. There were too few people

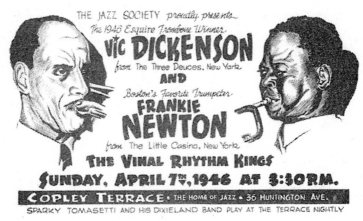

Postcard for a Jazz Society Sunday concert at the Copley Terrace, 1946.
Courtesy of Jack Bradley.

willing to do the work of keeping the group and the concert series going. Losing money certainly couldn't have helped. The Jazz Society wasn't quite done, though. The group came out of "retirement" in July 1948 to promote a benefit concert for Frankie Newton, to raise money so he could buy a new horn after all his possessions were lost in an apartment fire.

Of the many postscripts that could be added to a Jazz Society history, one is of particular interest to jazz scholarship. Sam Prescott and Dorothy Cooke met through the Jazz Society and later married. They accumulated a massive record collection, and Dorothy Prescott donated it to the New Hampshire Library of Traditional Jazz, which she founded in 1978. Housed at the University of New Hampshire at Durham, the Prescott collection is the foundation of the university's extensive jazz holdings.

The Copley Terrace, Home of Jazz

The Huntington Chambers Hall at 24-38 Huntington Avenue was a six-story office building on the edge of Copley Square, one in a block of such buildings that stretched from Dartmouth Street to Oxford Terrace, a street long vanished from the Boston map. It was a typical big-city office building with a few Boston twists. There among the dentists and magazine publishers and employment agencies were two rental halls, one often used by the Dixielanders, and a club at number 36, on the western end of the building, called the Copley Terrace. Next door, incidentally, was the Copley Theatre, which in 1944 staged the world premiere of *The Pooka*. The play's name was changed to *Harvey* before it moved on to Broadway. Despite his proximity to the Dixieland wailers, we don't know if the big bunny dropped by for the jazz, or if he even liked it.

The Copley Terrace opened at 36 Huntington Avenue in February 1945. Owner and manager Lycurgus A. Booras (better known as Al) was a friend of jazz, or at least he was until he went broke backing it in a few ventures. The Copley Terrace was a jazz-friendly place from its first day, and it enjoyed a lively season in the sun from September 1945 to June 1946.

Booras had music six nights a week, plus Sunday afternoon Jazz Society concerts. His most significant booking started in late October 1945 and played for 13 weeks. It was led by the hometown boy made good, trumpeter Max Kaminsky, ably assisted by the clarinetist Charles "Pee Wee" Russell. They assembled a top-notch Dixieland band and moved in for a long residency.

Max Kaminsky was a peer of Carney and Hodges, but his break from Boston hadn't been as lasting as theirs. When the jazz work was slow, he'd be back in town working society gigs for his longtime friend, Jack Marshard.

Born in Brockton in 1908, Kaminsky was raised in Dorchester, so close to the Franklin Park Zoo he could hear the lions roar at night. He was into music early, gigging at 14 and barely 20 when he went to Chicago and fell in with Eddie Condon, Jimmy McPartland and the rest of the Austin High Gang. This cadre of musicians became Kaminsky's lifelong friends, and they shared a lifelong musical affinity. He idolized Louis Armstrong and imitated the master's big tone in his own playing.

Back in Boston in the early 1930s, he played society swing with Leo Reisman and made the rounds in the clubs. He reached the big time in the mid-1930s, with stints in the Tommy Dorsey and Artie Shaw orchestras, and then in 1938 with the Summa Cum Laude band at Nick's in New York. He was a part of Condon's Town Hall concerts in 1940. Kaminsky changed jobs often; when he abruptly quit a job at Boston's Ken Club in April 1942, *Down Beat* wrote: "True to his record of having quit more jobs than any other star sideman in the country, Kaminsky left after a few days with no statement to the press."

Artie Shaw came calling again in 1943, when he recruited Kaminsky for his U.S. Navy Rangers band. *Down Beat* said of Kaminsky at that time: "At present he is thinking and playing big band music, because that is his war job; but he is a true hot jazzman with a preference for free and easy small group work, to which he will probably thankfully return after the war." And when the war was over, there was Maxie at the Copley Terrace.[5]

Kaminsky and Pee Wee Russell had been close friends since they first worked together in a Red Nichols band touring New England in 1929.

Russell was no stranger to Boston. Later that year he played in the orchestra for Gershwin's *Strike up the Band* (Gershwin himself conducted) at the Shubert Theatre, during which he roomed at the Kaminsky family home in Dorchester. He worked with Bobby Hackett in 1933 at the Crescent Club, and again with Hackett in his 1939 big band. Russell spent the war years in New York and Boston, and in late 1945 rejoined his old running mate at the Copley Terrace.

There were other Boston connections in that band, too. Pianist Teddy Roy was on that Crescent Club gig and at the Theatrical Club with Hackett. Trombonist Brad Gowans, from suburban Billerica, was at the Theatrical Club with Hackett, and at Nick's with Kaminsky and Russell. Rounding out the band were bassist John Field of the Vinal Rhythm Kings, and another Ken Club regular, drummer Benjamin "Buzzy" Drootin, whose family had moved to Boston from Russia when he was five years old. He was 25 at the time of the Copley Terrace gig, a veteran of the Ina Ray Hutton, Jess Stacy, and Al Donahue big bands, as well as of the small-group swing scene in the wartime Boston clubs.

Some of the Kaminsky/Russell sessions were broadcast over WHDH radio and transcribed by Jim Weaver, an MIT student and amateur sound engineer. These were eventually released on record and reissued more than once, usually with "Copley Terrace 1945" appearing somewhere in the title. Listening to the recording leaves no doubt that this band was deep in a Dixieland groove. They stayed at the Copley Terrace until the first week in February 1946. Gowans went to New York but everyone else stayed in Boston. Kaminsky had plans.

Al Booras worked hard to make the Copley Terrace a success, providing as it did the Savoy Cafe's most serious competition in 1945–1946. He tried everything. After Kaminsky departed in early 1946, Booras hired good musicians like stride piano master James P. Johnson, Chicago pianist Art Hodes and clarinetist Edmond Hall. He reunited Frankie Newton and trombonist Vic Dickenson, who had worked together in Boston in 1942–1943. He tried a modern group, that of trumpeter Neal Hefti and guitarist Chuck Wayne in February 1946. He presented Estelle Slavin's all-girl band, Estelle and Her Brunettes. But no matter what Booras tried, the Copley Terrace never achieved the success of the Savoy.

Booras even filed a lawsuit against the Savoy in November 1945 to prevent the Savoy's owners from calling the club the "home of jazz," a proceeding based on the registering of that title by the Copley Terrace, which already called itself the Home of Jazz in its advertisements. The lawsuit quietly disappeared.

Frankie Newton was the first jazzman Al Booras hired at the Terrace, in January 1945, and he was also the last, starting in May 1946 and continuing until the club shut down for the summer in mid-June. There was no September reopening; the club closed to make way for a new venture, the Show Bar. A year later Booras was managing the Down Beat Club on Tremont Street.

The Short, Distinguished Life of Maxie's

The big band days of Max Kaminsky, as we've just seen, were behind him in 1945 when he took up residence at the Copley Terrace. More than that, he was showing signs that he wanted to return to his home town. When the Copley Terrace gig ended, he put down his savings on "a little basement room in the cellar of a beat-up hotel on Huntington Avenue."[6]

The beat-up hotel was the Minerva, at 220 Huntington Avenue, just off Mass Ave. He cleaned up the place, installed a piano, and hung out the "Maxie's" sign, but he discovered he had no money left for a food license, or a liquor license, or any other kind of license. He opened anyway, despite the fact all he could provide was "music, chairs, and ashtrays."

When the Copley Terrace job ended, Gowans went to New York, but Russell and the rest followed the boss to Maxie's in February 1946. Sparky Tomasetti picked up the trombone chores.

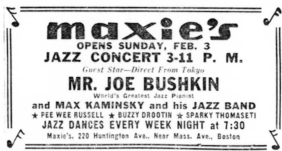

The grand opening of Maxie's. Ad ran in the *Boston Post*, February 2, 1946.

During his two-week run, Kaminsky claimed 1,500 paid admissions, but "I quickly found out that I would never learn how to run a night club…Despite all my years of experience in the music business, I was not the man to take care of the graft and the rackets and the liquor and the politics and the police payoffs, and I never would be." When the money ran out, "I folded up my empty wallet and stole back to New York."[7]

That's the story of Maxie's that Kaminsky told in his autobiography, *My Life in Jazz*. Others told it differently. One has it that the city offered a liquor license to Kaminsky, but to get it he had to dismiss Drootin, who had been charged with possession of marijuana. Kaminsky refused and opened anyway, without the liquor license.

Maxie's was a family affair on a tight budget. Nancy Kaminsky sold tickets, and Pee Wee's wife Mary ran the coat check. The band perched on a simple bandstand under an unshielded light bulb, and the crowd sat on folding chairs. Deluxe this was not! College students, artists and other musicians filled out the crowd. Photographer Bob Parent was there, and disc jockey Nat Hentoff. The improbable became probable at Maxie's:

> The music was nothing short of sensational—one of the truly great Dixie combos.
>
> One night a cat came in from Springfield or Worcester or Holyoke—somewhere out west—and a little crocked, climbed up onto the bandstand, produced a cocktail glass and ate it. Pee Wee's eyes popped. "We can never follow that act," he groaned. They could and did.
>
> At the end of each set, musicians and customers alike would emerge from Maxie's and go down the block to the Blue Moon, where they would inhale enough sauce to get them through the next set. Then, back to Maxie's for more music. It was an obvious prescription for bankruptcy. It lasted two weeks. Then, Maxie's bankroll being completely swallowed up, he locked the doors for the last time.[8]

Kaminsky stayed in Boston long enough to pay off his debts, and then went back to New York. So did Pee Wee, Teddy Roy, and Buzzy Drootin. John Field remained in Boston with the Rhythm Kings and became a mainstay of the Dixieland scene. Sparky Tomasetti also stayed in Boston, eventually winding up in Moe Solomon's house band at the Bradford Hotel. He also had a decidedly non-jazz gig as one of the Boston Troubadours, a brass trio who roamed the stands at Braves Field, playing musical encouragement behind the local nine.

How did Kaminsky sum up the experience? "It surer than hell was a disaster, wasn't it? And yet, if I had it to do over again, I would. Man, that was some band."[9]

Although Kaminsky returned to Boston quite often as a performer well into the 1960s, he never again attempted to set down roots in his hometown.

The Savoy Cafe's Dixieland Days

It was one of the most distinguished rooms in the annals of Boston jazz. Some claim that the Savoy started it all, that it was the room where jazz caught fire in Boston, and they'll get no argument from me. In its 15 years of existence, the Savoy Cafe survived an eight-month shutdown and relocation, launched the great band of Sabby Lewis, made adopted son Frankie Newton the most popular jazzman in Boston, was the home of 52nd Street-style swing in Boston, and served as the focal point for the resurgence of Dixieland music.

Dixieland days at the Savoy began in March 1945, with the arrival of two legends of New Orleans jazz: saxophonist Sidney Bechet and trumpeter Bunk Johnson. Both began playing around the time of World War I; Bechet had achieved supremacy on the soprano saxophone and was a major influence in jazz, while dental problems had forced Johnson into retirement in the early 1930s. He had only recently emerged from obscurity. The Boston engagement came about through the efforts of the members of the Jazz Society, who convinced manager Steve Connolly to hire Bechet. Connolly probably didn't need much convincing, given Bechet's lofty reputation in 1945.

The engagement wasn't entirely successful from a musical standpoint. One story has it that a frustrated Bechet let the band play while he set himself up at a table down front, shots of whiskey in a row before him. When Bunk made a mistake—and he made many—Bechet would down a shot and fling the glass at the stage. Bechet replaced Johnson with Johnny Windhurst after a month. These sessions, presumably without the sound of shattering glassware, were broadcast over WMEX radio, and many found their way onto record years later.

From that 1945 beginning, the traditional sound gained prominence. Throughout 1946 and 1947, small groups offering a "true jazz" sound trickled in; 1947 marked the tipping point between the Savoy's swing and Dixieland musical lives. It was the last year Sabby Lewis played the Savoy, and the first year Bob Wilber did. Over a period of time the Dixielanders at the Savoy eased the swing musicians out and never let the beboppers in. It became the meeting place for those obdurate fans uncharitably called "moldy figs." The Savoy emerged from the jazz wars as the Dixielanders' clubhouse. In 1948, Dixieland became the Savoy's steady diet, reigning until the place closed on New Year's Day 1956.

Bob Wilber was the dominant musical presence at the Savoy in 1948 and 1949, at one point working for six months straight. Wilber, a young clarinetist and soprano saxophonist and disciple of Bechet, was an enormous success. He took the world of Boston Dixieland by storm; he never lacked for work and there was even a "Bob Wilber Dixieland Jazz Club of Boston." The shenanigans reached a peak in January 1949 when Wilber and his band returned from New York to a tumultuous welcome at Back Bay Station, followed by a parade to the Savoy for a "welcome back" party. There are pictures of that parade, with Wilber's tailgating band in the back of a truck,

Postcard advertising Bob Wilber and Edmond Hall at the Savoy Cafe,
March 1949.

surrounded by cheering young people, all of them white. The band packed
the Savoy night after night.

Eventually Wilber tired of Dixieland, and unlike the college students who
were happy to hear the endless repetitions of "Muskrat Ramble," Wilber was
restless. In early 1950 he broke up his band, and later that year could be found
in after-hours jam sessions at Christy's Restaurant in nearby Framingham with
Gigi Gryce and Nat Pierce. And they weren't playing "Muskrat Ramble." By
early 1952, Wilber was studying with modernists Lee Konitz and Lennie
Tristano. Wilber added to his musical bag of tricks. Others at the Savoy did not.

In late 1950, Kathryn Donaghue, the Savoy's owner, fired longtime
manager Steve Connolly. No one remembers why. George Wein became
musical director for a brief time, but he had other plans and left the Savoy as
well. Both Connolly and Wein opened new clubs in 1950, and they siphoned
away much of the Savoy's talent. The imitators were left behind. Wrote
Metronome's Bill Coss:

> Just after the war, Dixie moved in with Bob Wilber at the new Savoy and,
> with Jimmy Archey, Henry Goodwin, Dick Wellstood, Pops Foster and a
> host of others, remained month after month as the young worshipped mon-
> etarily at the shrine of the old. The musicians found that what they did mat-
> tered little; the way they did it, the grimaces, foot-stomping and similar
> fakery was what sold. And they let down musically as have most who have
> played at the club with the exception of Vic Dickenson, trumpeter Ruby
> Braff and tenor man Sam Margolis, who are of too high calibre to relax their
> standards. At this writing, the Savoy is featuring Conrad Janis and his tailgate
> something, a carbon copy of the thing that sells best in Boston.[10]

In its last few years, the Savoy was locked in a Dixieland dungeon. Such was it that when the Savoy did present a Swing Street type of player, such as Dickie Wells or Charlie Shavers, the house would be empty, and management had little choice but to bring back the Dixielanders. It wasn't like the place was devoid of talent in those last years; Jack Teagarden's band with his sister Norma on piano made a fine stand over the Thanksgiving weekend in 1954, and the Excalibur Jazz Band, the Savoy's last house band, was anything but an imitative Dixieland crew.

The exuberant Leroy Parkins, leader of the Excalibur Jazz Band, ca. 1955. Courtesy of Leroy Parkins.

Clarinetist, saxophonist, and bandleader Leroy Parkins was surrounded by fine musicians in the Excalibur Jazz Band. There was Dick Wetmore, the musical chameleon, one of a handful of musicians who could play swing one night, Dixieland the next, and bebop the night after that—and play them all well. And Wetmore doubled on cornet and violin! The others were trombonist Cas Brosky, pianist Bob Pilsbury, bassist John Ronscheim, and the real veteran, drummer Tommy Benford. As a boy, Benford worked in circuses and minstrel shows, then went on to make jazz history with Jelly Roll Morton and Fats Waller in the 1920s. He spent the 1930s in Europe, the 1940s in New York, and a great deal of time in Boston and Cape Cod between 1948 and 1957. For much of that time, Benford played Dixieland music with Bob Wilber, Jimmy Archey, and Leroy Parkins.

Parkins himself was another changeling; a Boston native, his musical experiences ranged from playing in the Latin Quarter house band to studying saxophone with Big Nick Nicholas to being blown off the Savoy stage in a Sunday jam session by Arnett Cobb. Back in Boston in 1950 to attend the New England Conservatory, he played with jump bands at the Knickerbocker, the seminal bop bands of Dick Twardzik and Jaki Byard at the Melody Lounge in Lynn, and Harry Marshard's society bands everywhere east of the Mississippi River. By 1954 he was playing Dixieland at the Southward Inn on Cape Cod, and then from September 1954 until December 1955, at the Savoy. If ever there was a non-doctrinaire Dixieland band, it was the Excalibur band of Parkins, Wetmore, and Pilsbury.

What finally closed the Savoy? Perhaps it just didn't make enough money. In its last years tended to see crowds only on the weekends. ("College students. Beer drinkers. You can't build a clientele on that," sniffed Ray Barron, who booked bop bands at the Hi-Hat in the late forties.[11]) It wasn't a neighborhood place; people from the neighborhood were over at Eddie Levine's or Wally's. The college crowd thinned when the students started digging Dave Brubeck and Miles Davis. Perhaps the better musicians were being paid more to play elsewhere. But whatever the reason, the Savoy closed on New Year's Day, 1956. The Excalibur Jazz Band played the last stand on New Year's Eve. The last tune played before the doors closed forever was the "Original Dixieland One-Step."[12]

Hot Jazz Cools off

The Copley Terrace and Maxie's weren't the only Dixieland joints on Huntington Avenue. A few years later a series of rooms opened at the Copley Square Hotel at Huntington and Essex, including Storyville's false start in October 1950. George Wein barely had the doors opened when landlord troubles forced him to close after only six weeks. Wein had done business, though, and the landlord, hotel owner Bill Leonardi, wanted to capitalize on it. To do so, he opened the Music Box in the Storyville space in February 1951, the same month Wein reopened Storyville at the Buckminster Hotel on Kenmore Square.

The fortunes of jazz were always rising and falling, and in 1950 the club owners saw the fortunes of Dixieland rising. Although the Savoy was the best-known room at the time, there was plenty of competition for the Dixieland dollar in late 1950. George Wein had opened Storyville in October 1950, the same month that Steve Connolly opened his own club in the basement at 76 Warrenton Street, called Jazz at 76. The Bar of Jazz opened at Tremont and Stuart Streets with Dixieland in November 1950. Then in February 1951 along came Wein's reopened Storyville in Kenmore Square, and the Music Box. Where there had been just the Savoy, there were now five clubs, hiring the same musicians and competing for the same audience. Add in suburban clubs like Pelletier's in Lynn and the Log Cabin in Dedham, and there was a veritable Dixieland wave washing over Boston. This was great news for the Dixielanders but not for everybody else. Ray Barron, writing in *Down Beat* in May, lamented that Dixieland jazz was ruling the Hub, and only the Hi-Hat was bucking the trend.[13]

If one needed a scorecard to keep track of the clubs in early 1951, it was even harder keeping track of the musicians. There were all kinds of "Dixielanders." There was still a handful of the older black musicians who invented the style playing the circuit, and they played mostly at the Savoy. There were the white imitators playing the old tunes, rigidly adhering to the formula, and churning out "Milenberg Joys" and "Tin Roof Blues" night after night. And finally there was a cadre of small-group swing players who were playing "Nicksieland" in order to pay the rent, and it included Boston regulars like Bobby Hackett and Vic Dickenson. These were swing groups playing enough Dixieland to keep the audience happy, but playing music well outside the canon, and even employing saxophonists, which in some camps qualified them as heretics.

Nonetheless, whether the players were card-carrying Dixielanders or not, there was work. A musician working in the style could make the rounds, and Hackett and Dickenson did, working in Boston every night from September 1950 into April 1951 with long engagements at the Savoy, Jazz at 76, and the Music Box. Max Kaminsky was back working this local circuit as well.

It might have been too much of the same thing. The Bar of Jazz closed first. It was hardly fair to call it a closing, as the owners simply took down the "Bar of Jazz" sign and hung up another one that said "Silhouette Room." They didn't even fire the band. "Dick LeFave's Dixieland Band" changed overnight to the Dick LeFave Orchestra. This was probably a relief to trombonist LeFave, a smooth swinger who made his name in the big bands of Benny Goodman and Artie Shaw.

The Music Box went next. They had the right ingredients for success, according to the George Wein playbook: George's room, George's program, even George's musical friends. But they didn't have George—and by June they were back to hotel dance music.

Fall 1951 brought more changes. Wein had never intended for Storyville to be a Dixieland room, and when he reopened after the summer shutdown, it was with George Shearing, then Johnny Hodges. When Jazz at 76 reopened in the fall of 1951, the bands were locally based black bands playing jump music, with no Dixieland at all, and no Steve Connolly in evidence.

A year after Dixieland music exploded out of the Savoy to dominate the Boston jazz scene, the force of the blast was spent, and again it was only the Savoy presenting the music. It was not alone for long.

Mahogany Hall: Dedicated to Dixieland

Despite the decline of Dixieland in 1951, George Wein wanted a room for Dixieland music, and in 1952 he went ahead with his plans for a second club. Wein went back to the Copley Square Hotel that September, with his new venue, Mahogany Hall. As its advertising said, it was "dedicated to Dixieland." Wein's policy at Storyville was to feature the best entertainment in jazz, regardless of genre, but at Mahogany Hall, he featured the best in traditional jazz. Wein took a liberal view as to what Dixieland was, and he had no intention of being trapped by a formula. He assembled a fine band for his opening, the Mahogany Hall All-Stars, all familiar Boston faces—leader Pee Wee Russell on clarinet; a Savoy favorite, Jimmy Archey, on trombone; the young Dorchester cornetist, Ruby Braff; bassist John Field; and Wein himself on piano. The drummer was versatile Marquis Foster, a Bostonian better known at the Hi-Hat than in the Dixieland clubs, and just back from touring with George Shearing.

The next month the All-Stars began to assume a permanent face. Joining bassist Field in November were trombonist Vic Dickenson and drummer Buzzy Drootin, with trumpeter Doc Cheatham arriving in December. All stayed until December 1954. Claude Hopkins played piano for a year. Other regulars included Braff, Russell, Buck Clayton, and Buzzy's brother, clarinetist Al.

For Braff, as for Dickenson, Cheatham, and others, the "Dixieland" label was laughably inaccurate, but applied to them nonetheless. Cornetist Reuben "Ruby" Braff was born in Boston in 1927, and his Armstrong-inspired, melodic playing was always very much in the mainstream—he might have been one of the musicians the critic Stanley Dance had in mind when he coined the term.

Braff in the forties worked at Izzy Ort's and along Revere Beach, and aboard the *Steel Pier*, a ferry sailing between Boston and Cape Cod. He was at the Savoy by 1945, and recorded there in 1949 as a member of Edmond Hall's group. In 1950 he led a quintet at the jazz festival that was part of the Mid-

Century Boston Jubilee, and late that year was in the band that opened Storyville. This began an association with George Wein that lasted for decades. Braff worked frequently at Storyville and Mahogany Hall, often with Russell. In early 1953, Braff led a Storyville house quartet that included pianist Rollins Griffith, bassist Jimmy Woode, and drummer Jo Jones.

Braff left for New York in late 1953, but he returned to Boston often, playing at the first two Boston Arts Festivals in 1954 and 1955, headlining six times at Storyville in 1954–1957, and playing on numerous Storyville Records sessions in those years, including one of his own, *Storyville Presents Ruby Braff* (later reissued as *Hustlin' and Bustlin'*), in 1955.

Although the irascible Braff—he fired his first trumpet teacher at the age of six—spent a lifetime deriding the inadequacies of his early playing, it showed that he had absorbed the full vocabularies of the traditional jazz and swing styles early on, and used them to form a distinctive sound all his own.

Braff was popular in Boston, and perhaps if he'd stayed around, his presence might have improved Mahogany Hall's fortunes. It was never particularly successful, and in 1955 Wein cut the music back to three nights a week, using mostly area musicians, including Dick LeFave's band, and the Dukes of Dixie, then led by clarinetist Paul Nossiter. Perhaps an ever-busier Wein decided to throw in the towel in December 1955 when the club ran afoul of the Boston Licensing Board for serving drinks to minors. *Metronome*, in April 1956, said of the shuttered room that "the management found itself continually on the brink of disaster with eagle-eyed detectives and glib-tongued minors continually conspiring to supply the final push."

One can always argue about what marks the end of a musical trend, but for my money December 1955 marks the end of the Dixieland revival that began with Charlie Vinal in 1944. When Mahogany Hall and the Savoy both closed that month, it left the music homeless for the first time in a dozen years.

The Last of the Red-Hot Stompers

Mahogany Hall still had a bit of life remaining after December 1955. It reopened in October 1957 as a weekends-only operation, managed by Paul Nossiter, himself a fine clarinetist, with Leroy Parkins and the Excalibur Jazz Band providing the music. Parkins broke up his band in early 1958 and left for New York, and it was hit or miss at Mahogany Hall thereafter. Wein closed the club for the summer shutdown in 1959, and when he reopened in the fall, it was as the Ballad Room, a folk music club. That lasted one season.

Mahogany Hall's last gasp was in the fall of 1960, again as a weekends-only operation, with a Dixieland band called the Unquenchables. It lasted about a year. Those Unquenchables included Cas Brosky, longtime Excalibur trombonist, and clarinetist Mel Dorfman.

Mel Dorfman was another character well known in Dixieland circles, both as a clarinetist and for his seemingly indefatigable energy. From September 1958 to April 1960, his band worked at the Jazz Village, located, coincidentally, in the old Storyville space at the Buckminster Hotel. The Jazz Village promised the "world's finest Dixieland," and Dorfman led bands that included some of Boston's better Dixieland players, including ex-Excaliburs Brosky, pianist Bob Pilsbury, and cornetist Dick Wetmore. The band featured an unlikely drummer, Floogie Williams, a veteran of Lionel Hampton's orchestra and better known for his bop licks. Phil Wilson, then a student at the New England Conservatory, played trombone. The vocalist was Judy Powell, who once did a turn with the Jimmy Dorsey Orchestra and had been singing around Boston since at least 1946.

For a time, Dick Wetmore led the Jazz Village band, and sometimes strayed far from Dixie. It combined improvisational music with the work of other artists, like dancers, poets, mimes, and even with a locomotive enthusiast who played train whistles: "He had a table full of them, so we made up different sounds to enhance his act. He told stories about the trains, he'd heard them all, and a southern whistle does sound quite different from a whistle up here." Pianist Roger Kellaway, who later wrote the theme music for the *All in the Family* television program, was in and out of this Jazz Village band.

Another Jazz Village group was the Dukes of Dixie, which at that time included trumpeter George Poor and clarinetist Stan Monteiro, whose career path took him to Los Angeles and a long run on the business side of the recording industry, including a stint as vice president of promotions with Columbia Records.

In February of 1960, the Jazz Village closed, and Dorfman moved around the city like a jazz refugee, taking his Dixieland to any room that would have it—to the Brown Derby, Guys and Dolls, the Starlite Lounge in Allston, and finally Danny's, which ended his Sunday jam session to bring in rock and roll bands. Dixieland's heyday was long past, but it never disappeared; you'd find it in the Gaslight Room in Kenmore Square or the Gilded Cage on Boylston Street or the Red Garter in the Theatre District. Somebody, somewhere, is always ready for a Dixieland ramble.

Chapter 7

Reading, Writing, and Rhythm Physics

Boston has always been a city that valued education; Boston Latin School, the first public school in colonial America, was founded in 1635, one year before Harvard. That sense of value extended to music education as well. As early as the postwar years—the Civil War's postwar years—Boston could boast of two fine music conservatories, the Boston Conservatory and the New England Conservatory of Music, both founded in 1867. Both were classical in outlook and curriculum, and neither had a popular music program in the 1920s or 1930s. In those decades, though, they trained professional musicians, composers, and arrangers destined for the jazz field, like Mal Hallett, Milt Raskin, Don Redman, Slam Stewart, and Jerome "Don" Pasquall, who acquired his Donizetti-inspired nickname at school.

These institutions didn't reach the vast population of musicians working in commercial settings—in night club show bands, dance and society bands, theaters, and studio orchestras. A bandleader could never predict what kind of training the band members had. Maybe they played in a school band, or had private lessons, or learned riding in a band bus, or were completely self-taught. Maybe some of the talented ones had a year at a conservatory. It was haphazard, to be sure. It's not that there weren't good musicians. It's just that there were so many who weren't so good, even in the professional ranks. Songwriter Jimmy McHugh was music director at New York's Cotton Club in 1927. It was McHugh who hired Duke Ellington. "I heard Duke and I wanted him," He told *Down Beat* in 1960. "For one thing, he and his boys could read! The band I had to let go couldn't. I had to sit down at the piano and play every tune for them until they learned it." McHugh stated the training problem succinctly.[1]

Into this situation stepped two Boston educators who recognized this skills gap and had ideas on how to fill it. Quincy Porter formed the Department of Popular Music at NEC in 1942, and Lawrence Berk opened Schillinger House in 1945. Both recognized the commercial musician played a constantly changing book, with each night potentially bringing a different job and different music. Succeeding in this environment meant having a good ear and being an expert sight reader and transposer. Both knew that the musician who could also arrange music could earn more money. The audience for this practical training was large and poorly served.

Note we haven't said "jazz" yet. The emphasis wasn't on jazz musicians, and the idea of "teaching" jazz might not have occurred to Porter and Berk. They served the working commercial musicians, and taught them the tools of their trade. The jazz came later, first through the learn-by-doing approach taken by Charlie Mariano, Ray Santisi, and others at the Jazz Workshop in 1953, and then when the Jazz Workshop crew was integrated into the Berklee faculty in the mid-1950s.

Both of these programs succeeded after the war in part because there were students able to pay for the instruction, courtesy of the GI Bill, officially known as the Servicemen's Readjustment Act of 1944. The Boston Conservatory, although it did not have a popular music program, also benefited from the GI Bill, as did schools such as the Conn School of Music, affiliated with the instrument manufacturer, and private schools like Phil Saltman's School of Modern Music and the Arlington Academy of Music.

Both the Berklee College of Music and the New England Conservatory of Music thrive today, and each has prepared a history of its own.[2] Both have comprehensive websites, and first-person accounts abound in literature and around the web. This profusion of historical material allows us to be brief in our look at the early years of these programs. It would be a daunting task to list all the musicians who passed through the doors of these institutions during these years, but it is sufficient to say the list is quite long, and jazz lovers are the better for it.

New England Conservatory's Department of Popular Music

In examining the role of popular music over the years at the New England Conservatory, the school's first venture, the Department of Popular Music, is usually overshadowed by the more successful program established by Gunther Schuller and Carl Atkins in the late 1960s. But the earlier program had a 17-year history of its own. The Department of Popular Music started humbly in 1942, thrived in the postwar years, and vanished from the school's course catalog in the late 1950s.

The story started when the forward-thinking Quincy Porter, Dean of the Faculty and a man partial to the music of Stravinsky and Copland, became Director of the NEC in 1942. The war years were hard for the Conservatory, with its faculty depleted by the armed services and everyone coping with shortages and rationing. Porter saw past this, though, and his vision included an educational program for musicians working in popular music. In late

1942, he picked Ruby Newman, a commercial band leader, to lead the program. Newman in turn recommended that Porter bring in Sam Marcus to help organize it.

Violinist Newman was nothing if not well connected. A favorite with the society crowd since the 1920s, Newman led dance bands at the Ritz, the Copley Plaza, and the Statler in Boston and the Rainbow Room in New York. He was a favorite of the Roosevelts; he claimed to have played at more White House parties than any other bandleader, and he provided the music at the weddings of sons James and John Roosevelt. He was also a band booker with numerous bands working under his name out of his Newbury Street office. If anyone could open doors and create awareness for the new NEC program, it was Newman.

Newman, though, was rarely seen around the school. The real job of organizing the program fell to saxophonist Sam Marcus, another commercial bandleader with strong ties to the society scene. He booked and led bands for the Jack Marshard organization, worked as a staff musician at radio stations WBZ and WNAC, and was active in the musicians' union.

The new Department of Popular Music hobbled through the war while Marcus and his staff developed courses in practical theory, writing, and sight reading and transposing, a course Marcus called "rhythm physics." Their work paid off when the war ended and the program prospered, due in part to the many veterans taking advantage of the educational benefits of the GI Bill. When Porter left the NEC for a position at Yale in 1946, the program was flourishing.

Pent-up demand explains some of the program's success; here at last was a program tailored to the needs of the underserved population of commercial musicians. There was also a faculty with serious commercial credentials. Norman Carrel, who taught reed instruments, worked in the orchestras in the Shubert theaters. Trumpet instructor Ralph Fuccillo was a longtime orchestra member at the RKO Boston Theatre. Pianist Saul Skersey spent two years with Vaughn Monroe. Brass instruments instructor John Coffey was the real veteran, having played trombone for Jan Savitt, Joe Venuti, and Andre Kostalanetz, and was at the time a member of the Boston Symphony Orchestra. Every one of these instructors also worked as a studio musician at one or more radio stations. Practical experience was plentiful.

Porter's replacement was Harrison Keller, and Marcus felt that Keller didn't share Porter's commitment to the program. When it came time to negotiate Marcus's contract for the 1947–1948 academic year, Keller would not guarantee a base minimum salary. With the dispute unresolved, Marcus left the Conservatory.

Keller named Wright Briggs the new supervisor of the department, and though Briggs had good commercial credentials and taught arranging and choral writing, he was also a Harvard M.A. who studied with Walter Piston and was more acceptable to a "classical" man like Keller. To serve as the assistant supervisor and work with the orchestras, Keller hired another Harvard M.A., Avner Rakov, who had been music director at WBZ since 1936. Briggs hired his brother Loring, another Piston student, to teach arranging and theory. The new team had its own approach, and it wasn't to everyone's liking.

In 1948 Sam Marcus was back on the education scene with his own school, the School of Contemporary Music at 255 Newbury Street, a block from Lawrence Berk's Schillinger House. With him from NEC came Saul Skersey as co-director, as well as guitarist Ted Simonelli and bassist Georges Moleux. John Coffey joined the Marcus faculty for a year before moving on to Schillinger House.[3]

There was new faculty as well. Peter Bodge taught arranging; he had arranged for the Boston Pops and the Cleveland Symphony, and was the music director at WNAC radio. There were saxophonist Carl Rand, a former member of the Les Brown and Casa Loma Orchestras, and percussionist George Lawrence Stone, the author of influential method books such as *Stick Control*, which are still in use. The real coup, however, was the hiring of musicologist and composer Nicolas Slonimsky as musical advisor and teacher of composition and conducting. Marcus built a practical, commercially oriented program similar to the one he left behind at NEC. The school had some success, but as the competition for students increased and the number of GI Bill students decreased, Marcus closed his school in the early 1950s. He went on to became president of AFM Local 9 in the mid-1950s, and later left the music business for a career in commercial real estate.

Back at the New England Conservatory, the Department of Popular Music slowly wound down during the Keller years. The Conservatory was accredited and became a degree-granting college in 1951, which helped it attract students for whom the degree was important (Boston Conservatory was accredited in 1968, Berklee in 1973). Briggs left in 1955 and was replaced by Bill Tesson, a trombonist and arranger, who perhaps had the most varied resume of all. A graduate of Northeastern University and the New England Conservatory, he toured with the Fenton Brothers Orchestra and Red Nichols, led an Army band in the Philippines, and performed at the Folies-Bergere in Paris. Tesson tried to strengthen the program but despite his efforts it went under in 1958, the same year Harrison Keller retired. A dedicated educator and author, Tesson later taught for a dozen years at Northeastern University.

Many talented musicians passed through the Department of Popular Music. No list can do justice, but a few of the better known with Boston ties were Dick Johnson, Roger Kellaway, Andy McGhee, Don Stratton, Cecil Taylor, Al Vega, and Phil Wilson.

Significant as it was, the Department of Popular Music was but a prelude to a more sweeping commitment to jazz at the New England Conservatory. Gunther Schuller arrived at NEC as president in 1967, and in 1969 he appointed Carl Atkins to lead a new jazz studies program to encompass history, theory, and performance. It was the first such program at a classical conservatory in the United States. Working with George Russell, Jaki Byard, and others, Atkins and Schuller made the jazz curriculum a permanent part of the NEC. They also brought the Conservatory closer to the Boston community through outreach and teaching programs. But those are stories for another time.

Schillinger House and the Berklee School of Music

A story that considers only the years between 1945 and 1962 misses much of the Berklee history, as those years cover barely 20 percent of the institution's life span. It has become arguably the single most significant address in the whole 100 or so years of jazz in Boston. But it wasn't always that way. In the forties and early fifties Berklee didn't emphasize jazz instruction. Like the Department of Popular Music at NEC, in its early days Berklee's focus was on teaching commercial musicians the tools of the trade. The strong emphasis on jazz came later.

The school had three different names in its first 30 years. Named Schillinger House upon its inception in 1945, it was renamed the Berklee School of Music in 1954, and finally the Berklee College of Music in 1970. The man behind all of them was Lawrence Berk.

Born in Boston in 1908 and raised in the city's West End, Lawrence Berk was already a playing piano professionally in the mid-1920s, working society jobs around Boston with the Joe Rines Orchestra. He graduated from MIT with a degree in architectural engineering in 1932, but couldn't find a job in those Depression years, so he continued to work as a musician. He moved to New York in 1934, where he prospered as an arranger, eventually settling in with the NBC Studio Orchestra. While in New York, he learned Professor Joseph Schillinger's mathematics-based system for analyzing and composing music. Musicians found his methods intriguing, and among his students were George Gershwin and Glenn Miller. The "Schillinger System of Musical Composition" was complex, but Berk mastered it well enough to teach it, one of only a dozen "disciples" Schillinger certified before his death in 1943.

Lawrence Berk teaching the Schillinger System, ca. 1948. Courtesy of Berklee College of Music.

By that time Berk was back in Boston and working as an engineer in a defense plant, but he remained keenly interested in both music and Schillinger. He saw the future of music education in Schillinger's system, convinced it could be applied in any commercial writing or arranging situation. Berk set up a studio in the State Theatre Building on Massachusetts Avenue, down the hall from Charlie Shribman's office, and accepted his first three students. His method, which combined instruction in the Schillinger system with practical hands-on experience, caught on. In 1945 he made the jump into full-time teaching, and established his school, Schillinger House, at 284 Newbury Street in the Back Bay. Thanks to the GI Bill, he had more students than he could handle. The school was busy immediately, and Berk scrambled to hire staff.

His early hires were passionate teachers. Bob Share was a highly regarded harmony instructor who taught the Schillinger system as well; he became Berk's do-everything right-hand man in the institution's administration and was the school's provost at the time of his death in 1984.

In 1946 Berk hired Joe Viola, a local sax player who was born in 1920 in suburban Malden, and first played under the tutelage of older brother Tony.

Viola worked in the big bands of Ben Pollack and Red Norvo, and in studio orchestras, before serving four years in the army during the war. Back in Boston, he studied with Larry Berk, and shortly thereafter went to work for him at Schillinger House. Viola taught just about everything—ensembles, composition, theory, and various woodwinds. More interesting, though, is the idea that Viola might have been the Pied Piper responsible for much of the modern jazz that was made in Boston, as among his early students were Charlie Mariano, Herb Pomeroy, and Ray Santisi—the founders of the Jazz Workshop in 1953 and members of the Berklee faculty a few years later. Mariano for one always credited Viola for helping him develop his sound. Viola stayed at Berklee for 50 years, retiring as Chair of the Woodwind Department in 1985 but staying on to teach for ten years after that. Viola died in 2001.

His brother Tony, incidentally, while not on the Berklee faculty, was a renowned teacher in his own right, teaching some 2,000 students privately. The elder Viola was a member of the first Glenn Miller Orchestra and a sought-after saxophonist in the studio and theater bands. Although he taught jazz players such as Boots Mussulli and Jimmy Derba, he told an interviewer that "I have never enjoyed teaching jazz players. They are mostly characters and unreliable."[4]

Learning by doing was always a part of Berk's method, and so in 1948 he acquired a booking license to provide students with gigs on faculty-led dance bands during the school year. Berk started at least two bands, one led by Joe Viola and the second by Fred Guerra, who like Viola was an alto saxophonist with big-band experience. Guerra's came with Glenn Miller and Stan Kenton, and his commercial bands were quite popular in postwar Boston. *Down Beat's* Ray Barron counted six men in Guerra's orchestra with name-band experience in May 1948.

In May 1949, *Metronome's* George Simon reported that on a recent visit to Schillinger House, he came away impressed: "This is really an amazing place. It started a couple of years ago with an enrollment of two or three. Now it has over 500 students with more and more coming in." Berk reported that many of the students were in correspondence courses, and others in the branch studios in Worcester and Springfield. Ninety percent of the enrollment was made up of transfer students who heard what the school was doing. And what it was doing, Simon added, was "presenting a definite, working approach to the much discussed, mathematically based Schillinger system."[6] Though the Schillinger method was the school's calling card early on, over time its importance faded. One of the reasons for the name change to the Berklee School of Music in 1954 was that the school had diversified to the point that

Schillinger House was no longer a representative name. Schillinger system courses were dropped from the curriculum in the 1960s.

Most of the students in the forties and early fifties were professional musicians, and serving that market was Berk's vision, as it had been Quincy Porter's at NEC. Among the Bostonians mentioned in these pages who attended Schillinger House were Lou Allegro (who returned to teach theory in the 1960s), Tommy DeCarlo, Dean Earl (who joined the faculty in 1961 and taught piano for 41 years), Harold Layne, Eddie Logan, Joe MacDonald, Jimmy Neil, Joe Nevils, George Pearson, Ernie Trotman, Sonny Truitt, Al Vega (who taught piano in the early 1950s), Paul Vignoli, and Eddie Watson. Every one was a working musician before commencing his studies, and every one benefited from the GI Bill.

Television provided Schillinger House with the perfect vehicle for community outreach, and the school was involved in television as early as 1950, with its *Community Auditions* weekly show. Schillinger staff would select six acts for the broadcasts, and the viewing public would vote for their favorites by mailing in postcards. Berk estimated that in 1952 alone, school staff screened 3,500 applicants, and WBZ-TV sometimes received as many as 6,000 votes per contest. Later the school applied the same idea to *Tune Tryouts*, a show built around a songwriting contest. (Teddi King, then a Schillinger student, was the staff vocalist.) Still another television effort was the Sunday afternoon talent show *Star for a Day*, with faculty member Harry Smith directing the proceedings from the piano.

Joe Viola, Schillinger House instructor *extraordinaire*. Courtesy of Berklee College of Music.

The school's name changed to the Berklee School of Music in 1954, and what finally established Berklee as an institution synonymous with jazz education was the arrival of top faculty. Taught by Share and Viola, and committed to the practical, hands-on approach, some of the area's best musicians came to teach at Berklee in the mid-1950s. Herb Pomeroy joined in 1955, Alan Dawson and Ray Santisi in 1957, and Charlie Mariano in 1958. Others arrived in the 1960s: Dean Earl in 1961, John LaPorta in 1962, Phil

Wilson in 1965, Andy McGhee in 1966, and Lennie Johnson in 1968. Their ongoing presence in Boston was an important part of building the local scene, and their presence on the Berklee faculty attracted young students who wanted a career in music. This was all part of the Schillinger House to Berklee School transition.

Berk as a businessman had a good sense of his market, and was not afraid to take risks by adding new courses to the curriculum or exploring new ventures. His early entry into writing and arranging for television was one example. Other new ventures contributed to the school's growing reputation for jazz studies. Berklee students and staff produced jazz programs that were broadcast over the Voice of America radio network. The "Jazz in the Classroom" recordings began in 1957, emphasizing student writing and arranging; the first three volumes were released in the late 1950s and *Down Beat* awarded the first two four stars, and the third five stars when the magazine altered its ratings scheme.[7] The packages included the recordings as well as the scores of all the pieces. Berklee Press Publications was formed in 1958 to publish scores and instruction books.

With all these media activities, as well as its newsletters and magazine advertising, "Berklee" became a brand name with an international reputation, synonymous with jazz education.

In 1958, Berklee produced its first "Jazz Internationale" concert to feature the work of its growing number of non-American students, which that year included Japanese pianist Toshiko Akiyoshi, Malayan percussionist Ahmed Merican, Hungarian guitarist Gabor Szabo, and Turkish arranger Arif Mardin. World music enthusiasts would be impressed by the mix of musicians and instruments on stage that night. One Szabo-led group played jazz interpretations of traditional Malayan music; the band included Merican's Malayan drum, Charlie Mariano's recorder, and Jake Hanna's gong.[8]

Unlike the New England Conservatory, which had Jordan Hall, Berklee had no performance space of its own, a situation it finally resolved with its purchase of the Fenway Theater in 1973. In the intervening years, it conducted its concerts at the nearby John Hancock Hall. The biggest of these were the spring "Montage of Modern Music" concerts, some of which lasted four hours. The 1957 offering was a good example of the end-of-the-school-year concerts: it featured Richard Bobbit's 40-piece symphonic orchestra, Ray Santisi's Jazz Workshop Octet, Joe Viola's woodwind nonet, orchestras led by Herb Pomeroy and Toshiko Akiyoshi, and an orchestra of high school students. Among the musicians featured that April night who would go on to long careers in jazz were Charlie Bechler, Gordon Brisker, Joe Cardinale, Gene

Cherico, Alex Cirin, Paul Fontaine, Hal Galper, Everett Longstreth, Jimmy Mosher, Dan Nolan, and Tony Texeira.[9] Every spring concert was like that.

That students were making major contributions to the Boston scene was a fact of life, and the first students who studied under Pomeroy, Santisi, and Dawson at Berklee were graduating in the late 1950s. The roster was impressive: Hal Galper in 1957; Bill Berry, Gordon Brisker, and Jimmy Mosher in 1958; Toshiko Akiyoshi, Gene Cherico, and Joe Zawinul in 1959; Gary McFarland and Gabor Szabo in 1960; Jay Leonhart and Arif Mardin in 1961. Even for students who did not graduate, Berklee became the springboard to a jazz career.

In 1962, the Berklee School announced that it would begin accepting students into a degree-granting program beginning the following year, and in 1966 it graduated its first class of 13 Bachelors of Music. Between 1946 and 1966, the school had grown: enrollment went from fewer than 50 students in 1946, to about 300 in 1962, to almost 600 in 1966. The growth forced the school to seek new space and facilities, and in 1965 it purchased the former Bostonian Hotel at 1140 Boylston Street and moved to the renovated building the following year. It must have seemed ironic to Mariano, Santisi, and Pomeroy to attend student recitals in the space that had once been the Jewel Room, the hotel nightclub where they had played as young beboppers with Nick Jerret 15 years before.

The conservatories and Berklee contributed much to the reputations of the Boston musicians. It made them a known commodity, and that explains why the bands of Duke Ellington, Maynard Ferguson, Lionel Hampton, Woody Herman, and Stan Kenton kept coming to Boston for talent. Residency in New York did not automatically qualify a player as the best. The postwar crew of Boston musicians was solid musically, well educated, and able to step into the New York scene almost at will. Said Sam Rivers:

> All the musicians in New York knew about the musicians in Boston and vice versa. I would say, (we were) more harmonically grounded. Boston musicians, I mean, had a better musical education than New York musicians. We sort of looked down on the musical knowledge of the New York musicians because they were all there before they were ready. We all knew that. They got the on-the-job training. We waited and got ourselves together first and then we went to New York."[10]

What Rivers said about how educational preparedness gave the Boston musicians an advantage would have been music to Lawrence Berk's ears.

Berk had a broad vision, and he knew his industry and anticipated its needs. If he had a motto, it might have been "don't stand still." He understood the importance of growing and changing the curriculum, finding new opportunities, and integrating the media and new technology into courses and programs. In the school's first 15 years, Berk transformed his school from Schillinger House, a training program for working musicians, into the Berklee School of Music, a growing, internationally renowned institution at the forefront of music education. It was a good legacy for a kid from the West End. Berk stepped down as Berklee's president in 1978. He died in Boston, his city, in 1995.

Chapter 8

Scuffling

It's an old, old joke, localized for our town. Tourist in Boston stops a guy on Massachusetts Avenue and asks, "How do I get to Symphony Hall?" Guy answers, "Practice, man, practice." That is just what the "GI Bill generation" of young musicians did in Boston in the years after World War II. None of them started at Symphony Hall, although many took the stage there in later years. Instead there were nights playing in dive bars and on mundane dance dates. They often played for love, not money, even though money would have helped. They scuffled.

Scuffling in the late 1940s and early 1950s was about places in Scollay Square, on Washington Street, and on Columbus Avenue. They were gigs in what were called "buckets of blood," low-rent joints where the drinks were cheap and the music loud. For the gentlemen, jacket-and-tie were optional.

Fist Fights, Cursing Waitresses, and Scollay Square Dive Bars

The area around Scollay Square wasn't especially jazzy, so we're going to spend about as much time there as it would have taken to walk across it, from say Green Street at the western edge of Bowdoin Square to Cornhill Street at the eastern edge of Scollay Square. Of course, Scollay and Bowdoin Squares vanished decades ago. Despite all the nostalgia over Old Scollay Square, it was a down-on-its-heels part of town, a place where burlesque queens were the reigning royalty and the U.S. Navy provided their loyal subjects. Still, even in its dilapidated state after the war, there were a few places where one could hear jazz. That is, you could hear the jazz if you were close to the stage and the band played loudly.

Scollay Square joints were...boisterous. Places like the Paradise Grill on Green Street where the celebrated Roxbury drummer Roy Haynes worked one of his first professional jobs, with Mabel Robinson, as a teenager. There was the Imperial Hotel at Cambridge and Stoddard Streets, and the Pot of Gold on Hanover Street, and Jack's Lighthouse right on Scollay Square itself. These places were all dives, in keeping with the general character of the Square, but they all had live music of some sort, and they were all the kind of places where our young scuffling musicians might turn up.

As long as we're in the neighborhood, let us pay our respects to two master craftsmen who toiled a block off Scollay Square, at 40 Hanover Street. Theirs was a place of higher standards entirely. It was the shop of Charles A. Stromberg and his son Elmer, makers of acoustic guitars for the jazz trade. In the days before amplification, guitars had to be built that could project their sound over the band, and Elmer Stromberg built them—big archtop guitars, 19 inches across at their widest point. When strummed, a Stromberg could cut through the sound of the brassiest band. Among their best-known customers were Freddie Green of the Basie band, Fred Guy with Duke Ellington, and Irving Ashby, the Somerville native who worked with Lionel Hampton and Nat King Cole. These were fine guitars, much prized to this day. The Stromberg shop closed when Elmer died in 1955.[1]

The Crawford House at 15 Brattle Street was a cut above the standard Scollay Square fare, or at least it was in the 1940s, when the music director and leader of the house band was Preston "Sandy" Sandiford, a longtime presence on the Boston jazz scene who gave a start to many a jazz musician. In Sandy's time, the Crawford House lobby served as a late-night message center and ad hoc employment bureau. The contractors and managers of various shows would fall by when they were looking for substitutes or replacements, and the musicians knew to hang around the lobby to pick up the work when it came available.

What most people remember about the Crawford House, though, has nothing to do with jazz. The star performer there for years was Sally Keith, the queen of the tassel twirlers. She was so successful she even bought part ownership of the place in 1949. Although Keith worked with the Sandiford band for her Crawford House shows (she twirled to the sound of a Sandiford-arranged Duke Ellington medley), when she went on the road she had a second band, and trombonist Joe Ciavardone from Waltham was in it. He not only played growl trombone, he got to drive Sally's yellow Cadillac.

Bowdoin Square was a short block to the west along Cambridge Street from Scollay Square, with its own collection of dive bars and music haunts. Joe Ciavardone played in one, the Village Barn at 93 Cambridge Street:

> The Village Barn was a hillbilly place, but they decided to try some jazz. I played there one night with Sonny Truitt and Don Stratton—until the fight started. Guys were falling out of the balcony, pushing into the street…We were terrified. We hid behind the piano until the cops came. This place was across from the New Ritz, where we'd go to listen to the waitresses swear at us. What mouths![2]

Trumpeter Don Stratton played at the New Ritz Cafe, too, at 9 Bowdoin Square:

The New Ritz, down in a cellar, a narrow room, probably about 15 feet wide. Had a little stage, maybe four by nine feet. The door to the ladies room was on one side of it, so you'd be up there playing and somebody would get up there heading for the bathroom and be pushing you aside, "get out of the way, get out of the way," and usually a bit more colorfully than that. And the beer was stored behind the bandstand, and whenever the bartender would signal for more beer, the drummer would stop playing and carry a case of beer up to the bar, and the rest of us would keep playing without a drummer. And the other entertainment…There was a prostitute who hung around the New Ritz, Dry Run Annie, and when the bartender thought things were going a little slow, he'd come out from behind the bar and whack Annie on the breasts with a screwdriver, and the customers would think that was hilarious, and they'd be laughing…I worked there with another character who was hanging around Massachusetts Avenue and the New England Conservatory, Howie Small, a piano player. He was an expert on James Joyce and was working on the Great American Jazz Novel, which he never finished as far as I know. He would collect money for needy children, this was just after the war, and he'd collect the money in a can and he'd turn it in and get to keep half of the can. He'd set up at the New Ritz, put his can up there on the piano. So between the door to the john, and the drummer carrying the beer, and Dry Run Annie getting whacked with the screwdriver, and Howie trying to raise money…That was the New Ritz. Bowdoin Square made Scollay Square look like a park.[3]

All this is by way of illustration, so that in a later chapter when George Wein of the Storyville club tells us when he got into the business, there were mostly just joints that had some music, you'll have a frame of reference.

As a footnote, consider that all these places fell to the wrecker's ball as part of either the West End or Government Center redevelopments. It's a reminder that most of the places of Boston jazz are gone, torn down. I doubt anyone shed a tear over the passing of the New Ritz, but it had something in common with lots of other little places in Boston: It offered live music. Most everyplace had something going on, a trio or a piano player or some students passing the hat. It's what places did before the television age, when entertainment was mostly found outside the home. The Boston of the Village Bar and the New Ritz might as well be a place in a lost world.

Never a Dull Moment: Izzy Ort's Essex Street

In the late 1940s and early 1950s, the Bostonian walking south on Washington Street, away from the Old State House, would first arrive at the Washington Street shopping district and all the big department stores (Jordan Marsh, Gilchrist's, Raymond's, Filene's), and south of that was a stretch of four or five blocks of cheap hotels, theaters, restaurants, and clubs. This was a lively part of town, catering to a mix of working people, sailors (lots of sailors), movie-goers, tourists, and anybody else out to have a good time. The entertainment started at noon and lasted until closing, a time often loosely defined.

The bars here weren't high-class places. George Wein remembered Ort's and the Silver Dollar Bar, places where he made two bucks a night playing piano when he was a kid, as "buckets of blood," where "there was always music, dancing, and ample cheap booze, from noon until midnight."[4] Wein was just one of the young musicians who found work on Washington Street. Many jazz musicians remember it as a rite of passage, and if we linger here for a while, it's because the memories are strong and the stories plentiful.

The center of it all was the corner of Washington and Essex Streets, site of the RKO Boston Theatre, although its best days as a music venue were behind it in the late 1940s. By 1948 or so, the prism through which we see this area is a club called Izzy Ort's.

Izzy Ort in the 1940s. *Boston Traveler* photo, courtesy of the Boston Public Library, Print Department.

Isidore Ort was president and treasurer of Izzy Ort's Bar and Grille at 25 Essex Street, and Boston nightlife can boast of few more colorful characters. A grade school dropout, Izzy was a bartender on Coney Island in his native New York, in saloons where Jimmy Durante played piano, and the two became lifelong friends. Ort arrived in Boston in the early thirties in the employ of a bootlegger. He opened the Grille in 1935 and stayed with it for 34 years.[5]

Ort prospered in the downtown saloon trade, owning all or part of the Novelty and the Rex nearby on Washington Street, Hurley's Log Cabin on Albany Street, the Stage Bar on Stuart Street, and the Mayfair on Broadway. But the Grille, and its upstairs room, El Tropico, remained at the heart of his kingdom.

Many remember Ort for the weekly paid advertisement he ran for his club under the title, "I Wuz Thinkin'." Izzy (actually his publicist, Frank Cronin) concocted a Durante-like mixture of street talk, fractured grammar, and dese-and-dose-isms for his weekly missive from Essex Street. Here, for instance, is Izzy's contribution on Labor Day 1950:

> In de brite lexicon of I. Ort their are menny beliefs like de freedom of de
> seven sees, high tariffs, extinkshun of de boll weevil, opportunity fer all, de
> nickle ceegar an', as Labor Day brings up de subjeck ta closer focus—de wor-
> kin' man!

This claptrap appeared for years on Mondays in the *Daily Record*, always
accompanied by a photo of a fedora-clad Ort sporting a cigar.

Holidays always brought out the good will in Izzy. Here he is ringing in 1956:

> Happy New Year ta yez—ev'ry one of yez! Yep! I'm fulla good wishes today
> wid a New Year started off wid a bang an' wid hopes fer 1956!…Heer I am,
> wun yeer older an' not much wiser witch is pretty much de case wid de hole
> world. It's about time we get wise ta ourselfs an' put an end ta such t'ings as
> wars an' big-scale arguments. All in favor, raze dere hands![7]

Perhaps Cronin wrote this way because Ort's was only a block or two from
Raymond's Department Store, "the home ov Unkle Eph," the store "where U
bot the hat." But it is more likely that Cronin was trying to write the way
Durante talked. When Cronin died in 1956, "Wuz" switched to plain English, much to the disappointment of its regular readers.

Ah, de workin' man. Some of them were jazz musicians, and when they
worked for Izzy they worked long hours for short money. Many Boston jazz
musicians of all musical persuasions paid their dues here: Ruby Braff, Jaki
Byard, Bunny Campbell, Charlie Cox, Marquis Foster, Mert Goodspeed, Roy
Haynes, Dick Johnson, Sammy Lowe, Charlie Mariano, Leon Merian, Joe
Nevils, Ray Perry, Nat Pierce, Bob Pilsbury, Preston Sandiford. Everybody
worked at Izzy Ort's.

Izzy would keep an eye on things from his booth near the door, and he
carried one of those long heavy flashlights that he sometimes used to restore
the peace. He was never shy about mixing it up. Durante told a reporter in
1958 that when Izzy was tending bar back on Surf Avenue, his nickname was
"Knife in the Pocket."[8]

Quincy Jones, who played there during his Berklee days, called Ort's "a real
dive." Leon Merian was all of 16 when he first played Ort's: "It was always
very smoky and noisy, to the point where you could hardly hear the music…I
didn't like playing that room at all. As a matter of fact, I didn't even like being
there." Nat Hentoff called Ort's "a club that would have been right at home in
Dodge City before there were marshals in the town,"[9] and saxophonist Sam
Rivers agreed:

> It got rough sometimes. You'd get the Navy and the Marines in there, and
> they could destroy the place in five minutes. The police would come in and it

would be a shambles. I still don't understand why people weren't getting badly hurt—they were throwing bottles around in there.[10]

Herb Pomeroy recalled Ort's, too.

> I worked there in 1951. Terrible. There was a dance floor stage, up maybe four feet above the floor. So we were up on that stage, a quartet, we played for the strippers, everything. We worked there seven nights a week from 6:00 to 1:00... seven hours, seven nights, for $49. Joe Nevils was playing upstairs at the El Tropico, and I was playing downstairs with Eddie Schwartz, a drummer, and Dick Twardzik was playing piano, and Jim Clark was playing tenor. But Izzy... This is a sailor's joint and the fights, guys breaking bottles and going after each other, and Izzy would get right in there. He was short, I would say about five-five, and he'd be right in the middle of it. I never saw him get cut, but there were some awful fights. And I did learn about a slice of life there, I tell you.[11]

Even if Izzy sometimes used that flashlight to send a sailor or two to dreamland, Izzy loved the armed forces and they loved him. If you were in uniform on Thanksgiving or Christmas, Izzy served you a turkey dinner with all the trimmings, on the house. He sent countless cartons of cigarettes overseas. Wherever there were American outposts abroad, there were canteens and mess halls bearing the name "Izzy Ort's" over the door.

Trumpeter Don Stratton remembers working at Ort's:

> Charlie Mariano had a group at Izzy Ort's, and I'd sub with him sometimes. We played seven days a week, from one in the afternoon until one in the morning. I remember being paid $5 for the afternoon jam session on Sunday. Good band: Charlie on alto of course, and Willie Jones, piano; Marquis Foster, drums; Bernie Griggs Jr., bass, and Charlie Hooks, trumpet. Now Charlie Hooks...bands coming through town were always trying to hire him, but he wouldn't go. If he went on the road he'd lose money—he had a tonk game going in the basement at Izzy Ort's and he was picking up some good money. So he didn't want to leave. But Charlie, when he was playing, you knew it. When you'd get off the subway at Tremont Street, you could hear Charlie Hooks. He could play![12]

Charlie Hooks had been around Boston for years, as a member of the Alabama Aces with Joe Nevils, and as one of the trumpeters Sabby Lewis would call when needed to expand his group for New York engagements. Sam Rivers knew Hooks and a few others at Ort's:

> I was playing in a trio with Larry Winters on drums and Larry Willis on piano. Larry Willis was a genuine stride pianist, he played that style, and he knew all the tunes, all the standards, I don't know how he knew all those tunes, because I don't think he could read. He'd just get all these tunes by listening to them, and the chords were right every time. He just had this gift for

learning a lot of tunes, and if I didn't know a tune I'd just sit out and listen and learn it, learn the melody. He was a very knowledgeable fellow.

There were two bands at Ort's, there was the trio and we'd play with the singers, and then there was the band that played with the shows. Charlie Hooks had that band, four horns, that's the band Quincy Jones was in. Hooks was a trumpeter with a broad sound. He wasn't a soloist though, he was more of a first trumpet, a lead player. He couldn't solo. Whatever was written down, that's what he'd play…but nice and strong. Charlie Hooks was actually the guy who hired me. We'd play from something like 7 to 12 every night.[13]

Just because so many fine jazz musicians worked for Ort didn't mean he was a jazz fan. He was a club owner trying to make a living, and he brought in the music that was popular. In April 1953 he renamed the Grille the Golden Nugget, and because hillbilly music was the latest trend, he booked it there. In 1956, when rock and roll was here to stay, Izzy presented it.

Ort sold the Essex Street establishment in 1969, and it limped along for a few years without him before it closed. Izzy himself died in October 1975.

Today the building, with a rebuilt facade, houses offices and looks more and more out of place in the area now dubbed the Ladder District. It seems a long way from what Izzy Ort advertised: "No cover, no minimum, three floor shows, three dance bands, and never a dull moment."

One Outstanding Bar: the Silver Dollar

Essex Street wasn't alone in providing diversions that combined drink and music. Washington Street had its share of lively places too, and none was livelier than the Silver Dollar Bar, at 642 Washington Street.

The Silver Dollar opened in 1936, a year after Ort's, in what was then the Brigham Hotel. Customers entered into a long narrow room, with what advertisements claimed was the world's longest bar. In the back was the Blue Room, with the stage.

A parade of local musicians worked regularly at the Silver Dollar. Owner Harry Sher had something for everybody, and guitarist and singer Don Humbert had the theme song for everybody to sing: "Meet Me at the Silver Dollar Bar." Humbert, a Washington Street perennial, almost made it to the big time. It was unusual in the 1940s to find a singing guitarist, and Humbert was a fine singer with his own show on radio station WHDH. He got as far as the Palace Theatre in New York but no farther, and he ended up playing for 15 more years at places such as Ort's and the Silver Dollar.

In every Capital City thru-out the World there is one outstanding bar for instance: New York, Jack Dempsey's; Philadelphia, Benny's Bar; Los Angeles, Ptomaine Tommy's; Miami, 5 O'clock (5 to 5); Paris, Harry's Bar; Havana, Sloppy Joe's; Nassau, Dirty Dick's; Shanghai, The Internationale, (Bar of All Nations); London, The Savoy

and in Boston it's the

SILVER DOLLAR

Continuous Entertaiment from 11 a. m. till closing . . . . daily

642 WASHINGTON STREET
(Foot of Boylston Street)
See Location on Face of Map

You wouldn't mistake it for Jack Dempsey's: advertisement for the Silver Dollar bar in a tourist brochure, ca. 1940.

As at Ort's, the Silver Dollar entertained more than a few members of the U. S. Navy in the Blue Room in the postwar years. Saxophonist Paul Vignoli remembered: "When you were up on the bandstand there, all you could see were the white hats—all the sailors." It wasn't a place for quiet conversation. Vignoli had one word for it: "Loud!"[14]

The Silver Dollar was downright dangerous on some nights, and trumpeter Leon Merian described some mid-forties mayhem on a night he was working with Don Humbert:

This particular night, one of the girls dancing with one of the guys happened to "belong" to one of the wise guys.

When he saw his girl was dancing with another guy, one he didn't especially care for in the first place, he walked right out on the dance floor, pulled out his piece, and whacked him square in the chest, about six feet from the bandstand, right in front of me.

The guy dropped like a rock and there was blood everywhere. I ran into the kitchen with my horn and hid under the stove. Pretty soon the cops showed up and the commotion, the screams, and the carrying on lasted quite a while. It was an absolute zoo. Simply indescribable![15]

Never a favorite of the licensing board, the rollicking Silver Dollar closed in 1954, perhaps after a few too many nights like Merian's. Board Chairwoman Mary Driscoll wanted it to stay closed, too. She wouldn't approve additional liquor licenses in the area while there was still a chance the "rum-saturated" Silver Dollar might reopen.[16]

Its replacement was the Palace Bar, a place where the high-energy rhythm and blues of Fat Man Robinson served as an appropriate sound track. The Palace was robbed twice at gunpoint, and witnessed a few more well-publicized shootings and stabbings. This probably wasn't what Mrs. Driscoll had in mind when she sought to replace the Silver Dollar. It got worse though. Within 20 years, the Charlestown Navy Yard would be closed and all those sailors gone with it. Lower Washington Street would be home to the strip joints, peep shows and all-night cinemas of the Combat Zone, the home of the city's sex businesses. Had she known of that, Mrs. Driscoll might have accepted the merely rum-saturated readily, if not willingly.

Along Essex Street

A few doors from Ort's, at 47 Essex Street, was the Spotlite Cafe, on the corner of Harrison Avenue. An underaged Ray Santisi played piano there:

> It was on the corner of Harrison, a little joint called the Spotlite Cafe, a small place, a dive, you know? And in the afternoons they would have music for the early crowd: a "token amenity." We played with a singer, Peggy Mansfield…It was a trip. She'd make up her own words in the middle of the tune, often a verse made up to express her feelings about who was in the club just then. Or she would sing bawdy lyrics when she forgot the words to the song we were playing. Or at least she said she forgot them. We had a trio, clarinetist Don Houghton, and drummer Teddy Tedikus, and me. Just the three of us. No bass.

The Spotlite gave way to a joint called the Beantown in 1957, and Phil Wilson worked there sometimes as a piano player when he was a student. The piano was something less than concert quality—playing with sufficient force would send piano keys flying, and Wilson amused himself by timing his keyboard-banging so as to launch keys in the direction of other musicians on the bandstand.

Next door to Ort's at 21 Essex was Playland, a club with a long history as a gay bar and famous for the sign that hung over the bar: "Banks Don't Serve Liquor. We Don't Lend Out Money." Playland played a part in what might be the first use of the term "Combat Zone" to describe the area, and it had nothing to do with nude dancing or hookers. One night in April 1951, a member of the Marine Corps went AWOL, consumed a dozen drinks at Playland, and started a loud argument with his girlfriend. A Boston cop, himself an ex-marine, hauled the loudmouth out to the sidewalk. The sight of a policeman pushing around a serviceman in uniform proved irresistible to a passing navy veteran, one who had himself had earned 12 battle stars. He joined the fray and pushed the policeman to the pavement. The policeman drew his weapon and fired a shot, wounding the sailor and winging the marine's girlfriend, who had followed everybody outside. Police reinforcements arrested the lot of them. At the arraignment, Municipal Judge George W. Roberts proclaimed, "It's a combat zone, a bucket of blood all along Essex Street. They ought to award battle stars for service on Essex Street." He recommended that the military declare the streets off-limits, or at least station the military police there nightly, and not only on weekends.[18]

Just another night on Essex Street, training ground for a generation of Boston jazz musicians.

Chapter 9

The Jazz Corner of Boston

Over the years people have called it "the Avenue" or "Boston's 52nd Street," but whatever its name, for these 25 years Massachusetts Avenue was the most important street in Boston jazz, and its intersection with Columbus Avenue the most important corner. Disc jockey Symphony Sid Torin, riffing on the theme he had used in New York when he dubbed Broadway at 52nd "the Jazz Corner of the World," called Mass Ave at Columbus "the Jazz Corner of Boston" when he was broadcasting nightly there from the Hi-Hat.

Between 1937 and 1962, there were always two, or three, or four competing clubs: in the late 1930s, the Royal Palms and Little Harlem; during the war, the Savoy Cafe and Little Dixie; from the late 1940s through the mid-1950s, Wally's Paradise, Eddie Levine's, and the Savoy; in the late 1950s, Wally's, the Wigwam, and the Big M. The name-band room, the Hi-Hat, stood right on the corner itself. In the blocks surrounding the Jazz Corner were more rooms—Johnny Wilson's Swanee Grill, the 4-11 Lounge, the Pioneer Club, Handy's Cafe, Connolly's Stardust Room, the Professional and Business Men's Club. In the forties and fifties, the music was constant.

But more than nightclubs made this the Jazz Corner. The Local 535 union hall was here. Smilin' Jack's College Record Shop, an institution in its own right, was here. The musician-friendly rooming houses were nearby, as were the places musicians socialized. When Sabby Lewis went into the restaurant business in November 1947, he opened at 422 Massachusetts Avenue, just a few doors from Wally's Paradise. The stretch of Mass Ave from the railroad tracks to Columbus Avenue was the focal point of the Boston jazz scene.

And more than places made this the Jazz Corner. First was the presence of the black community, where the music enjoyed its greatest popularity. In the 1940s and 1950s, most of the black population of Boston lived in the South End and Lower Roxbury. Boston's black community was small (three percent of the city's population in the 1940 census, five percent in 1950, nine percent in 1960) but significant. Boston was home to 23,000 African Americans in 1940, and even with a jump in population in the postwar years, the black population still stood at only about 40,000 in 1950, out of a total city population of just over 800,000. This was a community, and all the institutions and businesses serving that community were centered on Mass Ave and its main cross streets, Columbus Ave and Tremont Street.

Mass Ave in these blocks was Boston's most diverse street at a time when "diversity" was not much in the minds of the people in tribal Boston. The South End had long been a point of arrival for newcomers, all races and nationalities mixed in this working class neighborhood, and everybody lived side-by-side. The Boston City Directories for these years show a proverbial melting pot living in these blocks of Mass Ave—Simonetti and Fung, Haddad and Johnson, Connolly and Courambis. People mixed here. It was a busy urban neighborhood and Mass Ave was its major thoroughfare.

The east side of the 400 block of Massachusetts Avenue, ca. 1955. Wally's Paradise is at 428. Chicken Lane replaced Sabby Lewis's restaurant at 422. The building with the glass-block panel is the Savoy at 410, and next door to that at 408 is Morley's, a preferred watering hole among the musicians. Detail of a photograph by Nishan Bichajian, Massachusetts Institute of Technology. Courtesy MIT Libraries, Rotch Visual Collections.

Living Rooms

Rooming houses and boarding houses often met the need for housing among jazz musicians, many of whom were young, single, or itinerant—or possibly all three. The obvious answer for the traveling musician was to stay in a hotel, but for the black musician that often posed a problem: they had a hard time renting rooms. There were no laws preventing it, but in the Back Bay hotels, there just never seemed to be any vacancies. The exception to this was the Bostonian on Boylston Street, which welcomed one and all, and many road bands stayed there. For many travelers, though, as well as for local musicians, private homes or rooming houses provided the necessary accommodations. Jazz musicians were familiar neighborhood figures. Ellington himself spent so much time in Myra McAdoo's home that she grew up calling him "Uncle Edward" and was shocked the first time she saw him on stage at the RKO Theatre. Up until that moment she hadn't connected the familiar visitor and the famous entertainer.[1]

In Boston's South End, a neighborhood teeming with rooming houses, it was inevitable that some would cater to the musicians, both local and transient. One such place operated at 417 Mass Ave from 1944 to 1965, under the proprietorship of Charles and Mary Jackson. The place was famous for Mary's restaurant, the Western Lunch Box. Everybody ate there, from celebrities like Nat King Cole to divinity students like Martin Luther King, then residing in a boarding house a few doors away at 397 Mass Ave. Perhaps the jazzmen liked Mary's place because her son, Chet King, was a longtime jazz bassist and bandleader in Boston.

Eddie Logan, down a few doors at 421 Mass Ave, also operated a rooming house from about 1948 to 1955. Logan's house was always popular with musicians because he was a musician himself, a saxophonist who came up in the Texas territory bands, served in the navy, and arrived in Boston in 1946 to attend the Boston Conservatory. He played saxophones in Jimmie Martin's Beboppers, worked all the South End clubs, taught himself the bass, and was accomplished enough to substitute for Johnny Hodges on some of Duke Ellington's forays into New England. His row house was home to many musicians.

> I had this place right there on Massachusetts Avenue and the musicians started finding out about it, and all the musicians came there. Mine wasn't the only rooming house, there was Mother's Lunch on Columbus, another one on Canton Street. But I had a lot of people staying there. Clark Terry, Wardell Gray, Russell Jacquet—Illinois didn't live there but he was always stopping by—Coltrane on the top floor in the front. Wyatt Reuther, the bassist, we called him "Bull" Reuther then, he worked with Erroll Garner after Boston. Fat Man Robinson and his wife lived there for a time. Gator Rivers and his wife. Joe Gordon. Percy Heath and Milt Jackson, and they used to do a lot of cooking. Percy would cook the dinners and Bags would bake pies.
>
> It was a convenient place for the musicians, close by the clubs where they were working, they could run in between sets to change, maybe sneak a girl up between sets. I was there for eight years, and it was always exciting. It's like Joe Perry said, that I had a place to play, and a refrigerator and a stove too.[2]

Mother's Lunch, close by at 510 Columbus Avenue, was another musicians' favorite. "Mother" was Wilhelmina Garnes, whom the *Chronicle* claimed "was known to the theatrical and music trade from coast to coast."[3] In its 1940s heyday, Mother's had a restaurant with a sidewalk cafe in the summer; the Tangerine Room, a second-floor club that operated into early morning hours; and a first-floor rehearsal space. ("Best jazz in Boston last week was at Mother's Lunch, where Louis Armstrong rehearsed his band daily," reported George Frazier in March 1942.[4]) It was not just Armstrong's band, but also Basie's and Ellington's, who found the atmosphere at Mother's congenial. Dizzy Gillespie stayed there. J. C. Higginbotham, who spent five years in Boston, was a longtime resident.

Wilhelmina Garnes and Mother's Lunch were in business until 1956, about the time the hotels were starting to wake up.

Eddie Levine's Intimate Lounge

In 1937, Israel E. Levine—Eddie—ran the Little Harlem nightclub at 428 Mass Ave. That was when he was selling liquor after hours and the city shut him down. But Levine was a player, and after Little Harlem closed, he tried to buy into Southland in the Theater District but was rebuffed, and there were persistent rumors that he wanted to get back to Mass Ave. In 1947, he did. He opened a small second-story room at 425 Massachusetts Avenue, across the street from his old place, where Wally's Paradise had just opened. It wasn't the first club at 425; for a short time in 1952 Johnny McIlvaine ran a jazz club there called the Green Door. Levine's place was called Eddie's Musical Lounge—or Eddie's Musical Cocktail Lounge, Club Eddie's, Eddie's Intimate Lounge, Eddie's Lounge, or Eddie's Cafe. Just plain "Eddie's" was good enough. The cab drivers knew where to drop you.

Compared to Wally's or the Savoy, Eddie's was small, accommodating perhaps 100 patrons on a good night. But its small size gave the room its character, and Eddie sold his place as "Boston's most intimate night spot." The man behind the piano in 1947, Dean Earl, became something of a fixture at Eddie's. Earl occupied the piano chair every day, for months at a time, until Eddie's closed in 1958. Earl and Levine had a long history together, going back to the 1930s when Dean led the Little Harlem Orchestra. Ron Gill recalled Earl holding court at Eddie's:

> The stage was on the left side as you came up the stairs, at floor level, one flight up, so as you came up the stairs, you rose to the level of the bandstand. The piano was on the end of the stage, so Dean could see everybody coming up. And as soon as he'd see me stick my head in the door, he'd say: "Ronnie Gill! C'mon up here and give us a song!"[5]

Eddie's Cafe at 425 Massachusetts Avenue, ca. 1955. A few doors away at 409 was the Local 535 union hall. Detail of a photograph by Nishan Bichajian, Massachusetts Institute of Technology. Courtesy MIT Libraries, Rotch Visual Collections.

Eddie's was always a singer's room. Earl knew the fine art of accompaniment, and the first singer to be featured in 1947 was Pat Rainey, not so much a jazz singer as a torch singer, dubbed "Boston's challenge to Lena Horne."[6] Rainey started singing in Boston during the war years, and by 1947 had appeared in films singing alongside Cab Calloway and Louis Jordan. Bigger days were ahead for Rainey.

There was something different at the Musical Lounge in the summer of 1948. It was saxophonist Jimmy Tyler, just off the Sabby Lewis band, with a quartet that included two young bebop players studying at the Boston Conservatory, pianist Curtis Brown and bassist Martin "Gator" Rivers. Although it was a small room, *Down Beat* reported it drew crowds.[7] In September, Tyler went across the street to Wally's, and Eddie replaced him first with trumpeter Phil Edmunds, then with a bop quintet led by saxophonist Charlie Mariano.

Despite using the occasional saxophonist as headliner (one was Ben Webster, who played for two unadvertised weeks in February 1953), piano trios were the perennial favorites at Eddie's. When Earl wasn't available, numerous Boston pianists filled in, among them Hi Diggs, Sammy Lowe, Melba Pope, Hillary Rose, Dick Twardzik, and Al Walcott.

Calypso music was quite popular in America in the mid-1950s, and it thrived at Eddie's with a well-known local exponent of the music, Gene Walcott, known as the Charmer. For about a year in 1953–1954, Walcott, a talented singer and violinist, led a group at Eddie's. Ron Gill, who sang in his group, recalled that "He could sing, play the violin, dance, tell a story and emcee a show. He was quite an entertainer, and popular. When the Charmer was performing, the streets were empty." Walcott eventually withdrew from the music scene to concentrate on his growing role in the Nation of Islam. Later he took the name Louis Farrakhan.

Levine, who had frequent run-ins with the licensing board in his Little Harlem days, had more trouble with the authorities in 1955. His liquor license was suspended for refusing to admit the police after hours that March, and in August it was suspended again for six weeks following a fatal stabbing on the premises.

Crystal Joy took over house band chores for six months in 1956–1957:

> I worked there for about six months, with all different configurations of musicians. They kept changing things around. First I went in with a trio, with Debbie Paulson, a good tenor player who had worked with Sabby Lewis, she actually got the gig. Then they asked me to work as a single—if you can sing and play piano, they'll fire the rest of the group right out from under you—so I did that. Then they wanted to have other musicians playing with me, so we tried that, and some worked better than others. One of my bassists was Mona Neves, John's wife. I also worked with a guitarist, Clarence Johnson, but our styles weren't compatible.[8]

After Crystal Joy's engagement, Eddie's Musical Lounge assumed a lower profile. It stopped advertising and Vin Haynes stopped mentioning the club in his *Chronicle* column. The club closed for a time in 1958.

Eddie's was reopened as the Wigwam in 1959. A storefront had been added to the building at street level years before to house a lunch counter, and bar patrons entered through this addition to reach the stairs. (The external stairway leading directly to Eddie's second-floor space had been removed and the front door bricked over.) The Wigwam made use of this addition by placing a teepee on it.

Although many musicians remember the Wigwam, not many remember much about it, but they do remember one of the bandleaders there, tenor saxophonist Roland Alexander. Born in Boston in 1935, Alexander was well known on the Boston scene in the mid-fifties as a member of Hy Lockhart's group at the Hi-Hat in 1953, Alan Dawson's at Wally's in 1957, and Richie Lowery's big band during his student days. He earned a bachelor's in music composition from the Boston Conservatory. A card-carrying Coltrane disciple, he played piano on Coltrane's Transition Records date in 1956, one track of which was released on the *Jazz in Transition* sampler LP. After his time at the Wigwam, Alexander moved to New York. His 1961 LP, *Pleasure Bent* on the Prestige New Jazz label, was very much in the hard bop school, but as Coltrane moved further out in the 1960s, so did Alexander. A footnote: Alexander walked away unhurt from the car crash that killed bassist Doug Watkins as they traveled to a gig in February 1962.

Eddie Levine died in 1961, and the Wigwam closed the next year.

Local 535's Union Hall

Although the Boston Musicians' Association, part of the American Federation of Musicians (AFM), spoke for all musicians during these years, in Boston the AFM spoke with two voices, with Local 9 representing whites, and Local 535 representing blacks. That was the way it was for 55 years, until 1970, when the locals merged. This was not an instance of racial separation unique to Boston. In fact, local jurisdictions were split this way all across the country in a pattern of institutional segregation.

Local 9 was chartered in 1897, and all musicians belonged to it in the early years of the century, but the black musicians soon wanted an independent local aligned with their own interests and identity. AFM Local 535 was thus chartered in 1915. The jazz musician was inextricably involved in this decision, because the black musicians were playing all of the jazz in those early years, and it was part of the new local's identity. Popular music was what the black musicians played; they were shut out of other types of commercial work—from classical ensembles, theater pit bands, and studio orchestras, for example.

Nineteen thirty-nine was a big year for both locals, with each occupying a new union hall. Local 9 relocated to the grand Musicians' Relief Society building on St. Botolph Street, and Local 535 bought a brownstone at 409 Mass Ave just off Columbus. Local 9's building included a performance space they christened Convention Hall, which saw use as a run-of-the-mill dance hall. Local 535's building had no performance space, but there were auditions and rehearsals and jam sessions on the first floor day and night.

No comprehensive list of 535's officers and dates of service has survived, but among those remembered are the local's Board of Strategy (president John Barkley, vice-president Newton Ball, and secretary Clemon Jackson) who in 1938 proposed the purchase of the brownstone; George Irish, president in the late 1940s and 1950s; and Preston Sandiford, president after Irish and through the 1960s. Joe Nevils was a longtime vice president, and Clem Jackson was secretary longer than anyone could remember. He was a fierce

Local 535 officers at the annual ball, ca. May 1958. Seated from left: Joe Nevils, Clem Jackson, Preston Sandiford, Charles Watson. Standing: Cliff "Smickles" Smith, Carlton "Blondey" Donaldson, Don Francis, John Long, Richard Lowery, Willie Moses, George Irish. Courtesy of Doris Clark.

enforcer of union work rules, driving from venue to venue to check union cards, collect fees, and assess fines. "Oh, he was tough," Elynor Walcott recalled of Jackson's visits to Wally's Paradise. "He was tough all day."[9]

The biggest affair of the year for Local 535 was the annual spring ball and benefit, an event much too large to hold at the hall. As many as a dozen jazz and dance bands played into the early morning at Butler Hall or Ruggles Hall or the Sherry-Biltmore Hotel.

In the years of this story, there were always a few musicians who carried cards in both locals, but for the most part the black musicians in Local 535 played jazz and filled the jobs in the Mass Ave clubs and downtown spots such as the Checker Cafe and the Crawford House. The Local 9 musicians filled the jobs in the hotel ballrooms, the Bay Village floor shows, and the theaters. Some in Local 9 said the work was distributed this way because the black musicians were good improvisers, but they couldn't read, and they needed to read to work the floor shows with their ever-changing book. Ridiculous on the face of it, but that was the story and some might even have believed it. The truth was more along the lines of maintaining control over the better-paying jobs. "It's still beyond my limited understanding why Boston, or any other city, for that matter, requires two locals—one for whites, the other for Negroes. Music is supposed to be the most democratic of the arts: what excuse, then, is there for segregation in that realm?" wrote Nat Hentoff in his *Counterpoint* newsletter in January 1947. Nonetheless, two locals remained the status quo through Hentoff's time and well beyond.

Locals 9 and 535 were eventually phased out of existence by the AFM itself. In late 1968, the AFM ordered Locals 9 and 535 to merge, a lengthy process finally completed in April 1970 with the birth of Local 9-535. The Mass Ave building, the symbol of the separate identity of the old Local 535, was sold soon afterwards.

Jazz Corner Joints

There were many joints around the Jazz Corner where there was music, and two, the 4-11 Lounge and Handy's, rate as jazz-worthy. Barely.

The 4-11 Lounge, at 411 Columbus Avenue near the corner of Holyoke, always had a dicey reputation. Sam Rivers remembered it:

> Oh, the 4-11, on Columbus Avenue. The gangsters were there, and the police too. The guy was a bookmaker. There would be the police, the pimps, the prostitutes, the gangsters all sitting together, and I learned how some things are done in this world there. But the owner liked the music. Gigi Gryce and I worked there, just before Gigi left for New York.[10]

First opened as the Monterey Cafe in 1937, it became the Golden Gate Cafe in 1944, the Sunnyside Cafe in 1946, and finally the 4-11 Lounge in October of 1948. There was always music. In its early years, the 4-11 offered a steady diet of both jazz and R&B, and most of the performers were locally based. Among them were trios led by pianists Mabel Simms, Eddy Petty, and Hank Mason; Fat Man Robinson's quintet, with Sam Rivers as his tenor man; and Ray Perry and his Perry Brothers band.

There was less live music as the fifties played out. It is likely other interests held sway. It was a "piano-over-the-trapdoor" kind of place. (They really *did* have a piano over a trapdoor, hiding the room that housed the bookmaking operation.) Newspaperman Bill Buchanan recalled that "in the 1950s and early 1960s, it was a mini-combat zone type of bar," and indeed in 1957 the joint was declared off limits to military personnel. In 1960 the owner, Abe Sarkis, was shot by a person unknown. He survived. Sarkis, a bookmaker and gambler with a rap sheet going back to 1935, was arrested for running a gambling operation out of the 4-11 in 1967, which led to its closing for good in 1968. The building was later demolished to make way for the Methunion Manor Housing Cooperative.[11]

The Handy Cafe, or Handy's Grille, at 723 Tremont near Concord Street, was a longtime neighborhood place, dating back to 1935. The Handy didn't buy much advertising, opting instead for a rolling promotion—an old ambulance with a sign on the roof.

The Handy earned unwanted publicity and the ire of the neighborhood in 1949 for refusing to hire black employees despite the fact that 95 percent of the club's clientele was black. It took a picket line protesting club hiring practices to change that

Jazz was strong at the Handy in the fifties. Pianist Hopeton Johnson led the house band for three years, then pianist Charlie Cox was in for at least one. Alto man Bunny Campbell and trumpeter Tommy Ball led bands in 1956–1957. Good music, but both musicians and patrons remember the Handy as a bucket of blood. "A real dive," recalled Herb Pomeroy, who would go there to hear Tommy Ball. It joined the 4-11 on the military's off-limits list at the same time in 1957.

The Handy survived until 1964, when it changed its name to the Jolly Cafe, then changed it again to the Lucky Lounge—surely the most interesting progression of adjectives-as-tavern-names on the city scene.

After Hours at the Pioneer Social Club

For the jazz lover, there was really only one place to be in the city after hours, and that was the Pioneer Social Club. It was Boston's all-time late-night leader in one category: mystique. It had, to use a word favored by George Frazier, one of its frequent visitors, *duende*. There was nothing in the city like it.

Housed in an unassuming two-story brick building at 2 Westfield Street, the Pioneer Club came to life late, serving drinks and food, and offering outstanding music until 5:00 in the morning or later. The Pioneer Club was the late-night place where jazz musicians went after their gigs, and they were joined by entertainers, athletes, politicians, news reporters, and plenty of people from the neighborhood. All they had to do was gain admittance.

Globe reporter Bill Buchanan, with a sharp reporter's eye, described how you'd gain entry:[13]

> If you were a regular, you rang the bell and waited for the doorman to move back a sliding wooden cover to the glass peephole. It was as dark as a pocket in the doorway, but in most cases you were recognized.
>
> On those occasions when the doorman could not recognize you, he opened the door, but kept the burglar chain fastened: "Who's calling, please?"
>
> If you were known, the door was opened and you stepped into a small foyer. The front door was closed and then the second door, which had to be unlocked with a key, was opened, and there you were in the Pioneer Club.
>
> Downstairs was a moderately sized bar with 14 stools. There were 11 wall booths, each seating four persons. Around the corner was a large square table that would seat 14. In one corner near the bar was a juke box.

The Pioneer wasn't in the business of advertising its late-night operations, and mostly things ran smoothly. Like the Theatrical Club in days past, the Pioneer Club avoided trouble. No narcotics, no hustling, no hassles…just a relaxed and trouble-free place. The Pioneer usually employed a couple of linebacker-sized doormen to ensure it. The few incidents that made the papers usually involved the police trying to gain admittance during club hours; one episode had two club employees accused of assaulting two plainclothes policemen trying to enter the club in the early morning of October 26, 1948. At trial, Judge Frankland Miles found both not guilty, and "as the judge's ruling was read, persons in the courtroom gave their audible approval."[14]

The Pioneer was one of those places blessed by jazz where blacks and whites mingled freely. The club was owned and operated by blacks for a clientele that was largely black, but it was one of the most integrated night spots in the city.

Pioneer Club favorite, Mabel Robinson Simms. Courtesy of Dan Kochakian.

The Pioneer Club began as a rooming house, became a speakeasy, and after Repeal, a legitimate club. The after-hours business began in the late 1940s, when Balcom and Silas ("Shag") Taylor, the owners of the Lincoln Pharmacy on Tremont Street, acquired the club. The Taylors were Roxbury's foremost practitioners of old-fashioned ward politics, and Shag, in fact, was nicknamed the "Mayor of Roxbury." His connections to the Democratic party establishment were as strong as any black Bostonian's could be in the late 1940s and 1950s. Taylor lined up support for Democratic candidates in black neighborhoods, and received political favors in return. One was a seat on the Massachusetts Parole Board, and another was the obvious complicity of the police in allowing the Pioneer to stay open until sunrise. The Pioneer avoided the rules governing regular nightspots by operating as a private club, to which patrons paid a membership fee. The membership records would make fascinating reading, but they've never been found.

The stage—really just an upright piano and a microphone—was a on the second floor in a room that seated perhaps 50. Some of Boston's best played there from 2:00 to 5:00 in the morning. Hi Diggs (who called the Pioneer a "musician's musical heaven") was one. Mabel Robinson Simms had a long-running trio with Bill Tanner and Frances Brown in the mid 1950s. Simms was deeply involved in the club, at various times working as both hostess and house pianist. George Pearson was another who occupied the piano chair.

All the royalty of jazz came through the door to relax and sometimes sit in: Miles Davis, Ella Fitzgerald, Erroll Garner, Dizzy Gillespie, Charlie Parker, Art Tatum, Sarah Vaughan, Dinah Washington, Lester Young, all of the Mills Brothers, and most of Count Basie's band somehow fit on and around that tiny stage. Some nights are the stuff of legend, for instance when Duke Ellington and Louis Armstrong played duets until six in the morning, or when Billie Holiday sang "Detour Ahead" to a packed and silent room with tears streaming down her cheeks. There were so many musicians dropping by that trumpeter Leon Merian compared the Pioneer to Minton's in Harlem, the late-night room where bebop was nurtured in the 1940s.[16]

Shag Taylor was struck by a car and killed while walking to work at the Lincoln Pharmacy on November 6, 1958, and ownership passed to Lincoln Pope, the Pioneer's last proprietor.

Times and tastes change, and the public's tolerance—or at least officialdom's tolerance—of after-hours clubs had faded by the early 1970s. After limping along for a time as a strictly legitimate club closing at one o'clock, the Pioneer shut its doors in June 1974 and a month later the building was razed. An apartment complex now stands on the site.

The Pioneer lives now only in glowing memories. "I only went there once," said one Boston jazz fan, "and I felt I had finally reached this ultimate place in Boston, the one place where everybody's hip."[17]

Connolly's Stardust Room

The well-known Connolly's Stardust Room wasn't actually on the Jazz Corner at all. The Stardust Room was at 1184 Tremont Street at Whittier Street, which was a bit of a hike from Mass Ave. It was in a five-story building so run-down that in 1959 Boston's Department of Building Inspection insisted that owner Jim Connolly remove the upper four stories, or shut down.[18]

Connolly's opened in summer 1957 and was in business for four decades. In the early years, the musicians most closely identified with Connolly's shared a Savoy connection with Jim Connolly himself. Hillary Rose arrived in July 1959 with his organ trio that included tenor saxophonist Dan Turner and drummer Baggy Grant. In December Jimmy Tyler replaced Turner, his old Sabby Lewis bandmate, and the Rose-Tyler-Grant trio remained at Connolly's until May 1962.

Tyler brought two things to Connolly's: his high energy and fiery play, and his extensive list of jazz world contacts, whom he invited to play with the trio for a week or two. The performers coming through Connolly's were well-known and represented a sound already being called "mainstream," and included players identified with both swing and bop. Among them were Buck Clayton, Vic Dickenson, Sweets Edison, Roy Eldridge, Paul Gonsalves, Coleman Hawkins, Johnny Hodges, Howard McGhee, James Moody, Charlie Shavers, and Sonny Stitt. His guests were all musicians he had known since the 1940s and whose musical experiences mirrored his own. For whatever reason, Tyler did not invite the younger hard bop players.

One of Tyler's great influences was Illinois Jacquet, the composer of Jimmy's signature song, "Bottoms Up," and the two must have staged quite a show when Jacquet played at Connolly's. Tyler played "Bottoms Up" every night, moving off the bandstand and blowing in every corner in the club. This included a stop at the women's bathroom, where he would pound on the door and enter, blowing, and emerge a few minutes later, still blowing, to much applause. His bar-walking ways, however, tagged him as just another honker out on the jump blues edge of jazz. Whether this reputation prevented Tyler's broader recognition is a debatable point, but it is not one that bothered the patrons at Connolly's.

John McLellan was a Connolly's regular during Tyler's tenure, and he saw both pluses and minuses. He didn't like Tyler's frantic style even if it was crowd-pleasing, but he noted that Tyler picked the musicians, and they were always first rate, so "it's worth putting up with some of the honking in order to get some of the swinging."[19] McLellan enjoyed both the small-group swing and the club's vibe, also due in no small part to Tyler: "The atmosphere there is one of conviviality and ready communication between jazzman and audience. This is a factor I haven't often seen discussed though its importance can't be underestimated."[20]

Come summer, Tyler and guests would decamp to the Rocky Manor, a night spot in coastal Wareham, and after Labor Day he'd return to Connolly's. But he didn't return in September 1962, and it isn't known whether that was Connolly's decision or Tyler's. The club diversified its schedule, continuing to pair Tyler's friends with local trios, but also inviting the younger musicians outside Tyler's sphere, such as Eric Dolphy, Herbie Hancock, and Jackie McLean. For his part, Tyler worked around Boston into 1963. In 1964 he signed on with Lloyd Price's road band, and when that ended he moved to Brooklyn, bringing to a close his 16 years as a part of the Boston scene.

Professional & Business Mens Club

The Professional & Business Mens Club, housed in a fine Chester Square brownstone at 543 Mass Ave, started out as a private club in 1947, and somewhere along the way it added music, and the room with the piano became known as the Flame Room. It was mostly a room where local musicians worked. Perhaps the most significant talent launched from there was pianist Dave Burrell, then a Berklee student, who had a band in the early 1960s.[21]

Longtime promoter John McIlvaine was managing the club by 1958. His career in promotion and management started in 1943, as president of the Younger Citizens' Co-ordinating Committee, a group organized to raise money for war relief. This they did by sponsoring concerts with stars such as Ella Fitzgerald and Lionel Hampton. He ran a short-lived club, the Green Door, at 425 Mass Ave before Eddie Levine got there. In the early 1950s he managed shows at Sugar Hill, a club in Bay Village, and it was there that he first hired Mae Arnette in 1952.

Mae Arnette and Al Vega, regulars at the
Professional & Business Mens Club. Courtesy of
Mae Arnette.

The show's headliner, Ida James, became ill and McIlvaine needed a replacement in a hurry. He called Arnette, his niece, in New York. Performing was in Arnette's blood; her father was a drummer and her mother had danced at the Cotton Club, and she had originally studied to sing opera. Arnette had recently won a Harlem Amateur Hour contest at the Apollo Theatre and was singing at Murrain's nightclub in Harlem. McIlvaine called and she came to Boston. "That was the first time I sang with Sabby's band, in that show," said Arnette. "I liked Boston…if you come from New York, this was like a miniature town, with its winding, narrow streets. I just fell in love with it and decided to move here."

When the Sugar Hill show ended, Arnette gravitated to Massachusetts Avenue and spent much of 1953 at Eddie Levine's, and then on to Wally's Paradise and the Professional & Business Men's Club. She recorded with trumpeter Buck Clayton and others in the 1950s but those sides were never released. Later in the decade she recorded one single for Big Top, and some pop tunes for the Aurora label, on which she sang English words to classical Russian melodies, all in preparation for a State Department trip to the Soviet Union. "But then Khrushchev pounded his shoe on the table at the United Nations in 1960, and that put an end to any plans for a trip."[22] Arnette's first influence was Sarah Vaughan, but over time she found her contralto was particularly suited for ballads, and it was as a ballad singer that Arnette earned the title of "Boston's first lady of song."

In the late 1950s the Professional & Business Mens Club was Mae Arnette's home base. During 1958–1959, Arnette sang as many as six nights a week with whatever trio was in the house. Often it was Al Vega's trio, and it was a place he remembered:

> That was another crazy club, with a piano on the second floor, and I had the trio that recorded the *All By Al* record, with Alex Cirin and Alan Dawson. I'd go upstairs and practice, and Alan would go in the kitchen and practice, and Alex would take his bass into some other room, and we'd practice like that for an hour and then the people would start coming in and it's: "Let's go, Sarah Vaughan just came in." And we'd play. A hell of a time.[23]

Mr. Vega had that right. It was a hell of a time, all around the Jazz Corner.

Chapter 10

Paradise

The year 1947 brought a new owner to the property at 428 Massachusetts Avenue. Joseph L. Walcott opened Wally's Paradise there on January 1, 1947, launching a Boston jazz institution that is still in operation and still a family-owned business, more than 60 years later. Sixty years is no small accomplishment for any small business, let alone one in the nightclub business. In 1947, Wally's first year, James Michael Curley was mayor, the John Hancock Building—the one topped by the weather beacon—opened its doors, and the Boston Braves drew a million fans to their Commonwealth Avenue ballpark for the first time. Curley went to prison, Hancock built a bigger tower, and the Braves moved to Milwaukee, but Wally's survived changes in popular taste, neighborhood decline, "urban removal," and racial unrest, and it still presents the music and still provides a place for local musicians to play. Of all the rooms mentioned in this book, it alone survived.

Joseph "Wally" Walcott, 1947. Courtesy of Elynor Walcott.

The Barbados-born Walcott arrived in Boston in about 1908 and worked at various jobs, but the one that was critical to his future was as operator of a taxi service. Prominent politicos were among his fares, and one was Curley, who was mayor of Boston (and under federal indictment for mail fraud) in 1946 when Walcott applied for his liquor license. Curley helped Walcott; the calculating Curley undoubtedly thought it could help him pick up votes in the black community. Without a good word from the mayor, it is doubtful that Walcott could have obtained the liquor license held by the Little Dixie's owners—in 1946, a black businessman simply did not have the clout or the capital to obtain the necessary permits and licenses to operate a nightclub. Walcott was the first, and he remained a part of the club until his death in 1998 at age 101.

Walcott had two reasons for opening a nightclub. First was to provide a place where black patrons were welcome. Other area clubs, like the Hi-Hat, admitted whites only, and the stories that make us shudder now, of "passing," and the "brown paper bag test," were everyday facts of African-American life in 1946. So Wally's was a place where the black community could relax and socialize. Second was a more typical reason for a man raising a family: economic security. "I wanted something to eat," he told an interviewer the year before his death. "I wanted to earn something independent of my friends or my family. I wanted something I could say was mine."[1]

A Jazz Corner Musical History

In the early years, Walcott built his business with good local jazz and relentless promotion. Sabby Lewis, the top name on the local scene, was already playing the club in 1947, at the peak of his band's postwar popularity. Saxophonist Jimmy Tyler, restive, broke away from the Lewis band in 1948 and brought a new band into Wally's that September, one featuring trumpeter Lennie Johnson, pianist Curtis Brown, and bassist Martin "Gator" Rivers, with the steady Bey Perry keeping time. They worked at Wally's until the summer of 1949. Lewis was back for the entire year of 1950, and trombonist J. C. Higginbotham led a house band for much of 1951, for a time featuring Frankie Newton. Wally's Paradise, during its first five years, was home to some of the best jazz in Boston. The peripatetic Tyler, who was always setting up a session somewhere throughout his career, for a time organized Sunday jam sessions at Wally's. A photo of one appeared in *Down Beat* in 1948, showing a stage full of musicians from the Tyler and Nat Pierce bands.[2] Every modernist in town was making the scene at Wally's in the late 1940s.

Bop was one development coming into its own when Wally's opened. Another was the jump blues, and Boston favorites Fat Man Robinson and Pete Brown brought this music to Wally's in the early 1950s. In fact, Wally's featured music from every corner of the jazz world except Dixieland in its opening years.

These were the best of the Jazz Corner years, when jam sessions were common and sitting in an accepted practice. Coleman Hawkins, Oscar Peterson, and Sarah Vaughan were among those who dropped by. One night in 1950, Lena Horne's trio, an all-star group of pianist Gerry Wiggins, bassist Joe Benjamin, and drummer Chico Hamilton, took over the bandstand after they finished their show at the Copley Plaza's Oval Room. It was a time when you might find a Roy Haynes or a Paul Gonsalves working for the night in a pickup band.

The early years were straight-ahead jazz, but starting in about 1952 Walcott scouted the "chitlin circuit" for entertainers, bringing to Boston Al Bryant's Harlem Swingsters, the dance troop of Lorraine Knight, Austin Powell's The Cats & The Fiddle, the comics Apus and Estrellita, and revues with names like *Mambo Rhapsody* and the *Harlem Gone Paris Revue.* "Yes!" read a Wally's advertisement in 1953. "The Show's That Good!" Even though such shows tailed off at Wally's by the mid-fifties, they played at other Boston clubs for another ten years.

Walcott worked hard at promotion. He went to the local college campuses and distributed handbills, advertised in the *Record*, and for parts of six years, sponsored his own program on the radio. Eddy Petty was broadcasting from Wally's as early as 1948 over WVOM, and he was followed by Art Tacker on WTAO and Speed Anderson on WVDA.

Caught in the act: Jam session at Wally's Paradise. From left: Curtis Brown, Gigi Gryce, Gator Rivers, Jimmy Tyler, Bey Perry, Gait Preddy, Frank Winters, Lennie Johnson, Charlie Mariano. Courtesy of the *DownBeat* archives.

Wally's Paradise, though not a hole-in-the-wall operation (when it first opened, the club had three bars, a full kitchen, and a dance floor), could not compete with Storyville and the Hi-Hat in the 1950s for the big-name, national talent. There were a few, such as Higginbotham, Pete Brown, and Milt Buckner, with reputations that went far beyond Boston, but they were the exceptions. Wally's started as, and remained, a room for local players.

Through the 1950s, a reliable core of Boston musicians provided Wally's music, including Fat Man Robinson, Bunny Campbell, Art Foxall, Herbie and Roland Lee, Joe Perry, Stanley Trotman, and Mabel Robinson. Jaki Byard led small groups there on and off through the decade, with his noteworthy Wally's effort being a short-lived Tuesday night big band in late 1958. Saxophonist Dan Turner, nicknamed "Hurricane," and a veteran of both the Lewis and Tyler bands, had the house band at Wally's in 1955, and stayed on to work with Eddie Logan, who took over the house band in late 1956:

I played at Wally's with Baggy Grant and Red Garland for about six months. I was playing bass. Red lived in Boston for about eight months back then. After Red left, I had a trio with guitar and drums, and I expanded that with Dan Turner on tenor. Then Alan Dawson came in on drums. No piano."[3]

Dawson himself led the house band at the club after Logan.

Walcott liked jazz, and it never occurred to him to replace it with the more popular sounds of R&B and soul music even when the popularity of those forms eclipsed jazz in the eyes of the public

There were times when he had to be a businessman first and a jazz fan second. Eddie Logan remembered one such instance in 1948:

He was tough, he was smart, and he was always looking out for the business. I remember that he was quite proud of the fact that he had Claude Hopkins coming in, and he'd be talking about that, how the great Claude Hopkins was coming to Wally's. I remembered Claude Hopkins from when I was a kid. So he's there, but it wasn't going well and people were just walking out. And Wally said to Claude, "you're ruining my business. You gotta get out of here." He was doing what he had to do for the business. Even though he put that effort into booking Claude Hopkins, he could see it wasn't working.[4]

Firing Hopkins was probably a difficult thing for Walcott to do, because Walcott, who was 50 years old when he opened his club, personally liked the style of swing rooted in earlier decades that Hopkins and other bandleaders in the early years (Sabby Lewis, J. C. Higginbotham) played. But he had to do what was right for the business.

Trumpeter Hy Lockhart remembered another aspect of working for Wally—being treated fairly. Sabby Lewis needed a place to break in a new band after his long-standing unit broke up in December 1949. Lockhart recalled how Walcott welcomed his friend Lewis:

This was the new band, with Alan Dawson and Lennie Johnson and Danny Potter and the rest, and we went into Wally's right after the first of the year and we played there for the whole year. And Wally treated us well. He always paid us on time, and he paid union scale. Not every club owner worked that way.[5]

One well-known presence at Wally's in the 1950s was drummer Alan Dawson. Dawson was born in 1929 in Pennsylvania but his family moved to Boston when he was a boy, and while in high school he was already gigging with the bands of Tasker Crosson, Hopeton Johnson, and Wilbur Pinckney. His first inspirations were Bobby Donaldson and Roy Haynes. After his high school graduation in 1947, he started five years of instruction with the well-known teacher Charles Alden. He began playing marimba and vibes in the late 1940s.

Dawson was a key player in the emerging modern jazz scene. He played in groups with Sam and Martin Rivers, Gig Gryce, Jaki Byard, and other leading lights of the time. In December 1949 he was with Frankie Newton at the Show Boat opposite Sabby Lewis, and when the Lewis band broke up that month, Lewis asked Dawson to join his new group. Dawson stayed with Lewis for a year until he was drafted. Out of the army in 1953, he toured Europe with Lionel Hampton, then returned to Boston and the Lewis band. He stayed until 1956. That's when he joined Eddie Logan's band at Wally's. In 1957 he led his own quartet at Wally's with tenor saxophonist Roland Alexander, then joined Al Vega's trio and recorded the *All by Al* album with Alex Cirin in 1958.

In 1957 Dawson joined the faculty at the Berklee School of Music. Then came trio work with Toshiko Akiyoshi, John and Paul Neves, and Rollins Griffith, and a stint with Herb Pomeroy's big band in 1961–1962. In the mid 1960s he was the house drummer at Lennie's-on-the-Turnpike, where he renewed musical associations with Jaki Byard and Booker Ervin, who had lived in Boston in 1950. In 1965 the *Down Beat* International Critics Poll named him a talent deserving of wider recognition, which he duly received as a seven-year member of the Dave Brubeck Quartet, starting in 1968. In 1975 he left both Brubeck and Berklee, and got off the road for good. Dawson remained a first-call drummer and sought-after teacher until his death from leukemia in 1996.

The 1960s brought changes to Wally's. For one thing, in 1960, the club changed its name from "Wally's Paradise" to "Wally's Cafe." The music changed, too. The early sixties were the time of organ duos and trios, and Boston had its share of notable combos: Hillary Rose, Jimmy Tyler, and Baggy Grant at Connolly's; Joe Bucci and Joe Riddick at Lennie's-on-the-Turnpike; and a few at Wally's as well, here remembered by Elynor Walcott, Wally's daughter and later club manager:

> The club had a Hammond organ, a 1937 Model A, and Wally was proud of it, he had a guy who came up from the South Shore to service it, keep it in tune. We've still got it in storage, and I hope to restore it to use some day. I remember very well two of the men who played it. Hopeton Johnson, he played at Wally's for a long time with his trio, four or five years. Hopeton, he always played with his eyes closed, looked like he was sleeping, off somewhere in another world. He'd rock back and forth, always with his eyes closed. Bunny Smith was his drummer, he'd come up from Connecticut to work here with Hopeton, and Jay Talbert played tenor.
>
> The other was Fingers Pearson, George Pearson, who was a perfect gentleman, very pleasant, very dignified, never raised his voice. Then he'd raise the

roof when he played. He'd just sort of lean back and let go. He had a day job, driving for a funeral home. I couldn't believe it when I heard that![6]

It was true; Fingers Pearson and his drummer Sammy Ellcock sometimes closed Wally's in the early morning and perhaps jammed a bit after that, and a few hours later, Pearson would arrive at the morgue in his hearse. When he could, Pearson practiced on the organ in the funeral home's chapel. Pearson had attended Schillinger House on the GI Bill and was an accomplished keyboard man, having taken over the piano chair from Mabel Robinson Simms at the Pioneer. He wasn't nicknamed "Fingers" because of his piano playing, however. It was because of his skill with a pool queue. Pearson, and then Johnson, kept Wally's in the groove when the clubs were filled with that big Hammond sound.

Sabby Lewis and an unidentified man outside Wally's Paradise, ca. 1948.
Courtesy of Elynor Walcott.

Perseverance

While the music inside Wally's put some swing into the early sixties, the scene outside was becoming more difficult. Although Mayor John Collins was busy building the "New Boston," people in Wally's neighborhood did not see much of it. What they saw were the ugly realities of racial inequality and a declining quality of life—in housing, in the schools, in public safety. Mass Ave and Columbus wasn't the Jazz Corner anymore. There was no Hi-Hat, no

Eddie Levine's, no Savoy. There was just Wally's, and Walcott kept his business going in spite of it. Said Elynor Walcott:

> What kept the club in business all those years? My father's tenacity. This club was his life, and he worked hard to keep it going. Even when the neighborhood went bad, with the robberies and the prostitution, he would be down here every day. He'd put on a suit and a white shirt and a tie and he'd go to work. He'd be down here first thing in the morning, with his pants legs rolled up, mopping the floor, cleaning the bathrooms. Then he'd roll 'em down again and open up.
>
> There was a bar up the street and my father used to say they ruined Massachusetts Avenue, with the prostitutes hanging around there. They'd be turning tricks in the hallways...my father eventually bought our building, and had to stand outside to protect the place, keep them out of the halls. And the drugs...people used to tape drugs to the inside of the toilet tank, and he'd find them and flush them down...He ran the place with a strong hand. He wasn't big, but he could grab a man by his collar and throw him out if he had to. If he told you to leave his club, well, you had to leave.
>
> That's how he stayed in business, it was his perseverance.[7]

The perseverance paid off, despite the hard times and the shutdown of the club's original location at 428 Mass Ave when the Boston Redevelopment Authority took the building in 1978. The club reopened in 1979 at its current location across the street, and has remained open since. Walcott himself accumulated numerous honors and accolades, among them from the City of Boston, the Commonwealth of Massachusetts, and the Berklee College of Music.

In 1997 the City of Boston's Business Heritage Project called the club "historic" because it had stayed in business for over 25 years, quite a feat for any small business.[8] Is that what makes Wally's historic? Walcott himself would probably have called that part of it "making a living." The historic part? That would be Wally Walcott himself, and his dedication to jazz and his willingness to do just about anything to keep the music going. And it would be the spirit of the countless musicians who came to blow at the jam sessions over the club's 65—65!—years of Sundays. In spite of a shrinking jazz audience, neighborhood turmoil, racial unrest, the Boston Redevelopment Agency, and the uncertain economics of the nightclub business, Wally's just kept making the scene. *That's* the historic part.

Chapter 11

Sabby Lewis, Jimmy Tyler, and the Last Days of Swing

In 1950, the midpoint of our 25-year survey, signs of change were everywhere. James Michael Curley finished the final days of his final term as Boston's mayor in January, having lost the election to the city clerk he openly derided, John Hynes. Hynes was in office for only four months when he rolled out the Boston Mid-Century Jubilee, a week-long affair designed to talk up Boston's then-feeble economic prospects, with a big party for the citizenry thrown in. One small piece of that was Boston's first outdoor jazz festival.

The Boston jazz world witnessed other events of note in 1950 as well. George Wein opened Storyville in November. John McLellan broadcast his first *Top Shelf* radio program on WHDH. Steve Connolly left the Savoy to start a new club, Jazz at 76, in the Theatre District. The Nat Pierce Orchestra recorded its most ambitious work, the Ralph Burns composition "Red Hills and Green Barns."

Perhaps all of these can be called "progress" more than "change." But one event did produce a major shift and clearly indicated times were changing. The Sabby Lewis band, the best and most consistent jazz band in 1940s Boston, broke up in the final days of 1949. On New Year's Eve 1950, Sabby Lewis, star of the Fitch Bandwagon program and leader of the house band at the Savoy for half a decade, did not have a gig. His former band did, though, at the Hi-Hat, under the leadership of the tenor player, Jimmy Tyler. Now *that* was a change.

Let's back up a few years. In 1945 Charlie Mariano, recently discharged from the U.S. Army, enrolled at Schillinger House, the new school started by Lawrence Berk. The following year, Jaki Byard, from Worcester and also recently discharged from service, arrived in Boston. Keep your eyes on these two, because they were the most influential musicians in postwar jazz in Boston. In later years, both became stars in the little world that is jazz.

What started with Byard, Mariano, and a handful of their colleagues was a whole new scene. The swing era ended with the collapse of the big bands and the changing economics of the postwar years. Tastes changed as well, and the brassy big bands gave way to a popular music dominated by crooners and "song stylists." In 1946, the Dixieland revival in Boston was just beginning in earnest following the engagement of Sidney Bechet and Bunk Johnson at the Savoy. The swing players—Sabby Lewis and Preston Sandiford among them—were still prominent and dominant. Bebop, the music made after midnight at Minton's in Harlem, was virtually unknown in Boston, but it was not unknown to Byard and Mariano. If you asked the swing or Dixieland players about bop, they dismissed it and kept doing what they were doing. And they were successful with it. No one was more successful in the postwar years than Sabby Lewis, who worked constantly and led recording sessions for Continental, Crystal-Tone, and Mercury.

Byard and Mariano and their friends changed that. It did not happen overnight, but it did happen, and they remade the face of jazz in Boston, just as others did in Detroit, Los Angeles, and Philadelphia. Byard, Mariano, and friends represented the changing of the guard. Boston jazz would have new stars for the new decade.

Although the focus here is on modern jazz and the musicians who played it, there was plenty of swing and Dixieland and jump music being played as well. These, however, did not shape the Boston jazz of the future.

We pick the story up in 1947, a year when, as we've noted elsewhere, Boston jazz was catching its breath. The ballrooms and the big bands were played out, and it was the small, affordable groups that were getting the work. The GI Bill students were arriving, and we'll meet many of them in the following pages. In Boston, Sabby Lewis was still on top.

Showdown at the Show Boat

Sabby Lewis was riding high in the late forties. An engagement at the Club Tondalayo in New York capped a busy summer of 1947, and when he arrived back in Boston that fall, Lewis branched out. Following a path not uncommon among entertainers, he opened the Sabby Lewis Restaurant in November, right in the thick of it, at 422 Massachusetts Ave, just off Columbus Ave.[1]

The Lewis band had survived the war years with its nucleus intact. Joe Booker, Maceo Bryant, Gene Caines, and Al Morgan had been with Lewis since before the war, and the saxophone section of Bill Dorsey, Dan Turner, and Jimmy Tyler had been together for about a year. There were recordings in 1947 on Crystal-Tone of the Hi Diggs arrangement of "Minor Mania" that became the band's theme song; the Al Morgan blues, "King for a Day;" a jaunty "I Can't Give You Anything but Love;" and a standout version of "Bottoms Up," with its blazing Jimmy Tyler tenor solo.

Nineteen forty-eight started with more trips to New York for appearances at the Club Ebony on 52nd Street and the Club Baron on Lenox Ave. There was a week at the Apollo in March, then back to Boston for three months at the Down Beat Club on Tremont Street. The summer brought engagements at three well-known theaters on the black circuit, the Regal in Chicago, the Royal in Baltimore, and the Howard in Washington. In September there was another week at the Apollo and another engagement at the Club Ebony. Then followed an extended engagement at Boston's Hi-Hat, from November 1948 into April 1949. Lewis and his band stayed very busy in the late 1940s.

In March 1949 the Lewis band was in the recording studio again, this time for Mercury Records. The *Record's* George Clarke was there that night:

> There was drama of a sort at the Boylston St. studios of the Ace Recording Co. the other early morning when, at 2 a.m., Sabby Lewis and his band from the Hi-Hat showed up to make their first recordings for Mercury Records. It was almost 3 a.m. before the band got set up and streaks of dawn were high-lighting the Common across the street before the session was finished.

> They cut four sides, one whole record of two parts being devoted to his sensational "The King," with Dan Turner's saxophone, while another record has Al Morgan singing "Ugly Woman Blues," a little piece stirred up by Sabby and Sherm Feller. The other side of that one has on it—ahem!—a piece called "Clarke's Idea."[2]

Following their Hi-Hat engagement, the band was again off to New York in April, for six weeks at the Royal Roost. The job had hardly started when the Roost closed its doors, throwing the band out of work and chasing it back to Boston and the Hi-Hat. Except for a few weeks at the Club Harlem in Atlantic City that summer, that's where they stayed until November.

Tyler left the band after Atlantic City to tour and record with the Count Basie band, returning in October. (Paul Gonsalves, himself an ex-Basie man, filled in.) Sabby strengthened his band further by adding trumpeter Cat Anderson. Having spent the past decade in the employ of Erskine Hawkins, Lionel Hampton, and Duke Ellington, the highly regarded Anderson was a major addition to the Lewis crew, and perhaps the ingredient they needed to attain sustained national recognition once and for all. There was no doubt it was a powerful lineup. In early December 1949, Sabby Lewis brought this band into the Show Boat.

Located on Huntington Avenue across from Symphony Hall, the Show Boat had a half-dozen names and just as many entertainment policies over the years, but nothing since the old Arcadia Ballroom had lasted very long. The best jazz club of the lot, the Zanzibar, lasted a month. But the Show Boat was trying jazz again in late 1949, first with Frankie Newton's small group, and then with the Sabby Lewis Orchestra joining the show. Clarke was ecstatic:

> Sabby Lewis is really rollin' at the Show Boat! And with Jimmy Tyler back in the fold, plus a new and fabulous trumpeter—he plays a triple optissimal high C, whatever that is—the band is hotter than ever.
>
> The new trumpeter is "Cat" Anderson, called so because of his eyes. His pyrotechnics lifted the brows of no less a person than Arthur Fiedler himself, famed conductor of the Boston "Pops" Orchestra, at ringside opening night. So Sabby tells you in all seriousness that the note is so high there's no way of writing it down on the music![3]

Clarke, ever the enthusiast, muffed a few details. A trumpet player will tell you a triple high C is a high note indeed, but would be mightily puzzled by the "optissimal" part of it. And the Cat got his nickname because of the way he fought on the playground as a boy, not because of his eyes. Even without Clarke's help, though, Cat attracted attention. A few days later, Eddy Petty wrote in the *Chronicle* that with Anderson in the fold, "when Sabby gives the green light, the gang will blow you into bad health."[4]

Clarke was back again on the 13th, writing about something that sounded more like a building collapsing than a band on a stage:

> First the chandeliers began to tremble a little bit. Next a kind of vibration seemed to seize the table, and presently, it jumped a little. Then the wall swayed, and at last—or so it seemed—the roof went soaring off up Huntington Ave., while the whole building rocked.
>
> Then it stopped quicker than it began, and Sabby Lewis was at the table, smiling apologetically towards Max Liebman, the theatrical producer, and saying softly, "I thought I'd hit you with the first one because I didn't know how long you'd stay."
>
> And it was so that Max was introduced to the Show Boat and to the kind of music, loud, raucous, but tremendously exciting, that Sabby and his men give out with. The opening number was "Bottoms Up," and if nine men ever sound louder it can only be on Judgment Day![5]

Finally Sabby had the band that should have achieved the recognition and success he sought all through the decade. The pieces were in place—a crack band with top soloists, good press both black and white, and records in the shops. But despite the press buildup, the audiences were small, and on the Sunday before Christmas, Lewis's band closed the night's show and left the bandstand for the last time. Every man resigned, and that was the end of the Sabby Lewis Orchestra, just like that. They formed a new band, elected Jimmy Tyler the leader and Gene Caines the business manager, and hired first Jimmie Martin and then Jaki Byard to fill the piano chair. Sabby was on his own.

Lewis was understandably bitter about the turn of events, because he had worked hard to keep the band together over the years, through the recording bans and wartime restrictions and the decline of social dancing and the rest of it. *Down Beat* attributed the split to the band's unhappiness with the Show Boat gig, but that was only part of the story. Trumpeter Hy Lockhart, then with Jimmie Martin, and friends with some of the musicians involved, said that in the end it came down to money.

> Sabby's band broke up because he couldn't pay them. He had been in partnership in a nightclub, the Show Boat, across Huntington Avenue from Symphony Hall, and for weeks he couldn't pay the band. So they got together and they chose Jimmy Tyler as their spokesman, and he told Sabby that "if we don't get paid at the end of this week, that's it —we won't play anymore." And Sabby couldn't pay them, so they quit. Tyler had probably talked to Julie Rhodes at the Hi-Hat already, because right after the first of the year the band, the Jimmy Tyler Orchestra, went in there.[6]

The Jimmy Tyler Orchestra, 1950. From left: Al Morgan, Jaki Byard, Joe Booker, Maceo Bryant, Dan Turner, Gene Caines, Bill Dorsey, Cat Anderson, Jimmy Tyler. Courtesy of Doris Clark.

Other factors were surely at work as well. Change was in the air, but Lewis was in a swing groove and unwilling to leave it. By his own admission, Lewis resisted the pull of bebop, and if his band reflected any of the schools of music pushing swing aside, it was the jump blues, with Tyler and Dan Turner honking like Jacquet. *The Billboard*, reviewing the Lewis band in Atlantic

City in August 1949, called it a "rock-rhythm band," one that "displays an enthusiasm matched by their musicianship in a manner that dispels the threat of be-bop smothering all musical initiative." Star soloist Tyler "plays a mess of sax...with thought-out improvisations rather than the be-bop rantings."[7]

Perhaps the band was tired of "staying the course" and wanted to give someone else a try at leadership. Lewis had been a bandleader almost from the beginning of his career, and Tyler, a sideman through all of his, might have been hungrier. Maybe the band thought the energetic Tyler would be a better promoter than the laid-back Lewis.

It could have been all of these things, or none. We can only speculate. But the fact remained that as the decade drew to a close, Sabby Lewis, the most important character in the world of Boston jazz in the forties, was without a band. There was a collective desire for change on the part of the musicians, and a recognition that the agent of that change was Jimmy Tyler.

Sabby's response was to organize a new band, a mix of younger and older musicians, and more modern in outlook than the band just left behind. Lennie Johnson and Hy Lockhart, from Jimmie Martin's band, came aboard to play trumpet. Veteran musicians Danny Potter and George Perry were on tenor and baritone, and one of the band's arrangers, Elwyn Fraser, who filled in for Dorsey in the 1948 band, was back to play alto. Joining Lewis in the rhythm section were bassist Champ Jones and drummer Alan Dawson. (Joe Gordon replaced Johnson after about a year, and possibly played trumpet on the group's lone recording on the Trison label). The new band opened at Wally's Paradise the first week of January 1950, and stayed for the entire year. That same month, the Jimmy Tyler Orchestra was down the block at the Hi-Hat. It was a real battle of the bands—just that both of them happened to be Sabby's

Sabby Lewis never again reached his 1940s heights. He continued to work in a succession of small groups through the 1950s, but each seemed to be a little less successful than the one before it. Sabby tried radio in 1952, joining WBMS as a disc jockey and remaining for five years. He led the house band at Sugar Hill, then at Showtime and the Jazz Box in the mid 1950s, where they advertised "rock and roll with Sabby Lewis," and the records he made for ABC-Paramount at that time confirm that's what he was playing. That band broke up in 1957. Lewis led another quartet at the Trinidad Lounge in the late 1950s, this one with another forties stalwart, trumpeter Phil Edmunds.

In the early 1960s, Lewis was regularly working as a single, playing intermission piano in the downtown lounges. Driving home from a job in Rhode Island in October 1962, his car was struck from behind, and Lewis was badly hurt in the ensuing crash and rollover. Some of his fingers were broken, and there was a real danger the accident might mark the end of his professional career. Happily this was not the case, but Lewis was off the scene for much of the 1960s. In 1964, Lewis became a housing investigator for the Massachusetts Commission Against Discrimination. He began playing again in the early 1970s and continued to do so almost until the time of his death in 1994.

Jimmy Tyler and the Swing-to-Modern Transition

Jimmy Tyler was born (1918) and raised in Kittrell, North Carolina, where even as a boy he was playing a saxophone on the street corner. He grew up on the go, moving from the home of one relative to another, which eventually took him to an aunt in New York while still a teenager. There he found work with Edgar Hayes, Chris Columbis, and the Savoy Sultans before entering the U.S. Army. While stationed at Fort Devens in Massachusetts, he played in bands with Bostonians Joe Nevils and Ernie Trotman, and when his service ended, he moved to Boston. He played in the Lewis band from 1946 to 1948, recording his signature piece, "Bottoms Up," with Lewis in 1947.

Jimmy Tyler in 1952.

Tyler played a pivotal transitional role on the Boston scene. When he struck out on his own in 1948, Tyler played in the jump style typified by "Bottoms Up," playing inspired by the song's writer, tenor saxophonist Illinois Jacquet. As with Jacquet, there was some bop in Tyler's playing as well. But like Jacquet, he never wandered far away from his swing roots. He wasn't a bopper, although it flavored his playing, and he certainly hired his share of bop players. In 1948, Tyler formed a quartet with pianist Curtis Brown and bassist Martin "Gator"

Rivers, both then students at the New England Conservatory. Bey Perry settled in as the drummer. The band worked at Eddie Levine's that spring, then with trumpeter Lennie Johnson added, opened at Wally's Paradise starting in September. They worked steadily at Wally's until April 1949, helped no doubt by their radio exposure on Eddy Petty's show on WVOM. Tyler also organized the Sunday jam sessions at Wally's; a photo of one of these sessions, showing a stage full of musicians from the Tyler and Nat Pierce bands, appeared in *Down Beat* in November 1948.

Tyler rejoined Lewis for the Royal Roost and Atlantic City jobs in 1949 (Sam Rivers filled in for him at Wally's), then went with Basie, and again rejoined Lewis for that fateful December engagement at the Show Boat. At the time of the split, Tyler was two years into his exploration of new sounds, and at least a few others in the Lewis orbit were exploring with him.[8]

Tyler's restless movements in 1948–1949 offer clues as to why he was chosen to lead the breakaway Lewis contingent. First, he found work for his small group and was probably confident he could find work for the larger group in Boston and elsewhere. Then there was the matter of the music. Like many players of his generation, Sabby, by his own admission, was resisting the pull of bebop. Tyler, although only four years younger than his boss, worked to incorporate it. As the new decade dawned, the hope was that Tyler would bring the band more work and an updated book.

The Jimmy Tyler Orchestra stayed at the Hi-Hat through the spring, then hit the road. Tyler did indeed find work, from New York all the way to Miami. When they returned to Boston in April 1952 for an engagement at the new Sugar Hill nightclub, it was as the road band for Larry Steele's *Smart Affairs*, a popular touring show on the black circuit. By then Joe Booker, Maceo Bryant, and Jaki Byard were off the band. Gene Caines was still writing and arranging for Tyler but no longer performing or touring. Cat Anderson had rejoined the Duke Ellington Orchestra. But the saxophone section was still intact, Al Morgan was still playing bass and singing the blues, Bostonian Clarence Johnston came on as drummer, and trumpeter Little Benny Harris, well known in bebop circles, added his skills as writer and arranger. If any band could be called "rollicking," it was this one, and their small recorded legacy on the Federal label is a mix of ballads (Tyler sounding like Ike Quebec) and mid-tempo jump blues numbers. "Little Jim," written by Harris and Tyler, shows the band to best effect.

Tyler stayed with *Smart Affairs* until its touring season ended. Then he broke up the band. That September, he was back at Wally's leading a small group with Joe Gordon. That same month, Booker, Dorsey and Morgan rejoined Sabby Lewis, then leading the house band at Sugar Hill. Al Morgan stayed with Lewis until 1957, when he moved to Los Angeles, thus ending his 16-year association with Lewis and the Boston scene.

Jimmy Tyler remained a fixture in Boston jazz for the next decade, beginning with the short-lived 1953 band with Joe Gordon. He played with just about everyone at just about every place, finally finding some stability at Connolly's Star Dust Room, where he anchored the house band from 1958 to 1962. Tyler also led the house band at the Shanty Lounge in 1963. He continued to record for Federal, and these recordings demonstrate Jimmy Tyler's dilemma. Throughout his Boston career he seesawed between his role as a bar-walking honker ("Callin' All Chickens" from 1954) and artful jazz soloist ("Pink Clouds" from 1956). Some thought that the frantic showman overshadowed the skilled saxophonist, and being labeled "the wild man of the tenor saxophone"[9] inhibited rather than helped Tyler's career. But he was what he was, a showman and a fiery player.

As the Boston jazz scene tapered off, Tyler found work first in New York and Atlantic City, then in Florida and Europe. He toured with Lloyd Price's big band in 1964, recorded with Johnny "Hammond" Smith and Buck Clayton later in the 1960s, and formed a quartet with organist Wild Bill Davis in the mid 1970s, which recorded one LP, the obscure *Blue Waters of Bermuda*. In later years Tyler worked on jazz cruises with Lionel Hampton, Dizzy Gillespie and Ella Fitzgerald. Jimmy Tyler died in Florida in 1998.

It wasn't just Lewis who had to adapt as a performer and bandleader as the times changed in the 1950s and 1960s. The whole contingent of Boston-based pianists who came up playing swing music had to adapt as well. It was a role call of top-notch talent: Charlie Cox, Hi Diggs, Dean Earl, Hillary Rose, Preston Sandiford, Mabel Simms, Ernie Trotman. "Boston used to be a town that turned out jazz pianists by the dozens," Teddy Wilson told John McLellan in 1961.[10] They were caught in a bind. There were fewer places to play and fewer jobs available on the one hand, and there was a tendency for those jobs to go to more modern players on the other. So they adapted and made the best of it. Charlie Cox and Hi Diggs played R&B, Dean Earl joined the Berklee faculty, Hillary Rose formed an organ trio, Preston Sandiford concentrated on teaching and arranging, and Mabel Simms worked as a single at the Hotel Vendome for ten years. Ernie Trotman moved to New York in 1960 and was out of music. It was the same story in other cities. But all this is getting ahead of our Boston story.

Chapter 12

Big Bands, New Sounds: Nat Pierce and Jimmie Martin

With big bands collapsing from coast to coast, small combos of all types on the ascent, and popular music wallowing in the syrupy concoctions sung by the crooners, the late 1940s seemed like a risky time to launch a big band. Here and there across the country, though, a few bandleaders were applying the lessons of modern jazz to the big band setting. Billy Eckstine was the first, and then followed Dizzy Gillespie, one of Eckstine's trumpet players. Gerald Wilson's band was exploring sophisticated harmonies on the West Coast. And there were composers and arrangers writing for these bands, such as Gil Evans, Gerry Mulligan, and George Russell. So even though the late forties were not kind to the big bands, there were a few modern ones at work. It should come as no surprise that there were two such bands in Boston. One was the Nat Pierce Orchestra, the white band. The other was the Boston Beboppers, the black band organized by Jimmie Martin. We'll devote this entire chapter to these thoroughly modern units.

Mert Goodspeed, a trombonist with Pierce in the late 1940s, recalled a conversation with one of his opposite numbers in the Martin band that summed up the two styles of play: "the Pierce band looks for precision, but we're looking for an animal sound."[1]

Regardless of sound, both bands were loaded with the talent abundant in Boston then. Players in both bands were young. Many were veterans. Many were studying at the Boston or New England Conservatories, or at the new Schillinger House. All of them were modernists, excited by the new bop sounds. None played Dixieland, even though the Dixielanders worked more often.

Sam Rivers was one of the Beboppers, and he remembered the scene:

> There were a number of us around, studying in the conservatories. And we were all working. There were other things going on, other people around. Charlie Mariano was at Schillinger House, and Quincy Jones, and Herb Pomeroy. We were all connected, all jamming. Other people were getting bands together, Herb was getting a band together, so it's not like we were the only ones.[2]

The Nat Pierce Orchestra

Nathaniel Pierce Blish, known to the jazz world as Nat Pierce, was born in Somerville, Massachusetts in 1925. Pierce attended the New England Conservatory briefly and started playing piano professionally at 17. In the mid-1940s, he jammed in sessions at the Ken, worked at the Silver Dollar Bar with Nick Jerret, and played in a trio at Izzy Ort's with drummer Marquis Foster. Then he played and arranged for the Boston bands of Pete Chase and Carl Nappi, and did a turn with Shorty Sherock's big band, where he first met his longtime colleagues Goodspeed and drummer Joe MacDonald.

Nat Pierce, ca. 1948. Courtesy of the Frank Driggs Collection.

In 1947 Pierce joined the Ray Borden Orchestra. Borden was a trumpeter who organized his first Boston band in 1941. That one fizzled, and Borden spent the next five years working for a string of big bands, including those of Bobby Sherwood and Jack Teagarden, but the most significant one from a musical development point of view was that of Stan Kenton, in 1942–1944. In 1946 he joined a band led by Whitney Cronin, a bassist and guitarist from Boston. Eventually Borden assumed leadership of the band, and Pierce came on as pianist and arranger. Over time they were joined by Charlie Mariano, trumpeters Gait Preddy and Nick Capezuto, and the aforementioned Goodspeed and MacDonald. The band recorded six sides for Manny Koppelman's Crystal-Tone Records in 1947, under the guidance of Reuben Moulds, who was either handling publicity for Borden or doing legwork for Koppelman, or both.

Borden's was a good band. Their Crystal-Tone sides wear well and have been reissued more than once. They were well rehearsed and well played, the soloists were first-rate (listen to Charlie Mariano on "What's New?"), and Pierce's up-tempo arrangements already showed the rhythmic drive that would mark his best work. But Borden was not cut out to be a bandleader. ("He was a screw-up" was the uncharitable opinion of one musician.) Personal differences were compounded by financial problems, and in July 1948 the band members fired Borden and selected Pierce to replace him because, as Goodspeed recalled, Nat captured the spirit of the band. But Pierce couldn't find work, and he disbanded in November. In early 1949 Pierce and five band mates hit the road as members of the new Larry Clinton Orchestra.[3]

Pierce regrouped for another try in the spring of 1949, and in April the band recorded its first sides for the new Motif label, "Autumn in New York" and "Goodbye Mr. Chops." The 1949 recording of "Autumn in New York" featured the alto saxophone of Charlie Mariano, whom Nat Hentoff called the best local man on that instrument since Johnny Hodges.[4] The flip side was "Goodbye Mr. Chops," the recording debut of vocalist Teddi King, and a record she never particularly liked. Mariano, who had joined Ray Borden's band in 1947, was the best-known and most highly regarded member of the Pierce orchestra, and a real catalyst for the growth and acceptance of modern jazz in Boston.

The recordings of 1949 are still gems. Mariano was already playing with great feeling on his Hodges-influenced "What's New" with Borden, and again on "Autumn in New York" with Pierce. "King Edward the Flatted Fifth," recorded for Motif with a Ralph Burns/Serge Chaloff septet, and "Sheba," with his own sextet, show the Parker influence. These recordings marked Mariano as a special talent. He remained with the Pierce orchestra until its demise in 1951.

Brockton-born trombonist Mert Goodspeed entered a diploma program at Bentley College following his wartime army service, "but that's when I was really getting into music—in fact I missed my graduation ceremony because I had a gig that night."[5] He worked with Johnny Bothwell and Shorty Sherock before joining the Ray Borden band, and he was one of the group who wanted Pierce to lead it. When Pierce disbanded in 1948, Goodspeed joined Pierce with Larry Clinton.

Goodspeed made the rounds in Boston, jamming at the Ken Club with Pee Wee Russell and Vic Dickenson, and playing in a group at Izzy Ort's with Charlie Hooks and Marquis Foster. He was accomplished enough to work with Sabby Lewis and Phil Edmunds. When Pierce reformed his band in 1949, Goodspeed and Sonny Truitt formed a dynamic duo in the trombone section, where Goodspeed remained until 1950.

Sumner "Sonny" Truitt arrived in Boston after his wartime navy service to study at Schillinger House, and in late 1947 he too was in the Borden band. Truitt was another multi-instrumentalists who could seemingly play anything. Primarily known as a trombonist, he also played piano, tenor sax, clarinet, and even bassoon. He composed and arranged, and despite the fact he was a stutterer, he was a fine singer as soon as he got on the bandstand.

The Nat Pierce Orchestra, Fall River Mass., 1950. Pierce, piano; Frank Gallagher, bass; Joe MacDonald, drums. Back row, trumpets, left to right: Roy Caton, Nick Capezuto, Perry Wilson, Don Stratton. Middle row, trombones: Sonny Truitt, Mert Goodspeed, Ace Lane. Front row, saxophones: George Green, Dave Figg, Dave Chapman, Charlie Mariano, Randy Henderson. Courtesy of the Frank Driggs Collection.

Although Truitt stayed with Pierce until the band broke up in 1951, its frequent downtime gave him time for other projects. In 1949 he was a regular at the Hi-Hat as a pianist and trombonist, and while Pierce was on the road with Larry Clinton in 1949, Truitt joined another Boston contingent, which included trumpeter Don Stratton, trombonist Joe Ciavardone, and pianist Roy Frazee, on the road with Tommy Reynolds, who had rehearsed his New Sound band in Boston. Said Stratton of Sonny Truitt:

> Sonny Truitt played everything well, and I never thought the trombone was his best instrument. With Reynolds he was playing a two-piano thing with Roy Frazee. I think he was getting an extra $5 a week for writing arrangements—and that was lousy money then, too. But he arranged the music we played between the juggler and the balloonist in the floor shows.[6]

Metronome reviewed all the Pierce Motif recordings, but it was an octet date released under Mariano's name that drew the highest praise. "Babylon" earned a grade of B in May 1950: "Boston baked bop, clean and clever in a Miles Davis mold, with only a tuba missing to make Miles's sound really stick. The leader's alto, Mert Goodspeed's trombone, Don Stratton's trumpet, and Nat Pierce's piano deserve recognition; the ensemble is unusually precise for their kind of skipping line."[7]

The Pierce band rehearsed before a live audience, albeit a motley one, at Philip Amaru's Mardi Gras, a bar at 863 Washington Street, in 1949–1950. Numerous young musicians would fall by for the late afternoon sessions to listen, but the regular daytime crowd was attracted by the 15-cent beers and couldn't have cared less about jazz.

Trumpeter Don Stratton remembered the scene at the Mardi Gras:

> For us, the Mardi Gras was an important place. The Pierce band rehearsed there in the afternoons for close to two years. And the owner let us play there for nothing. Well, not quite nothing, he did ask us to play for his daughter's wedding. An Italian guy. Imagine, here's this bunch of young guys with a bebop band playing for a traditional wedding in the North End!

> When we started playing in the late afternoons at the Mardi Gras, there wouldn't be many customers, a few drunks at the bar, the regulars, and we'd start to play and they would get upset with it, didn't like it. And Nat, he went out and got an arrangement of a polka, the "Beer Barrel Polka" or something, and we'd play that and they would cheer us on. So that was Nat, playing something for the regulars.

> They did have shows at the Mardi Gras, and they did have good jazz players at night there, like Bill Wellington playing saxophone and Danny Kent on piano. It was a gay bar, and the band was in there playing for the show, and the main attraction was a guy, Alan Vey, and he was up there in a wig and makeup. This was Boston and it was tame stuff compared to what I saw in New York working in gay bars a few years later.[8]

Part-time jazz bar and full-time dive, the Mardi Gras was a key location for the Pierce band and the development of modern jazz in Boston, but it's been gone for 40 years. The building was demolished around 1970 to make way for the New England Medical Center.

Spring 1950 brought the group its most consistent work. Charlie Shribman hired the Pierce band to work two nights per week for 12 weeks at the Symphony Ballroom, the spot known as the Play-Mor back in the Ballroom District days. George Shearing heard the band and liked it. He hired Teddi King to sing with his celebrated Quintet, the only singer ever to do so. Basie heard the band and liked it. He turned his piano over to Nat Pierce for last set chores on his subsequent trips to Boston, and the two began a musical relationship that lasted more than 30 years, until Basie's death. Woody Herman heard the band and liked it. After the Pierce band's 1951 breakup, he hired a half-dozen of its members, including Nat himself.

Pierce's band earned an invitation to the Local 535 Musician's Ball in May 1950, at the Red Roof in Revere, where Eddy Petty in the *Chronicle* noted they acquitted themselves well:

> Nat Pierce and his 15 piece band and girl singer opened their phase of the program with one of their own compositions, titled "Spirit of 1950" (which you will soon hear on record) and rocked the joint from top to bottom. Charlie Mariano, Mert Goodspeed and Joe MacDonald gave out with the good feature work. Ruth Mann, the vocalist with the band, gave a splendid rendition of Ellington's "I Got It Bad and That Ain't Good." This band was definitely the greatest band to hit the stage that night, and their music was what the crowd begged to hear more of.[9]

The mystery of this night is the band that failed to show. Jimmie Martin and his band were scheduled, and their vocalist for the evening, Barbara Jai, was backstage and waiting. But the Martin band didn't show, and it is possible that some of the band members did not want to share the stage with a white band at a function staged by the black local. Instead Pierce's band ruled the roost…but what a night it would have been for a battle of music!

Looking Back on the Pierce Orchestra

Working sporadically, the Pierce band grew in reputation but not in financial security. If there was one guy who had no illusions about the band, it was Pierce himself. Talking with Les Tompkins in 1966, Pierce played down his band's significance:

> Most of the guys were all single, like I say, in those days. We didn't have a dime, we couldn't care about making money—as long as we had enough to exist on. So we had a very good thing going there. We had a certain amount of professionalism. I guess when I listen back to some of those records now, they sound kinda trite—with all the so-called bebop licks that we wrote into the arrangements. Double-time trumpet figures and everything—it was kinda patterned after Woody's band at the time.
>
> We made one record date, to which a lot of the guys from Woody's band showed up—Lou Levy, Earl Swope, Zoot, Serge and so on. They all came around to help us on our way. It was nice. It was a very friendly situation up there in Boston at that time. So my direction was towards the Herman noise. It was a little cruder then, though. Some of the voicings were strange, and then we wrote too many notes. We did things that were completely uncomfortable to play. In fact, we couldn't even play 'em!
>
> I don't think this band or any other could play some of the things we played up in Boston. We just killed ourselves, trying to get these things down, you know—for no reason at all. It was just a lot of flash. But we thought we were

doing something that was good. Most young people do play many extra notes. It takes many years to learn what to leave out.[10]

One of those kill-the-band numbers was among the last pieces the Pierce band recorded, an ambitious Ralph Burns composition, "Red Hills and Green Barns." Scored for two pianos, played by Burns and Pierce, it was recorded at an overnight session in the studios of WCOP radio in December 1950. Longtime band members MacDonald, Mariano, Stratton, and Truitt were present. The band broke up before a record could be made, and it was 25 years before "Red Hills and Green Barns" was finally released.

Lack of steady work doomed the Pierce Orchestra. Nat Hentoff reported in *Down Beat* in October 1951 that Nat Pierce, "leader of the city's most musically advanced and most thoroughly unemployed band, has left town to take over the piano chair with Woody Herman." (He took Dave McKenna's place.) A weary Hentoff closed his article with, "Unless you have a boom-chick beat and a 1924 mind, this is no town for a progressive local jazzman."[11]

Pierce of course went on to a long, stellar career in jazz. He arranged and played piano for Woody Herman for five years, freelanced for five, then went back to Herman for five more. Pierce arranged the music for the landmark 1957 television program *The Sound of Jazz*, filled in for Count Basie on many occasions, recorded prolifically as leader and sideman, and finally formed another big band, Juggernaut, in 1975 with drummer Frank Capp. Although he experimented with bebop with his own Boston orchestra, over time he settled into a swing-oriented groove—but it was swing chipped off the same block as Basie's and Herman's. Nat Pierce died in Los Angeles in June 1992.

The Pierce band scattered to the wind, some going on to long careers in music and others leaving the field completely. Of the former, saxophonist and arranger Dave Figg must have set a road warrior record, as between 1950 and 1964 he was with the big bands of Louis Prima, Tony Pastor, Ray McKinley, Claude Thornhill, Hal McIntyre, Thornhill again, Billy May, Sam Donahue, Jimmy Dorsey, Buddy Morrow, and Woody Herman.

Four other members of Pierce's 1951 band followed him to Herman's: saxophonist Art Pirie, trumpeters Roy Caton and Dud Harvey, and bassist Frank Gallagher.

Don Stratton went with Buddy Morrow, Claude Thornhill, Tony Pastor, and Elliot Lawrence before settling in New York, where he played jazz, Broadway shows, and modern classical music. Stratton was the only member of Pierce's Boston band to work with him again, in New York in 1956. George Green settled in New York as well, and became a sought-after copyist.

Sonny Truitt was bitten by the same modernist bug as Charlie Mariano. He was an early member of Mariano's bop groups at the Melody Lounge, and took part in Mariano's *The New Sounds from Boston* recording in 1951. Truitt, Mariano, and drummer Joe MacDonald toured with Bill Harris and recorded under Mariano's name on the West Coast. In New York, Truitt recorded with Miles Davis in 1953, and played in innumerable bands before forming The Six, a sextet with Bob Wilber, in 1956.

A few members of Pierce's band returned to Boston. Nick Capezuto was with Harry James, Tex Beneke, and Louis Prima before returning to Boston and the Herb Pomeroy Orchestra. Dave Chapman entered the U.S. Air Force, and joined Capezuto with Pomeroy after his discharge. Joe MacDonald joined Woody Herman in 1954, but after less than a year returned to Boston, where he worked as an engineer and played music part-time, eventually becoming president of AFM Local 9. Trombonist Bob Carr worked with Manny Wise in the mid-1950s. Phil Viscuglia from the 1949 band taught at the New England Conservatory and played bass clarinet with the Boston Symphony Orchestra.

Mert Goodspeed was one who left music. He remained with the Pierce band until 1950, when he went with Dean Hudson, a dance band working seven nights a week across the southeast. When that ended, he moved to New York and worked with Buddy DeFranco while he waited for his union card. In 1951, though, he left music and enrolled in business school. He faced the realities of the business: "Why did I quit? Six months of one-nighters, you get real tired of that. And guys like Urbie Green were getting all the studio work and I didn't see any way past that."[12]

There were never any revivals or reunions. For all its importance to Boston's jazz scene, the Nat Pierce Orchestra was forgotten until Art Zimmerman collected its music for an LP he released in 1977. At the time, Pierce was surprised anybody was interested.

The Boston Beboppers

Like Jimmy Tyler and Nat Pierce, Jimmie Martin represented another step in the swing-to-modern transformation in Boston jazz. If Jimmy Tyler owed his inspiration to Illinois Jacquet, and Nat Pierce owed his to Basie, then Jimmie Martin owed his inspiration to Billy Eckstine.

Jimmie Martin came to Boston in 1946 to study at the Boston Conservatory, moving from Florida with his mother and sister. He played piano, studied composing and arranging, and sang like Billy Eckstine. And he wanted to organize a modern big band modeled on Eckstine's. He did, serving mainly as the front man and vocalist. Then he disappeared from the scene. Not much more is known today about him.

Although it did not have a popular music program, the Boston Conservatory was an interesting place in 1946 for young musicians with a mind for modern jazz. Jimmie Martin was in good company. During his time, Gil Askey, Gigi Gryce, Sam Rivers, and Eddie Logan attended the Conservatory. All would be a part of Martin's bebop experiments.

Martin organized his first band shortly after arriving in 1946. He advertised it as Jimmie Martin's Nightingales, but who they were, and how often they worked, are unknown. By late 1947 the band was called Jimmie Martin's 17 Exponents of BeBop, and Joe Gordon and Gigi Gryce were counted among the Exponents. Martin broke up this band in spring 1948 and re-formed it in February 1949 as the Boston Beboppers, but most people called it the Jimmie Martin Orchestra.

Martin might have been the leader, but Jaki Byard supplied the drive. Byard, born in 1922 in Worcester, started with violin and piano lessons as a boy, picked up the trumpet at 16, and was gigging around his hometown by the late 1930s. After his wartime army service, Byard gravitated to the expanding scene in Boston. He worked in Boston and New York with Ray Perry, but unfortunately the recording they made has not been found. In 1947–1948 Byard went on the road with Earl Bostic at a time when Bostic was still playing jazz, but the two weren't especially compatible musically, and Bostic fired him. Byard spent part of 1948 working in Canada, then came back to Boston where he got involved with Martin's Beboppers as an arranger and performer.[12]

The band of Martin and Byard is almost forgotten. Unlike the Sabby Lewis band, it wasn't written up regularly in the *Daily Record* or *Down Beat*. Unlike Jimmy Tyler's Orchestra, it wasn't at the Hi-Hat for weeks on end. Unlike the Nat Pierce Orchestra, it didn't record. Its output was limited to just four sides on the Motif label, and on two of those they're backing vocalists. But from one end of the bandstand to the other, the Beboppers were loaded with talent and quite capable of holding their own in a battle of music.

Hiawatha Lockhart was an Alabama-born navy veteran who worked in the Midwest territory band of Nat Towles before his arrival in Boston in 1947 to study at the New England Conservatory. He became one of the Exponents/Beboppers:

> I was with Phil Edmunds first, and then I went with Jimmie Martin, and that band was the talk of the town among the musicians. Jimmie heard me play somewhere and he asked me to come to a rehearsal, and then he asked me to join the band. I bumped another trumpet player out of the band, and I knew

the guy I replaced and I felt bad about that but that's the way it is in the music business.

Our trumpet section had Gil Askey playing lead, he was later Diana Ross's music director. Then there was Joe Gordon, and Gordon Wooley, and Lennie Johnson, he was the high note man. He was the power in the section. And me.[14]

Saxophonist Eddie Logan was from Texas, a place known for its big-toned tenor saxophonists, where he played in the territory bands of Clarence Love and Boots (Clifford Douglas) & His Buddies. He came to Boston in 1946 after his navy service to study at the Boston Conservatory, where he met Jimmie Martin. He recalled the trombone and reed sections in the Beboppers:

Have you heard of Hampton Reese, trombone player and arranger? He was B. B. King's musical director for about 25 years after he left here. He was with B. B. almost from the beginning. Hampton was in the trombone section, and Jimmy Taylor, and Jack Jeffers, and Jaki Byard—yeah, he played trombone in that band, he could play *anything*.

The reeds, there was Frank Kidd on alto and clarinet, he was far ahead of his time. He worked with Josephine Baker when she brought her show to town. And there was Gigi Gryce and Wally Brodus on alto, and Sam Rivers and Gump Whitman on tenor, and I doubled on tenor and baritone. I played tenor on the record we made, "Second Balcony Jump." Joe Gordon and I had the solos. We recorded it at Ace Studios on Boylston Street.[15]

Neither Logan nor anyone else remembers what was on the flip side of "Second Balcony Jump." Today the record is quite rare.

Gigi Gryce came to Boston to study composition at the Boston Conservatory in 1947, where he met Martin and the rest. His writing was profoundly influenced by Alan Hovhaness, who came to the Conservatory in 1948. Perhaps his closest friend and certainly his most constant musical companion was Sam Rivers. Both spent time in the Martin band and played together in numerous small groups. A devotee of Parker and Monk, Gryce played with both in Boston. His composing skills were recognized even while still a student, as he contributed a half-dozen compositions to Stan Getz's book.

Sam Rivers recalled some of his bandmates:

The name had it right, that's what we were, beboppers. We worked mostly in Boston. Jaki Byard did most of the writing for the Beboppers and he was one of the biggest influences on my own writing. Jimmie was a singer, he sang like Billy Eckstine. Hampton Reese, the trombonist, was also writing, and he was an excellent composer, and another one of my influences as a writer, as close to a genius as anyone I knew. Joe Gordon played trumpet, and Hampton and Joe Gordon did excellent unison things, play together and then each play his own solo. We all did that. Play a whole record note for note, and then go on from there. Hampton Reese became B. B. King's music director in the 1950s and I toured with them.

Frank Kidd was playing alto. He was doing things like Eric Dolphy back in 1949, if you can believe that. He had his cane, and his cigars, and he had a real interesting style. I don't know what happened to him.[16]

Eddie Logan completed the personnel by naming the rhythm section:

Bill Grant was our drummer, but there were always other drummers around, like four drummers, but Bill was the main drummer. There was Clarence Johnston, he went with James Moody, and then Alan Dawson, he was the youngest, and also Larry Winters. Gator Rivers was the bass player. Stephen Peters played piano. He went over to Africa to teach many years ago.[17]

Hy Lockhart also remembered Grant and Johnston, and recalled that Martin sometimes liked to use two drummers in some arrangements. Larry Winters distinguished himself in the Beboppers drum circle by playing the bongos. Another Roxbury-born drummer, Floyd "Floogie" Williams, later a longtime member of Lionel Hampton's big band, was also in the mix, playing maracas.

Sam Rivers was a masterful musician who played an outsized role on the Boston jazz scene. He was not Boston-born, but he spent about a dozen years in the city. Rivers was born in Oklahoma in 1923, where he started on the saxophone at age 13. He enlisted in the navy during the war, and while stationed in Vallejo, California, he worked nights with blues singer Jimmy Witherspoon in the Bay area clubs.

Upon discharge, Rivers joined the veterans converging on Boston, entering the Boston Conservatory in 1947 to study composition and theory. That's where he met Jimmie Martin and joined the Boston Beboppers, but he found many other ways to stay busy musically. He worked with Hopeton Johnson, with Gigi Gryce and drummer Floogie Williams at the 4-11 Lounge, with Fat Man Robinson's jump band, and at Izzy Ort's with Larry Willis and Larry Winters. He worked gigs with Tasker Crosson and subbed in the Sabby Lewis band. He led a significant bop band at Louie's Lounge in 1950–1951, with Martin, Joe Gordon, the unheralded tenor saxophonist Gladstone Scott, his bassist brother Martin "Gator" Rivers, and drummer Bey Perry.

Rivers transferred to Boston University in 1952 but dropped out, and spent the next two years in Boston concentrating on his writing. In 1954 he moved to Florida, organized a group with tenor saxophonist Don Wilkerson, then played R&B with his brother Martin, and toured with B.B. King, likely at the invitation of Hampton Reese. Rivers returned to Boston in 1958, and we'll pick up his story again in Chapter 15.

The band members were talented, but so were the arrangers. The Martin band had superb writers. While Byard and Reese did the bulk of the writing, Gil Askey wrote some arrangements, Nat Pierce contributed a few, and another New England Conservatory student, Paul Broadnax, also pitched in. Lockhart: "Paul Broadnax arranged "Flamingo" for us. It was a masterpiece. I'll never forget it."[18] Broadnax, a saxophonist, singer, and pianist, was at the time writing arrangements for Sabby Lewis.

Good Reviews, No Gigs

One of the few items written about the Martin band appeared in the *Boston Chronicle* in April 1949, reviewing their performance at Local 535's Annual Musicians' Benefit Ball:

> The ball is ended, but the melody, and Jimmie Martin, lingers on. The Martin band, composed of the most modern of young, energetic musicians, returned to Boston's musical whirl after a year's absence to "Bop-tize" 1,250 dance enthusiasts at the Annual Musicians' Benefit Ball and Show last Thursday at Mechanics Hall.

> Complete with assorted Afro-cubanisms, an over-enthusiastic bongo drummer, flailing maracas, Joe Gordon's bop phrasings and the Parker-ish tenor of Andy McGhee, the twenty-piece outfit provided an unexpected thrill to the audience lured by the big names of New England jazz.

> Playing four numbers, one of them an original, the Martin entourage presented bop, the new American art form, to an attentive audience. Their pulsating music was at times ragged but it never lost its youthful drive or its emotionality.

> As the Martin outfit took the stage, groups of dancers sauntered on the floor. When the first lusty notes of "Our Delight" hit the lofty ceiling, burst, and fell dizz-ily forward—one by one—the dancers stopped. The tumult died away—silent before the Great Sound. When the music stopped—hushed silence—then all hands registered approval.

> A bop standard, "Wouldn't You," followed. Backed by a nice arrangement, leader Martin sang "Summertime." The band completed the set with "Edna," an original composition by an unnamed musician.[19]

> Just two months had elapsed since the band had organized to rehearse for the show. Into those months were crowded a wild variety of episodes, starting with chronic absentee-ism and proceeding through many organizational mishaps, to the happy ending which was wildly applauded by stomping, whistling, excited dancers and musicians.[20]

Martin broke up the band in fall 1949. The much praised appearance at the Local 535 Annual Ball led to little work. There were a few one-nighters at the

Rio Casino, and some concerts in Butler and Ruggles Halls, but not much else. For whatever reason, the band failed to appear at the 1950 Local 535 affair, although it was on the program.

It is hard not to ask "what if." Had this band been in New York, it might be held today in the same esteem as the Gillespie big band of the same era. But the Martin band in Boston had the same problem the Gillespie band had in New York: You can't eat esteem. Martin once paid his musicians with IOUs. Lockhart, though, recalled how the band almost made it to New York:

> Billy Eckstine caught one of our rehearsals and he just loved the band. He wanted to take the band with him back to New York. Minus Jimmie. He just wanted the band. So of course we said no way, and we laughed about it later. But that's how we didn't go to New York.[21]

If the band did not do well, its individual members did better. Lockhart, Johnson, and Alan Dawson were members of Sabby Lewis's band of 1950, and when Johnson left, Joe Gordon replaced him. Hampton Reese went with B. B. King, serving as King's music director for about 25 years. Gil Askey went to Detroit and was instrumental in the development of the Motown Sound. In 1972, Askey was nominated for an Oscar for his score of *Lady Sings the Blues*, the film version of the Billie Holiday story that starred Diana Ross. Askey was then Ross's musical director.[22]

Gigi Gryce spent a year studying in Paris, returned to Boston to complete his degree in 1952, and moved to New York. He and Joe Gordon worked with Art Blakey in 1954, and Gryce went on to form the Jazz Lab with Benny Golson. Jack Jeffers went on to a recording and performing career that included stints with Lionel Hampton, Clark Terry, and Count Basie. He subsequently formed his own big band in New York. Andy McGhee played R&B with Fat Man Robinson, then toured with Lionel Hampton and Woody Herman before joining the Berklee faculty. Jaki Byard, Joe Gordon and Lennie Johnson helped create the Jazz Workshop and all the fifties excitement at the Stable. Others were mainstays in the South End clubs—Eddie Logan at Wally's, Hy Lockhart at the Hi-Hat, Sam Rivers at Louie's Lounge, Bill Grant at Connolly's.

And the enigmatic Martin? He was in New Jersey for a time, then went west. By one account, he became a preacher. Hy Lockhart knew this much:

> Jimmie Martin just dropped out of sight. The last time anybody I know heard from him or about him, was Wally Brodus some years ago, out in Los Angeles, where Brodus went after he left Boston. Someone told Martin to look Wally up, and they got together and Martin asked Brodus if he could keep a box of music out in his garage for a short while. As far as I know, it's still there, because he never came back for it.[23]

Jimmie Martin…pianist, singer, composer, arranger, bandleader, and in the end, man of mystery. But there is no denying the role he played in the changing of Boston's musical guard.

Chapter 13

The Hi-Hat: America's Smartest Barbecue

The Hi-Hat, at 572 Columbus Avenue, was the most celebrated of all the clubs around the corner of Mass Ave and Columbus. It was the busiest jazz club on the city's busiest jazz corner, and between the summer of 1948, when it launched its jazz policy, and December 1955, when it was closed by fire, the Hi-Hat was one of the most important jazz spots in New England.

The Hi-Hat opened in 1937, around the same time as its neighbors Little Dixie and Johnny Wilson's, but other than being another white-owned club in a black neighborhood, it wasn't like them at all. Its closest kin in the nightclub trade were the upscale spots in Bay Village, with which the Hi-Hat competed for customers. It didn't take long for the Hi-Hat to become known throughout the city as a restaurant with outstanding barbecued chicken, with its rotisserie strategically placed, turning the birds right in the front window.

The Hi-Hat claimed to be "America's Smartest Barbecue"—an urbane gathering place, with a top hat and cane prominent on everything from the dinner plates to the menus to the matchbooks, and even the club's doorman wore top hat and tails. There was a restaurant at street level and a nightclub upstairs. The music of those first years was dine-and-dance fare played by white hotel bands or novelty trios for an exclusively white audience. The only blacks in the place were cooking the food and serving the liquor. And so the Hi-Hat went through the war years, and into the postwar years, with an outdated approach to business and no real ties to the neighborhood around it.

1948: A Jazz Club at Last

Finally in 1948 things changed. Julie Rhodes (Julian Rosenberg) was the Hi-Hat's president, treasurer, and keeper of the secret barbecue sauce recipe. He looked at his neighbors and saw clubs doing business with jazz. Where there had once been just the Savoy, now there were new competitors. The Savoy was still there, featuring the Dixielanders in their ascent, but so was Wally's Paradise, Eddie Levine's, and the 4-11 Lounge.

People were digging small-group jazz all over the neighborhood, and in summer 1948 Rhodes made his move to grab some of the excitement. He hired a trio, its members all part of the Ray Borden Orchestra—pianist Nat

The Hi-Hat, sometime in the late 1930s, prior to the addition of a second floor on the right of the building to match the one on the left. Courtesy of the Bostonian Society/Old State House Museum.

Pierce, alto saxophonist Charlie Mariano, and drummer Joe MacDonald. It was an easy commute for Pierce, who lived a few doors away at 458 Mass Ave. It was a big summer for Nat, too, because in July the members of the orchestra voted for a change in leadership and put Pierce in charge.

Years later, when Pierce returned to the Hi-Hat bandstand as pianist with Woody Herman, Rhodes recalled those early days when he hired Pierce for five dollars a set. Woody got a bit more than that.

As good as that trio might have been, however, having a jazz policy meant employing black musicians, and the first ones Rhodes hired that September were the local stars of longest standing—Sabby Lewis and his band. As Sabby had played an important role in the emergence of the Savoy in 1942, Rhodes hoped he could play a similar role in helping the Hi-Hat emerge in 1948. For Lewis, the timing was good. His style of music had been pushed out of the Savoy by Dixieland, and the location where he planned to work in the fall of 1948, the Down Beat Club on Tremont Street, failed to reopen after its summer shutdown.

Rhodes had misgivings about booking black acts at his club, because it would also mean admitting black customers. He didn't want the Hi-Hat to "go colored," which might scare away the free-spending white clientele he had already developed. And he still wanted to maintain that "Nightclub-with-a-capital-N" aura as the top night spot in the area. The popular Lewis band was the ideal choice. Their ability to take care of business on the bandstand had built a sizable following of both blacks and whites. As it turned out, Rhodes needn't have worried because he got the patrons he wanted. He just had to stick to his plan of hiring those musicians, black or white, who would attract patrons, black or white, with a few dollars to spend.[1]

Not surprisingly, though, there was a problem with the plan. Rhodes didn't know how to find jazz musicians. "What Julie Rhodes knew about," recalled pianist Al Vega, a fixture at the Hat between 1950 and 1953, "was making chicken." Rhodes needed allies to build his club, and his first was Lewis, who was featured from September 1948 through March 1949. Lewis suggested that Rhodes get Ray Barron to organize Sunday jam sessions, which were doing well at Wally's Paradise. Lewis and Barron had worked together at the Down Beat Club, where Barron booked bands and organized the Sunday sessions. Barron had jam sessions underway at the Hi-Hat by November. What Rhodes had, with Lewis and Barron, were eyes and ears in the jazz community. Recalled Vega:

> Ray Barron would tell Julie who Charlie Parker was, that he should hire Charlie Parker. So he'd do that, but he still couldn't evaluate quality. Julie worked by the numbers. He'd tell me, we've got a trio coming in, so you should hire a band. Who's the trio? Oscar Peterson. He didn't know how good Peterson was, and he thought that since it was only three guys, we'd have to hire another seven, eight guys to compensate.[2]

Rhodes solved the management problem by hiring Dave Coleman. Coleman, a college-trained chemist and frustrated musician, had been around the Boston club scene for years, managing bands and such downtown rooms as Izzy Ort's and the Crawford House. He knew the club business, and he'd been bit by the modern jazz bug.

Modern Jazz Mecca

The Hi-Hat jam sessions in 1948–1949 were an important incubator for modern jazz in Boston. Its Sunday matinees and Tuesday "boppers nights" became magnets for anyone interested in playing the new music. It was the meeting place for the members of Nat Pierce's "white contingent" led by Charlie Mariano and Sonny Truitt, and Jimmie Martin's "black contingent" led by Jaki Byard and Joe Gordon. The Sunday jam sessions proved popular, often playing to full houses.

The Hi-Hat was a haven for local jazz players, particularly the Local 535 musicians. The club featured continuous entertainment, with the headliner, the house band, and the intermission pianist each getting their turns. Intermission pianists included Dean Earl, Mabel Simms, Dick Twardzik, and Al Vega. Earl and Vega also led the house band, as did Jaki Byard, Charlie Cox, Trudy Jones, Hillary Rose, Serge Chaloff, Clarence Jackson, Hy Lockhart, Jay Migliori, and Fat Man Robinson. And though the Hi-Hat put many local musicians to work, money was always tight. Said Hy Lockhart:

> After I got out of the navy, I was back in Boston and stopped by the Hi-Hat to say hello to Julie Rhodes. Julie asked me if I wanted to bring a band into the Hi-Hat, to work as the house band. So I formed a quintet and we were there for a year or so, in 1952, '53. I was one of the few bandleaders that got Julie to pay union scale, he usually tried to hire guys for less, and the reason I was able to do it is because I said I'd forgo the extra fee the bandleader normally gets. That way all the guys could get scale, and I was paid the same as they were. It was a quintet, with Rollins Griffith on piano, Bernie Griggs on bass, Al Johnson on drums, and J. J. Johnson on tenor, and yes, his name did sometimes cause some confusion but he was a tenor player, a good one, from Atlantic City.[3]

Lockhart's pianist and bassist, Rollins Griffith and Bernie Griggs, were key members of the Boston scene in the 1950s. Rollins Griffith graduated from the New England Conservatory of Music in 1949 and gigged around town, but his first significant job came in 1952, at the Hi-Hat with Lockhart. When that ended in 1953, he moved over to Storyville, first in a trio with Slam Stewart and Marquis Foster, then with Jimmy Woode and Jo Jones. In January 1954, Griffith, along with Foster and Woode, played with Charlie Parker at the Hi-Hat, a session later released on record. Then we don't hear much from him (possibly because he was earning two masters degrees, one in music from Boston University and the other in education from Boston State College), although he surfaces as the intermission pianist at Storyville in fall 1957. In 1959, though, he was back on the scene, rolling out a nonet for the Boston Arts Festival in June. He led the house trio at Storyville at the Bradford Hotel in 1960–1961, but after that, his day job subsumed his jazz career.

Griffith started as a music teacher in the Boston schools in 1951. He was named an assistant principal in 1966, a principal in 1969, and an assistant superintendent in 1970, the first black chosen for this position. He served through the very worst years of Boston's public school crisis as a leader in the struggle for equal education. He apparently had Jackie Robinson's ability to tolerate abuse, of which there was much hurled his way from all sides. Perhaps it wore him out. Griffith died of leukemia in 1978, at age 52.

Bassist Bernie Griggs—more precisely, Bernie Griggs Junior; his father had been a bassist also—worked with Charlie Hooks at Izzy Ort's, in Jimmie Martin's Orchestra, and with Charlie Mariano's small groups. Wider recognition came following a stint with Dizzy Gillespie in 1952; Gillespie heard Griggs in Lockhart's group and hired him. In March 1953 Griggs worked with Charlie Parker at Storyville, then spent about a year in 1953–1954 at the Hi-Hat in a trio with Dean Earl and Marquis Foster. In 1954 he joined a "pre-Messengers" Art Blakey unit with Gigi Gryce and Joe Gordon, recording *Blakey Featuring Art Blakey* for EmArcy in May. When Griggs came back to Boston, he moved increasingly into commercial work, backing singers and forming a calypso band in 1957. He played jazz again in 1959–1960 as a member of Rollins Griffith's nonet, but poor health forced him to withdraw from music. He died in 1984 at the age of 53.

Bostonians all. From left: Sonny Stitt, Marquis Foster, Dean Earl, Bernie Griggs. Courtesy of Berklee College of Music.

Boston musicians had opportunities at the Hi-Hat, but the club earned its reputation as a name-band spot. In September 1949, name bands started splitting time with Lewis and the other local outfits. Milt Buckner, Eddie Heywood, Slam Stewart, Earl Bostic, and finally Buddy DeFranco were scheduled. The December appearance of DeFranco, in fact, represented a coup for the club, in that DeFranco had just won the annual *Down Beat* Readers Poll as top clarinetist, and Ray Barron, the Boston correspondent for the magazine, arranged to have the award presented to DeFranco at the Hi-Hat, and he further arranged for the presenter to be none other than Arthur Fiedler, of the Boston Pops. Fiedler presented the award December 29.

That would be "Cat" Anderson in Tyler's band on New Year's Eve. Ad ran in the *Boston Daily Record* December 31, 1949.

Nineteen-fifty started with the breakup of the Sabby Lewis band, which came undone after an unsuccessful engagement at the Show Boat, recounted in Showdown at the Show Boat, page 157. The entire band quit to form a new unit under Jimmy Tyler's leadership, and it rolled into the Hi-Hat for New Year's Eve and stayed until April 1950. Lewis assembled a new band and worked a few doors away at Wally's Paradise

Among the visitors appearing in the spring of 1950 were two prominent musicians closely associated with bebop, trumpeter Howard McGhee and pianist Thelonius Monk. Pianist Hi Diggs, a member of Clarence Jackson's Four Notes of Rhythm, one of the early Hi-Hat house bands, recalled that Monk visit in a 1988 interview:

Julian Rosenberg was a great guy to work for and knowledgeable about running a restaurant, but was smart enough to hire someone else to book the talent. Nevertheless, he took a great interest in every phase of the business.

One particular week, Thelonius Monk had been booked in and I don't think poor Julius was ready for him. Come rehearsal time, Monk sat down at the piano and played to a small group of people who was there at the time. Julie was not to be considered a square as he dug Sassy and Mel Torme, Diz and Hamp, but when Monk started playing some of his own sounds, poor Julie was completely baffled. Now I'm not the hippest guy in town, but I knew that what Monk was putting down was really bad and when Monk turned to his audience and asked, "You dig?" Julie turned to me and asked, "Is he really good?" I put on my hippest look and said, "He's a genius," which of course he was and for the sake of this gig, I was convincing.[4]

Joe Gordon was on that gig, and Don Stratton recalled what Joe said about Monk and one of his well-known predilections: "I asked him how it felt to play with Monk and he replied, 'I don't know, he hasn't finished dancing yet.'"[5]

The early 1950s were the peak time for the Hi-Hat, with musical gem after musical gem taking the stage for the eight-day week, Monday through Sunday nights plus the Sunday afternoon jam session. There were jazz stars, but the Hi-Hat brought in musicians from across the blues-based musical spectrum. There were blues shouters like Wynonie Harris, New Orleans R&B with Fats

Domino and Ivory Joe Hunter, doo-woppers like the Ravens and the Five Keys, and honking saxophonists like Al Singer and Big Jay McNeely.

It was jazz, though, that the Hi-Hat brought to Boston in those years. It was the first Boston club to:

- Present as bandleaders Miles Davis, Erroll Garner, Dizzy Gillespie, Thelonius Monk, Charlie Parker, and Oscar Peterson.

- Present as headliners the singers Ruth Brown, Carmen McRae, Jeri Southern, and Sarah Vaughan.

- Present the big band survivors with their new-look small groups— Count Basie's Sextet, Charlie Barnet's Drifters, and Artie Shaw's Gramercy Five.

Certain artists were enormously popular and made annual or even semiannual visits. Earl Bostic, Erroll Garner, Stan Getz, and Charlie Parker each appeared five times, Milt Buckner and Oscar Peterson six times, Dizzy Gillespie seven times, Illinois Jacquet eight times, and the undisputed champion was Slim Gaillard, with 11 appearances. Almost everything going on in jazz between 1949 and 1955 was on the Hi-Hat's schedule, except for big bands. They cost too much. But even for the exception there was an exception: Rhodes brought in Woody Herman's big band in 1954. Dixieland, of course, was a nonstarter.

The Hi-Hat competed for musical talent at the highest level, far outpacing any other Jazz Corner club and in fact outpacing any club in town except Storyville, the other name band room. The two clubs battled for bookings for the most popular artists, and the names on the marquees speak to the character of the clubs. The Hi-Hat and Storyville were like two windows offering a different view of the same landscape.

It became an increasingly expensive competition, eventually won by Storyville. George Wein could offer a better room, as well as concert and festival bookings. Rhodes had only his club.

Some bands and musicians played both rooms, but many did not. Some of the Hi-Hat's most popular artists, such as Bostic, Gaillard, and Jacquet, never appeared at Storyville. By the same token, some of Storyville's most popular artists, like Dave Brubeck, Gerry Mulligan, and George Shearing, never appeared at the Hi-Hat. At the Hi-Hat, jump music was in, cool school was out. At Storyville, the opposite was true. Whole categories of music heard regularly at the Hi-Hat (R&B, doo-wop, and those frantic honkers) never played Storyville, while the folk musicians and Dixielanders on the Storyville schedule didn't play the Hi-Hat.

Erroll Garner, Ella Fitzgerald, Billie Holiday, and Charlie Parker appeared multiple times at both clubs in the early 1950s. (Holiday and Parker worked frequently in Boston in those years because they had lost their cabaret cards and were shut out of the New York clubs.) By 1955 most of the "mainstream" names were moving to Storyville. Dizzy Gillespie, in fact, was playing his first Storyville engagement at the time of the Hi-Hat's 1955 fire. Regardless of payday implications, some artists may have had a sense of loyalty to the Hi-Hat. Some of its popular artists—Miles Davis, Carmen McRae, Oscar Peterson—did not appear at Storyville until after the Hi-Hat closed.

There was one other difference, though, and it was significant: ambiance. Storyville always prided itself on being a listening room, with soft lighting and good sound equipment, where artists were respected and audiences attentive. The unruly were asked to leave. The Hi-Hat, though, was loud and bright and a long way from being a listening room. Columnists George C. Clarke, Nat Hentoff, and John McLellan did not agree often, but they all thought the Hi-Hat had too many distractions and too much noise.

Broadcasting Live from the Jazz Corner of Boston

Radio was important to the success of the Hi-Hat. It started with Steve Allison on WVOM in 1950. Allison, a late-night talker, was on from midnight to three, and though the music stopped at one, Allison stayed on with guest interviews into the wee hours.

The most identifiable Hi-Hat voice was that of Symphony Sid Torin. Starting in May 1952, Torin broadcast nightly from the Hi-Hat, from ten to midnight over WCOP, and later over WMEX when WCOP went Top 40. It was Symphony Sid who first called the Hi-Hat "the Jazz Corner of Boston." Sid emceed sessions led by Charlie Parker, Sonny Stitt, and Miles Davis that were eventually released as recordings. In 1953, the Hi-Hat built Sid a booth, and he did his whole show from there, spinning records from within and emerging for the live portion.

Al Vega, who was the intermission pianist, remembered how Symphony Sid set up the live broadcast:

> First I'd play a few tunes, then the headliner's bass player would sit in for a few more—some of them were Ray Brown, Oscar Pettiford, and George Duvivier—and then the headliner would take over. I'd play 20 minutes and the headliner would play 40. When Bird came in, though, he only wanted to play 30-minute sets, and that's how I got my trio in there, I put together a trio with Frank Gallagher and Jimmy Zitano and we'd play 30 minutes and Bird would play 30. Other guys, sometimes I'd play the 40 minutes, if somebody didn't show up or didn't want to play the last set.[6]

Al Vega achieved legendary status in Boston. In a career spanning almost seven decades, the pianist played with every bassist and every drummer, backed every singer, and worked every room. Born in 1921 in Everett, Massachusetts, Vega's career began as a substitute for just-drafted musicians at the Roseland-State Ballroom and in the jam sessions at the Ken Club before he himself entered the army in 1943. Immediately following the war, he formed a quintet with saxophonist Ted Goddard, and studied at the New England Conservatory of Music on the GI Bill. He and Goddard made the rounds, playing jazz at the Ken Club and dance music with George Graham's orchestra. When money was tight and jobs were few, they worked society dates for Ruby Newman. In 1949, Vega joined the dance band of Syd Ross and began teaching at Schillinger House. Then came the Hi-Hat.

Bostonians all: Pat Rainey, Fat Man Robinson, Al Vega, and Trudy Jones. Ad ran in the *Boston Daily Record,* September 7, 1951.

Vega moved into the local limelight in 1950 at the Hi-Hat, first playing intermission piano and then fronting the house trio. He was there for three years. Everybody coming through Boston knew Vega, which probably explains why he got the call to record for Prestige in October of 1951. His trio recorded enough music to make an album, but only one 78 was actually released, of "Cheek to Cheek" and "Makin' Whopee" with bassist Jack Lawlor and drummer Sonny Taclof. In November 1951, Nat Hentoff predicted national recognition for Vega, "one of Boston's few regularly employed modernists...who combines a full day of teaching piano, modern theory, and improvisation with nightly pyrotechnics at the Hi-Hat."[7] Vega had better luck with Prestige in January 1953, recording and releasing the album *The Al Vega Trio*, with Lawlor and drummer Jimmy Zitano.

Vega was in residence at the Hi-Hat from fall 1950 to spring 1953, and with his departure he commenced a jazz odyssey that lasted almost 60 years. It included stops at Storyville, the Darbury Room, the Jewel Room in the Hotel Bostonian, the Music Box, and the Cactus Room. Starting in January 1954, Vega's trio kicked off three years at the 1-2-3 Lounge, and some of his notable accompanists included bassists Rosemary Stairret and Joe DeWeese, and drummers Joe Locatelli and Johnny Rae, who doubled on vibes. In 1958, Vega recorded the LP *All by Al* with bassist Alex Cirin and drummer Alan

Dawson. Then came three years in Revere Beach clubs, followed by a berth at Ralph Snider's Storyville at the Bradford Hotel.

This brings us to January 1962, and Vega was only getting started. He never attained the national recognition Hentoff predicted, but he worked steadily—in fact, he had a gig on the night of his 90th birthday. He died later that year, in December 2011.

"In Flames from Cellar to Garret"

But Vega's saga takes us away from the nightclub at hand. For all its musical glory, the Hi-Hat was a bit of a hard-luck operation. The first blow came in January 1953, when manager Dave Coleman died of a cerebral hemorrhage, stricken at his desk.

The second blow was the fire in the early morning hours of December 19, 1955, which started in the kitchen and spread upstairs to the club, then to the office and dressing rooms above, and finally through the roof. The two-alarm blaze injured two firefighters and caused extensive damage. The club had no choice but to close, and it stayed closed in 1956. This marked the end of the Hi-Hat as a spot on the national jazz map.

The next two years proved to be difficult for the Hi-Hat. Its clientele moved on to other clubs, and in 1957 Symphony Sid moved back to New York. Music was in an on-again, off-again pattern. The entertainers were all local.

In December 1958, the Hi-Hat came back under new management for what would be its last hurrah. The space was completely renovated, with the first-floor ceiling removed and what remained of the second floor becoming a balcony. For the grand opening, the club brought in an old favorite, Illinois Jacquet, and followed with other big draws from earlier years, Max Roach and Arnett Cobb. Back, too, came a gang of Boston musicians, including the Jones Brothers, Sabby Lewis, and Pat Rainey. Hillary Rose led a house band powered by drummer Baggy Grant. The club had a good winter with this gathering of old friends, and it appeared that things were back on track when Red Prysock and Betty McLaurin opened for a week on March 9, 1959. Then bad luck struck again.

The next morning's *Herald* carried the story on page 1, with an **EXTRA!** banner at the top of the page for good measure. The story was short, it broke just before press time, but it had detail enough to sink the hearts of the most optimistic of the club's patrons. The fire that swept through the Hi-Hat in the early morning was a stubborn four-alarm blaze. The club closed at one a.m. and the fire was discovered by a passing Boston police officer shortly after three a.m. "The four story brick structure was in flames from cellar to garret," reported the *Herald*. The afternoon *Traveler* had the whole story. Ice, snow, subzero temperatures, thick smoke, and thick clouds had the firefighters working in what amounted to a dense smog. A thousand residents fled surrounding buildings while the blaze burned out of control for two hours. Streets were closed and the morning commute was a mess. There was no saving the place. It was a total loss, and what was left standing was leveled as a safety precaution a few days later. That was the end of the Hi-Hat.[8]

For the musicians, what remains are shimmering memories. Herb Pomeroy remembered June 1953, when Charlie Parker worked with a local band of pianist Dean Earl, drummer Baggy Grant, and bassist Bernie Griggs. Joe Gordon, Parker's preferred trumpeter, was not available, so Pomeroy got the gig:

> I remember working with Charlie Parker for the first time at the Hi-Hat. I probably had heard Bird there several different times before I worked with him. The club was upstairs on the second floor, and I can remember walking up the stairs, and my knees were shaking, literally shaking, at the thought that I was going to work with Charlie Parker, June of '53. It was the very month, the very week, that I would have graduated if I had stayed at Harvard. Some of the guys from the class came to hear me play with Charlie Parker and they said, "oh yeah, you graduated." He called me Herbert... "you're wailing, Herbert!" he'd say.[9]

There was still jazz around the neighborhood at Connolly's and Wally's, but without the Hi-Hat, the Jazz Corner wasn't really the Jazz Corner any more. Julie Rhodes opened another club in Boston's Allston neighborhood in the early 1960s, but not much came of it. He belonged on Columbus Avenue. In later years other commercial structures were built on the Hi-Hat's corner, but there was nothing that could call itself "America's smartest barbecue" or offer America's finest jazz.

Chapter 14

The Melody Lounge Gang

When Nat Pierce joined Woody Herman in late 1951, it brought an end to the modern big band experiments in Boston and the focus settled on the small groups. For the cohort of young, modern-minded musicians who filled out those bands, it was a time to make decisions. For some, it was a matter of finishing their studies and moving on. Others left Boston when their bands broke up to follow the work. The Korean War was underway, and military service claimed a few more. Still, there remained a core of young modernists who would chart the course of Boston jazz in the decade to come, and with the exception of the Herb Pomeroy Orchestra, they would steer that course from their small groups. We've already met some of the musicians who would lead the charge: Jaki Byard, Joe Gordon, Charlie Mariano, Sonny Truitt. We'll meet others in this chapter, at their unofficial clubhouse, the Melody Lounge.

Though they aren't much in evidence in this chapter, Herb Pomeroy, Ray Santisi, John Neves, and Varty Haroutunian are well covered elsewhere. Their adventures merit a place of their own, in Chapter 15, Stablemates.

Our story is primarily about Boston, which precludes our digging into the more interesting stories in the suburbs, but those stories are out there—the after-hours jam sessions at Christy's in Framingham, the big band nights at Moseley's-on-the-Charles in Dedham, Boots Mussulli's Crystal Room in Milford, the Sunday sessions on summer afternoons on Revere Beach. But one suburban outpost was important to the growth of modern jazz in Boston, so we'll make an exception to the rule and visit Lynn, on the North Shore, in the early 1950s.

Why Lynn? Well, if you were playing modern jazz, there weren't too many options in Boston itself. The Hi-Hat could only hire so many men at once, and other club owners were only beginning to discover they couldn't all make money on Dixieland. Besides, Lynn was a good town for jazz. There were a half-dozen spots in and around Central Square, like the Alibi Club, Gus Dixon's Red Fox, Primo's, Michaud's, and the Melody Lounge, Nate Finkelstein's place on Washington Street. Leroy Parkins recalled how it was when he arrived in 1951:

> The Melody Lounge was a dive, plain and simple, but all the bebop players worked there. Jaki Byard, Charlie Mariano, Dick Wetmore. A piano player

named Al Walcott, he played like Milt Buckner. The Melody Lounge was just a rite of passage, a stop you made on the way to New York. But places like the Melody Lounge were the native home of jazz, places where you played seven nights a week, and there aren't places like that anymore, examples of what I call the "grit 'n' shit" of jazz.

That was the tail end of bands playing with little nightclub shows, cheap vaudeville acts, and even at the Melody Lounge there were acts. Those days were almost over when I was there. One night it might be Tiny, a 300-pound, $100 a night whore who could move in very sexy ways, and always dressed so you could see her body. And there was Iron Jaw, a guy with a mouth full of gold teeth, and his act was to pick up a table, one of those tables with a round metal base, and hang on to it with his teeth and balance it up there on his face while he danced. And we'd play.[1]

Sound like Izzy Ort's and places like it? It was. Even as Iron Jaw and Tiny were being phased out, the boppers were being phased in, and they played week after week. Indeed, Nat Hentoff called the Melody Lounge "the only consistent local bastion for modern jazzmen."[2] This was a whole new scene, quite apart from that of the swing players like Sabby Lewis, or the Dixieland revivalists. These musicians were young, talented, and passionate about bop.

It wasn't a perfect musical place at the Melody Lounge. Heroin was a serious problem in the bop community, including Boston's bop community, and we'll see some of its tragic effect in this chapter. It was around the Melody Lounge. But let's focus on the music rather than the drugs, and turn the story over to the Melody Lounge regulars: Jaki Byard, Charlie Mariano, Joe Gordon, Serge Chaloff, Dick Twardzik, Dick Wetmore, Jimmy Woode, and Jay Migliori. And we'll include Gladstone Scott and Toshiko Akiyoshi as honorary Loungers, although they never visited the Lynn club themselves.

Jaki Byard

Nat Hentoff called Jaki Byard "a pervasive influence on nearly every young Boston musician who was interested in discovering new jazz routes."[3] His story, though, goes back to Worcester, where he was born in 1922. Jaki started piano lessons at the age of eight and learned the trumpet at 16. In 1938, he and five other Worcester musicians formed a cooperative, the Saxtrum Club, where they hosted after-hours jam sessions. It was an anchor for jazz activity in central Massachusetts, and Byard was right in the thick of it.

In 1941 Byard moved to Boston; the draft made his stay short and we don't know about his musical associations, but the *Chronicle* did advertise at least one job in Providence featuring "Byard's Orchestra" in June 1942, shortly before he entered the service. It was in the army that he took up the trombone, later his principal instrument with Jimmie Martin's Boston Beboppers, to play in the marching band. After his discharge, Byard gravitated to the expanding scene in Boston. He worked with Ray Perry and Earl Bostic, toured in Canada, and finally got involved with Martin's orchestra as an arranger and trombonist. He acquired a working knowledge of the saxophones and the strings to make himself a better writer, and it made him a leader in the Martin band. That part of Byard's story is told in Chapter 12, Big Bands, New Sounds: Nat Pierce and Jimmie Martin.

Byard spent part of 1950 touring the east coast with Jimmy Tyler's Orchestra but was back in Boston by 1951. There was work but not a lot of it; Jaki had a young family, and to make ends meet he worked in a venetian blind factory by day and with his trio at Wally's by night. He also played society gigs and dance dates, and for three years he was part of the evolving scene at the Melody Lounge. He recorded with Charlie Mariano and Herb Pomeroy in 1953, was a charter member of the Jazz Workshop that same year, and joined the growing number of modern jazz players congregating at the Stable, initially as an intermission pianist. That's when Pomeroy asked him to join his still-forming orchestra in 1955.

Byard joined the Pomeroy orchestra as a composer, arranger, and saxophonist, and remained until September 1957. He organized a big band of his own in November, working once a week at Jazz Village in the Buckminster Hotel, and again led a trio at Wally's, which included Al Francis on drums and vibes, and Ray Oliveri on bass and cello. It wasn't, Byard later recalled, "the average piano trio."[4]

In 1959, Byard finally gave up on Boston. Hoped-for recording contracts never materialized, and he had exhausted the musical possibilities of the city. He joined Maynard Ferguson's big band as pianist and arranger in 1959, staying until 1962. In 1960, he finally recorded an album of his own for the Candid label, a collection of solo piano pieces eventually released with the title *Blues for Smoke,* and followed with a trio recording on Prestige, *Here's Jaki,* in 1961. He reunited with Charlie Mariano in 1963, on Mariano's own *Jazz Portrait* LP and on Mingus's *The Black Saint and the Sinner Lady,* and with Sam Rivers in 1964, on *Fuchsia Swing Song.*

Creativity and individuality marked Jaki Byard's playing, in Boston and beyond. From his earliest days, Byard demonstrated an encyclopedic knowledge of jazz piano and a rather remarkable facility for integrating bits and pieces from across the spectrum into his improvisations, combining and recombining these elements to create passages wholly new. His first influences were Earl Hines and Erroll Garner, but he went further, absorbing everything from James P. Johnson to Art Tatum to Bud Powell, and in later years he'd add the avant-garde to his resume as well. The style he derived was all his own. In Boston he worked with everybody who was at all forward looking, and this only became more pronounced over time, as his definition of "forward looking" moved further out.

Byard flourished in the 1960s, playing alongside Charles Mingus, Eric Dolphy, and Roland Kirk. Byard capped the 1960s by joining the faculty at the New England Conservatory of Music at the invitation of Gunther Schuller. There he started a new big band, the Apollo Stompers. He was still teaching in New York at the time of his death in 1999.

Of Jaki Byard, Dan Morgenstern wrote in 1965: "There are musicians who have worked the vineyards for years. Known mostly among musicians and serious listeners, they are often praised but rarely rewarded. Jaki Byard is such a man, but now perhaps his time has come."[5] Whether Byard received reward enough is open to debate. There's always room to recognize a master.

Charlie Mariano

In the early 1950s, Charlie Mariano was the most important musician in Boston jazz. He did not seek such recognition and probably would have disputed it, but he earned it the only way that mattered: through his playing. It was Mariano who was invited to record on the Prestige and Imperial labels, and it was Mariano who came up with the idea for the original Jazz Workshop. Between 1951 and 1953, he was the man to call.

Don't get the idea, though, that his phone was ringing off the hook. It wasn't. The jazz work he loved was not plentiful, and he took his share of work with bands like Baron Hugo's Totem Pole Orchestra. He wasn't above day jobs outside of music, either. He was working in a department store as late as 1953, doing what a guy with a young family had to do.

Born in 1923, Charlie Mariano grew up in Boston's Hyde Park district. He took up the alto saxophone in his late teens, and by 1942 he was making the rounds on Boston's buckets of blood circuit. The following year he was drafted. It was Mariano's good fortune to spend his two years in the service playing in an Army Air Corps band in California, where he heard Charlie Parker for the first time. Mariano, whose strongest influence to that point was Johnny Hodges, was deeply affected by Parker. For years he battled the label of Parker wannabe.

When he returned to Boston, Mariano enrolled at Schillinger House, where he studied with Joe Viola, whom he often credited for his sound, and he joined the Ray Borden/Nat Pierce orchestra. The Pierce band didn't work often, and Mariano had his own quartet at Eddie Levine's as early as 1948 and recordings under his own name for Motif in 1949.

In 1951, Ira Gitler at Prestige Records wanted to produce a series of recordings showcasing regional talent, and the first place he came was Boston, and the first musician he contacted was Mariano. (The second was Al Vega, then leading the house trio at the Hi-Hat.) In December, Mariano made his first recording, with ensembles ranging in size from quintet to octet. Mariano assembled some of the area's best modernists: Joe Gordon on trumpet; trombonist Sonny Truitt and baritone saxophonist George Myers from the Pierce band; Jim Clark, a tenor saxophonist from Chicago stationed at an army base near Boston; Pianist Roy Frazee, a New England Conservatory student who had worked with Tommy Reynolds; and Jack Lawlor, the bassist in Al Vega's trio. Gene Glennon and Carl Goodwin shared the drum duties. Pianist Dick Twardzik sat in on one tune, his first known recording.

Charlie Mariano, ca. 1953. Courtesy of Cynthia Mariano.

The result was the LP *The New Sounds from Boston.* Said producer Gitler: "I hope this album has shown you that good modern music is being produced in areas other than readily acknowledged places such as New York and Chicago."[6]

Mariano recorded his second Prestige LP, *Boston All Stars*, with a quintet in January 1953. Alongside Mariano on that one were Twardzik; trumpeter Herb Pomeroy; Bernie Griggs, at the time the first-call bassist in Boston; and drummer Jimmy Weiner, who with Twardzik was previously in Serge Chaloff's group.

In November 1953, Mariano was in the studio again, recording enough material for a pair of LPs on the Imperial label, *Charlie Mariano with His Jazz Group* and *Modern Saxaphone* (sic) *Stylings of Charlie Mariano.* His quintet on these sessions included Byard, Pomeroy, bassist Jack Carter, and drummer Peter Littman. Despite the mediocre sound quality, opined *Down Beat* in its four-star review, "This is really a remarkable illumination of Boston's jazz talent. Stan Kenton's new altoist has never sounded better on record and yet he's overshadowed by brilliant trumpeter Herb Pomeroy, who misses only in the occasional edginess of his tone."[7]

All this recording was important because it introduced people like Byard, Pomeroy, and Twardzik, in fact the whole Boston modern jazz scene, to a wider audience. Mariano, though, wasn't done. In June 1953, he proposed to his fellow musicians that they form a "jazz workshop," a school for musicians to focus on the practical and hands-on. There were no "jazz schools" at the time. Schillinger House and the NEC's Department of Popular Music were more on the line of trade schools for commercial musicians. The workshop idea was ahead of its time, and Mariano and a core group of Pomeroy, Ray Santisi, and tenor saxophonist Varty Haroutunian started it, a tale told in Chapter 15, Stablemates.

Mariano's time at the Jazz Workshop was brief. In October 1953, he went west to replace Lee Konitz in Stan Kenton's band, and he stayed in California for almost five years. Mariano returned to Boston in 1958, to teach at Berklee and play in Herb Pomeroy's Orchestra. At Berklee he met the sensational pianist/student, Toshiko Akiyoshi. They formed the Toshiko Mariano Quartet in 1959, married that November, and moved to New York. Boston was never far away, though. There were gigs at Storyville and an appearance at the Boston Jazz Festival at Pleasure Island in August 1960. It was at this time that Mariano finally shook off the reputation as a card-carrying member of the Parker school. The release of their recording, *Toshiko Mariano Quartet*, on Candid in 1961 showed Mariano playing with authority and inventiveness, well beyond the shadows of Hodges and Parker. As he said in the liner notes, "For good or bad, I'm playing my own way."

"His own way" led Mariano to record his *Jazz Portrait* LP in 1963, serve a stint with Charles Mingus, seek out musical destinations in Japan and India, and encounter major figures in fusion and the avant-garde. He found more work abroad than he did at home and became a jazz expatriate, settling in Germany in 1977. He was living in Cologne at the time of his death from cancer in 2009.

Joe Gordon

Byard left Boston and played alongside jazz royalty. Mariano wandered the world and became one of the foremost exponents of world music long before anyone thought to call it that. Both lived for decades after their Boston years. Joe Gordon left Boston in 1958 and died, a long way from home, just five years later.

By all accounts, Joe Gordon, born in Boston in 1928, was the town's top trumpet player: big ears, a crisp attack inspired by the Eldridge-to-Gillespie lineage, the one Charlie Parker wanted on the bandstand when he worked in Boston. Gordon started in his teens as a bugler in a marching band, and from there found his way to the trumpet and lessons at the New England Conservatory. At 18 he was with pianist Hopeton Johnson, and went from there to Jimmie Martin's Beboppers, then to a sextet with Sam Rivers and Gladstone Scott, and then to a spot with Sabby Lewis in 1950–1951. "Between gigs with Sabby I had a chance to really play like I wanted with Charlie Mariano,"[8] said Gordon, and he was featured on Mariano's *New Sounds from Boston*. He was with Hillary Rose in 1952, and played with Charlie Parker and others at the Hi-Hat that same year. In 1953 he co-led a quintet with Jimmy Tyler, and in 1954 he teamed with alto saxophonist Bunny Campbell.

In 1954 Gordon left Boston for a stint with Art Blakey and Gigi Gryce, and in September he recorded his first album as a leader, *Introducing Joe Gordon* on EmArcy. *Down Beat* gave the record four stars and praised Gordon's "comet-like imagination that heralds one of the exciting newer voices of the year," and called the effort "a bracing sample of somewhat raw but always moving jazz," but *Metronome* wasn't impressed, grading it a C+: "This is old-time bop and it just won't do today."[9]

Joe Gordon, 1960. Photo by Ken Palmer. Courtesy of *Jazz Journal*.

In 1955 Gordon, too, joined the scene at the Stable, as part of Varty Haroutunian's group, but he was gone again in 1956, on an international tour with Dizzy Gillespie. He recorded well-received sessions with Donald Byrd and Horace Silver. Back in Boston that fall, he returned to the Stable and a spot in Herb Pomeroy's big band. In May 1958 Gordon left Boston again, this time for Los Angeles, where he had no trouble finding work.

Joe Gordon first started using heroin in 1954, around the time he worked with Blakey, and he struggled with the drug for the rest of his life. Drug use caused friction with Gillespie, perhaps led to his abrupt departure from Boston in 1958, and certainly led him to admit himself to Synanon for treatment when he got to California. He left, against the recommendations of the staff, to join Shelly Manne's group in November 1958. In his 18 months with Manne's Men, Gordon achieved his greatest success.

After Manne, he freelanced and recorded his second album, *Lookin' Good*, on Contemporary in 1961. *Down Beat* gave the record three and a half stars, noting Gordon's "clean, crisp attack with a bright, brassy sound and a singing quality that make his solos flow easily."[10] But he continued to struggle with personal issues and was arrested on drug charges in 1962. He was just getting himself righted and playing well when he died in November 1963, the result of injuries sustained in a house fire the previous month. Evidence indicated Gordon was smoking in bed. At the time of his death, he was scuffling, living in what was described as a "beach slum," a condemned building with no electricity. Joe Gordon, the promising trumpeter who played with the giants of jazz, was just 35.[11]

Gordon in performance, wrote one reviewer, "displays a fertile musical mind, a keen lyric sense and a powerful tone, which he combines with a considerable measure of self-assurance. He charged into tunes like the end of the world was at hand." That's a memory of Joe Gordon worth keeping.[12]

Serge Chaloff

Serge Chaloff was the biggest name on the Boston bop scene in the Melody Lounge years. Chaloff, born in 1923, grew up in one of Boston's premiere musical families. His father Julius was a composer and concert pianist, and his mother Margaret was a highly influential teacher. Among the pianists mentioned in this book who studied with Madame Chaloff are Toshiko Akiyoshi, Ralph Burns, Crystal Joy, Steve Kuhn, Ray Santisi, Dick Twardzik, Al Vega, and George Wein, not to mention Leonard Bernstein.

Chaloff was a product of the big bands, playing tenor and baritone with Tommy Reynolds in the early 1940s, then climbing the name-band ladder through the war years and after, with Dick Rogers, Shep Fields, Ina Ray Hutton, Boyd Raeburn, Georgie Auld, and Jimmy Dorsey. Finally in September 1947 he went with the Woody Herman Orchestra, the band that came to be known as the Second Herd, and there he was one of the famous Four Brothers, one of the most distinctive saxophone sections in all of the big bands. Chaloff was featured on such Herman tunes as "Keen and Peachy," "Lemon Drop," and of course "Four Brothers."

In reviewing Chaloff's work on "The Goof and I," in January 1949, Mike Levin wrote in *Down Beat* that "Serge Chaloff's baritone solo is pretty well beyond reproach." In another review in July, he wrote: "At this point, he is certainly one of the best young musicians in the country."[13] There were other accolades in 1949 as well. That year he took first place in the *Metronome* readers poll, the first of five consecutive awards, and first place in the *Down*

Beat readers poll, the first of three consecutive awards. When Woody broke up the band in December 1949, Chaloff was a star.

Serge Chaloff, early 1950s. Courtesy of the Institute of Jazz Studies.

It all came at a price, and that was the wreckage of Chaloff's off-stage life. He first tried heroin in 1945 to relieve the drudgery of life on the road. By the time he joined the Herman band in 1947, Chaloff was the most notorious junkie in a band that had a few. He was a star on stage, but his off-stage behavior veered between erratic and outrageous, marked by misadventure and overshadowed by the death by overdose of his close friend, trumpeter Sonny Berman. When Chaloff came back to Boston in 1949, he left many burned bridges behind him.

Chaloff organized a short-lived big band with a string section but abandoned it to tour with Count Basie's small band in 1950, and he toured the Midwest with a quartet in 1952. But he behaved like an addict— dishonest, unreliable, and consumed by his habit. He left Boston after a drug bust in 1952 and was off the scene for almost two years.

In spring 1954 Chaloff returned to activity in Boston. Trying to reestablish himself despite his tarnished reputation, he worked in any room that would have him. One was Storyville. George Wein hired Chaloff and former Kenton altoist Boots Mussulli to work there, and he recorded the pair on the *Serge Chaloff and Boots Mussulli* LP on Storyville Records that April. Finally, Wein put Chaloff and Charlie Mariano together in a group for the Boston Arts Festival in June.

Chaloff made another trip to the studio for Storyville in September 1954, for *The Fable of Mabel* sessions. The octet session featured the group of musicians coming together around the Jazz Workshop and the Stables nightclub: Mariano, Pomeroy, Twardzik, tenor saxophonist Varty Haroutunian, trombonist Gene DiStasio, bassist Ray Oliveri, and drummer Jimmy Zitano.

In late 1954, Chaloff voluntarily entered the rehab program at Bridgewater State Hospital in an effort to end his nine years of addiction.

In 1955, WVDA disk jockey Bob Martin arranged for Chaloff to appear on *The Tonight Show*, then hosted by Steve Allen, and helped him land a recording contract with Capitol Records. Chaloff, with Mussulli, Pomeroy, Zitano, Ray Santisi, and Everett Evans, recorded the now-classic *Boston Blow-Up!* album in April. *Metronome's* B+ review praised Mussulli's writing, Pomeroy's playing, and Chaloff's landmark version of "Body and Soul," "an especially eloquent solo not to be missed."[14]

In March 1956 Chaloff journeyed to Los Angeles to record his masterpiece, *Blue Serge*, for Capitol Records, with a quartet of Sonny Clark, Leroy Vinnegar, and Philly Joe Jones. While in Los Angeles he worked with Sonny Stitt at Jazz City. But he fell ill on the West Coast, the most outward symptom being paralysis of the legs. Back in Boston, doctors discovered a tumor pressing against his spine.

Even from a wheelchair, Chaloff played well. He worked regularly with Pomeroy's big band, and in February 1957 went to Los Angeles for a session with his brothers from the Herman band. In May he performed at the Stable for the last time, standing to take his solos, but weakened to the point where he leaned against the wall to do it. Two months later, on July 16, 1957, Chaloff died at the age of 33.

There is every reason to believe that Chaloff could have achieved the same long-term success as his Herman brothers Stan Getz and Zoot Sims. The *Boston Blow Up!* and *Blue Serge* recordings showed a musician playing better than ever, and his personal life had settled considerably. He could have prospered in the coming decades as his sometimes rival (and recovered addict) Gerry Mulligan did. But none of that could stop the cancer that killed him.

Dick Twardzik

You can't tell the Serge Chaloff story without also telling the story of his close friend, the pianist Dick Twardzik.

Richard Twardzik was born in 1931 and raised in suburban Danvers. He was playing piano at age nine, and studied classical music for seven years, at the Longy School and with Madame Chaloff. He was influenced by Art Tatum and Bud Powell, but also by Arnold Schoenberg and Alban Berg. He sat in for the first time at a Melody Lounge jam session when he was 17. Twardzik joined Chaloff's group in late 1950 and stayed for two years, touring the Northeast and Midwest as well as playing in the Boston area. After Chaloff, Twardzik worked at the Hi-Hat and the Melody Lounge, took part in Charlie Mariano's Prestige sessions, and in January 1954, joined the orchestra of Lionel Hampton. It wasn't a good fit, however, and he was back in Boston by April.

Twardzik had memorable encounters with Charlie Parker, whom he met at the Hi-Hat early in 1952 when he was playing intermission piano there. Parker hired Twardzik when he returned to that club in December. Some of that collaboration, which also included Charles Mingus, Joe Gordon, and Roy Haynes, eventually found its way onto record. And somewhere during these years around Chaloff and Parker, Twardzik became another victim of the plague years. He discovered heroin, but those who knew him said his behavior was nothing like Chaloff's.

Twardzik rejoined Chaloff in 1954, in time for the *Fable of Mabel* sessions. *Mabel*, Twardzik's composition, was another step forward for its writer as he approached his creative peak. In later years critics pointed out all manner of stylistic touches, from the varying tempos and abrupt transitions to its use of dissonance and approach to harmony. At the time, though, it was drubbed by the reviewers. *Metronome* noted that the engineering was awful, the piano out of tune, the bassist behind the beat, and the drummer a Max Roach copycat. "This record should never have been…The only guy who makes it throughout is Dick Twardzik," who "wrote well and played better," and whose solos were "inventive and daring."[15]

A month after the *Mabel* session, Chaloff's trio opened at Storyville for Chet Baker. With Chaloff were Twardzik and drummer Peter Littman, until recently the Jazz Workshop Trio's drummer. Born in 1934 and from the Boston suburb of Medford, Littman at 18 was already a Jazz Workshop regular who had recorded with Mariano in 1953 and Boots Mussulli in 1954. Littman was a close friend of Twardzik's and his drummer of choice. He also used narcotics. He had just joined Chaloff's group—creating, what one musician ruefully remembered 50 years later, "Boston's all-junkie band."

Twardzik impressed Russ Freeman, Baker's pianist. "His playing struck me as being fresh and very uninhibited, especially harmonically." Freeman arranged a recording session for Twardzik with Pacific Jazz Records, and in late October 1954, Twardzik, Littman and Carson Smith, Baker's bassist, recorded four jazz standards and three Twardzik compositions of startling originality. Six of these tracks were released in 1956 to a four-star *Down Beat* review. Wonderful as his work on "I'll Remember April," "Summertime," and the other standards was, it is his own writing, "A Crutch for the Crab," "Yellow Tango," and "Albuquerque Social Swim," that are the crown jewels of Twardzik's pianistic life. Said *Down Beat*: "He is clearly his own man at base on these, surging through with a strongly identifiable musical personality that was not yet matured but that already could turn emotions."[16]

When Chaloff emerged from Bridgewater State Hospital in February 1955, he encouraged Twardzik to enter their program as well, and Twardzik did (some reports have Joe Gordon there at the same time). Littman, meanwhile, joined Chet Baker's group and performed with them at Carnegie Hall.

After Bridgewater, Twardzik rejoined Chaloff and the rest of the *Boston Blow-Up!* band in a successful appearance at the Boston Arts Festival and the subsequent summer tour. In August, Twardzik replaced Freeman in Chet Baker's Quartet just prior to the start of a planned European tour.

Twardzik went to Europe with his eyes wide open and over the objections of family and friends. Baker's own troubles with drugs were well known even then, and Littman's presence certainly wasn't a plus. Leroy Parkins recalled a dinner party Twardzik attended shortly before leaving for Europe. "Why," he was asked, "are you going off with all those junkies?" "To prove that I can do it," was his reply. But he couldn't.[17]

The Chet Baker Quartet came undone as the band crisscrossed the continent, and the behavior of Twardzik and Littman grew increasingly erratic. October 21 found them in Paris with a recording session scheduled. Twardzik was late, and Littman went to the hotel to fetch him, only to return with the news that Twardzik was found dead in his room, an apparent overdose. He was 24. Predictably, there was shock on both sides of the Atlantic.

Shortly after Peter Littman returned to Boston, George Clarke reported a meeting on the street:

> There will be no report on police blotters, but a little drama worked itself out the other night with but few witnesses. A talented Boston youngster recently died suddenly in Paris. He was a musician, a member of an American outfit, then there. Some time ago, he had voluntarily entered Bridgewater to be cured of drug addiction, as had another, even more famous. So his friend, cured now for a solid year, met another member of the band on the street, and asked what happened, although he already knew. The other temporized, then admitted that the youngster had returned to drugs. The cured one slugged him and walked away…a small drama of city life.[18]

The two, of course, were Chaloff and Littman, and the encounter happened in front of the 5 O'Clock Club. The slightly built Chaloff was no fighter, and the punch he threw was glancing. Its momentum carried him, and not Littman, to the ground.

We don't know how it was for Littman after he got back to town, but he too was grieving, and he didn't stay around Boston for long. Littman went to Los Angeles and rejoined Baker in 1956, but later he dropped out of sight.

It's hard not to wonder "what if." Twardzik was only 24, and there is no telling how far his talent would have taken him. Chet Baker, then at the height of his own poll-winning popularity, would have showcased Twardzik as both composer and performer. And after that? He had been studying harp at the New England Conservatory, and perhaps he would have been the first bebop harpist. Perhaps he would have followed an adventurous path, as did his mentor Jaki Byard. Or given his deep knowledge of classical music and its forms, perhaps Twardzik would have been a leader in the Third Stream movement just then developing. One thing is for certain, he would have traveled far beyond his Bud Powellish beginnings. And it was all lost.

Chaloff, Gordon, and Twardzik made choices and all were dead by the age of 35. Byard, Mariano, and Pomeroy made different choices and all were still contributing to the music 40 and 50 years later. It's a cautionary tale.

Dick Wetmore

Dick Wetmore was another member of the Melody Lounge gang, one who doubled on violin and cornet. He also played trumpet, baritone horn, cello, bass, and maybe one or two more, and was remembered by Jaki Byard as a "fabulous musician."[19] A few years later, Wetmore and another Melody Lounge type, tenor saxophonist Bill Wellington, famously worked together in Boston at Danny's Cafe.

Wetmore was born in upstate New York in 1927, and took up the violin before he was 10. He only started playing trumpet because his army band, the wartime version of Bob Crosby's Bobcats, didn't need violinists. After his discharge in 1946, he worked in New York with Alvino Rey, and then, like numerous other musician-veterans, made his way to Boston. For a few years he was employed by the MCA booking agency, touring with performers such as Peggy Lee and Rosemary Clooney; one of his road trips in 1948 was up and down the East Coast as one of Pat Rainey's Rain-Beaus. In 1950 he entered Boston University to study violin, and after a year moved to the New England Conservatory of Music to study composition. There he immersed himself in modern classical music.

Wetmore's willingness to play any style of music kept him working, but strictly as a horn player. ("I only played horn for years. I thought the violin was just for classical music. Didn't even bring it into the clubs. The clubs thought you were putting on the dog—acting superior to the people in the place."[20]) Modern jazz, though, was a revelation, and through it he found a way to add the violin to his repertoire. Inspired first by the blues-based music of Stuff Smith and Eddie South, he added his own modernist sensibilities and classical influences, and derived a unique style. Dick Wetmore was one of the first violinists in modern jazz, but he never abandoned his horn.

Dick Wetmore, ca. 1955. Photo by Jack Bradley.

There have always been doublers in jazz, musicians with equal facility on two or more instruments, but not too many doubled on the violin. At the time, there was Ray Nance in the Ellington Orchestra who also played trumpet and cornet, and Ray Perry of Boston, who doubled on the alto saxophone. "Ray Perry was Wetmore's idol!" recalled Leroy Parkins.[21]

By the early fifties Wetmore, with his violin, was a key part of the modern jazz vanguard in Boston, playing regularly at the Hi-Hat and Melody Lounge. He organized two groups of his own in those years, one playing cornet alongside saxophonists Bill Wellington and Dick Johnson, and the second as a violinist with pianist Dick Twardzik and bassist Jimmy Woode. This second group entered into the realm of chamber jazz, playing the compositions of Bob Zieff. Wetmore recorded the music, with Ray Santisi replacing Twardzik, for a 1954 LP, *Dick Wetmore* on Bethlehem Records. Wetmore also recorded with a band formed by arranger Dave Coleman for Transition Records, but only one cut from their session was released on the *Jazz in Transition* LP.

In 1956 Wetmore moved to New York City. He was on the *Tonight Show* band, recorded with Gerry Mulligan, and formed a quartet with guitarist Chuck Wayne. He again explored chamber jazz as a member of Vinnie Burke's String Jazz Quartet in 1956, and on Nat Pierce's *Chamber Music for Moderns* in 1957. The late 1950s also took Wetmore to Las Vegas with a Woody Herman sextet.

All of this activity in modern jazz made Wetmore memorable, but there was a another facet to his music that made him truly distinctive: his versatility. Just as he was equally at home playing either brass or strings, so he was equally at home blowing bop one night, straight-ahead swing the next, a Broadway show the next, and Dixieland the night after that. Said Wetmore: "I just like playing music. All styles, they're all good. Anything from "Jeannie with the Light Brown Hair" to "Round Midnight."[22]

Wetmore's Dixieland credentials were as formidable as his modern ones. He was a member of Leroy Parkins's mid-fifties Dixieland group, the Excalibur Jazz Band, which worked extensively at the Savoy, Mahogany Hall, and the Southward Inn on Cape Cod. Upon his return to Boston in 1959, Wetmore again demonstrated his versatility, playing Dixieland with Mel Dorfman's unit at the Jazz Village, and more modern jazz with Ernie West's quartet at Danny's Cafe. There he reunited with Wellington. Wetmore worked with the Danny's Jazz Quartet for the better part of three years.

Bill Wellington did not leave much behind—a few early 1950s recordings from the jam sessions at Christy's in Framingham, a tune or two recorded with Bird at the Hi-Hat on which he does not solo—but the regulars who frequented Danny's remember the extraordinary rapport he enjoyed with Wetmore. Some of the musicians who knew him, including Herb Pomeroy and Dick Johnson, put Wellington in a class with Charlie Mariano among the modern saxophonists working in Boston.

At some point after Danny's, both Wetmore and Wellington dropped out of the Boston jazz scene. Wellington became a teacher. Wetmore moved to Cape Cod and painted houses for years before returning to music in the 1970s. True to form, in the ensuing decades he played everything—blues, concert music, Dixieland, bop. Although he eventually gave up the cornet, he continued to play violin until shortly before his death in 2007.

Jimmy Woode

Although he was active at the Melody Lounge, if anyone could be called the house bassist at Storyville in its Hotel Buckminster days, it was Jimmy Woode. Woode came to Boston following his army discharge in 1946 to study first at Boston University, then at the Boston Conservatory. He was one of Clarence Jackson's Notes of Rhythm in 1948 before getting into the modern jazz scene with a quartet at Wally's in 1949. He went on the road in 1950–1951 with Flip Phillips and Bill Harris, but by late 1951 he was at Storyville, backing the likes of Sidney Bechet, Ethel Waters, Lee Wiley, Billie Holiday, and Charlie Parker. A few Storyville Records sessions highlighted his versatility: one was with the New Orleans master Bechet, the other with modernist Serge Chaloff.

Nineteen fifty-four found him working in a duo with Jaki Byard and in a trio with Dean Earl, and by then Woode was the first-call bassist in Boston.

He continued to back the biggest stars in jazz in 1954, working with Parker and Ella Fitzgerald at the Hi-Hat, and in 1955, with Miles Davis there.

In 1955, a new chapter opened for Woode, when Duke Ellington picked him to play bass in his orchestra, a position he held for five years. In 1957 he recorded his only album as a leader, *The Colorful Strings of Jimmy Woode*, on the Argo label, with fellow Ellingtonians Clark Terry and Paul Gonsalves. In spring 1960, after leaving Ellington, Woode moved to Sweden. He spent the next 40 years in Europe as an expatriate. Woode was again living in the United States when he died in April 2005.

Gladstone Scott

Gladstone Scott (Scott converted to Islam and changed his name to Ghulam Sadiq, but continued to use Gladstone Scott professionally), one of the forgotten ones of Boston jazz, was by all accounts one of the best bop tenor players in Boston. Born in Boston in 1927, Scott studied the clarinet and tenor saxophone at the New England Conservatory as a teen, and like many young Boston musicians, worked as one of Tasker Crosson's Ten Statesmen. When he was of draft age near the end of the war, Scott declared himself to be a conscientious objector and served his equivalent time with the USO as a touring musician. When the war ended, his band went to occupied Japan and was stationed near Hiroshima. When he later developed lung cancer, Scott attributed it to his prolonged exposure to radiation in that environmentally poisoned Japanese city.

In the late 1940s, Scott worked with Hillary Rose in the mill towns along the Merrimac River, and with Sam Rivers at Louie's. Rivers compared Gladstone Scott's big sound to that of Lucky Thompson, while Eddie Logan recalled that Scott "played in the style of Don Byas, and there was not a faster guy on his instrument." Scott, though, was one of a number of Boston jazzmen who found work in Canada. He arrived in Montreal in about 1952, and he remained an integral part of the jazz community there until his death in 1957. Legal problems involving child support made him an infrequent visitor to Boston in his later years, so he missed out on the modern jazz at the Melody Lounge and Hi-Hat. But it is as one of the Melody Lounge gang that he should be remembered.

Jay Migliori

Jay Migliori didn't arrive in Boston until 1952, when he enrolled at Schillinger House following his discharge from the air force. Born in Erie, Pennsylvania in 1930, he started with the saxophone at 12 and studied music before enlisting. After Korea, he came to Boston and became a member in good standing of the Melody Lounge gang as a no-holds-barred bebopper.

Primarily a tenor saxophonist, he caught Charlie Parker's attention at a Hi-Hat jam session one Sunday in January 1954, and Bird invited him back to play that evening. Some of that session was broadcast live on Symphony Sid's program, and much later released on record. This kicked off some busy years for Migliori. He led the Hi-Hat's house band for long stretches in 1954 and 1955, and in February 1955 worked two weeks with Miles Davis, another performance that was eventually released on CD. From September to December 1955, Migliori led the band at the Downbeat on Boston's Park Square. This quintet included Tommy Ball, trumpet; Danny Kent, piano; Wyatt Reuther, bass; and Floogie Williams, drums. They recorded enough music for Transition Records to make an LP, to be called *Downbeat Jazz*, but the record was never released. One tantalizing number was included on the 1956 *Jazz in Transition* LP.

In December, Migliori's band moved to Storyville; advertisements had Serge Chaloff joining Migliori in January and February 1956, just prior to his leaving for Los Angeles for the *Blue Serge* sessions. Finally, later in the year Migliori had his most ambitious group yet, a septet working at Showtime on Warrenton Street, including trumpeter Bill Berry, trombonist Joe Ciavardone, baritone saxophonist Wally Brodus, and the rhythm section of Kent, Reuther, and Williams.

For about two years, Migliori led some of the finest modern jazz groups in Boston, playing in some of the best rooms—a fact overlooked by most of his biographers. He was well established here, but when Woody Herman called in 1957, Migliori accepted the offer, and remained with Herman for about 18 months. He later settled in Los Angeles, where he worked prodigiously in the studios, and became a member of Supersax, the five-saxophone group that played sophisticated arrangements of the music of Charlie Parker. Migliori died in California in 2001.

Toshiko Akiyoshi

Toshiko Akiyoshi was not the typical Berklee undergraduate. For one thing, she started her freshman year at age 26. For another, she was from Japan. And, of course, she was a woman in what was then mostly a man's game. The whole idea of "Japanese woman jazz pianist" was something of a novelty, and ten weeks after arriving in Boston, Akiyoshi appeared as a guest on the television game show, *What's My Line?*

Toshiko Akiyoshi never played at the Melody Lounge, at least not the one in Lynn. But if you translated "Melody Lounge" into Japanese, and put it on a sign and hung the sign out in front of a bar in Beppu, her hometown…she played in that one.

The Toshiko Akiyoshi Trio, with Jake Hanna and Gene Cherico, ca. 1957. Courtesy of Jack Bradley.

Akiyoshi started playing in clubs in 1945, when she was 16. Oscar Peterson heard her in a Tokyo club in 1952 and on his recommendation, she made her first recording in 1953 for Norman Granz. She formed her own nine-piece group and did all the writing for it, and despite the fact that her group appeared on radio and television for three years, work was scarce. "We did not have too many jobs," she told *Down Beat*. "We did not play commercial."[23] So there, too, she fits in with the Melody Lounge gang, as a veteran of a modern ensemble that did not work much.

Akiyoshi applied to Berklee in 1955, and was granted a full scholarship. In January 1956, she arrived as the school's first Japanese student. But she had to *play*, too, and by February she was co-leading a quartet at Storyville with Boots Mussulli. They stayed for four months. From the beginning she played with great intensity and a knack for compelling rhythmic changes.

Her trio, with fellow students Gene Cherico and Jake Hanna, was back at Storyville for the fall of 1956. More engagements followed, as did a pair of recordings for the Storyville label, the first a trio date, *The Toshiko Trio*, and the second *Toshiko, Her Trio, Her Quartet*, with Mussulli. It is a wonder she found time to study, but she did, with Herb Pomeroy and Madame Chaloff among others. She graduated in 1959.

In 1958 Charlie Mariano returned to Boston after five years on the West Coast, to a teaching position at Berklee. He and Akiyoshi began working together as the Toshiko Akiyoshi Trio with Charlie Mariano. He was not happy at Berklee, though, and left after the spring term in 1959.

For Charlie and Toshiko, the year at Berklee was only a beginning. Mariano divorced in 1959, and he and Akiyoshi married in November. They moved to New York and formed the Toshiko Mariano Quartet with Cherico and Eddie Marshall, a drummer from Springfield, Mass. In December 1960 they recorded an LP for the Candid label, *Toshiko Mariano Quartet*, which earned a four-star review in *Down Beat*.[24]

Pianist Marian McPartland, writing in *Down Beat* in October 1961, best described how the Toshiko Mariano Trio was stepping into the sixties:

> Her style and conception seem different from the Bud Powellish ideas of a few years back, her playing seems to have outgrown the similarity it once had to Powell, and she plays in a more personal style, clean lines, clearly executed with fire and intensity.
>
> Nor can Charlie still be identified, as he once was by some, as another Charlie Parker imitator. Fresh jets of sound, emotional, yet with a dry-ice quality, spurt from his horn. His ideas are fresh, the feeling lyrical yet full of virility. Charlie and Toshiko seem to inspire one another to play excitingly.
>
> When Toshiko plays, she puts her whole being into the effort. It is interesting to see this small, slim woman perform with such furious power and concentration. She is uncompromising on stage. No designing crowd-pleaser, she bends over the keyboard, lost in what she is doing. She does not look up or smile until the end of a number.[25]

In January 1963, the quartet played one of its last, if not the last, gig at Connolly's on Tremont Street before disbanding. Toshiko and Charlie moved to Tokyo later that month.

* * *

In summary, it's safe to say that Boston in the early and mid-1950s was home to exceptional talent, making striking modern jazz. Can we call it a "Boston sound"? Perhaps not, because apart from the oldest (Byard, born in 1922) and the youngest of this gang (Twardzik, born in 1931) these were musicians playing good but not exceptional bebop. All the surviving musicians went far beyond that as they developed musically. They left these formative days behind as surely as they left behind Iron Jaw and Tiny.

We noted earlier that the difference between this modern jazz generation and the swing generation that preceded it was the length of time these players stayed in Boston before they moved on. Byard and Gordon both spent over a dozen years here in their time as professional musicians, and Chaloff, Mariano, Wetmore, and Woode were all in Boston for at least seven years in the late forties to mid fifties. Byard, Chaloff, Gordon, Mariano, Scott, and Twardzik were raised in the area, while Akiyoshi, Migliori, Wetmore, and Woode were drawn to Boston by the schools.

The Melody Lounge declined in importance as Boston became more hospitable to modern jazz. The Jazz Workshop was started in 1953 by some Melody Lounge regulars, the Stable started its jazz policy in 1954 with Melody Lounge regulars, and as the gang gained seasoning, more and more of them worked at Storyville, the Hi-Hat, and Wally's. But the Melody Lounge filled an important function for the jazz community in the early 1950s.

Chapter 15

Stablemates

Modern jazz was already established in Boston when two institutions that came to embody it came into existence just outside of Copley Square in the mid-1950s. One was the Jazz Workshop, a school for jazz musicians formed in 1953, and the other was the Stable, a club that began presenting jazz in 1954. Both loom large in the telling of the Boston story. This Jazz Workshop was the forerunner of the Boylston Street club of the 1960s and 1970s, and its founders played an important role in the growth of the Berklee School of Music.

This chapter looks at the origins of the Jazz Workshop, and introduces the Stable and the Stablemates: Herb Pomeroy, Ray Santisi, and Varty Haroutunian—and their well-regarded friends John Neves, Jimmy Zitano, Gene DiStasio, and others. And we'll catch up to some Boston characters we've met in earlier chapters, including Jaki Byard, Joe Gordon, Lennie Johnson, and Sam Rivers.

All in all, it was a remarkable group making music in a remarkable place. Everyone who was there wishes they could have captured the essence of it in a bottle and doled it out, drop by drop, through some of the less jazz friendly years that were to come.

The Jazz Workshop: A "Striking New Concept"

Despite its significance, though, if we were to try to place an historic marker at the site of the original Jazz Workshop, nobody would know exactly where to put it. The actual address has been forgotten and the building was torn down in the 1980s. Everybody remembers it was on Stuart Street between Huntington and Dartmouth, hard by the train yards, but that block no longer even exists.

It's what the Workshop represented that put it on Boston's jazz map. Nat Hentoff in *Down Beat* called it "a striking new concept of jazz instruction...aimed at providing opportunity for musicians—advanced and beginners—to work and experiment with all phases of jazz under actual playing conditions." Emphasis, said founder Charlie Mariano, was on "simulating on-the-job conditions...Through pragmatic experience the student will be able to originate and exchange ideas ordinarily not a part of formal instruction."[1]

Ray Santisi recalls how it started in spring 1953:

> The Jazz Workshop was Charlie Mariano's idea. We were at a gig with Jesse Smith at the King Philip out in Wrentham and Charlie started talking: "why don't we start a school, a workshop, where we can teach classes and give private lessons and have jam sessions." It sounded like a good idea, so we rented space in an office building on Stuart Street—Charlie, Varty Haroutunian, Herb Pomeroy, and me.[2]

Herb Pomeroy continues:

> It was spring of 1953 when we started the Jazz Workshop. The space we rented was on Stuart Street, on the right side as you're going west, right where the Westin Hotel is. We got the pianos for free but we didn't have any money to move them, so we borrowed $500 from a guy named Peter Morris and got them moved. And once we finally got all the pianos moved, we started to play the pianos, and the building tenants complained—so much that we had to move again, across the street. So we had to hire the piano movers again to move the pianos out of one and into the other building, and we didn't have any money, and they're going up two and three flights with these things. That's how it started.[3]

Santisi again:

> So we had ourselves a workshop. We had a desk by the door, and Varty would sit there and collect a buck for each lesson, half for the instructor and half for the school. We had good people in there, Jake Hanna teaching drums, Serge Chaloff was there, Jaki Byard. And Storyville was right around the corner, and musicians from there would come by, like Jo Jones. So we were getting by, running sessions, doing a few concerts.[4]

The faculty comprised one of the best gatherings of talent in Boston. Others teaching included Jaki Byard, Dick Wetmore, and a trio of bassists in Bernie Griggs, Jack Lawlor, and Jimmy Woode. The "drop-in" faculty was also impressive, including Louie Bellson, Kenny Clarke, George Shearing, and Cal Tjader.

The Jazz Workshop was the right idea in the right place at the right time, but times change, and activity slowed, then stopped. One reason was the departure of Mariano in October 1953 to join Stan Kenton. He stayed on the West Coast for five years. Pomeroy, too, left late in 1953, to tour with Lionel Hampton. At the same time, Lawrence Berk invited Santisi to run some Workshop-styled Saturday afternoon sessions at Schillinger House, pointing the way to a future home for the Jazz Workshop approach. Then Santisi and Haroutunian got involved with a little joint around the corner that carried on the Jazz Workshop name and turned into one of Boston's best jazz rooms. That was the Stable. The musicians infused the spirit of the Workshop into the Stable, and kept "Jazz Workshop" as the unofficial name. The Workshop's practical orientation paid off a few years later as Pomeroy, then Santisi, and then Mariano joined the faculty at the Berklee School and helped it achieve its preeminent position in the field of jazz instruction. But that's getting ahead of the story.

Jazz in a Stable

Close your eyes. It's May 1959, you're at 20 Huntington Avenue, and it looks and sounds like this:

> At quarter to nine on a recent Thursday evening, we entered the Stable (Huntington Avenue at Copley Square), passed between the bar on the left, booths on the right, down the ramp, through the half-padded, half-glassed door to the Jazz Workshop—a pine-paneled room (ninety seat capacity) filled with small, sturdy tables, red-padded kitchen-type chairs, a rumpus room-sized bar with some half-dozen stools, and a tiny bandstand jammed with music stands, a piano, a set of drums, a bass fiddle, and the sixteen musicians of the Herb Pomeroy Orchestra who twice weekly (Tuesday and Thursday) practice this version of Telephone Box Squash and play powerful and exciting big band jazz.
>
> We found a table and sat down as Herb Pomeroy delivered a typical introduction...Turned and clapped and counted a slow, ballad tempo, which the band, looking frighteningly disorderly until the last instant possible, picked up and carried as effortlessly as if they were in the middle of a number they had been playing for some time.
>
> The beat fell easily, like water dripping from a faucet; saxophonist Dave Chapman floated on a calm sea of reeds and brass which now and then surged and subsided like a huge wave, leaving the soloist drifting as calmly as before. Alto saxophonist Charlie Mariano followed with another ballad, "My Old Flame"...Mariano, half-bent over, his horn pushed back between his legs, played in his paradoxically halting and swinging style, his high-pitched, biting voice crying out in the night.[5]

This is as good a description as you'll find of the room that was the Stable. It was less than a third the size of its neighbor Storyville, but that basement space became one of Boston's most distinguished jazz rooms and its primary incubator of local talent. The Stable was the name in neon out on the street. The Jazz Workshop was what they called it.

The owner of Storyville, George Wein, was well aware of the Stable and its place in the Boston jazz community:

> The Stable was a good breeding ground for the musicians in town, Herb Pomeroy and Jimmy Zitano, and a good piano player, Ray Santisi. They

didn't become major jazz artists but they were good musicians and the big names would go over there to sit in. It wasn't a name-band place, but the Stable was very important for the growth of jazz locally. Charlie Mariano played there. Boots Mussulli, Sam Rivers played there. So many guys![6]

The Stable itself was a modest affair. Said Ray Santisi:

> One day I'm at the Workshop with Varty, and Dick O'Donnell comes in. He's managing a bar around the corner, and he doesn't have much going on there. He asked if we wanted to bring in some music. I sent him over to Varty, he was the one with the head for managing. And that was the beginning of jazz at the Stable. A real bucket of blood, small, you had to fall down the stairs to get into the men's room.[7]

The Stable, 20 Huntington Avenue, 1959. Courtesy of Elsa Hart.

Dick O'Donnell's place was a sleepy hillbilly bar that came complete with horse heads sticking out of fake windows on the walls. Although the Stable in past years had featured members of WCOP's *Hayride Jamboree* program and the occasional Grand Ole Opry star, O'Donnell was looking for a way to attract new customers. Haroutunian lined up a trio with himself on tenor, Santisi on piano, and Peter Littman on drums. Thus was the Stable's jazz policy born in April 1954. Haroutunian and Santisi would be there for eight years.

Vartan Haroutunian was born in Everett, Massachusetts, in 1922, and by the time he graduated from Everett High School, he was already on the scene as a tenor saxophonist. He played on the buckets of blood circuit and jammed at the Ken Club, one of the few teenagers with the chops to do so. Recalled Al Vega, another teenage jazzer from Everett: "Varty, he played with me in a big band. He was fearless, he'd go to the Ken and he'd say, 'Vega can *play*,' and he was convincing, so Varty and I got to sit in."[8] Then Haroutunian went to war. With the U. S. Army Air Forces, Haroutunian flew 37 missions and was awarded the Distinguished Flying Cross. After his discharge, he studied at the Boston Conservatory of Music, hit the road with Freddie Slack in the last days of the big bands, and drifted back home when that ended. Then came the scene at the Melody Lounge. That brought him to the Jazz Workshop. Haroutunian was a swing player gone bebop, a tenor saxophonist out of the Lester Young school via Zoot Sims. But he also brought talents as a manager and an organizer, and he led the Wednesday, Friday, and Saturday groups at the Stable until the club closed.

Ray Santisi, born in 1933, was both the youngest of the Stable's core group, and the one with the most formal education. From the Jamaica Plain section of Boston, Santisi was still a teenager when he met Herb Pomeroy at Schillinger House, and worked with him in Jesse Smith's dance band. Santisi graduated from Schillinger House in 1951 and went on to further studies at the Boston Conservatory (class of '55). He was barely 20 when he joined Boots Mussulli's quartet in 1954, recording what would be Mussulli's only album as a leader, *Kenton Presents Boots Mussulli*. In 1955 Santisi played on Dick Wetmore's self-titled LP for Bethlehem Records, and in 1956 he was on Donald Byrd's *Byrd Blows on Beacon Hill* session for Transition. He occupied the piano chair in the Herb Pomeroy Orchestra for its first six years. In 1957, Santisi joined the faculty at the Berklee School of Music and was instrumental in shaping its jazz curriculum.

That first Jazz Workshop Trio got something started, and other musicians heard about it. Bassist John Neves, just out of the service, started sitting in, riding in from East Boston every day on the subway with his instrument—a ride made all the more treacherous by the fact that Neves didn't have a case for his bass at the time. He just hauled it uncovered and hoped for the best. Neves had graduated from East Boston High School, where he was a three-sport star in the late 1940s. He followed that with a season as a second baseman in the Cleveland Indians farm system in 1950, then served as an army corporal in the Korean War. A combat injury ended his baseball career. He turned to music. "I was 16 when I went to hear Roy Eldridge at the Hi-Hat," Neves later told the *Boston Globe*. "The bass player was Bonnie Wetzel. I approached the bandstand and Bonnie Wetzel looked down at me and asked, 'Can you play bass, Face?' Naturally, I said yes, and proceeded to raise five blisters on my right hand."[9]

The original Jazz Workshop Trio, 1954: Peter
Littman, Ray Santisi, and Varty Haroutunian.
Courtesy of Elsa Hart.

Neves made the band better, and Haroutunian and Santisi convinced
O'Donnell to put him on the payroll. By late 1954, Jimmy Zitano, formerly
with the bands of Al Vega and Serge Chaloff, had settled in as the regular
drummer. Then Pomeroy was off the Kenton band in late 1954, and he
started sitting in. The quintet sounded better than the quartet, and
O'Donnell hired Pomeroy too.

This was the unit that made the live recording, *Jazz in a Stable*, for
Transition Records in March 1955, the first record produced by the fledgling
label. It was an auspicious debut for both quintet and record label, garnering a
five-star review in *Down Beat*. Said *Metronome*: "Trumpeter Pomeroy is
certainly the standout, but the other four are also good, among Boston's best
and indicative of what you can hear there on the modern kick; mostly familiar
and nicely turned and almost always exuberant."[10] One writer dubbed the
Stable's style of jazz as "warm"—modern jazz with a voice clearly between the
cool school jazz coming from the West Coast and the hard bop coming to
dominate in New York.[11]

The quintet was playing six nights a week and the joint was jumping. Pomeroy left that summer, back on the road with Serge Chaloff, which created an opening for Joe Gordon, Boston's top trumpeter. Pomeroy never expected to get his job back that fall, but O'Donnell decided to use both trumpeters. Under Haroutunian's leadership, the Jazz Workshop Sextet became the most prominent unit working in Boston.

There was another key addition to the Stable in October 1955: the innovative Jaki Byard was hired as intermission pianist, and he regularly amazed the patrons with his ability to play just about anything in just about any style. The multitalented Byard—composer, arranger, pianist, saxophonist—was a already a veteran of the Boston scene, the force behind Jimmie Martin's Boston Beboppers in the late 1940s, and known in jazz circles for his work with Ray Perry, Earl Bostic, and Charlie Mariano. He played a significant role at the Stable in 1956.

Byard was not the first intermission pianist at the Stable. There was Rene de la Osa, who would abandon his mambo band down the block at the 5 O'Clock Club to play a fast set at the Stable. In 1954, there was Dick Twardzik, who became so involved in his playing that he'd lose track of time and play beyond his allotted 20 minutes. Haroutunian finally set an alarm clock, and when that alarm went off, Twardzik would stop playing then and there and turn the piano over to Santisi. There was Bob Freedman, who would later join Serge Chaloff's sextet and then the saxophone section in the Pomeroy Orchestra. He knew Twardzik from earlier days together on the Tommy Reynolds band. Twardzik was a disciple of Jaki Byard's, and perhaps even a future collaborator, but it was not to be. Jaki Byard was hired at the Stable the same month Dick Twardzik died in a Paris hotel room.

Birth of a Big Band

The energy and excitement at the Stable was not happening in a vacuum. Late 1955 was a lively time in Boston, and a glance at the newspapers from around Thanksgiving that year shows a jazz scene in high gear. Looking back on it, the level of activity is hard to believe, an embarrassment of jazz riches, the high-water mark of jazz in Boston not only in the fifties, but in all of our 25-year span. Across the street in the Copley Square Hotel, Storyville was on a piano kick that November, presenting Garner, Tatum, and Shearing, while in their cellar, Mahogany Hall featured Wild Bill Davison, Vic Dickenson and Jimmy McPartland. The Miles Davis Quintet, with its new tenor player, John Coltrane, had just closed at the 5 O'Clock two blocks away. Jay Migliori and Tommy Ball had the house band at the Downbeat on Park Square, where Mabel Simms played intermission piano. Downtown, the Sabby Lewis band, then including Alan Dawson and Lennie Johnson, was in the midst of a long engagement at Showtime on Warrenton Street, and Al Vega's trio was similarly employed at the 1-2-3 Lounge. Altoist Tom Kennedy was just starting his long run at the Brown Derby in the Fenway. On the Jazz Corner of Boston, Dean Earl had the group at Eddie's, saxophonist Dan Turner the group at Wally's, and Roy Hamilton was breaking the box office record at the Hi-Hat. Fingers Pearson was playing until dawn at the Pioneer Club.

Boston was *jumping*, and the Stable crew was about to make it jump even higher. Herb Pomeroy:

> I had a 12-piece band back in the early Fifties. Varty and I talked it over, about how we'd like to get a band like that started. We had seven musicians employed, and we were making enough money to do that. And Jaki, who was playing intermission piano, also played tenor. So if we could get Dick O'Donnell to give us a little more money, we could hire five more horn players to fill out the instrumentation we needed to play my band's book. We'd have a 12-piece band, and we'd work one night a week.

> And in November of 1955, we did that. Well, the joint was mobbed, and the band sounded wonderful, and we did so well that Dick said, in March of 1956, let's go to two nights a week. So we had the big band in on Tuesdays and Thursdays.

> I still look back on this and shake my head. This band, which was doing very well, had started out as a trio in April 1954, and grew—first to a quartet, then a quintet, then a sextet, then adding an intermission pianist, then adding five more guys one night a week, then two nights a week...all in two years. We could not have planned it this way. It just happened.[12]

Pomeroy quickly expanded the band from 12 to 14, adding many who became longtime associates: saxophonists Byard, Dave Chapman, and Serge Chaloff (although health issues led to his early replacement by Deane Haskins); trombonists Joe Ciavardone and Bill Legan; and trumpeters Nick Capezuto, Lennie Johnson and Everett Longstreth. Another expansion, to 16 men, added trombonist Gene DiStasio and alto saxophonist Boots Mussulli. These horns joined the Stable Sextet of Gordon, Haroutunian, Neves, Pomeroy, Santisi, and Zitano. It was an impressive roster.

At this point, Herb Pomeroy becomes central to this story. Gloucester, Massachusetts-born Irving Herbert Pomeroy III was 11 in 1941 when his mother took him to a movie in which Louis Armstrong had a part, and that bit of celluloid inspired Pomeroy's career as a trumpet player. He was gigging at 14 with his own high school dance band and he discovered bebop in the mid-1940s. He began studies at Schillinger House in 1948, although his vague career plan was to be a dentist like his father, and he did spend a year at

Harvard before quitting school to be a musician. He had worked at the Jewel Room with Nick Jerret, and at Izzy Ort's, and at the Melody Lounge with Charlie Mariano and Jaki Byard. Pomeroy also had a musical day job, with the Jesse Smith Orchestra at the King Philip Ballroom in Wrentham:

> That was not a jazz band, it was strictly a dance band. If there was any jazz, individual guys brought it. Ray and I were on that band. I was glad to have that job, we played every Friday and Saturday night, and in the summers on Wednesday night. I'd make about $21 a night, and I had a young family and that was good money. I stayed with Jesse until I went with Lionel Hampton in 1953.[13]

Nineteen fifty-three was a watershed year for Pomeroy. He recorded two LPs with Mariano on Imperial Records, played a week with Charlie Parker at the Hi-Hat in June, and in December joined the Lionel Hampton Orchestra for about four months. He was involved with the Jazz Workshop in its early days, and after leaving Hampton, Pomeroy started playing at the Stable. He didn't stay long, however, going with Stan Kenton in fall 1954. By January he was back at the Jazz Workshop. That summer Pomeroy went on the road again, with Serge Chaloff's Sextet. Tired of the road and with a family to support, he joined the faculty at Berklee in September 1955 (he stayed for 40 years), and started auditioning musicians for his big band. It made its public debut at a meeting of the Teenage Jazz Club in November 1955.

The Stable was swinging and invariably packed with enthusiastic listeners enjoying the sextet four nights per week and the big band on two more. The music expanded again when orthodontist-turned-trombonist Gene DiStasio stepped out of the big band to take over the Monday night chores. Business was good.

The 1956–1959 Herb Pomeroy Orchestra was a Boston phenomenon, as the earlier band of Sabby Lewis had been. Their home was at the Stable but there were numerous notable engagements away from it, including two weeks at Birdland in May 1957 and a week at the Apollo Theatre in Harlem in December 1958. There were the festival appearances—the North Shore Festival in 1957, the Boston Jazz Festival at Fenway Park in 1959, and the annual performances at the Boston Arts Festival. The 1962 Arts Festival crowd numbered about 20,000, the largest crowd Pomeroy ever played, with or without the big band.

The Pomeroy Orchestra appeared at the Newport Jazz Festival in 1958, and John McLellan enthusiastically wrote that "Boston can well be proud of the Saturday afternoon appearance of the Herb Pomeroy band. It was a big-time debut which completely flipped critics and musicians as well as the audience...The band was easily the surprise hit of the Festival! Their driving

The Herb Pomeroy Big Band at the Stable, ca. 1958. Front row, left to right: Jimmy Mosher, Joe Caruso, Dave Chapman, Bob Freedman, Varty Haroutunian. Second row: Bill Legan, Joe Ciavardone, Gene DiStasio, Jimmy Zitano. Top row: Bill Berry, Nick Capezuto, Lennie Johnson, Augie Ferretti. Ray Santisi seated at piano. Standing: John Neves, Herb Pomeroy. Courtesy of Elsa Hart.

finale, "The Lunceford Touch," left the critics and musicians agog at the sound of one of the greatest brass sections anywhere."[14]

"The Lunceford Touch" had its origins in the *Living History of Jazz*, an ambitious history of the music arranged primarily by Jaki Byard and narrated by John McLellan of WHDH. The *Living History* incorporated field hollers, blues riffs, African polyrhythms, touches of Louis Armstrong and Charlie Parker, and Byard's prediction of how the music might sound in the future, "Jazz Suite, Opus 3." It also included "The Lunceford Touch," an original composition contributed by bassist George Duvivier, Jimmie Lunceford's last arranger. Duvivier had challenged Pomeroy, saying the *Living History's* first Lunceford piece didn't do the band justice, and he would write an arrangement to remedy that. Herb Pomeroy:

> Duvivier and Jimmy Crawford, Lunceford's longtime drummer, were in Boston working at the Colonial Theatre in a Lena Horne show. Now, the way we worked it was to rehearse between 7 and 8 and hit at 8:20, and we rehearsed "Lunceford Touch" and we might have even played it in the first set. But George and Jimmy came down after their show was over and sat in and we played it again, and the guys said they'd never been through anything like it.[15]

The Pomeroy Orchestra also recorded. There were the LPs, *Life Is a Many Splendored Gig* recorded for Roulette in June 1957 (5 stars in *Down Beat*), included the most requested tune in the Pomeroy book, Jaki Byard's "Aluminum Baby." *Band in Boston,* recorded on United Artists in late 1958 (4½ stars in *Down Beat*), showcased the writing and arranging of Bob Freedman, Neil Bridge and Arif Mardin. They also recorded *The Band and I*, with Irene Kral, for United Artists in 1958.[16]

While all this was going on, the Pomeroy band enjoyed two advantages. First, it rehearsed regularly and worked twice a week, every week, at the Stable, without the distraction of living out of a suitcase. Second, the band's personnel remained stable in a business where change was the norm. Besides Pomeroy himself, nine of the original 16 members were still together in January 1959. The band had the opportunity to develop its book and its sound. That it chose to stay in Boston was ultimately part of its undoing: the road to greater recognition and success ran through New York, not Boston.

It would be a mistake to overlook lead trumpeter Lennie Johnson's contribution to the Pomeroy band. Just as he was the powerhouse in Jimmie Martin's trumpet section, so too was he the powerhouse in Pomeroy's. His bandmates called him "The King." It is a mystery why Johnson did not attain greater recognition in his lifetime. Born in Boston in 1924, he started making a local name for himself in 1948, when he was playing with Jimmie Martin and working in Jimmy Tyler's small group. In 1950 he went with Sabby Lewis, and remained with Sabby until 1953. In 1955 he joined Pomeroy's big band, where he stayed until 1959. He was in and out of the Pomeroy band after that, first with Quincy Jones in 1959–1960, then with Count Basie, replacing Joe Newman; he took part in the *First Time!* sessions, the Basie/Ellington collaboration of 1961. He worked regularly in Boston all through the 1960s and into the 1970s, often with other Pomeroy alumni like Alan Dawson, Ray Santisi, and Dick Johnson. He joined the Berklee faculty in 1968. Even with this resume, he remains well known in the business and little known outside of it.

In the early 1960s, Johnson sometimes played with the house band at the Surf, a Revere Beach nightclub. Manny Wise, then the drummer there, tells a story that shows the respect insiders had for this musicians' musician:

> At the Surf, we used to play the shows, and sometimes we had to build the band up for that. For Al Martino we played, and Teddi King, Julius LaRosa... Some of these people wanted more than five men, because usually in a show band you'll need a trumpet player. For Julius, we had Lennie, we got Lennie Johnson to play the trumpet. When LaRosa came in, he had his own piano player, and he asked us to play a couple of charts, to get a feel for the band. He asked who we had on trumpet, and I said Lennie Johnson. And he just

said, "Oh man, we don't have to run through it, don't worry about it." That was all he needed to know.[17]

Lennie Johnson was the one man in this story who worked with every significant Boston band and band leader in the late 1940s and 1950s, and with Basie and Quincy Jones besides, yet until he began teaching at Berklee in 1968, he worked a day job as a hospital attendant to make ends meet. Pomeroy called him the heart and soul of the band, and if anyone qualifies as an unsung hero in this Boston jazz story, it is Lennie Johnson, who died of cancer at age 49 in 1973.

Standards, "Saints," and Singers

There are countless good stories about the Stable, and here are three. One of the better ones is the genesis of the Benny Golson standard, "Stablemates." Recalled Herb Pomeroy:

> Joe Gordon worked with Benny in 1953, with Tadd Dameron at the Club Harlem in Atlantic City. Joe came back to Boston and told us about Benny: "this guy writes great jazz tunes and we should get him to do something for the band."

> Benny came through town with Earl Bostic, and they dropped by the Jazz Workshop, and we told Benny that we'd love to have him write something for the sextet. And he said OK, but he was going to be gone with Bostic and he'd have something when he came back. And he came back with five original tunes, fully arranged, and they were complex arrangements. And he had copied the parts himself!

> Varty was handling the business, and he asks Benny how much we owed him. And he said $50 for all five! Remember, these were not slapdash, simple pieces—they were elaborately arranged. And they were great tunes: "Park Avenue Petite," "Hassan's Dream," "City Lights," "411 West," and "Stablemates." He wrote that one for Varty and Ray and me. Miles Davis recorded it, and that's when it became a standard.[18]

Musicians on the road always fell by the Stable when they hit town, especially those featured at Storyville, who would cross Huntington Avenue on breaks to hear the Stable groups. The scene was lively, and the Stable remained a room where everybody wanted to sit in, and even singers like Tony Bennett and Frank D'Rone took a turn on the bandstand with bands that did not have singers of their own. Elsa Hart remembered one guest vocalist in particular:

> Varty was not crazy about vocalists. He said they got all the credit while the guys in the band doing all the work got none. One night a guy Varty knew from New York came in, and he had a singer with him, and wanted to know

Stablemates: Herb Pomeroy, Varty Haroutunian, Ray Santisi, Alan Dawson ca. 1960. Courtesy of Elsa Hart.

if she could sing with the band. Varty put him off, but he came back another night and asked if she could sing. Varty said maybe later. When it was getting late, the guy said, "is it gonna kill you to let her sing?" So Varty finally said OK. She started to sing with the rhythm section, and everybody was just amazed. It was Barbra Streisand.[19]

The Stable was across the street from Storyville, and there was a bit of a friendly rivalry between the two. Dan Morgenstern, who had a long career in jazz journalism before becoming director of the Institute of Jazz Studies at Rutgers University, was then a student at Brandeis, and a regular at both clubs:

The Stable, that's where we used to go to listen to Herb's band and Varty's band. Those were fine bands, with Joe Gordon, and Jaki Byard playing tenor on "Aluminum Baby" and his other tunes. And one night here's George Wein, he came in from across the street to see what was going on, and Varty gave him a little tongue-in-cheek introduction. George always liked to play, and he sat in with Varty's band, and Varty called "Saints." Now, that's a tune that they never played at the Stable, but they did it to poke a little fun at old traditional George. And George played a hell of a solo filled with bop licks, so he poked a little fun right back.[19]

The End of a Club, a Band, and a Place in Time

The Jazz Workshop, Herb's band, Varty's band...It couldn't last, and 1959 was the turning point on several fronts. First, the musical climate was changing as the 1950s drew to a close. Folk music, R&B, and rock and roll were claiming larger shares of the audience. Second, the entertainment landscape of Huntington Avenue had changed. By 1959, the neighborhood had grown quiet. The 5 O'Clock closed in 1958, Mahogany Hall became the Ballad Room and switched to folk music in 1959, and Storyville moved to the Theatre District in 1960. The healthy competition among the clubs was gone, and fewer people were drawn to Copley Square as there was less to do there. And the Stable was a familiar nighttime destination—it was no longer *the* place to go, as it had been. Third, there were simply fewer people, as an important slice of the demographic, young working adults, were moving to the suburbs. Finally, there were multiple personnel changes at the Stable, and that changed the dynamic of the music itself.

Boots Mussulli departed in 1958, replaced by Bob Freedman, as did Joe Gordon, who left suddenly for California, and Jaki Byard, who left in search of a new musical direction. In 1959 Gene Cherico replaced John Neves, Augie Ferretti and Bill Berry went with Maynard Ferguson, Lennie Johnson went with Quincy Jones, and Joe Ciavardone went with Woody Herman, as did Berry's replacement, Paul Fontaine. Freedman left, replaced briefly by Charlie Mariano, in turn replaced by Dick Johnson...and so it went.

Nonetheless, the Jazz Workshop crew carried on, despite the fragmenting scene and frequent personnel changes. Haroutunian's small group became a quintet on some nights and an octet on others. Pomeroy reorganized and downsized his band in 1960. New stars emerged, like alto saxophonist Dick Johnson and tenor saxophonist Sam Rivers. "Sam," said Pomeroy, "was the excitement factor."

Rivers, who a decade before had played with Jimmie Martin, returned to Boston in 1958 and was music director at Louie's Lounge. The following year he started the quartet that he would anchor for the next four years:

> I had the quartet with Hal Galper in 1959, with Hal and Tony Williams, Henry Grimes on bass. Tony was all of 15 at the time. We played in Cambridge, Harvard Square, at the Club 47. A little coffeehouse. We had John Neves on bass sometimes. In summer we used to work on Cape Cod, and up in New Hampshire.[21]

In November 1960, Rivers replaced Jimmy Mosher in Pomeroy's orchestra:

> Very exciting, his big band. I was glad to be there. He had great writers with that band, Jaki Byard, Chris Swanson. Mike Gibbs. I wasn't doing anything

as a writer then, so I didn't bring my music in there. I had the Monday quintet at the Stable with the trombone player, Gene DiStasio, as well as playing in the big band.[22]

John McLellan in December 1960 called Rivers a jazzman worth listening to:

As soon as he starts to blow, you're aware of two things. One is the big, fat sound he gets. That's rare enough these days. The other is the facility he has on his horn. The ideas seem to flow out smoothly and easily. But, of course, there has to be more. After all, there are plenty of fly cats with big sounds— and empty heads. What I especially like about this man is the way he builds his solos. Sometimes it's a short phrase, repeated and lengthened, and finally built to a climax and resolved. And the ideas sound to me like his own, too."[23]

In 1964, Rivers went on the road with bluesman T-Bone Walker, and then at the urging of Tony Williams, joined Miles Davis. He eventually moved to New York in the mid-1960s and became a major force in the avant-garde movement. Dick Johnson sat next to Rivers for two years in the Pomeroy sax section, and drew nightly inspiration from him:

I was in awe playing beside him, he was far ahead of all his peers. He was an 'out' player, but not like most out players—he could play 'in' so well. And he was a really nice guy. One of my best memories is of sitting beside him at the Stable, and he played a cadenza on the end of a tune, like a flamenco guitar, on his tenor. I just flipped, I'd never heard anything like that in my life, and he was laughing... I could not do what Sam did, he was one of my favorites, and just so far ahead.

When I was just starting to play, we used to go down to this joint off Mass Ave where Sam was playing, Louie's, and we couldn't get in, we were too young to drink, so we'd just stick our heads in the door to listen. He was playing all these bop tunes... and then he'd just reach out and go beyond. Even then he was his own man. He always went his own way.[24]

Even a stellar soloist and section man like Rivers couldn't bring the crowds back to Copley Square. Given the weakness of the Copley Square scene, club owner Harold Buchhalter contemplated closing down, but the musicians convinced him to turn the place over to them, and for a time the Stablemates found themselves in the bar business. Like managers of small businesses everywhere, they found ways to lower expenses. They cut back to six nights a week, closing on Sundays. Santisi took over the intermission piano chores, Haroutunian tended bar, and Pomeroy restocked the cooler. Then the word came from the Commonwealth of Massachusetts that the building was to be torn down to make way for an on-ramp for the Massachusetts Turnpike Extension. There were many in the Back Bay community for whom this was not welcome news, and civic groups like the Defend Copley Square Committee fought the transportation plan, but it was a done deal.

Other musical opportunities were beckoning as well. Pomeroy spent an extended period teaching in Asia in 1962. Santisi got involved with the annual Stan Kenton summer band camps in 1960, and in 1962 he joined Buddy DeFranco's band for a European tour. John Neves joined Byard in Maynard Ferguson's big band in 1961. Lennie Johnson went with Basie and Bill Berry with Ellington that year as well.

Buchhalter found a new space for his club, beneath the Inner Circle Restaurant on Boylston Street, and he closed the Stable in October 1962. In early 1963, Pomeroy broke up the band. Only Haroutunian and DiStasio remained from the days of the band's formation in 1955.

Where does Pomeroy's band fit into the overall picture of Boston jazz? Sabby Lewis led an "important" band in Boston. So did Nat Pierce, and Jimmie Martin. Herb Pomeroy, however, might have led the most important of them all because of everything it brought together.

As Pomeroy filled out the big band in late 1955, he assembled it from all the elements of modernism that had been percolating since the late 1940s. He picked up veterans of the Pierce band (Dave Chapman, Nick Capezuto), the Martin band (Jaki Byard and Lennie Johnson), and the progressive big bands of the day (Serge Chaloff and Everett Longstreth from Woody Herman; Boots Mussulli and Joe Ciavardone from Stan Kenton). These blended with the *Jazz in a Stable* quintet, all of whom were part of the Hi-Hat and Melody Lounge bop scene. The final ingredient was the best trumpet player in Boston, Joe Gordon, a veteran of the Martin band, the club scene, and Art Blakey's hard bop band as well. The Pomeroy band was the finest modern band to emerge in Boston.

The Pomeroy Orchestra was also unique because of its local roots. Pomeroy was from Gloucester, Santisi from Jamaica Plain, Haroutunian from Everett, Neves from East Boston, Gordon and Lennie Johnson from Roxbury, Capezuto from Hingham, Ciavardone from Waltham, DiStasio from Revere, Chaloff from Newton, Mussulli from Milford, Byard from Worcester. Many of the later players were also locals: Alan Dawson, Charlie Mariano, and Bill Chase (Chiaiese) from Boston, Joe Caruso from Everett, Jimmy Derba from Chelsea, Hal Galper from Salem, Dick Johnson from Brockton, Jackie Stevens from Worcester, Jimmy Mosher and Paul Fontaine from Lynn, Dan Nolan from Lawrence.

It was, well and truly, a band in Boston. "I can't help feeling that just as we are proud of and help support the Boston Symphony, so we should be equally proud of and support the Herb Pomeroy Orchestra," wrote McLellan at the time the *Splendored Gig* album was released.[25]

The Stablemates had been together musically since the early 1950s, but that changed when Buchhalter opened the new Jazz Workshop in September of 1963. Haroutunian set aside his tenor and became the new club's full-time manager. Pomeroy and Santisi, meanwhile, chose instead to concentrate on teaching and performing. When Stan Getz inaugurated the new Jazz Workshop, they were both in the band (as was John Neves), and Haroutunian was counting the house.

Pomeroy and Santisi were core faculty at Berklee and regulars at clubs like Connolly's and Lennie's-on-the-Turnpike, as well as the Workshop, in the 1960s. Both were still deeply involved in the Boston jazz scene as the new century dawned. Haroutunian left the Jazz Workshop shortly after Harold Buchhalter sold it. He opened Varty's Jazz Room in the Hotel Bradford in 1966, but it was not successful; he left the music business after his club closed. Pomeroy and Haroutunian died within a month of each other in 2007.

The Stable's closing went unreported in the Boston papers. October 1962, after all, was a big month for news—President Kennedy's October 22 announcement that the Soviet Union was building secret missile bases in Cuba touched off some of the most anxious days of the cold war. That month astronaut Wally Schirra orbited the earth six times in his Mercury capsule, John Steinbeck was awarded the Nobel Prize for Literature, and Johnny Carson replaced Jack Paar as host of NBC's *Tonight Show*. The New York Yankees triumphed over the San Francisco Giants in a dramatic World Series that went to seven games. Given everything else happening in the world, the closing of a small jazz club in the basement of a doomed building probably didn't strike the city's news editors as much of a story. In retrospect, though, one wishes they had taken notice, because the passing of the Stable marked the end of a jazz era. When the Stablemates blew their last notes in that cellar bar, the swing-to-modern years, Boston's Southland-to-Storyville years, were over and done. Boston hasn't seen the likes of them since.

Chapter 16

Dynamo

There was simply no keeping up with George Wein during his dozen years of activity in Boston. The man was tireless. Name something that needed to be done between 1948 and 1960, and Wein did it: pianist, club owner, artists' manager, concert promoter, newspaper columnist, disc jockey, talent scout, television producer, university instructor, festival organizer, record company executive. His work defined how jazz is presented, indoors and out, to this day. He was more than an entrepreneur; he was a ground-breaker and a trendsetter and later he was acknowledged as *the* impresario of American jazz. Lovers of music owe him much and Boston is proud to claim him as a native son.

Describing all this activity would itself take a whole book, and fortunately Wein has already written *Myself Among Others: A Life in Music*. He's also been the subject of countless articles and interviews. There are, however, a few more nuggets particular to Boston that we can add here.

George Wein was a dynamo in the 1950s, accomplishing one achievement per year throughout the decade. In 1950, at the age of 25, Wein opened Storyville. In 1951, Wein opened his first "summer Storyville" in Gloucester. In 1952, he opened his second club, Mahogany Hall. In 1953, Wein formed his record company, Storyville Records. In 1954 he introduced Jazz Night at the Boston Arts Festival. This was the same year he founded the Newport Jazz Festival. Wein began teaching jazz history at Boston University in 1955. He began writing his column, "The Jazz Beat," for the *Boston Herald* in 1956. He started his jazz show on radio station WVDA in 1957. The *Storyville Show*, on television station WBZ, debuted in 1958, as did the summer jazz series at Castle Hill in Ipswich. Finally, Wein staged the first Boston Jazz Festival at Fenway Park in 1959.

Nothing like that has happened in Boston since. Nothing like that has happened *anywhere* since. Some of these ventures were successful, some were not, but what impresses is the sheer number of ways Wein found to put the music in front of an audience, and his willingness to take risks to do so.

George Wein, born in 1925 and raised in suburban Newton, first set out to be a piano player. He started in the war years, while still in his teens, hitting the jam sessions and playing on the buckets of blood circuit, in places like Izzy

Ort's and the Silver Dollar Bar. He studied with the fabled Madame Chaloff and the New England Conservatory's Sam Saxe. He got to know his musical mentor, trumpeter Frankie Newton. Everything was put on hold, though, when he was drafted into the army.

After his discharge in 1946, Wein returned to a different jazz landscape. He wanted to play swing music at a time when other prominent young piano players, such as Jaki Byard and Nat Pierce, were exploring the emerging sounds of bebop. In the late 1940s, Wein was among the many players pushed into something labeled "Dixieland," for better or worse. One of the strange side effects of the jazz wars of the 1940s was that for a time anyone playing any pre-bop jazz style was assigned to the category of Dixieland. However inaccurate the label, many of the musicians so branded could swing like mad and still play the melody, and Wein cast his lot with them.

In 1948–1949 Wein worked with Pee Wee Russell, Max Kaminsky, and numerous local men at the Ken Club and the Savoy. These included bassist John Field of the Vinal Rhythm Kings, cornetist Ruby Braff, Vic Dickenson, and big band trombonist Dick LeFave. These names—Braff, Dickenson, Field, Kaminsky, LeFave, Russell—became the foundation of Wein's first years at Storyville, and Braff, Dickenson, and Russell were regulars until Storyville folded. All three traveled in Wein's touring group, the Newport All-Stars, for years after that. There were others with their roots in swing and Wein hired them all often, including Doc Cheatham, Buck Clayton, Buzzy Drootin, and Bobby Hackett.

Wein had his first taste of promotion in 1949, staging a sold-out Edmond Hall concert at Jordan Hall. He started his first club that year, in the Hotel Fensgate, a short-lived venture called *Le Jazz Doux*, "The Soft Jazz," featuring his own trio with trumpeter Frankie Newton and bassist Joe Palermino. Then came Storyville.

Storyville: Boston Nightlife's Brightest Star

There is no denying the importance of the Storyville nightclub to the Boston jazz story. It had three things going for it. First was the indefatigable Wein. Second, Storyville set the standard as to how a club should be run and how jazz should be presented. Third, Storyville was a showcase for the best in jazz in the 1950s, a magnet that attracted the music's top talent to Boston. Storyville is the story of the right person in the right place at the right time. Did this guarantee the club's success? It did not. Wein himself claimed operating Storyville left him in a "constant purgatorial state of debt," and he closed for financial reasons, not artistic ones.[1]

Storyville made a solid start on October 25, 1950. Wrote George Clarke a few days before, in the first of many mentions of Wein in Clarke's column:

> There is the imminent opening of a new jazz spot in the basement of the Copley Square Hotel in what used to be the Backstage Room. It's to be called "Storyville" after the famous New Orleans red light district from which, many believe, came the first Dixieland jazz. The room will have a New Orleans decor and is being opened by George Wein, a pianist, who graduated from B.U. last year. It will also feature a rotating exhibit of the paintings of contemporary artists.[2]

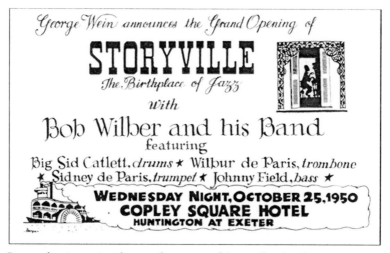

Postcard announcing the grand opening of Storyville, October 25, 1950. Courtesy of Nick Puopulo.

For the record, the band on opening night was that of soprano saxophonist Bob Wilber, the star of the Savoy. It included trombonist Wilbur DeParis, pianist Red Richards, bassist John Field, drummer Big Sid Catlett, and Ruby Braff filling in on trumpet for Sidney DeParis, who was unable to make it to Boston for opening night. Braff and Dick LeFave replaced the DeParis brothers after three weeks, about the time that Louis Armstrong and his band, who were performing at Symphony Hall, created a local splash by dropping in to enliven the festivities.

By the second week in December Storyville was closed. Clarke wrote:

> It is apparently an extremely prosperous enterprise, but profitable or not, Storyville, one of the most successful of the recent crop of jazz spots, is leaving its basement quarters in the Copley Square hotel in most precipitous fashion.

Its departure is so hurried and so unexpected, as a matter of fact, that the evacuation may have been completed by the time you read this. Reasons for the departure are not wholly explained by entrepreneur George Wein, the pianist, who almost built an idea into an institution, but seem to stem from a lack of understanding between the young impresario—after all, he's only a year out of Boston University—and Bill Leonardi, the hotel's owner. There was some kind of a sharing agreement between them which apparently didn't work out successfully.

At any rate, George is taking his idea elsewhere—he thoughtfully registered the name with the Secretary of State—and if not already in action at another place by now, probably will be soon. The Bostonian and the Buckminster hotels were both mentioned as possible havens.[3]

The success of Storyville led to the mushrooming of jazz places all over town—there are seven such now in action and more are said to be planned.

Wein reopened in early February 1951 at the Buckminster, but what to make of that final sentence? Did Storyville lead to a mushrooming or was it just another mushroom? Wein was good, but not good enough to refashion the city's nightlife. If anyone could have moved the jazz community like that, it would have been the Savoy's Steve Connolly. Regardless of how elastic you make the definition of "jazz club," it is hard to make the count reach seven in December 1950, but it was nice of Clarke to note the increase in activity.

Storyville at the Buckminster opened February 8, 1951, again featuring the popular Bob Wilber. Wein's first season featured a great deal of Dixieland. In fact, except for a late-season engagement by the Johnny Hodges All-Stars, the music was all Dixieland. Wein was competing with the Savoy and Steve Connolly's new club, Jazz at 76. It wasn't until the start of his second season in September 1951 that he worked out the formula that made Storyville iconic. That September Wein opened his season with George Shearing, then one of the most popular figures in jazz, for ten sold-out nights.

Wein figured he was in the money. He was wrong. Almost nobody had Shearing's drawing power, and Wein lost money on many of the acts he presented that season. But it was the season where he learned the formula of mixing the old-school players like Wild Bill Davison and Sidney Bechet, new-school modernists like Dave Brubeck and Lee Konitz, and singers such as Ella Fitzgerald, who worked the borderline between jazz and pop. In 1952–1953, there was only one traditional group scheduled, Louis Armstrong—sandwiched between Dinah Washington and Erroll Garner. That season also brought Charlie Parker, Bud Powell, and Lennie Tristano.

In 1951 Wein hired Charlie Bourgeois as publicist, and over time Charlie became trusted advisor, troubleshooter, and all-around right-hand man.

Postcard advertising a Sunday jam session at Storyville with Frankie Newton, March 18, 1951.

Bourgeois was no stranger to jazz promotion when he joined Wein. He had organized the jazz concert at the Boston Jubilee in 1950, staged a Lennie Tristano concert at the John Hancock Hall the same year, and arranged record dates for Nat Pierce and Marion McPartland. His expertise proved invaluable to the new club owner, and perhaps Bourgeois introduced Wein to some of the new sounds that were soon heard regularly at Storyville.

It doesn't hurt to mention a few of the high points of Wein's two-and-a-half seasons at the Buckminster: four appearances each by Dave Brubeck, Erroll Garner, and Lee Wiley; three appearances each by Ella Fitzgerald and Josh White; two appearances by Sidney Bechet, Billie Holiday, Pee Wee Russell, George Shearing, Art Tatum, and Sarah Vaughan; employment for many local musicians including Braff, Field, LeFave, Marquis Foster, Alice Ross Groves, the Jones Brothers, Herb Pomeroy, Pat Rainey, Al Vega, and Jimmy Woode; Wein's own house trio with the marvelous Jo Jones on drums; a night of Leonard Bernstein doing his best to play the blues with Pee Wee Russell; live broadcasts over WMEX and WHDH; and what must have been the most unusual week in Storyville history, in April 1952, when John Carradine recited Shakespeare, Johnny Windhurst played Dixieland, and Sam Gary sang folk songs.

Where did all the players of traditional and Dixieland jazz go if they were cleared off the calendar in 1952? They went to Wein's second club, Mahogany Hall, which he opened in the basement at his once and future home, the Copley Square Hotel, in September 1952. Wein loved this music and he wanted a place for it. That story is recounted in Mahogany Hall: Dedicated to

Dixieland, page 111. This action cleared the way for Wein to realize his goal of presenting the best of jazz at Storyville, regardless of style

In 1953 the Saunders family bought the Copley Square Hotel. They were friends of jazz, having bought the Broadway Hotel in 1939 and given the Ken Club a home there. Storyville returned to Copley Square in September 1953, George Shearing opening, and remained for seven seasons. After altering the room's configuration, Storyville's seating capacity was about 360.

Storyville was a nice place in a nice location. Jazz clubs still had a seedy reputation, and to counter that impression Wein ran the place strictly on the up-and-up. The lighting and décor were tasteful and the sound system was good. Men wore jackets, ties were optional. There were no photographers or cigarette girls, staples of the big nightclubs of the previous decade. And though the idea of Wein's bartenders working with B-girls was ludicrous, they were a problem in the city and Wein allowed no margin for error. Unescorted women were not allowed at the bar.

Storyville was trendsetting in its approach to the music, the musicians who made it, and the people who listened to it. Nat Hentoff in 1953 noted:

> From its very beginning, Storyville made it discreetly clear that it considered its attractions artists who deserved as much consideration as artists in any other medium. Once in a while, the manager of the room would point this out in a whisper to a garrulous customer, but in time even that was rarely necessary. It just became understood that you went to Storyville to listen…Compared to the other clubs in town, listening to a jazz musician at Storyville is like sitting at home with a pair of earphones…By contrast, in another club recently, I saw Billie Holiday singing to a crowded, noisy room…for those who hadn't look up for a while, there was little indication that anyone was singing at all.[4]

Hentoff was referring to the Hi-Hat, where Holiday performed that May.

Wein himself took on the role of jazz spokesman and good citizen. His club hosted benefits for organizations like the NAACP and the Damon Runyon Cancer Fund, and he gave Storyville (and sometimes its performers) over to the Teenage Jazz Club for their monthly meetings. He was a first-call participant for panel discussions or speaking engagements. It was all part of building the brand, and it reached the point in Boston and elsewhere that ticket buyers knew a concert advertised under the banner "George Wein Presents" would be worthwhile.

Wein advertised relentlessly, and in this he took a page from Charlie Shribman's playbook of previous decades. Wein bought radio time on the AM stations, first on WMEX, then WVDA, and finally on WHDH. He advertised in all the daily newspapers and in some of the college papers.

Often—quite often—Wein couldn't fill his 360 seats, but he filled more of them by booking singers. The Latin Quarter was doing the same thing, and the clubs booked some of the same acts (Armstrong, Holiday, Nat Cole, Buddy Greco). He also featured double bills, pairing a singer with a jazz group that couldn't carry the room alone, for instance Chris Connor with J. J. Johnson, Carmen McRae with Sonny Stitt, or Teddi King with Don Elliott.

George Wein at Storyville, 1956. *Boston Traveler* photo, courtesy of the Boston Public Library, Print Department.

The double bills were always interesting: singers with singers (Lambert, Hendricks and Ross with Jimmy Rushing), old comrades-in-arms (Anita O'Day and Roy Eldridge), established stars with new talents (Miles Davis and the Australian Jazz Quintet), like minds (Max Roach and Sonny Stitt), unlike minds (Jeri Southern and Charles Mingus) and even husband and wife (Marion McPartland's Trio and Jimmy McPartland's Sextet). Sometimes half a double bill was given over to a comedian judged to be on the same wavelength as the Storyville jazz audience, such as Harvard mathematician-turned-satirist Tom Lehrer, and "America's only working philosopher," Mort Sahl. Groups worked it out between themselves as far as the schedule and sitting in were concerned.

Although Storyville was a name-band place, Wein provided plenty of work for Boston musicians in house bands, as intermission pianists, and backing the artists who worked as singles. Rollins Griffith, Nick Jerret, and Joey Masters led house trios. Jay Migliori led the house band for seven months in 1955–1956, and for much of that time it included Serge Chaloff. Pianist Toshiko Akiyoshi, still a student at Berklee, led a quartet in 1956 featuring Boots Mussulli, and a trio after that with fellow student Gene Cherico and Jake Hanna. Lou Carter, Rollins Griffith, Dizzy Sal, Ernie Trotman, and Al Vega were intermission pianists with lengthy tenures. Sabby Lewis worked a bit as an intermission pianist. Ruby Braff (six times) and Teddi King (five times) were among the Bostonians who were headliners in their own right.

Wein was a believer in sure things. With rent to pay and payroll to meet, he had to be. It made the schedule look repetitive from year to year, especially in the late fifties, but audiences wanted to hear the same music from year to year, and they turned out for the crowd-pleasers. Erroll Garner was by far Wein's most popular attraction, appearing 14 times. Sarah Vaughan and nightclub bluesman Josh White each appeared 11 times, Gerry Mulligan and George Shearing nine, the Ellington Orchestra seven. Wein took some criticism for this repetition, but his audience grew less adventurous over time and he had seats to fill.

Storyville was hurt in the end by the changing nature of the jazz business; its best attractions wanted to go to the biggest rooms to achieve the biggest paydays. All these artists could fill a concert hall, which made nightclubs less appealing, and old standbys Garner, Mulligan, and Shearing skipped Storyville in Wein's last season. Wein also had to contend with Blinstrub's, the barn-like South Boston club with seating for about 1,100 in 1960. Crossover stars Louis Armstrong and Sarah Vaughan chose to play that room in Storyville's last season instead.

The final year was a struggle for other reasons as well. The jazz wave had crested locally and Copley Square wasn't as prosperous as it had been a few years before. Mahogany Hall, which had been open only sporadically since 1956, was replaced in 1959 by the Ballad Room, a folk music club. Folk music was featured upstairs, too. Twice the schedule fell back on quickly assembled configurations of "the Storyville All-Stars," bands basically organized around Pee Wee Russell. The whole operation shut down for five weeks in the spring of 1960 because, as John McLellan sardonically observed, "too many people gave up jazz for Lent."[5] Dinah Washington played the final set in May 1960.

During the spring shutdown, Wein sent a letter to friends and supporters shortly before reopening to finish the season. John McLellan excerpted parts of that letter in his April 14 *Traveler* column:

If Storyville is successful, or even moderately successful, in this six-week period, then we will go ahead with some plans for the fall. If business is as dismal as it has been all winter, then I don't know what the future of Storyville will be... Frankly, I will keep it open if it only loses a little money. I'm willing to subsidize it up to a point, but there is just so much I can do.[6]

It was typical for Storyville to close in late May and adjourn to the seaside, first to Gloucester and later Harwich on Cape Cod. Around Labor Day Wein would reopen the Boston room. That pattern continued until 1960. But when Storyville reopened that September, it was under new ownership and in a new location. Wein was out of the club and in New York, concentrating on his latest venture, Production and Management Associates (PAMA).

Wein may have been out of Storyville, but he and the club had made their mark. Said Wein in 1966:

The thing about Storyville, is that it was one of the very few jazz clubs in the country to give the musicians a fair shake. Before Storyville, there were mostly joints. We tried to do right by the musicians as well as the music— little things, like having the piano in tune and having good acoustics. We set some decent standards in what was then a pretty crummy business, and we also booked a lot of good talent, which nearly ruined me."[7]

Wein mentioned setting standards, but there was something else that went further—the respect shown to both performer and patron. Wein always maintained that jazz was a true American art form, and in his club it was treated with the respect due an art form. That's why Storyville was Boston's brightest star.

Miss Teddi King

Storyville is an apt place to talk about Teddi King, because she recorded her best jazz work for the Storyville label, and when she was in the regular club rotation in the mid-1950s, George Wein was her manager.

To start with, there were two Teddi Kings. There was Teddi King the jazz singer, who sang with Nat Pierce and George Shearing, made splendid recordings on the Storyville label, and was named Female Singer of the Year in *Metronome's* 1956 Yearbook. That Teddi was "the most gifted vocalist this city ever produced."[10] Then there was Teddi King the pop singer, who worked the high-end show-biz circuit at Mr. Kelly's in Chicago and the Fontainebleau in Miami, and made a series of recordings for RCA-Victor backed by full orchestras and strings. That Teddi King was the biggest pop star to come out of Boston since Vaughn Monroe.

Theodora King was born in 1929 in the North Shore city of Revere, and even before she was out of high school she was creating a name for herself, winning a Dinah Shore sing-alike contest at the RKO Boston Theatre in 1945. Then she started singing with dance bands—George Graham, Jack Edwards, George Jones, Ray Dorey. With Nat Pierce in 1949, she found something better.

Teddi King in the mid-1950s. *Boston Traveler* photo, courtesy of the Boston Public Library, Print Department.

King wasn't Pierce's only vocalist, but she's the only one to record with the Pierce band. The first was "Goodbye Mr. Chops," from spring 1949, a number she never liked. Better were songs from the Great American Songbook, like "You Don't Know What Love Is," and two from the team of Burke and Van Heusen, "You May Not Love Me" and "Oh, You Crazy Moon." She was singer-as-storyteller, with perfect diction and pure tone. George Shearing heard her, and hired her to sing with his quintet in 1952, the only singer he used with that group.

Back in Boston in 1954, she made three records for Storyville, the second of which was *Miss Teddi King*, on which she was backed by a Ruby Braff-led quartet. It attracted attention; in January 1955 *Metronome* made the unusual decision to review it in both the jazz and pop categories. Jazz reviewer Barry Ulanov called King a major vocal talent and said the album was one that "admirers of jazz singing of quality should not miss." He gave it a B+, while George Simon, the pop reviewer, gave it an A–: "Here is one of the best vocal LPs to come along in ages. Teddi King emerges here as a truly topnotch gal singer who phrases wonderfully, has great rhythmic sense, a sensuous and musical timbre and just about all the attributes required of a great vocalist."[11] She also made four sides for MGM, including the Mildred Bailey standard, "I'll Never Be the Same," which were subsequently licensed to Decca and released on the Coral label.

Teddi King the pop singer made three LPs and a slew of singles for RCA, and one LP for Coral. She was caught up in major label politics and spent more time than she liked on the purely commercial. It discouraged her, and it dismayed critics like Hentoff and McLellan, who thought it damaged her jazz career. Yet her stage presence was nonpareil and her performances were electric. McLellan, reviewing a December 1957 performance wrote: "Teddi King in person is something else. An alternately charming, wistful, tender and dynamic show stopper. This is the show biz Teddi King."[12] She might not have been singing jazz that night, but she put on a first-class show.

A disillusioned King walked away from the recording industry in 1959, not recording again until 1973. She spent the 1960s on tour, and even after rock and roll washed away most of the singers like King, she stayed on the road, working exclusively for the Playboy Corporation.

In 1970 she contracted lupus. The disease weakened her immune system, and led to her death in November 1977.

Storyville Records

The nightclub was George Wein's primary business, but there were others. Wein partnered with record distributor Cecil Steen to form Storyville Records in October 1953. Just as the Storyville club presented the best in jazz regardless of genre, so did the Storyville label. Their first recording was of Sidney Bechet, a no-frills session recorded at the Storyville club on a Sunday afternoon. The albums that followed came from the modern end of jazz (Lee Konitz, Bob Brookmeyer), the traditional (Pee Wee Russell, Wild Bill Davison), the mainstream players in between (Joe Newman, Mary Lou Williams), and singers (Teddi King, Jackie & Roy, and Lee Wiley). One of Wiley's releases caused a minor stir.

George Frazier wrote the liner notes for *Lee Wiley Sings Rogers and Hart*. These were not your normal liner notes; they were vintage Frazier, personal and provocative. *Record* columnist George Clarke labeled them "Rabelaisian." Others called them tasteless. Bill Coss in *Metronome* was especially annoyed, calling the notes "gilded outrages," "delivered in a Madison Avenue, check-this-virile-guy manner, more rightly expected from anxious teenagers than from a mature man." In the very first sentence Frazier called Wiley "one bitch of a singer," a phrase she insisted be removed, and he went on to discuss her sophistication and her ability to sing with devastating sex appeal. The notes got more reaction than the music.[8]

Boston jazz musicians did well by Storyville Records. Some made records of their own, notably Toshiko Akiyoshi (*The Toshiko Trio; Toshiko, Her Trio, Her Quartet*), Serge Chaloff (*Serge Chaloff and Boots Mussulli; The Fable of Mabel*), and Teddi King (*Miss Teddi King; Now in Vogue*). Among the group that was close to Wein and later formed the nucleus of the Newport All-Stars, Ruby Braff (*Storyville Presents Ruby Braff*, later reissued as *Hustlin' and Bustlin'*), Vic

Dickenson (*Vic's Boston Story*) and Pee Wee Russell (*We're in the Money*) released records on the Storyville label. And Wein hired the better local men as session players. Braff and Dickenson were regulars in the studio groups, as were Jimmy Woode and Buzzy Drootin, often in a rhythm section with Wein himself. Jo Jones was on so many Storyville sessions he might as well be considered the house drummer.

Like the Storyville club, the Storyville label was a success artistically but a financial struggle from day one. Wein and Steen sold the company in 1955. Included in the sale were the rights to the recordings, something that in hindsight Wein came to regret. At that point, though, it was time to cut losses and move on.[9]

"The World Series of Jazz"

Wein first met Louis and Elaine Lorillard, of Newport, Rhode Island in late 1953. They wanted to do something involving jazz to enliven the Newport summer scene, and they wanted Wein to produce it. He agreed. The Lorillards provided the local connections and $20,000, and gave the final go-ahead in April 1954. The First Annual American Jazz Festival at Newport was set for the weekend of July 17–18, 1954.

Wein the entrepreneur saw an opportunity to use the format of the outdoor classical music festival at Tanglewood to present jazz. He counted three factors in his favor. One, in those pre air-conditioned days, city clubs (including Storyville) shut down as the audience retreated to the shore. Jazz could be heard seaside every summer from Maine down to Cape Cod, and fans might be willing to travel to Rhode Island for a good event. Two, there were fewer jobs for musicians in the summer. Not only were the clubs on hiatus, but many of the summer dance halls and pavilions, big employers of years past, were closed permanently. Third, this wasn't a carnival like Revere Beach, this was Newport, the summer retreat of American high society, and an event here would assume an immediate touch of class. The conclusion? People could be lured to Newport to hear music, musicians could be lured there to play it, and the Lorillards could be the founding patrons of the major event of the season.

He was right on all counts. Eleven thousand fans attended the two-day event staged on the lawn of the venerable Newport Casino. It rained, and for Wein the enduring images of that festival were the wire service photos showing the canopy of open umbrellas held by die-hard jazz fans spreading out from the stage. The musicians, too, came to life in the photos taken over the weekend. Newport introduced the media to the photographers' pit, occupying its prime location in front of the stage.

And there was music, far too much to note here, but Wein stayed true to his idea of presenting all styles of jazz, and this Newport introduced the programming staples that have marked the festival ever since. There were unpredictable musical pairings, long-overdue reunions, and no-holds-barred jam sessions. One session included Eddie Condon and Stan Kenton in the same rhythm section. Who could have imagined that?

It wasn't all perfect ("We had some trouble at Newport in 1954 when blacks couldn't find rooms, but that was taken care of by 1955."[13]) but it was widely declared a success. In just a few years Wein's own promotional copy would be hailing Newport as "the World Series of jazz."

Great press and iconic status are fine, but the festival made a profit of $142.50, and it only did so because Wein declined his salary as promoter and manager. Although he missed his payday in 1954, in the end he made out all right on the festival scene, and summers have never been the same.[14]

Incidentally, Newport wasn't the only outdoor event being planned by the Wein machine in 1954. Also in the works was the first Jazz Night at the Boston Festival of the Arts, a June night of joyous employment for a dozen Boston jazz men, with one band led by Braff and Dickenson, the other by Chaloff and Charlie Mariano. That story is told in Chapter 19, as are those of Wein's other Boston festivals, the first Boston Jazz Festival in 1959 and the Jazz Festival at Pleasure Island in 1960.

Man in the Middle, Man in Motion

Although Wein came up playing swing and continued to play it on the bandstand at his own club, he had the unshakable conviction that for the club, the record label, and the festivals to succeed, the musical base had to be broad. So on Wein's watch Storyville hosted them all, from Sidney Bechet to Ornette Coleman, and Charlie Parker was supposed to be on stage at Storyville the night he died. Still, at times the public's reaction left him somewhat bemused. He lamented in *Jazz Today* that even though he presented and recorded many modern jazzmen, he was so closely identified with older styles that no one believed him when he said he liked contemporary music. And because he presented so much contemporary music, the old guard accused him of desertion.[15]

So Wein became the man in the middle, looking forward and backward, patrolling the no-man's-land between the traditional and modern camps in the jazz wars. He berated the young moderns for their smug disregard of the earlier masters, and berated the elders for closing their ears and minds to the innovations of the young Turks. It was Wein who put Thelonius Monk and Pee Wee Russell together at Newport when no one else would dream of it.

Wein called Storyville his learning tree, and it was while he was on the Boston scene that he began listening to all the voices in jazz regardless of style or genre. He used these Boston lessons to take the jazz scene to a whole new level and bring the music to countless new listeners.

For Wein, the closing of Storyville in May 1960 was a defining moment. His concert business was doing well, his Newport All-Stars were performing across America and Europe, he was using Newport as the springboard to form new festivals in other cities, and he had his first corporate partner, the Sheraton Hotels company, sponsoring jazz events at a major level—yet another first achieved during his Boston years. But he couldn't make a go of his nightclub, and when he closed it, he chose to move forward with his other enterprises from a base in New York. His first months there were a struggle; the 1960 Newport Jazz Festival was marred by beer-fueled riots and the chain reaction hurt the gate everywhere, including the second Boston Jazz Festival at Pleasure Island. He recovered from the events of that summer and never looked back.

Boston Red Sox fans talk endlessly about how much was lost when Babe Ruth was sold to the New York Yankees. When George Wein left Boston for New York, the Hub's jazz scene suffered a loss every bit as serious. Ruth's home run records were subsequently surpassed, and the Red Sox won world championships. But no one ever filled the hole in the line-up left by Wein's departure, and the Boston jazz scene never recovered its 1950s verve. The dynamo was gone.

Chapter 17

Stories from the Fifties

Most of the people and places at the center of the peak of Boston jazz in the mid-1950s—George Wein and Storyville, Byard and Mariano, the Hi-Hat, the Stablemates—are found in other chapters. Here we pick up a few more faces and places. There was Tom Wilson, student and entrepreneur, who founded Transition Records, and the Teenage Jazz Club, whose members undoubtedly listened to some of them. There was the Latin Quarter, the crossover capital of New England, and a whole gang of jazz musicians employed around the corner of Tremont and Stuart Streets. There were jazz sounds in the Back Bay's refined Darbury Room, and the Fenway's raucous Brown Derby. Finally, there's a visit to two clubs that featured modern jazz in late 1955. In fact, 1953 to 1956 were very busy years for Boston's musicians, and although there was much more to come, the peak might have been reached right about the time the crowd was singing "Auld Lange Syne" in the early hours of January 1, 1956.

At the Theatre District Crossroads

There was always an abundance of nightlife around the busy intersection of Tremont and Stuart Streets in the heart of the Theatre District, and at no time more so than in the 1950s. There were not only theaters and the businesses they spawned, but also innumerable clubs presenting live entertainment, and two hotels favored by the theatre crowd, the Bradford and the Broadway. There were no name-band rooms, but there was plenty of work at the Knickerbocker, the 1-2-3 Lounge, the Silhouette Lounge, the Frolic, Showtime, Stuart Manor, and others. "There must have been a hundred musicians working on Stuart Street," recalled Al Vega.[1]

"Do you want to know how many musicians were working then?" asked drummer Manny Wise, who led the band at the Frolic on Tremont Street:

> One night at the Frolic our piano player, Tony Parker, got sick during the first set, and he couldn't finish the night, he had to leave. There were so many clubs around with piano players…guys working in different clubs nearby came in and played a set, just to help out, get us through the evening. Bob Winter did a set, Al Vega did a set. There were so many working musicians around you could get away with something like that.[2]

The first stop is the Knickerbocker Cafe at 117 Stuart Street, the home base of Paul "Fat Man" Robinson, whose band worked the room for months at a time between 1950 and 1956.

Robinson was a high-energy alto saxophonist and vocalist whose combo played jump blues in the style of Louis Jordan's Tympany Five. His was a familiar band around the Theatre District, playing in the Petty Lounge, the Rio Casino, and the Silhouette Room as well as the Knickerbocker. Robinson worked just about everywhere else around town, too, and traveled as far south as Florida and as far north as Montreal. Robinson made his first record for Boston's Motif label in 1949, "Lavender Coffin," by the Cambridge-born songwriter Shirley Albert. Like Jordan, Robinson was a storyteller whose sets always included several humorous vocal numbers; he followed "Coffin" that same year with "Fill That Gap in Your Mouth with Teeth 'Cause Daddy's Tired of Kissing Gum," in which a frantic Fat Man pleads with his girl to invest in some false teeth. He later recorded for Regent and Decca.

Robinson's band was a well-rehearsed working unit whose membership included trumpeter Oscar Dunham, who had been a member of Sabby Lewis's first band in 1936, tenor saxophonists Sam Rivers and Andy McGhee, bassist Bill Tanner, and pianist and arranger Charlie Cox. For a time in 1952, trombonist J. C. Higginbotham worked with the band.

Robinson and his jump music set the pace in the 1950s in the Theatre District. Leroy Parkins recalled the scene:

> Soon after I came back to Boston in 1950, I moved into a seven night a week steady gig on Stuart Street, in downtown Boston. The Korean War was raging, the Boston Navy Yard was overflowing with sailors and marines, and it took a lot of clubs to keep them occupied. Sam Rivers was across the street from me with Fat Man Robinson, an obese, marvelous black R&B alto player/singer, who would chant periodically between tunes, "I'm as cool as a fool in a motor pool." Mostly blues and early rock tunes had to be numbingly boring for as gifted a man as Sam Rivers. He amused himself and the crowd by playing with his right hand behind his back, reaching around to grab the lower keys of his horn from behind. I spent as many set breaks there as I could digging him, night after night, until we both moved on to other gigs and he vanished for a spell.[3]

Parkins was wrong about Rivers being bored by the blues; Rivers later toured extensively with B. B. King and T-Bone Walker, and in the late 1950s was music director at Louie's Lounge, an R&B room in the South End.

Izzy Ort bought the Knickerbocker in late 1954 and changed the name to the Stage Bar, and over time the Stage got rather raunchy. Its license was

Fat Man Robinson and Band, ca. 1951. From left: Sam Rivers, Emmy Johnson, Fat Man Robinson, Bill Tanner, Charlie Cox. Courtesy of Dan Kochakian.

finally revoked in October 1961 following a police raid and the arrests of 14 men and women, all charged with lewd and lascivious behavior and staging indecent shows. A plainclothes policeman noted one B-girl (or "bar girl," a woman employed by the bar to be companionable and help customers spend money) hustled him for $45 in drinks plus bottles of champagne, and he was solicited for "immoral activities" on five consecutive visits. Even the U.S. Navy declared the place off-limits to its personnel.

Ada Bullock's at 243 Tremont Street was just a restaurant with a bar, but in 1950 it, too, jumped into jazz and named the room the Bar of Jazz, installing trombonist Dick LeFave and His Dixieland Band there. This seems like an unlikely working name for a LeFave group, given his association with the big bands of Sam Donahue, Benny Goodman and Artie Shaw. When Dixieland didn't work, the management renamed the spot the Silhouette Room, brought back LeFave, and presumably let him blow. For a few years the Silhouette Room featured bands like LeFave's, Sammy Lowe's, and Fat Man Robinson's.

If there were any name bands around the corner, they were at the Petty Lounge, at 233 Tremont Street, between 1949 and 1952. Red Allen, Roy Eldridge, Hot Lips Page, and Buddy Tate played during those years, but the Petty also featured local bands, including Clarence Jackson's Notes of

Rhythm, Fat Man Robinson, Jimmy Woode, and finally in February 1952, Serge Chaloff. Chaloff closed on February 17, and the next night the club said goodbye to its jazz policy by opening with "Hawaiian Holiday," where, the advertisements claimed, "every night is a tranquil delight." We can only imagine what a shock that was to any sailor who wandered in looking for Chaloff's bop band.

The 1-2-3 Lounge, at 123 Stuart Street between the Knickerbocker and the Plymouth Theater, was a clothing store until 1953, when Willie Oxman and Lee Fields opened the club there. They also owned the Saxony Lounge around the corner in Park Square, and both featured singers from all across the jazz-pop continuum with trios in support. There was a seemingly endless supply of singers working in Boston in the mid 1950s, some quite good and all now mostly forgotten, such as Jo Thompson, a cabaret singer from Detroit; Barbara Jai, a singer and actress who left Boston in the mid-fifties with drummer Max Roach; Terry Swope, who sang with Al Haig, and with Benny Goodman's short-lived bop band; Judy Tremaine, "the Bombshell of Song," who sang with Charlie Barnet and Tommy Reynolds and recorded for the Signature, Stellar, and Coral labels;[4] and Charlene Bartley, who might have been the best of them all. She sang with Al Donahue's big band, worked in the studio at WHDH radio and television, and recorded *Weekend of a Private Secretary* for RCA in 1957 with guitarist Don Alessi and the orchestra of Tito Puente.

With a policy of providing continuous entertainment, the 1-2-3 employed two trios and three singers at a time, plus a singing bartender. Al Vega's trio worked the 1-2-3 seven nights a week for about three years. Others with long stays there were the Jones Brothers; the Paul Clement Trio featuring vibist Lou Magnano; the Storm Trio, with the husband-and-wife team of pianist Bob and drummer Fran Tyler; Jes 2, the duo of pianist Gerry Gottschalk and bassist Tony DeFazio; and Two Kings & A Queen, with pianist Trudy Jones, bassist Jimmy Alford, and drummer and saxophonist Don Francis. These were all versatile groups, with their members singing as well as playing.

Our last corner stop is the Frolic and Musical Bar, which opened on the street level at 245 Tremont Street in 1952. By 1953, drummer Manny Wise's band was providing the music, first as a quintet (Serge Chaloff liked to sit in) and then as a well-regarded septet that featured three trombones.

Wise was a Londoner by birth who arrived in the United States in 1949. It was while working in upstate New York that he acquired his stage name. Latin music was all the rage, and "Manny Wise" just didn't sound very Latin. So he became Manuel Denize, and that's what people called him when his band played at the Frolic, the Hi-Hat, and Storyville in the 1950s. As for the band, Wise recalled:

I started my own group at the Frolic, not the one in Revere, this one was downtown, facing the Metropolitan Theatre. The club owner was interested in the group, it was trombone and trumpet and three rhythm and he liked the sound, because we worked hard on the arrangements. I used to get the good arrangers from around the area, like Harry Rodgers and Bill Leavitt, and a piano player named Neil Bridge. Bob Freedman did some charts. We built up a nice book. The club owner was one of those rare ones who was very interested in the music, and he said to me one day, "I like the sound of the trombone, why don't you hire two more trombone players?" I told him it would be expensive, you can't just buy arrangements for three trombones, you have to write them. He said he'd give me extra money, and in 1955 I organized the band with three trombones, saxophone, and rhythm section. It was unique, and a lot of the musicians used to stop by to hear the arrangements. There were some good guys in the band, like Will Kaslick, and Bob Carr, a trombonist from Nat Pierce's band, and the bass player Joe DeWeese. Later I had Harry Rodgers and Tak Takvorian and Will Kaslick. With that band, we did the Teenage Jazz Club at Storyville, and George Wein said it was the loudest seven-piece band he ever heard![5]

Wise could have mentioned that Rodgers and Takvorian had long histories in the music. Harry Rodgers went all the way back to the Theatrical Club with Herbie Marsh, and worked his way through the big band hierarchy, with Glenn Miller, Artie Shaw twice, and Harry James. Rodgers emerged as an arranger with Shaw in his first peacetime band, and he wrote numerous arrangements for Wise's book.

Vahey "Tak" Takvorian joined Wise after a long, long time on the road. He started with the prewar Boston bands of Larry Cooper and Lew Bonick, and worked his way through the hierarchy with Sam Donahue, Artie Shaw's navy band, Donahue again, Claude Thornhill, Larry Green, Tex Beneke, Tommy Dorsey and finally the reunited Dorsey Brothers. After Jimmy Dorsey's death in June 1957, Tak spent the summer with Ray McKinley, and finally arrived back in Boston, where he settled into a teaching career. He stayed active musically, playing jazz with Wise and others, and working in the house band at Blinstrub's.

Soft Winds

Although jazz musicians worked steadily at the Darbury Room at 271 Dartmouth Street, it wasn't so much a jazz club as it was a shrine to the Great American Songbook. That status was bestowed between November 1949 and April 1950 in a series of month-long tributes to the great composers of that songbook—Rogers and Hammerstein, Irving Berlin, Cole Porter, Jerome

Kern, and George Gershwin. Reed man Al Drootin led the band, but the standout was a young Broadway-bound singer, Barbara Cook.

As clubs go, the Darbury Room was definitely not a sailors' joint. People were drawn to the elegant room by the Back Bay setting and the quietly insistent swinging on the bandstand.

The house trio from early 1949 to late 1952 was the Soft Winds, with Herb Ellis on guitar, Lou Carter on piano, and John Frigo on bass. Ellis, Carter, and Frigo first played together as the rhythm section in Jimmy Dorsey's orchestra. In 1947 they went out on their own as the John Carlis Trio, and adopted the breezier name about the time they arrived in Boston. This group set the Darbury Room's standard for quiet jazz well played. Frigo departed in fall 1952 and was replaced by bassist Bonnie Wetzel. When Ellis joined Oscar Peterson's group the following year, Carter and Wetzel continued as a duo and played at the Darbury Room on and off until 1956.

Others spending time on the bandstand in 1950s were Teddi King, and the trios of pianists Al Vega, guitarist Don Alessi, and bassist Paul Clement. For just over three years beginning in January 1957, the house band was the duo of pianist Maggie Scott and bassist Eddie Stone. At a time when Boston had more than enough joints where loud music served as background noise, the Darbury Room is fondly remembered as a room pleasing to both its musicians and their listeners.

Latin Quarter

Lou Walters opened the Latin Quarter in 1939 in an old church at 46 Winchester Street, and almost from the start it was Boston's most famous nightclub. The biggest stars of the day performed there, accompanied by the splashiest press coverage. It wasn't a jazz club, but when jazz interest was peaking in Boston, the Latin Quarter often featured jazz artists, particularly those with star power, who appealed to an audience wider than the usual crowd at Storyville. Long before the term "crossover artist" became popular, the Latin Quarter presented a steady stream of them.

The Latin Quarter was not the first club to be housed in the old Winchester Street church. That honor belonged to the Club Karnak, a speakeasy where Warren Hookway, Frankie Ward, and other hot men prevailed; Eddy Duchin, then studying to be a pharmacist, played piano. The Club Karnak was a mandatory after-hours stop for traveling bands like Paul Whiteman's, and among those sitting in were Bix Beiderbecke and Bing Crosby. But that was the twenties.

The years 1950–1951 were the best ones for jazz entertainers, or jazz-influenced entertainers, at the Latin Quarter. The club presented Louis Armstrong, Pearl Bailey, Josephine Baker with Buddy Rich's band, Cab Calloway with Jonah Jones, Billy Eckstine, Billie Holiday, Lena Horne and the Mills Brothers, as well as jazz-flavored pop talents like Billy Daniels, Buddy Greco, Frankie Laine and Fran Warren. Jazz, yes, but the pattern is evident: singers all. Only singers could attract the desirable crossover crowd. But good singers need good support, and the house band in those years was the Latin Quarter's best. Led by Dave Lester, brother of bassist Jack Lesberg, it was loaded with big band veterans, such as trombonist Dick LeFave, trumpeter Tommy DeCarlo, saxophonist Carl Rand, and bassist Joe Carbonaro.

The management changed in 1952, and the new man was one Rocco "Rocky" Palladino of East Boston, a character with a cloudy past, a stable of race horses, and a history of run-ins with the Boston Licensing Board. There were no more Armstrongs or Holidays on Palladino's watch, but he brought in one of the biggest crossover artists of all, Sammy Davis Jr. He also had a special fondness for the Italian-American boy singers who rose to prominence in the 1950s, such as Tony Bennett, Tony Martin, Al Martino, and Jerry Vale. In January 1953 Palladino brought in the biggest Italian-American boy singer of them all, Frank Sinatra, in what was his only Boston nightclub appearance as a single.

In January 1953, Sinatra was beginning an unprecedented comeback, and while in Boston he learned he had won the part of Maggio in *From Here to Eternity*, for which he earned the Oscar for Best Supporting Actor. Sinatra was ebullient, singing 70-minute sets featuring his current single, "Birth of the Blues," and songs from *Porgy and Bess*. He enjoyed his time in Boston, hanging around Storyville where the Ellington Orchestra was playing, and taking an afternoon shift on WORL, spinning records and reading commercials.[6]

Sinatra wasn't the only game in town in January 1953, as Blinstrub's in South Boston featured Frankie Laine going voice-to-voice with Sinatra. Late January 1953 marked something of a high-water mark for Boston nightlife. There was more than Frank and Frankie, more than the Ellington Orchestra at Storyville. The Hi-Hat featured Coleman Hawkins and Roy Eldridge. Vic Dickenson and Doc Cheatham led the band at Mahogany Hall. Red Allen held forth at the Savoy, and alto saxophonist Bunny Campbell was down the street at Wally's Paradise. Nick Jerret's trio played nightly at the Moulin Rouge in the Vendome Hotel, the Soft Winds were at the Darbury Room, and Sabby Lewis provided the music at Sugar Hill. If musicals suited your taste, Rosalind

Russell had just opened in the Broadway tryout of Frank Loesser's *Wonderful Town* at the Shubert.

Has Boston ever seen bigger nights than those in January 1953, when Sinatra, Laine, and Ellington were packing the houses, and when you could satisfy an urge to hear some jazz trumpet by catching Red Allen, Doc Cheatham, and Roy Eldridge on the same night? When one room did well, it meant a little more business all around. When all these rooms did well, it spilled over across the whole of Boston nightlife, and that nightlife thrived for the next three years.

It came apart for the Latin Quarter a year later with *l'affaire Christine*. In January 1954, Palladino announced Christine Jorgensen was coming to the Latin Quarter the following month. Ms. Jorgensen was much celebrated because of her sex-change operation, and she was touring with a low-key nightclub act that had played in New York and Las Vegas (not to mention Holyoke) without incident. She was an undistinguished singer, getting by on her notoriety. But Boston was not New York or Las Vegas or even Holyoke, and here the mere idea of Christine Jorgensen was, in certain quarters, a call to arms.

Inevitably, it was Mary Driscoll, the feisty chairwoman of the Boston Licensing Board, who prevented Jorgensen's appearance. Driscoll, joined by Mayor Hynes and District Attorney Garrett H. Byrne, succeeded in blocking Ms. Jorgensen's appearance by claiming she violated the city's ban on female impersonators. Upon being told Jorgensen wasn't *impersonating* anybody, Driscoll's board suspended the Latin Quarter's operating license for the duration of the show. That done, they began a pursuit of Palladino himself that did not abate until he quit the club and the downtown scene in February 1955.

The Latin Quarter closed in May 1955, a victim more of increasingly unfavorable nightclub economics than of action by the licensing board. It was sudden. Even the employees were surprised when the place was shuttered after Eartha Kitt's last show.

The Latin Quarter closed because the rules of the game changed suddenly as well. Big names were asking for big money, and they were getting it in the concert halls and the television studios. It put smaller clubs such as the Latin Quarter at a disadvantage. They shelled out $15,000 to hire Jimmy Durante for 12 days in June 1954, which would be more than $126,000 in 2012 dollars. Wrote Clarke:

> It was a profitable engagement, but customers were alienated by the necessity
> of charging considerable sums; large minimums, entertainment charges and
> the like.

There is no such obligation at a place like, say, Blinstrub's, where an enormous capacity makes it possible to play the biggest stars in the business without materially increasing prices to the customers. When Blinstrub's first opened, Your Reporter pointed out that only such places can hope to survive.

There was no compromise with quality at the Latin Quarter right up to the end. Service was good. The food was excellent, and for the most part, the shows were fine. There just wasn't enough money coming in.[7]

For the next three years, rumors persisted that the Latin Quarter was going to reopen (one rumor even involved Lou Walters), but it never did. The wrecking crew arrived at the old church in January 1958 and ended the speculation.

The Real Jazz Is on Transition

Transition Pre-Recorded Tapes, Inc., released its first record in 1955. Transition was the brainchild of Thomas Blanchard Wilson, a transplanted Texan and 1954 *cum laude* graduate of Harvard. There he worked at radio station WHRB and founded the Harvard New Jazz Society. He started Transition in 1955. Said Wilson: "We plan to specialize in folk songs, jazz, and American classical music. One of our main objectives is to record neglected American compositions which we feel deserve recognition."[8]

Wilson was a study in the unexpected. He was a black man from Texas, yet he was president of the Harvard Young Republicans Club. Although he was a pioneer and the first to record major figures in the jazz avant-garde, it is for his later work producing rock music that he is best known.

His first recording was *Jazz in a Stable*, recorded live in the Huntington Avenue club and featuring the Jazz Workshop quintet. Other recordings followed, some 14 in all, among them LPs by Dixieland trumpeter Johnny Windhurst, hard-bop trumpeter Donald Byrd, saxophonists John Coltrane and Pepper Adams, and pianists Cecil Taylor (his first), and Sun Ra (also his first). Wilson also released folk and contemporary classical music. The label's musical sampler, *Jazz in Transition*, included one tantalizing cut by a Boston group co-led by Jay Migliori and Tommy Ball, and another featuring violinist Dick Wetmore, but subsequent LPs were never released and the tapes have yet to emerge. In 1957 Wilson ran out of money and closed up shop. He sold his master tapes to other record companies.

Collectors don't come across a Tom Wilson Transition recording too often. Few were made, and most probably became unplayable over time because they were made of polystyrene, not higher quality vinyl, and the brittle polystyrene was easily broken or scratched. And some Transitions were poorly recorded. Groused Nat Hentoff in his review of Johnny Windhurst's album,

"It's about time Transition did something about its engineering…an over-all thinness of sound, insufficient presence for trumpeter Windhurst, and a rhythm section that sounds, to borrow a phrase from Mike Levin, as if it had been recorded on fudge."[9]

After his Transition days, Wilson produced jazz for Savoy, United Artists, and Audio Fidelity. In 1963 he was hired by Columbia Records, where he began a 15-year career as a prolific and influential producer of rock music. Wilson was responsible for the first recordings of Bob Dylan, Frank Zappa, the Velvet Underground, and others. Sadly, Wilson never returned to jazz, his first love. He was only 47 at the time of his death in 1978.[10]

The Teenage Jazz Club

Live jazz was mostly out of reach for teenagers in the mid-1950s. Clubs served alcohol and thus could not admit minors. The Teenage Jazz Club came into existence in April 1955 to provide young people with access to the music. Attendees at a typical club meeting heard professional musicians playing their music in a proper atmosphere, but club members also had opportunities to learn about the music, and even how to play it. The only requirement for membership was to be under 21.[11]

The guiding lights behind the TJC were John McLellan of WHDH, its first advisor, and high-school student Stephani Saltman, the energetic organizer. Saltman had grown up with music; her father Phil was a longtime bandleader and instructor at his own Newbury Street music school, and her mother was a voice coach. All the kids in the Teenage Jazz Club were serious about the music, but Saltman was more serious than most. She sometimes skipped her study sessions at the Boston Public Library to dig the first set at Storyville, standing by herself in the hallway behind the stage door while the club's proprietors looked the other way. This was quite risky on their part: Mrs. Driscoll would have busted Storyville in a heartbeat for allowing the underage teen to enjoy the show.

Those proprietors, Charlie Bourgeois and George Wein, were major supporters of the Teenage Jazz Club. They hosted the club's monthly meetings at Storyville after school on Fridays—soft drinks served at the bar during intermission—from the club's first days. The admission charge was 80 cents, later raised to one dollar. The first meeting set the tone. Father O'Connor opened the meeting, Wein gave a short history lesson accompanied by recordings, and drum instructor Stanley Spector passed out pairs of brushes and showed how to use them. Then Spector demonstrated the styles of some of the popular jazz drummers, and Roy Haynes demonstrated his own style by playing an extended drum solo. Club member Steve Kuhn, then 17 and attending high school in Newton, played a short set with a quartet. (A year earlier, Wein called Kuhn "the second Leonard Bernstein.") The meeting closed with music by a pickup trio—Erroll Garner, Roy Haynes, and bassist Stan Wheeler.[12]

Not bad for a Friday afternoon, wouldn't you say?

By November 1955 the club boasted 92 members, and membership peaked in November 1956 at almost 700. (Despite the high number, a typical meeting drew a crowd of about 50.) Among the members were Kuhn, Serge Chaloff protégé Dom Turkowski, trumpeter and future author Richard Sudhalter, and soon-to-be WBUR disc jockey Ron Della Chiesa.

The club thrived in the middle of the decade, to the point of establishing a scholarship fund. In January 1957, the Teenage Jazz Club established the fund to further the musical education of its members, to be financed by dues and proceeds of the Pomeroy band's *Living History of Jazz* concerts. The first recipients were announced in September 1957, when two student club members from Lynn Classical High School each received a $250 scholarship to Berklee. They were trumpeter Paul Fontaine and saxophonist Jimmy Mosher. Both went on to play with Herb Pomeroy and Woody Herman, and Mosher spent six years with Buddy Rich as well. Later that year the club awarded $500 to a Berklee-bound Swedish student. The success of the Teenage Jazz Club caught the attention of *Metronome* and *Down Beat*, both of which ran features on the club and covered its events.

Many artists from Storyville and the Stable performed or presented at these meetings, all with the blessing of the musicians union. The best local groups of all styles played at the meetings, including Jaki Byard playing solo, the Toshiko Mariano Quartet, Serge Chaloff's sextet, Manny Wise's septet, the Excalibur Jazz Band, and the sextet of Jay Migliori and Tommy Ball. There were stellar guests, among them Art Blakey, George Shearing, and Shelly Manne. Duke Ellington dropped by to take requests from the piano. Serge Chaloff sat in with the Max Roach/Clifford Brown Quartet, the only time Serge and Clifford played together. Herb Pomeroy debuted his new big band at the November 1955 meeting. Woody Herman ran a rehearsal at one. And when schedule problems forced last-minute cancellations, the club could count on George Wein to assemble a group of Storyville All-Stars on short notice. From an entertainment point of view, club members undoubtedly got their money's worth.

The club lasted about six years, until the end of the spring semester in 1960. Stephani Saltman was a student at Boston University by then, hosting her own jazz show on WBUR radio and preparing for a career in broadcast journalism. At about the time club patron George Wein left for New York, the club quietly disbanded. Waning jazz interest among teens in general certainly couldn't have helped its fortunes. But for a time in the 1950s, it was the best deal to be had for a dollar, as long as you were under 21.

Eight Years of the Fabulous Four

Out in the far reaches of the Fenway, at 1358 Boylston Street at Kilmarnock, was the Brown Derby, a good-times place, and the home of the Fabulous Four, the quartet led by alto sax man Tom Kennedy. Kennedy had a long run, by Boston standards or any other, starting in the fall of 1955 and continuing into 1963.

Kennedy started his musical career singing in a traveling church choir, and he learned saxophone playing in the Boston Police Junior Band as a teenager. He started playing professionally in the late 1930s around his home town of Somerville, and he organized his own groups in the war years while holding down a day job at the Charlestown Navy Yard. With the end of the war, Kennedy joined Hillary Rose's house band at the Savoy, and he stayed with Rose until 1951. Kennedy then crossed the street to join Dean Earl at Eddie Levine's, where he played calypso with Gene Walcott and backed the singing of Mae Arnette. In 1955 came the Brown Derby and the Fabulous Four. Altoist Kennedy was strongly influenced by the bluesy saxophone style of Earl Bostic, and like Bostic, Kennedy reached across musical styles at the Brown Derby to achieve popular success. The Fabulous Four (pianists Ernie Trotman or Rudy Riley, bassist Jim Clark, drummer Harold Layne) mainly played jazz and standards but added R&B, rock, Dixieland, and if the occasion called for it, probably "When Irish Eyes Are Smiling," too. They were entertainers and good at it. Kennedy recorded the *On His Way* LP for Golden Crest in 1957, but he didn't like it because the label used New York studio musicians instead of his Fabulous Four.

The good times rolled on for eight years, but the Brown Derby changed to a rock policy in 1963. With the Fabulous Four out of work, Kennedy broke up the band and as the decade progressed, gravitated to the suburbs as the jazz jobs in Boston dried up.

The Greatest Rama of Them All, Until It Wasn't

When the interest in Dixieland music was at its peak in 1950–1951, a number of clubs became Dixieland rooms overnight as their owners attempted to cash in on the craze. Some of the latecomers lasted only three or four months, and when the dust settled, the Savoy stood alone. In late 1955, that same rush to cash in befell modern jazz.

In September a restaurant at 54 Park Square renamed itself the Downbeat and brought in Jay Migliori's quintet to provide the music. Migliori had a very good working band at that time, with trumpeter Tommy Ball, pianist Danny Kent, bassist Wyatt "Bull" Reuther, and drummer Floogie Williams. (This band recorded an LP's worth of music for Transition Records, called *Downbeat Jazz*, but the record was never released.) Mabel Robinson Simms was the intermission pianist. The music was good but the writer from *Metronome* who dropped by thought the band was too loud and the sound system "was reminiscent of a short wave broadcast during a snow storm." When Migliori's group took over house band duties at Storyville in December, the always-popular Jones Brothers moved in for the holidays and into January.

Just down the street from Storyville was the 5 O'Clock Club a long, narrow room at 78 Huntington Avenue, near the corner of Irvington Street. Its entertainment policy was always shifting, and at the end of 1955 it became a major jazz destination. The club's neighbors, Storyville and the Stable, were going full bore with jazz and doing good business with it, so in September 1955, Bart Buchhalter, manager of the 5 O'Clock (and brother of Harold Buchhalter, owner of the Stable), jumped into the jazz business. Just after Labor Day, Buchhalter started advertising that the 5 would soon unveil "the greatest Rama of them all."

What Buchhalter unveiled on September 22 was Jazzarama, a renamed 5 O'Clock, featuring the Serge Chaloff Sextet, with alto saxophonist Boots Mussulli, trumpeter Joe Bovello, pianist Bob Freedman, bassist Everett Evans, and drummer Paul Drummond. The club followed that with Miles Davis. What a coup for Buchhalter to secure the services of Davis, ahead of the better-known Hi-Hat or Storyville! This was an engagement of interest to Davis's followers as well, because it marked only the second appearance of John Coltrane with the quintet. He had replaced Sonny Rollins earlier that month, and he was so new, some of the Boston newspaper advertisements still listed Rollins as a band member. Every Boston jazz fan of a certain age claims to have been there.

More modern jazz followed in November with Don Elliott and Teddy Charles, and it appeared that Storyville had some neighborhood competition for booking the name bands. But it didn't last. There was only room enough for one. As 1956 rolled around, the club dropped the Jazzarama label and the name band policy.

Early 1956 marked the end of a peak period in Boston nightlife, and jazz nightlife was hit particularly hard. Perhaps the harbinger of that trouble was the death of Dick Twardzik in late October. Then in December clubs started closing and winter settled in. First was the Hi-Hat fire of December 19 that knocked the club out of business, and it never regained its former glory when it opened again a year later.

Then came George Wein's decision to close Mahogany Hall, his Dixieland room in the Copley Square Hotel. It had been a weekends-only operation for some months, but there had been a run-in with the licensing board in mid-December over serving alcohol to minors. Except for a few special events, Wein kept the club closed in 1956.

Next was the closing of Jazzarama and the return of the 5 O'Clock club with its assorted lounge acts. That was followed by the closing of the Savoy at year's end; when the last notes of "The Original Dixieland One-Step" faded in the early morning hours of January 1, the Savoy Cafe ended its historic run.

The Stage Bar on Stuart Street, a longtime home for R&B bands and Fat Man Robinson's home away from home, burned early one January morning and stayed closed until May. Finally, on Park Square, the Downbeat closed in January. If the demise of Jazzarama showed that there were only so many people willing to buy tickets to name-band modern jazz, the demise of the Downbeat showed there were only so many people willing to support local modern jazz bands, and the Stable was their place.

It all meant many closings and many jobs lost in the span of one month. The Stage Bar and Hi-Hat closed because of fire, the Savoy and Mahogany Hall closed because their owners had seen the Dixieland audience dwindle. For the first time since the beginning of the Dixieland revival, there were no rooms in Boston featuring the music. The two modern jazz rooms closed because there just wasn't enough audience to go around. All of this left the musicians with fewer places to play—and fewer paychecks.

There were good working bands in town—the Stable's sextet, Migliori's quintet, Chaloff's sextet—but not enough listeners. That was true about all kinds of jazz in 1956 and 1957. Many clubs that couldn't be called jazz clubs had jazz entertainment in the mid-1950s because that was the trend. Even the hotels were booking jazz, and they only booked sure things. But in 1956 and 1957 the trend changed, and all those places that ride the trends started booking calypso bands. Even a jazz club like Eddie Levine's brought in calypso bands; Crystal Joy was out and the Trinidad Steel Orchestra was in.

Storyville, the Stable, and Wally's were still going strong and some of the very best jazz Boston would ever hear was still to come. However, in terms of commercial activity, the local jazz scene had reached its 1950s peak.

Chapter 18

Telling It

Stories go to waste without good people to tell them, and Boston had good people through these 25 years. With all the colleges and universities, and the tradition of great writing that is part of Boston's identity, it was perhaps inevitable that there would be writers writing about jazz here, and jazz writers dabbling in broadcasting, and jazz broadcasters becoming writers. Add in a few graphic artists and photographers, and there was a very busy core of people active in the business of telling the Boston jazz story, of helping people learn about it and develop an ear for it. They did it through writing, speaking, radio, and finally television.

This chapter introduces a few of them. There's Symphony Sid, the celebrated disc jockey; John McLellan, the one-man jazz media machine of the 1950s; Vin Haynes, a part-time teller who did it strictly for love; and Father Norman J. O'Connor, the Jazz Priest and philosopher. And we'll take a peek at television, the technology that took the country by storm in the 1950s, to see how jazz fared locally on the small screen. Although jazz music made only a small splash in the big pond of television broadcasting, McLellan and O'Connor could take credit for some of its ripples.

Jumpin' with Symphony Sid

All through the 1950s, quirky, locally owned AM stations kept jazz on the air in Boston with a string of talented deejays. John McLellan was on the air, and we'll meet him presently. So was the erudite Bob "the Robin" Martin, whose daily program from Storyville on WVDA from 1953 to 1955 came to an abrupt end when the station switched formats, and Martin, a fiercely partisan fan of good jazz regardless of age or genre, quit rather than play bland pop music. He ended up at WCOP, first doing overnights and later a four-hour afternoon show. Martin helped revive the career of Serge Chaloff, arranging an appearance on Steve Allen's *Tonight Show*, and supervising the recording of Chaloff's classic *Boston Blow-Up* album in 1955. Chaloff thanked his friend by writing the tune "Bob the Robin" and including it on that album. When WCOP went Top 40 in 1956, Martin left town for WGBS in Miami.

Then there was the minor uproar that was WBMS. Norman Furman, who introduced all-black programming to WLIB in New York City, became the general manager of Boston's WHEE in April of 1952, and he immediately converted the sleepy station into one featuring jazz, gospel, and R&B. Within a month he had changed the call letters to WBMS (perhaps standing for "World's Best Music Station"), hired Boston jazz icon Sabby Lewis as a disc jockey (he stayed for four years), and topped that by hiring his friend, the celebrated New York deejay "Symphony Sid" Torin. Later he brought Ken Malden over from WVDA. There was nothing else on the radio like WBMS.

Symphony Sid Torin (Sidney Tarnopol) was nationally known through his broadcasts from Birdland on New York's WJZ, and he became a powerful presence on Boston radio between 1952 and 1957. Furman actually did Sid a good turn by bringing him to WBMS, because Sid was blacklisted in New York after being charged with possession of marijuana. Sid had an unusual working arrangement as a two-station disc jockey, working out of the WBMS studios by day and on WCOP live from the Hi-Hat at night (some time after the Hi-Hat fire he moved to WMEX). It was Sid who dubbed the Hi-Hat at Mass and Columbus "the Jazz Corner of Boston," a play on his calling Birdland at Broadway and 52nd "the Jazz Corner of the World." He had two shows on WBMS, his daily *Interlude in Jazz* and his Saturday afternoon *Brother Sid's Gospel Hour*. Boston, like New York in earlier years, was "jumpin' with Symphony Sid."

Symphony Sid Torin at WBMS, ca. 1955. Courtesy of Jack Bradley.

There are a thousand Symphony Sid stories and some of them are undoubtedly true. He was the quintessential fifties hipster, with a Beacon Hill flat, British sports car, flashy clothes, and shades day and night. All agreed that he loved the music and did well by his advertisers. Many also agreed that his hipster routine could be tiresome. ("Sid," said one Boston musician who knew him, "was basically full of shit.") But to this day you can hear Sid announcing tunes by Parker and Stitt on "Live at the Hi-Hat" sessions, regularly reissued on CD almost 60 years later.

Ken Malden (Milton Tokson) went into broadcasting after his navy service and was at WVDA with Bob Martin, playing jazz and blues until 1954, when he jumped to WBMS. He mostly played R&B, even sending some records to a convalescing Dwight

Eisenhower in 1955 in the hope that the president would "look alive and dig the jive."[1] With Malden alongside Sabby Lewis and Symphony Sid, it was jazz and jump all the time at WBMS.

When WBMS changed ownership in 1957, Norman Furman returned to New York and station WEVD. Symphony Sid soon announced he'd join him there, and he closed out the Boston portion of his career as emcee at the North Shore Jazz Festival in August 1957. In September, Bartell Broadcasting completed its purchase of WBMS and changed its call letters to WILD. Ken Malden stayed on, as both as deejay and program director until 1960, when he headed south to Miami, reuniting with Bob Martin at WGBS.

Having Symphony Sid working in Boston for five years certainly made the city's radio waves more jazz-savvy, but he himself wasn't as important as Nathan Furman, who put programming of interest to the black community in a place of prominence on WBMS. He also hired black announcers, including Sabby Lewis. Sabby wasn't the first black deejay in Boston; that was Eddy Petty who started at WVOM in January 1949. Lewis, however, was the better known by far.

In 1954, in the midst of WBMS's run, Boston first heard the sound of jazz radio to come, when *Trends in Jazz* debuted on WBUR-FM, the Boston University station. The once-a-week program was directed by Father Norman O'Connor, with students doing most of the announcing and interviewing. In 1957 O'Connor started a second program, *Jazz Anthology*. A year later, Ron Della Chiesa followed with *The Sound of Jazz*, and in March of 1959, Stephani Saltman introduced *Jazz for a Saturday*. WBUR was noteworthy because it marked the start of jazz's transition from AM to FM in the Boston market, and because it started the shift of jazz programming from commercial to non-profit stations.

The Top Shelf

John McLellan (John Fitch) was born in Shanghai in 1926 and raised in Boston. He enlisted in the navy, and after his discharge enrolled at MIT. He graduated with a degree in electrical engineering, but even as a student he threw himself into the world of Boston jazz.

McLellan started at WHDH radio in 1950 and remained on that station until 1961. During his time at WHDH, McLellan created what was arguably the best jazz program on Boston radio during that decade, *The Top Shelf*, which first aired in 1951. The show was a success despite indifferent station management and an uncertain schedule, which sometimes had him on one night a week and at other times six nights.

For three years, McLellan hosted the remotes from Storyville, sometimes taping the proceedings for his own enjoyment. His tapes of Charlie Parker at Storyville in 1953 were good enough to merit commercial release years later, in 1990.

John McLellan at the WHDH microphone. *Boston Traveler* photo, courtesy of the Boston Public Library, Print Department.

The articulate and knowledgeable McLellan went well beyond radio, however. He wrote the "Jazz Scene" column for the *Boston Traveler* from 1957 to 1961, was one of the founders of the Teenage Jazz Club, emceed the first two Newport Jazz Festivals in 1954 and 1955, worked with Herb Pomeroy as narrator of the acclaimed "Living History of Jazz" concert, was instrumental in putting jazz on television in Boston and hosted his own show from 1958 to 1961, wrote LP liner notes, and reviewed records for *Metronome*. On top of all this, he studied clarinet with Berklee's Joe Viola. Ron Della Chiesa remembers McLellan as "the most learned, professorial even, of the broadcasters. He could put any tune in context, relate it to its time, describe how it fit into what the artist was doing." *Metronome* called him the "purest jazz jockey in town."[2]

"The Jazz Scene"

Jazz writing in Boston goes back to *Down Beat's* George Frazier in the late 1930s and early 1940s. He passed the Boston correspondent's torch to his followers in the Hot Club of Boston, most of whom, like Frazier himself, had Harvard connections (he was class of 1933). The best of them was Mike Levin (Harvard '42), and after his wartime service, Levin became *Down Beat's* New York editor. He introduced the four-star rating system for grading recordings still used today. He remained in the editor's post until 1951.

Between 1951 and 1953, *Down Beat's* man in Boston was Roxbury's Nat Hentoff (Northeastern '45), best known as WMEX disc jockey and author/editor of the *Counterpoint* newsletter. He became the magazine's New York editor in 1953, and in that decade went on to edit three noteworthy jazz collections and serve as artistic director for *The Sound of Jazz* on CBS television. Hentoff's place as Boston correspondent was taken by Dom

Cerulli (Northeastern '51), Boston-born and a former *Globe* reporter. In 1957, Cerulli succeeded Hentoff as the *Beat's* New York editor. Apparently *Down Beat* used the Boston correspondent's post to groom its future New York editors, the Chicago-based magazine's eyes and ears on the East Coast.

There were more strong Boston ties over at *Metronome*, where George Simon (Harvard '34) wrote "Simon Says," the must-read column for the big band set. He became the magazine's editor in 1939. Simon yielded the editor's position in 1954 to Bostonian Bill Coss, who for a time had the Dorchester-born artist and photographer Burt Goldblatt as his art director. *Metronome*, while putting fewer Bostonians on the payroll, at times covered the Boston scene in more depth. In fact, we owe *Metronome* a debt for the issue of April 1956, which included a long survey of the Boston scene by Coss himself, as well as shorter pieces on Toshiko Akiyoshi, Charlie Mariano, John Neves, and Transition Records. Stretching across eight pages with 11 photos, plus a clever Burt Goldblatt cover that superimposed a photo of Teddi King on another of the Boston skyline, the package forms the most complete picture of the Boston scene taken during this entire period.

Eventually the editorship passed to Dan Morgenstern (Brandeis '56), and when *Metronome* shut down, Morgenstern became the first editor at *Jazz* magazine in 1962, and editor at *Down Beat* in 1964.

That was a lot of talent by any measure, and it is fair to say that Boston writers defined much of the personality and heft of postwar jazz journalism.

Not everyone who wrote about the music in Boston took a job in New York, however. One who stayed was McLellan at the *Traveler*. He wrote "The Jazz Scene" for that paper twice a week for four years, from September 1957 to September 1961. His column was the first in the daily papers since Frazier's "Sweet and Low-Down" in the *Herald* in 1942.

His first column appeared in August 1957, but before others could be published, a strike shut down the Boston papers for three weeks. With that resolved, the *Traveler* began publishing regular columns on September 3, and posted two per week thereafter for four years, until September 14, 1961. The odd thing about the start and finish of McLellan's tenure was how quiet it was. The first column just appeared one day, without any fanfare on the part of the editors or opening statement by the writer. McLellan just started writing. When the column ended four years later, there was no "hail and farewell" either. The column simply stopped running.

McLellan wrote close to 400 columns in his time at the *Traveler*, a vast body of work, and the best ongoing account of the scene available at this or any other time. McLellan reported all the Boston news—upcoming concert and club dates, band personnel changes, venues opening and closing, meeting and lecture notices, and related events in the community and the arts. McLellan reviewed his share of records, television programs, movies, books, and of course performances, in clubs and concert halls, suburban dine-and-dance places and festival stages, music tents and school auditoriums.

McLellan was especially interested in bringing jazz to young people. No scholarship opportunity, award recipient, summer jazz camp, or public performance featuring young musicians went without mention. As a founder of the Teenage Jazz Club, McLellan was committed to bringing jazz to the youth audience. Nurturing the music's future audience was a recurring theme, and at a time when many jazz people complained about the diminishing youth audience, McLellan did something about it.

Musically, McLellan found something of interest in all styles and schools, from Louis Armstrong to Cannonball Adderley, if it was genuine and well played. Like Hentoff, he had no patience for those too stubborn to open their ears. Even though he recognized Dixieland music for what it was in the mid-1950s ("Let's face it, the college crowd and the perpetual adolescents form the last bulwark of Dixieland"), he still acknowledged its place as good-time music. Writing in October 1957 about the Excalibur Jazz Band, then playing weekends at a reopened Mahogany Hall:

> It's good to have the place open again. Boston needs a place for Dixieland. The music that Parkins' Excalibur Band plays is valid and should be heard. That is, unless you're such a moldy fig that you think jazz died with King Oliver, or such a young "hippie" that you think Stan Kenton invented jazz.[3]

He liked the mainstream swing played by the likes of Buck Clayton and Vic Dickenson, older players stuck stylistically between the Dixielanders and the modernists and finding little work because of it. Capable of playing in bands both big and small, they were "swing era musicians playing in a collectively improvised context...The ensemble choruses are the spontaneous polyphony of traditional jazz. But the rhythmic flow is the smooth 4-4 of the Basie band."[4]

McLellan prized originality and fresh approaches, and found much to like in the work of the modernists. On Jaki Byard's arrangement of his tune "Septet:"

> The Byard arrangement, like so much of his work, was simply bursting at the seams with unusual ideas from his seemingly unlimited imagination. He's a Boston arranger-composer who, though strongly influenced by Duke Ellington, has written a good deal that is startlingly fresh and original.[5]

McLellan believed that the new directions of men such as Byard would define the future of jazz. Describing the Ken McIntyre Quartet in 1960, gigging at 47 Mt. Auburn in Cambridge:

> The music these men play is full of surprises, shocks and delights. Unusual construction of tunes, varying rhythmic patterns, and above all an emphasis on complete freedom of improvisation are the characteristics most immediately noticeable. Their music may be tortured on occasion, too intense at times, even immature in a showoff way at other times. But, make no mistake: these musicians are going to change the sound of jazz.[6]

McLellan appreciated Pomeroy and his musical associates, writing at least a dozen columns about the band and even more about its individual members, including his favorite, Lennie Johnson, whom he called the soul of the Herb Pomeroy Orchestra, "one of our prize possessions in Boston...One whom we ought to listen to with great respect and admiration." In the same column, he effusively praised the Pomeroy big band as a whole, just reformed with a new concept in mid-1960:

> It's a band with some of the exuberant shout of the old Herman Herd. And the roughness of the Dizzy Gillespie big bands. Yes, and maybe even the ragged swing of the Fletcher Henderson bands before that—when big band jazz was still young and thrilling to play. It's a band that'll make you feel that life is worth living. And jazz is worth hearing. I, for one, am glad to have the Herb Pomeroy band back on the jazz scene.[7]

McLellan, as a rule, was tough on singers and he thought jazz singing was a dying art. In one of his first columns in 1957, he wrote that the Four Freshmen were good vocalists but "their kind of music isn't jazz for one simple reason. It doesn't swing. It's as rhythmically corny for our time as Red Nichols and his Five Pennies were for their day." They "exist in a musical limbo somewhere between the Four Aces and Count Basie. Somewhere between Blinstrub's and Storyville. Somewhere between popular music and jazz." But they packed Storyville on Labor Day night, "about as dead as any night you could find on the calendar."[8] Nor did he see any redeeming qualities to Chris Connor, Helen Merrill, or Nina Simone. Of the local singers, he liked Mae Arnette and not too many others. Then in October 1958, he heard Lambert, Hendricks and Ross on their first visit to Boston:

> After years of pseudo-hip singing by the Four Freshmen and Hi-Los, it was a revelation to listen to this refreshing trio of jazz singers at Storyville last week... Here at last is a group that understands that jazz didn't begin and end with Stan Kenton. That jazz means more than spread harmony and clever arrangements... All in all, it was a heartening experience to listen to this new and unique jazz vocal group. The enthusiastic audience response overwhelmed them.[9]

McLellan believed the jazz musician should be respected and given an atten-tive hearing, and he had no use for the boorish beer drinkers at festivals and had nothing good to say about rooms with noisy audiences. He put the Hi-Hat on that list, and he rarely mentioned any of its Mass Ave neighbors, per-haps for the same reason. On a visit to the Showbar to hear bassist Tony Tex-eira's trio: "There was simply too much interference from telephones, the 'big show' in the back room, and all the conversations, to make any kind of eval-uation. Let's just say they play and sing jazz and leave it at that."[10]

On the Scene with Vin Haynes

Cameron Vincent "Vin" Haynes, brother of drummer Roy Haynes, wrote his "On the Scene" column for the Boston *Chronicle* from February 1953 until February 1960. Unlike the *Daily Record* or the *Traveler*, the *Chronicle* was a slim tabloid, published each week on Saturday, for a primarily African-Amer-ican readership. It published into the early 1960s.

Vin Haynes was a fan first and a reporter and critic second. He was not a professional journalist, and other than writing record reviews and an annual report from the Newport Jazz Festival, he confined himself to reporting on the Boston area jazz scene. He didn't limit himself to music, either; he probably wrote as much on youth sports as he did jazz. He used his space to promote the up-and-coming talent who caught his attention, such as Ron Gill and Crystal Joy. The Haynes version of the jazz calendar was different from the daily papers too, because he included places like Eddie Levine's and Wally's Paradise, which generally weren't mentioned in the mainstream press unless they bought advertising.

Sometimes Haynes was in the right place at the right time. Because the Boston newspapers were on strike during the North Shore Jazz Festival in 1957, Haynes was the only Boston reporter to cover it. And sometimes he caught something that otherwise went unreported. It was Haynes, for instance, who noted that the Storyville audience booed Lee Konitz, who had the unenviable task of filling Charlie Parker's spot on the Storyville schedule the week Bird died.

Writing was a sideline for Haynes, and his work at the *Chronicle* was a part-time avocation. Haynes had a full-time job, and he listened to new records early on Saturday mornings and wrote his reviews for the next week's column, because that was the only time he could find to do it. Haynes's later passion was photography, which he pursued with notable success until his death in 2004.

Haynes inherited a *Chronicle* column that had been written on and off by a long procession of scribes writing about jazz and entertainment from at least the early 1930s. The longest tenured prior to Haynes was Eddy Petty, who started "Eddy Petty's Musical Moments" in 1949 and wrote for more than two years. Petty was a jazz pianist himself who worked around the Jazz Corner, as well as a disc jockey on WVOM. Actually, Eddy Petty had a split personality. One wrote about Boston jazz news, and the second wrote about national entertainment issues of interest to the black community. This second writer was better by far than the first. This was never an issue for Haynes, who kept his eye on the local scene and reported on it in a straightforward style.

The Jazz Priest Meets Jazz Broadcasting

Norman James O'Connor was born in Detroit in 1921. He was just a kid when he took up the piano and played in a dance band or two. He was a big Benny Goodman fan. He'd hear Goodman on the radio and he'd go to the piano and work out what he'd just heard, an exercise he abandoned when he entered first college and then the seminary. He was ordained a Paulist priest in 1948, the Reverend Norman J. O'Connor CSP.

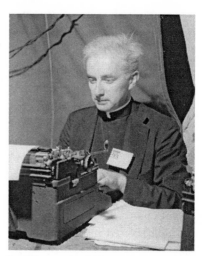

O'Connor arrived in Boston in 1951, appointed to serve as Boston University's chaplain and director of the Newman Club. He also taught history and philosophy at B.U., and he always put in a full day performing his priestly duties—saying daily mass, hearing confessions, counseling the Catholic students. His day started at six a.m. and ended at about one in the morning. Late in the evening, though, he could often be found at Storyville digging the band. Father O'Connor's nickname was "the Jazz Priest."

True to his priestly calling, he befriended many in the jazz world, some of whom he discreetly helped in

Fr. Norman J. O'Connor, ca. 1957. Photo by Popsie Randolph. Courtesy of Michael Randolph.

solving the problems of their everyday lives, arranging for medical care, family counseling, financial assistance, or housing. Nobody will ever know how many members of his jazz flock he helped this way.

O'Connor was into everything that had anything to do with jazz. His energy seemed inexhaustible. He found a place for jazz music in church services. He was emcee at the first Newport festival in 1954, and every festival thereafter for his time in Boston. As a member of the Newport Festival's board of directors, he often served as a spokesman for that event. He was not only the Jazz Priest, he was also the Jazz Ambassador.

O'Connor began writing about jazz in the early 1950s, coupling his knowledge of music and familiarity with jazz history with the constant writing he was doing at his day job at Paulist Press. Today Father O'Connor would be a blogger. He wrote LP liner notes. He wrote a biweekly column in the Sunday *Globe* starting in 1956, as well as for all the national jazz publications. He claimed to have written a novel running to hundreds of thousands of words called *Death Is All Metaphors*, a line borrowed from Dylan Thomas; the novel was always coming out "next year" but never did.

O'Connor was a talker; his insightful participation on panels garnered a positive response, and he hosted programs on WBUR radio, and later on WCRB. His approach to radio, he told *Metronome*, was simple: "Little preparation, lots of records, some talk about the background, occasional interviews, and no gimmicks."[11] He was outgoing, curious, and knowledgeable. People couldn't help but like him.

Through it all O'Connor remained an avid listener, happily nursing soft drinks through late-night sets at Storyville.

O'Connor not only wrote for the jazz magazines, they wrote about him, too, and *Down Beat* put him on the cover of the November 14, 1957, issue. Reporters found him just plain interesting. The question he heard most often was a variation on "how does a priest end up being a jazz expert?" and he'd reply along the lines of, "My feeling is a priest should never be a stranger in any area. Like you, we all have our preferences and I happen to like jazz." He saw no contradiction in it: "There's a common ground between the creative artist and religious attitudes. In the past, the Church sponsored art."[12]

The Catholic church could have complained about O'Connor's secular activities but did quite the opposite. In fact, in November 1960, O'Connor was feted at a testimonial dinner at the Statler Hotel, and Richard Cardinal Cushing of Boston was the featured speaker. Among the attendees were O'Connor's friends Duke Ellington, Teddi King, and Marion McPartland.

Small Screen Scene

McLellan and O'Connor were both forward-looking thinkers with a keen interest in the future. Both were communications professionals, and it was only natural that they'd take on the biggest communications challenge of the 1950s together. They wanted to put jazz on television.

Looking back now, even considering the impact of the Internet, it is hard to believe the massive cultural shift brought about by television in the 1950s. It replaced the public's fancy with radio at lightning speed. Early television producers, though, stumbled in trying to find the formula for presenting live music. They thought four people making music together wouldn't be enough. They added visual effects: fancy sets, dancers, swirling smoke. The result was often overproduced and not at all relaxed. Honesty turned out to be the best policy—all that was needed was those four musicians and their music. McLellan and O'Connor stuck to that policy and were successful with it.

On the set of *Jazz with Father O'Connor* in 1959. From left: Gabor Szabo, Chet Kruley, Alan Dawson, Fr. Norman O'Connor, Ahmad Merican, John Neves, Berklee School administrator Robert Share, WGBH producer James Healy, and Charlie Mariano. Courtesy of Berklee College of Music.

Nineteen fifty-seven was a good year for jazz programs on television, both locally and nationally. In January, McLellan and O'Connor started the weekly series on WGBH, *Jazz with Father O'Connor*, a live program that featured local and touring artists conversing with the Jazz Priest and playing a few numbers. Coleman Hawkins and Dinah Washington were guests on the first program. Later in 1957, O'Connor teamed up with George Shearing on WGBH to produce 17 episodes of *Jazz Meets the Classics*, a program bankrolled by the Ford Foundation.

Then came the landmark CBS broadcast of *The Sound of Jazz* on December 8, 1957, generally acknowledged to be the medium's greatest success with jazz. It had everything the jazz fan could want—the spontaneity, the emotion, and the inventiveness that marks jazz at its best. It was "honesty is the best policy" at its finest. There were no elaborate sets, no dancers, no celebrity hosts. There were simply musicians, in casual settings, blowing. The story was on their faces and in their music, and people will be talking about Billie Holiday and Lester Young and their rendition of "Fine and Mellow" as long as people talk about jazz. The show was a triumph.

The old WMEX deejay, Nat Hentoff, was the program visionary and a key figure in its success. He and Whitney Balliet served as artistic directors. (Nat Pierce wrote the show's arrangements.) *The Sound of Jazz* succeeded because Hentoff and Balliet were able to keep control of the show. They played it straight and put the focus on the musicians. Later network efforts, cluttered with product tie-ins or promotions, proved their vision was correct. Programs that followed in 1958 to capitalize on the success of *The Sound of Jazz—Stars of Jazz, The Subject Is Jazz, The Timex All-Star Jazz Show*—couldn't compare.

Surely O'Connor and McLellan watched *The Sound of Jazz* and learned from it, because on their programs, they too always played it straight. Their programs were unrehearsed, the music and the conversation improvised, with the emphasis on the music maker. A few years later, O'Connor summed it up thusly: "Jazz is the most vital music we hear today. Its vitality comes from its originality and the fundamental respect it has for the person and personal expression."[13]

With O'Connor off and running, McLellan started *The Jazz Scene* on WHDH-TV in May 1958. On the first Wednesday every month, McLellan took over the slot of that station's popular *Dateline* program. His first guest, not unexpectedly, was trumpeter Lennie Johnson, who talked and played through the history of the trumpet in jazz.

McLellan mixed it up on his show. There were the touring musicians such as Coleman Hawkins and Charles Mingus. But more interesting were some of his jam sessions, for instance pairing the folk musicians Pete Seeger and Sonny Terry with jazzmen John Neves and Jimmy Zitano, or assembling members of Basie's Old Testament and New Testament bands. There was an abundance of exposure for local musicians: Don Alessi, Toshiko Akiyoshi, Jaki Byard, Alan Dawson, Champ Jones, Charlie Mariano, Herb Pomeroy, Ray Santisi and Manny Wise were among the guests on *The Jazz Scene*.

Bill Coss wrote about *The Jazz Scene* in December 1961:

> However it is constructed, the program is pre-eminent, quite beyond its
> uniqueness. On that program he gives sureness, dignity, and understanding
> to jazz. In that turvy-topsy world he pays his dues, pays them for many, and
> the results have been splendid and prolific. This is a program about which
> jazz can be proud, as Boston can be proud of its jazz, and, most particularly,
> its strongest jazz advocate, John McLellan.[14]

Coss likely knew what was ahead when he wrote those epitaph-like words, because weeks later McLellan ended his show after a four-year run. He had already dropped his newspaper column and radio program. After more than a decade of involvement, McLellan stepped away from the Boston jazz scene:

> I enjoyed the interviews, and the TV shows, and the contact with the great musicians... but I was bored, so I moved on, even though I took a cut in pay when I left. I had said everything I had to say, and I was starting to repeat myself... I just decided it was time, so I left broadcasting.[15]

As it turned out, McLellan only left jazz broadcasting, as he went on to host WGBH's *MIT Science Reporter* program for six years.

Losing *The Jazz Scene* was a blow to local jazz, to be sure, and it would soon be followed by another. In late 1962, O'Connor was transferred to New York, where he became director of the radio and television division of Paulist Communications, a job for which he was quite well prepared. Weekly jazz programming continued on WGBH until 1969, but Father O'Connor's enthusiasm and knowledge were irreplaceable.

Nineteen sixty-two was not a good year for the storytellers in Boston. McLellan and O'Connor left the jazz scene that year, and the local small-screen scene seemed even smaller. Although Vin Haynes remained, he had no paper to write for, as the *Boston Chronicle* ceased publication. Other notable radio voices, such as Symphony Sid, Bob Martin, and Ken Malden, were on the air in other cities. Even George Clarke was gone, having retired from the *Daily Record* in 1961. As 1962 wound down, there were not only opportunities for the next generation of storytellers, there was a crying need for them.

Chapter 19

Into the Great Outdoors

Musicians and promoters have always found ways to perform in the great outdoors, New England weather permitting. In the late 1930s, the Boston Symphony Orchestra began its annual trek to Tanglewood for the summer season, and for those more interested in popular music, there were summer dance pavilions and dancing under the stars on the Ritz and Bradford Hotel roofs, and war bond rallies and U.S.O. Buddies Club dances on the Common.

Offshore jazz was almost a given in the port city of Boston; summertime harbor cruises and excursion boats to Cape Cod were a pleasant way to beat the heat. Preston Sandiford and Joe Nevils played the moonlight cruises in the late 1930s aboard the *S. S. Steel Pier*, and although such pleasure cruises were banned during World War II, they were quickly revived in 1946. The Wilson Line ran the profitable Boston-Provincetown excursion ferries from Foster's Wharf in the 1950s. The ever-popular Mal Hallett was a regular on Wilson's *S. S. Pilgrim Belle* until his death in 1952. Wilson claimed its *S. S. Boston Belle* had the largest marine ballroom afloat. Musicians remember it as a shipwreck waiting to happen. The Ford Theatrical Agency handled the bookings for the Wilson Line from 1946 until 1957, and hired every kind of band, from Tom Kennedy's jazz quartet to Baron Hugo's Totem Pole Orchestra. Calypso bands proved quite popular on these boat rides in the 1950s.

The 1950s, though, really brought jazz to the great outdoors, in single-concert offerings and festivals stretching over two or three days. The first was staged as part of the Mid-Century Boston Jubilee in 1950 (page 76). It was Boston's first jazz festival, and the press mostly ignored it. The Boston Arts Festival featured a Jazz Night concert in the Public Garden every year from 1954 to 1963. Lynn's Manning Bowl hosted the three-day North Shore Jazz Festival in 1957. The decade ended with two multi-day festivals, the first Boston Jazz Festival at Fenway Park in 1959, and the Pleasure Island Jazz Festival in 1960.

We visited the biggest festival of them all, the Newport Jazz Festival, in Chapter 16. The man behind it, George Wein, organized Boston-based concerts and festivals as well, and his right-hand man, Charlie Bourgeois, staged the festival at the Boston Jubilee in his pre-Storyville days.

The outdoor concerts fared well with the critics, but the festivals were not universally acclaimed. Although the *Traveler's* John McLellan emceed jazz festivals himself, they were not high on his list. He knew how important festivals were to jazz, especially Newport. "What is happening in Newport," he wrote in July 1958, "is what is happening in jazz."[1] But he didn't like festivals, even while granting that musical meetings took place in a festival setting that couldn't happen in a club, and getting out of the smoky clubs into the open air did give everyone a different point of view. But time limits and curfews interfered with the music, the folding metal chairs were hard on the bones, and festivals tended to book groups that were borderline jazz, or worse. He deplored the appearance of rock and roll at the 1958 Newport festival, calling it "the fifth annual Carnival of Jazz." "The scar left by the atrocious Chuck Berry...may never be healed...Previous Newport spectacles may have been disillusioning. This one was disgusting!"[2]

Musicians often had artistic differences with the festival's procedures, but the more serious problem was the crowd. Wrote McLellan after the 1959 Newport festival: "They didn't have any outright rock and roll this year. But they've got a new problem—Joe College and His Beer Bottles—a growing collection of collegians out for a wild four-day beer brawl."[3] Things were better at the 1959 Boston Jazz Festival, but writing in June 1960 about the upcoming Newport festival: "All the popular artists in the jazz world will be there. Along with the college kids and the beer and the broken glass... All that carnival under the guise of festival is too frightening for me."[4] That was the year of the riots, when some festival goers ran amok, performances were canceled, and the National Guard mobilized to restore order. The very future of the Newport festival was in doubt.

So there were pros and cons to the festival scene, and we'll see in coming pages how that played out in events held in Boston and environs.

Jazz Night at the Boston Arts Festival

The Boston Arts Festival was an annual outdoor exhibition celebrating the arts in New England, honoring writers and poets, painters and sculptors, musicians and dancers. It ran for about two weeks in June or July from 1951 through 1964, in Boston's Public Garden. To accommodate the lively arts, the festival erected a stage on the southeast quadrant of the Garden abutting the lagoon, with the performers facing forward toward Boylston Street. Beginning in 1954 and continuing through 1963, jazz took its place among the arts, and one evening's public performance was given over to jazz bands—and the musicians on the bandstand were almost always local artists.

The 1954 show offered both talking heads and wailing musicians. The talkers (Father Norman O'Connor, MIT music professor Klaus Leipman, *Christian Science Monitor* music critic Rod Nordell, and WHDH radio's John McLellan) discussed various aspects of jazz, and the musicians demonstrated it before the concert. George Wein assembled the musicians, one group more traditional, a second more modern. Wein himself played piano with the first group, which included Ruby Braff and Vic Dickenson. Wein recorded this group and released the results on his Storyville label as *Jazz at the Boston Arts Festival*, with Nordell's liner notes. Charlie Mariano's modern group went unrecorded. Nonetheless, it was a good showing, drawing a crowd of from 5,000 to 10,000, and as Rod Nordell noted, "even the stately elms were seen to rock."

Jazz has always struggled to attain respectability, and there was a bit of struggle associated with the 1955 Boston Arts Festival. Publicists embarrassed themselves with promotional drivel like "the jazz night will be a chance to come cool at the Garden for a gig. The cats from two combos will flip you with funky music."[5] Local 9 of the American Federation of Musicians union did not help matters when they allotted money for the services of all musicians who participated in the festival, *except* for the jazz musicians, who had to play on their own time, without pay. Nonetheless, the cool cats again fielded two combos, one led by Braff, the other by saxophonist Serge Chaloff, with the band that had just recorded the *Boston Blow-Up!* album for Capitol Records. Wrote Robert Taylor in the *Herald*:

> The ingenuity of Chaloff as a soloist is enormous and his use of dissonance always conveys a strength of purpose and of form. In "Body and Soul" he exhibited his capacities vigorously, taking a deliberate tempo and treating the music from a lyric, delicate, tonal standpoint. Pomeroy, the trumpeter, is in every way his match rhythmically, in the articulation of difficult registers and in tonal nuance, while Mussulli in "Kip" and "No. 6" disclosed a rapport with the rest that proved to be the very heart of the ensemble. As a whole the harmonies of the group are tense and the melodies resourceful and they play with a kind of controlled abandon.[6]

Almost everyone in an Arts Festival crowd had a good time; the exception was a reporter sent by the *Boston Globe*, which in those days did not recognize jazz as respectable art. Their writer, Paul Benzaquin, ridiculed the proceedings and ended his column with "Big Serge Chaloff played the baritone sax, Little Ruby Braff blew upon a trumpet so loud that those who didn't like it couldn't lump it. Each one led his own combination, then they joined together for some super syncopation. Dee-da-diddle ba-ba nonny oh Boom!"

In hindsight, it does make one realize that the jazz community's trad-versus-modern battle was just so much hot air. The warring camps had more in common than they admitted at the time, and one of the things they had in common was a detractor like Benzaquin. Times would change. In 1966, the *Globe* would sponsor its own jazz festival.

Regardless of what the *Globe* printed, jazz night brought people to the festival. Attendees in 1955 filled the 12,000 temporary seats and spilled over to anywhere they could sit. Some estimates put the crowds in later years at 16,000 and even 20,000.

Beginning in 1956, jazz night belonged to Herb Pomeroy and his Orchestra, who played four years in a row. In 1956 they shared the bill with Cannonball Adderley, in 1958 they featured Gerry Mulligan as guest soloist, and in 1959 they shared the bill with Rollins Griffith's nonet. The 1957 performance was something special, however, as Pomeroy's crew presented their *Living History of Jazz* program. This whirlwind tour through the world of jazz was narrated by John McLellan and featured bits of blues and ragtime, a sampling of Bix Beiderbecke, the rhythms of Duke Ellington, the precision of Jimmy Lunceford, Benny Goodman and his Fletcher Henderson arrangements, the swing of Count Basie, the saxophone of Lester Young, the jam sessions of the World War II years, the bop of Charlie Parker, the Afro-Cuban music of Dizzy Gillespie, the cool of Miles Davis, the Second Herd of Woody Herman, the counterpoint popular on the west coast, and finally big band music the way Pomeroy played it in 1957. Much of the credit went to Jaki Byard, who wrote and arranged extended portions of the work.

Woody Herman stepped in for 1960, performing as a soloist with the Festival Jazz Orchestra, a band organized by his former drummer, Joe MacDonald, and starring his former pianist and arranger, Nat Pierce.

Nineteen sixty-one was marred by controversy. June 20 was to feature Langston Hughes joining Jimmy Rushing, Sonny Terry and Brownie McGhee in a presentation titled, "The Blues: Words and Music." They were joined on the program by the Festival Jazz Orchestra, again directed by Joe MacDonald. Father O'Connor was the evening's emcee. The day before the performance, however, the *Herald* reported that Hughes would be picketed by protesters claiming he was "a communist sympathizer and a danger to the children of Boston." Festival organizers, to their eternal credit, would have none of it, and Hughes and company went on as scheduled. Another big crowd (the *Herald* said a record-breaking throng of 20,000) was on hand, along with extra cops and the picketers. All 28 of them. They were orderly, with their protest mainly confined to distributing literature that portrayed Hughes as anti-Jesus and pro-communist. Hughes, in his post-concert press conference, said the charges were nonsense and he had testified under oath to that effect, and nothing more came of it. But the problem in the eyes of his many supporters was that Hughes was forced to address the issue at all, and that a couple dozen reactionaries could so easily transfer Boston's attention from the art to the artist.[7]

And how was the show? In the following day's editions, the *Herald* didn't say. Its reporters were too busy covering the picketing, and the Hearst papers ignored the issue completely. Besides, there was other big news in Boston on June 21. Early in the morning, the Old Howard Theatre, Boston's bastion of burlesque, went up in flames. Only two days before, the shuttered big-band venue Nuttings-on-the-Charles in Waltham also burned. Nuttings, once a Charlie Shribman holding, was being used as a warehouse. Both fires were of suspicious origin.

Pomeroy was back for his final turn in 1962, with George Wein's Newport Jazz Festival All-Stars, and "even the swans in the lagoon trumpeted a few notes of Dixie," claimed a now enthusiastic *Globe*. "It was the hipsters' night, and things really swung." The *Globe's* only omission? They didn't mention the music at all.[8]

The year 1963 brought a night of the "real" traditional jazz to the Arts Festival in the form of the Preservation Hall Jazz Band. Emceed by Reverend Alvin Kershaw, clarinetist George Lewis led a band of New Orleans musicians, the very musicians who gave birth the traditional style and never stopped playing it: trumpeter Kid Howard, trombonist Big Jim Robinson, bassist Alcide "Slow Drag" Pavageau, and drummer Joe Watkins. These men, all but forgotten now, were jazz stars in their fashion, and four of them were dead before the decade was over. On this night, though, the band was "up there having a ball for themselves, with no affectations, no idiosyncrasies. They just swung, and as they did they lifted the crowd with them," reported the *Globe*.[9]

The year 1963 marked the end of jazz night at the Boston Arts Festival. Despite the fact that thousands of people turned out for jazz night year after year, festival organizers dropped jazz from the 1964 program. Perhaps giving the 20,000 jazz-loving people a reason to stay home wasn't such a good idea, though. The Festival itself, chronically short of funds and plagued by mismanagement, made its last stand in 1964. Maybe they could have used some of that dee-da-diddle ba-ba nonny after all.

The North Shore Jazz Festival

The North Shore Jazz Festival took place over three days, the weekend of August 23–25, 1957. Of all the events described in this chapter, North Shore is the only one George Wein did not produce, but it was well planned, with a good stylistic variety, although not many Boston-area musicians were scheduled. Lynn was a good choice for location, as the city had a stronger jazz tradition in the postwar years than any other North Shore community, having been home to clubs like the Melody Lounge and the Red Fox.

Producer Harold Leverant fully expected that all three days of his North Shore Jazz Festival would be held at the Manning Bowl in Lynn, but Mother Nature had other ideas. Unseasonable cold kept people away on opening night, and steady rain forced the Sunday session indoors. Leverant's scramble for available space took him to the Boston Arena on St. Botolph Street.

Weather wasn't the only thing out of Leverant's control. The Boston newspapers went on strike two weeks before the festival and stayed out for the duration, seriously hampering promotion and preventing the next-day buzz normally generated by reviews. And on Saturday night, Stan Getz ran up against the curfew and only played two numbers. "One of the few things that didn't happen at the North Shore Jazz Festival," reported *Down Beat*, "was an invasion by Martians."

Nonetheless, about 22,000 chilly fans attended the three-day festival, including 6,000 who managed to find their way to the Boston Arena on the final night, thanks to blanket announcements on radio and television.

Reverend Alvin Kershaw, then the pastor at All Saints Church in Peterborough, N.H., was emcee on the first night. John McLellan hosted the second night, and Symphony Sid Torin the third. This was Symphony Sid's last Boston appearance; he had already announced he was returning to New York, and Sarah Vaughan serenaded him with a farewell song.

With everyone else on strike, the Lynn *Daily Evening Item* was the only daily covering the festival, and the only jazz writer covering it in depth was Vin Haynes of the *Chronicle*. He noted good sets by Billie Holiday, the Four Freshmen, Oscar Peterson and George Shearing; liked the trumpets of Lennie Johnson and Joe Gordon in the Pomeroy band; and reported the festival's surprise was Lee Konitz sitting in with Gerry Mulligan's band. Haynes declared the weekend a success.

Leverant said his festival would be back in 1958, "bigger and better than ever," but it wasn't back in that or any other year. Still, it was the first multi-day festival held locally, and as such, was an important step in getting jazz outdoors in the Boston area.[10]

Leverant had yet more bad luck in 1957; a Dizzy Gillespie/Sarah Vaughan show he produced at Boston's cavernous Mechanics Hall in December was an utter disaster. The show started an hour late, the shrill metallic sound system ruined the music, the overhead fluorescent lights could not be shut off, and the emcee appeared lost. Moaned McLellan, "This set jazz concerts back to the level of a rock and roll record hop."[11]

The First Boston Jazz Festival

Festivals were definitely on the move in 1959, and George Wein was the man moving them. He wanted to do something in his home town, so his Newport Jazz Festival company, in partnership with the Sheraton Corporation, organized a Boston Jazz Festival for Fenway Park to run August 21–23 that year.

Wein had been in the jazz business in Boston for ten years by then, and had started an outdoor series in suburban Ipswich the previous year. His Newport Jazz Festival would run for the sixth time in 1959. If anyone could put a festival over in Boston, it was Wein. He planned to sell 11,000 tickets each night, with seating under the grandstand on the first-base side, to avoid the weather problems faced in the open at the Manning Bowl. The stage was erected on the infield and surrounded by a tall curtain. Fenway's acoustics problems were solved by the same technicians who had designed the sound system at Newport.

The talent was exceptional; it was as if a whole year of Storyville artists played in three nights at Fenway. From Thelonious Monk to Coleman Hawkins to Dinah Washington, every night promised a listener's delight. Did it deliver? George Forsythe, who filed festival stories for both the *Traveler* and *Down Beat*, commented: "Although they had all the ingredients for good concerts, it was as if the people didn't much care, as if they were up to their ears in festivals. I got the feeling that if they hadn't heard the music, they wouldn't have much cared."

Father O'Connor, then the Sunday jazz columnist at the *Globe,* estimated first-night attendance at about 5,000. He was rather circumspect about the night's proceedings, saying that "jazz festivals are a sometimes thing," and that opening night wasn't one of those times. He blamed the stadium setting, the distance between stage and listeners, the small crowd, and the generally lackluster music for the off night.

Saturday night fared better, despite Sarah Vaughan's last-minute cancellation. John McLellan, writing in the *Traveler,* praised Dick Johnson's alto work with the Pomeroy band, Blue Mitchell's trumpet work with Horace Silver, Buck Clayton's trumpet work with Eddie Condon, and the Brubeck Quartet for finally achieving the relaxed groove that had long eluded them. The crowd was bigger on Saturday, too, drawing 8,500 fans, as did Sunday's.

The Sunday finale went well, with Ruby Braff and Oscar Peterson turning in good sets; the vocal trio Lambert, Hendricks and Ross, then billed as "the

Take me out to the jazz fest! View of the stage at the Boston Jazz Festival at Fenway Park, August 1959. *Boston Traveler* photo, courtesy of the Boston Public Library, Print Department.

hottest new group in jazz," turned in a crowd-pleasing set, and Duke Ellington's orchestra closed the festival. Both O'Connor and McLellan declared the festival a success, calling it a good start to an annual tradition. Both thought Wein and the Sheraton Corporation should be pleased with the result, and ready to roll in 1960.

Wein, however, lost money ("too many free tickets," he told *Down Beat*). If the show was to go on, he would need to overhaul it.[12]

Jazz Festival at Pleasure Island

Changes there indeed were for Wein's second Boston festival in 1960, everything from festival site to sponsorship to reducing the festival to a two-day event. Even the name changed. Even though everyone called it the Boston Jazz Festival, it was actually the Jazz Festival at Pleasure Island, named for the amusement park in suburban Wakefield where the festival was staged.

The 80-acre Pleasure Island (1959–1969) was modeled after Disneyland, offering diversions like the Old Smokey narrow-gauge railroad, whale hunting in Pleasure Island Bay, and Diamond Lil's old west saloon, where the sheriff and the bad guys shot it out several times a day while the band, the

Disgruntled Threesome, played the lighthearted "Getting to Know You" from *The King and I.* The park's executive vice president, Norm Prescott, a former Boston disc jockey who had lost his job in the payola scandals, approached Wein with the idea of staging the jazz festival in the park's 7,000-seat Outdoor Show Bowl. The fest, pared down to two days, was set for August 26 and 27.

Again the entertainment would be first-rate, drawing on Wein's regular stable of stars, among them Dave Brubeck, Vic Dickenson, Duke Ellington, Oscar Peterson, Pee Wee Russell, Dakota Staton, and Dinah Washington.

Again circumstances beyond the control of the promoters interfered with their best-laid plans. This time it wasn't weather or a newspaper strike; it was the events that took place at the Newport festival earlier that summer. That was the year of the beery, destructive riot at Newport, started by people who couldn't gain entry to the sold-out festival grounds. It forced that festival's early shutdown and caused a chain reaction that affected festivals everywhere.

At Pleasure Island, it meant a strong police presence, with 200 state and local officers, including contingents from nearby communities and the military police, and a ban on alcohol inside the park. To make sure festival-goers got the message, Wakefield's package stores closed early and police were posted at stores in nearby Lynnfield. The sellout crowd was well-behaved, and the police made sure they stayed that way, planting undercover men in the crowd and even going so far as to eject a number of fans who were dancing in the aisles when Gene Krupa's band broke into his signature piece, "Sing, Sing, Sing."

Far more press coverage was given to law enforcement than to the music itself. One review of opening night started with: "There were more cops than beatniks at the Pleasure Island Jazz Festival tonight." And the music? The informality of nightclub jazz was absent. "It seems to be a case of too much and too little. There is too much commercialism, too much regimentation, too much scheduling. There is too little rapport, too little joy in playing from the heart and even, perhaps, too little cigarette smoke and tinkle of glasses." Efficiency won out over spontaneity. There were some good sets, such as those by Dinah Washington and Art Blakey, and Duke Ellington's closing set on Saturday night was buoyant, but in the midst of a medley of Ellington's hits, which was "stirring the audience into its most jubilant mood," the police inexplicably stopped the show.[13]

The festival did near-capacity business both nights, but still, there were too many cops and too many rules. In early 1961, John McLellan reflected on the troubled Newport festival of 1960 and the prospects for future festivals: "What will probably happen is a jazz festival conducted in the midst of an armed camp. Sort of like the one last summer at Pleasure Island…And you can just imagine how much fun that was. It's no way to relax and listen to jazz, I can tell you that."[14]

Perhaps the site or the timing were wrong, or perhaps there were too many police checkpoints and too few jam sessions. Whatever the reason, there was no third Boston Jazz Festival.

With the failure of the Boston Jazz Festival and the end of Jazz Night at the Boston Arts Festival, local jazz went back indoors. When the *Boston Globe* sponsored its first jazz festival in 1966, it was a concert-like, mid-winter affair staged in the War Memorial Auditorium. Jazz would wait until the late 1960s, with the city's Summerthing program and Elma Lewis's Playhouse in the Park, before it returned to the great outdoors.

Chapter 20

Looking Forward, Looking Back

The early 1960s mark the end of our chronicles. Storyville closed in May 1960, and the Stable in October 1962, and the period in between was a transitional time on the local scene. Key people moved on, popular tastes continued to change, economic realities were reshaping the way music was presented. The early sixties act as a vantage point from which we can both look back at what was ending, and look forward to the decade to come.

A City Changes

One thing certainly was in a state of transition: Boston itself. The city was changing physically and that changed where music was played. Consider the closing of the Stable. That marked the end of jazz on Huntington Avenue, which began with James Reese Europe's ill-fated concert at Mechanic's Hall in 1919 and lasted through dance halls, Dixieland, and Storyville. The nightclub closings were a small part of the change overtaking Huntington Avenue itself. Mechanic's Hall was demolished in 1959 and the Prudential Center was rising in its place. The buildings that housed the Stable, Copley Terrace, and Huntington Chambers Hall were razed to make way for a turnpike on-ramp, which itself replaced the railroad corridor that once moved goods inland from the port. Later in the 1960s, the Christian Science Center expanded from Mass Ave east to the Prudential Center, removing all traces of the old Strand and Uptown Ballrooms. Across the street, construction of a new hotel claimed the Ritz Plaza Hall and the Hotel Minerva, where Max Kaminsky opened his little jazz club.

Changes such as those that remade Huntington Avenue were wiping out the old jazz spots all across the downtown and nearby neighborhoods as the "New Boston" took shape. Perhaps it did not change the music being played, but it changed where people went to hear it. Boston was becoming a different place, finally awakening from a slumber of 40 years' duration, and coming to resemble the city we know today more than the city Jimmie Martin knew in the late 1940s. It came at a price. Neighborhoods were demolished and people were displaced, and the displaced ones did not share in the progress promised by the New Boston. The downtown prospered while inner city neighborhoods collapsed.

There was still jazz on the Jazz Corner, but the music had lost its prominence. Connolly's and Wally's continued as jazz clubs, even as the neighborhood turned harder and white faces became scarcer. Other clubs came and went, but nothing could replace the Hi-Hat and the Savoy, because nothing could replenish the spirit of their time.

Changes in Time, Changes in Taste

People danced to swing music; that's what it was for. In the first eight years of our story, swing was the unrivaled popular choice on the radio, dance floor, and theater stage. Then came bop and other types of listening-not-dancing jazz, and the audience began to drift away. Young people in particular didn't want to listen to music, they wanted to move to it, and the uncomplicated beats of R&B and rock and roll suited them just fine. This was the time of those "why are they listening to this trash?" parental laments, but they did no good. In 1961, it seemed like everyone was twistin' the night away. It marked the beginning of the generational split in musical taste that would lead to the rock revolution of the mid-1960s, and jazz would never recover its diminishing audience share.

Nor should we overlook folk music, which claimed a growing share of the college crowd, a reality acknowledged by George Wein when he closed his Dixieland club in 1959 and reopened it as the Ballad Room. "Mary Hamilton" was in, "Muskrat Ramble" was out.

No place in the city embodied this shift as much as the clubs opening near Mass Ave and Washington Street. When the Trinidad Lounge opened at 1844 Washington Street in November 1958, R&B was up front and jazz was in the back seat. Pianist Hopeton Johnson, a graduate of the New England Conservatory who organized his first jazz group in 1944, opened the club. The Hurricanes, his band at the Trinidad Lounge, wasn't a jazz band, and except for the Sunday jam session, the Trinidad Lounge wasn't a jazz club. Johnson's group played the dance-oriented R&B popular at the time.

In December 1960, the Trinidad Lounge closed and John McIlvaine opened a new, more sophisticated club there called Basin Street South, on New Year's Eve, with Arthur Bragg's *Idlewild Revue*, a major touring show on the black entertainment circuit. Basin Street South sometimes presented jazz, but it wasn't a jazz club. It featured the biggest names in black entertainment regardless of genre, its schedule heavy on floor shows built around singers and comics. It was, like the Latin Quarter in the decade before it, a room for name acts with crossover appeal.

Louie's Lounge, at 1788 Washington Street, had already been a blues and R&B club for close to ten years. Its musical director in the late 1950s was Sam Rivers. For all his jazz credentials, Rivers enjoyed playing mainstream black music, and he gave that side of his musical self full reign, leading the Louie's Lounge house band that backed up Maxine Brown, Jerry Butler, and others.

Jim Mellen's Shanty Lounge, at 1781 Washington Street, opened in June 1961 with a jazz policy, and Sam Rivers and Jimmy Tyler both had groups there, but by mid-1963 the Shanty, too, offered mostly blues and R&B.

In late 1962, the Washington Street clubs were serving a predominantly black clientele and presenting the music that clientele heard on the radio— Sam Cooke, King Curtis, Mary Wells, Jackie Wilson—musicians one generation removed from jazz. Jazz was still part of the mix, but it was no longer the first choice for the young urban audience. Although jazz wasn't unknown in the clubs they frequented (organ trios were popular at the time), it was far from being the focus.

Modern Jazz Matures

The obvious answer to "what happened here?" is that a modern jazz scene developed in Boston between the late forties and the mid-fifties, and it happened away from the limelight of New York. In spite of the better efforts of *Down Beat* and *Metronome*, it remained relatively unknown to many jazz fans. In earlier years, musicians of the caliber of Joe Gordon, Lennie Johnson, John Neves, Herb Pomeroy, or Ray Santisi would have left Boston in their late teen years, as Roy Haynes and Dave Lambert did. But in the postwar years they were joined by others of an equal caliber, courtesy of the GI Bill, and they stayed in Boston and built their scene. The prewar trickle of jazz musicians studying at the conservatories became a flood after the war, bringing Gigi Gryce, Sam Rivers, Sonny Truitt, Dick Wetmore, and others to Boston. In terms of talent, Boston reached a critical mass. The merging of the students with the locals created bands such as those of Jimmie Martin and Nat Pierce, and culminated in Herb Pomeroy's orchestra.

Big Thinkers and Risk Takers

While the musicians were creating the sound of Boston, other individuals were being just as creative on the media, education, and business sides. In 1937, Charlie and Cy Shribman built a music empire with splash publicity and good management, proving themselves the exception to the rule that the music business must always be a tawdry one. In the 1950s, though, another businessman, George Wein, showed how a jazz club should be run at Storyville, and produced the first Newport Jazz Festival, and in the process became the most important figure in Boston jazz in the 1950s.

There were others who took risks on a smaller but still important scale. Joseph Walcott was a pioneer, the first black man to open a nightclub in Boston. Given the racial and political climate, that was no small accomplishment in the Boston of 1947. Tom Wilson formed Transition Records in 1954. He wasn't the first Bostonian to form a record company, but his independent company was recording and releasing long-playing jazz records in Boston in 1955. Like Walcott, he was an African-American finding his way in the local business community. That he was less successful than Walcott takes nothing away from his status as a pioneer.

Although Boston had George Frazier as its local jazz journalist between 1937 and 1942, his work—and his narrow outlook—were surpassed by Nat Hentoff, Bob Martin, John McLellan, Father Norman O'Connor, and others in the writing and broadcasting fields, all ardent and articulate spokesmen for jazz. These men, as well as Dom Cerulli, Bill Coss, and Dan Morgenstern, had Boston in their blood, and even after they moved on, they kept a close watch on the city and gave Boston a prominent place in *Down Beat* and *Metronome*. It was through their efforts that the jazz world came to know the likes of Jaki Byard and Herb Pomeroy.

Walcott still ran his club in 1962, but the others were gone or out of the business by 1962, and Boston faced a talent shortage not on the bandstand, but off it. There were no Weins or Hentoffs or O'Connors. One big thinker remained, though, and he was going stronger than ever. That was Larry Berk.

The Ascent of the Berklee School

Although the New England Conservatory phased out the Department of Popular Music in 1958, the Berklee School of Music was unquestionably one of the success stories of the fifties. As it consolidated its position at the forefront of jazz education in the late 1950s, it anticipated more growth in the 1960s. In 1962, the saxophonist, composer, and author John LaPorta joined the faculty, perhaps Berk's most significant hire to that point. That same year Berklee started its guitar department, continuing to shape its course of study to meet changes in the music industry. And it announced that as of 1963, Berklee would begin accepting students into a new degree-granting program.

That students were making major contributions to the scene was a fact of life, and the days of relying on veterans to fill out the student body were past. Berklee's students came from all over the world. Approximately 300 full-time students were enrolled in September 1962, a number constrained by the limited space on Newbury Street. That problem was addressed a few years later with the acquisition of the Boylston Street building, where the school moved in 1966, the year its first bachelors of music graduated. With the new facilities, the degree program, and an opportunistic curriculum, Berklee's steady growth became explosive. About 600 students were enrolled in 1966, and more than 900 in 1969.

A Change in Venue

If jazz was music aimed at an adult audience, the audience in Boston was shrinking as young adults left the city in large numbers. The U. S. Census reported a Boston population of about 801,000 in 1950, a number that fell to 697,000 thousand in 1960, while at the same time the metro area as a whole grew through suburban expansion. With fewer people residing in the city, the legislature reasoned that Boston needed fewer club and cafe liquor licenses, so they reduced the number available from 811 to 700 in May 1958.[1] This meant that as urban renewal shuttered places in the West End, South End, and Scollay Square, their licenses came off the books. Even though many of these places did not offer musical entertainment, every lost license represented a lost opportunity for a music venue in another part of town.

Perhaps the decline didn't matter from a jazz point of view. In the early 1960s, the clubs were giving ground to alternative venues, and that meant more than college auditoriums and concert halls. Jazz was in coffeehouses, churches, museums, and other places that did not sell liquor. But there was always a need for a name-band room where customers could order a drink, and in fall 1960, Storyville had another go under new management.

Storyville's final iteration opened in the Hotel Bradford in September 1960, with Duke Ellington's Orchestra presiding. Ralph Snider, the Bradford's owner, ran the club, and Rollins Griffith led the house trio. Dakota Staton recorded her *Dakota at Storyville* LP for Capitol Records during her season-ending engagement in April, capping a good first year. Everyone looked forward to reopening in September. Al Vega had the trio that second year and recalled:

> We had Stan Getz. Josh White came in, and he brought along some friends, a new group—Peter, Paul and Mary. We had the Shearing Quintet, and Chico Hamilton, and Ahmad Jamal, and Cannonball Adderley. My band played for Betty Carter. The musicians liked it, and we were 95 percent full...and we didn't make it to Christmas. It was getting hard financially, with groups asking for a lot of money. Groups could go to Symphony Hall and other big rooms and skip clubs completely. If you ran a club and if you weren't doing 100 percent, selling every seat, you couldn't survive.[2]

Cannonball Adderley's Quintet played the last set in December 1961. It was a closing reminiscent of the Latin Quarter's in 1955. "There just wasn't enough money coming in," George Clarke wrote at that time, and if he hadn't retired in October 1961, he could have written it again.

Storyville's last act underscored the jazz nightclub's choices in the early 1960s: keep increasing cover charges and drink minimums, or find more seats to sell, or close up shop. For the name bands, the economics favored the concert hall and festival stage—a one-nighter schedule minus the bus rides.

Some name bands found their way to Lennie Sogoloff's spot in West Peabody, Lennie's-on-the-Turnpike. Lennie's became a much-heralded stop for musicians on tour. It started its full-time jazz policy in October 1962, the same month the Stable closed. Lennie's, like an ever-larger number of jazz listeners, was out in the suburbs.

New Faces

This story is mainly about people who already had a horn in their hands during the World War II years. They were the ones at the Melody Lounge and the Hi-Hat, and they created the Jazz Workshop and were enrolled at Schillinger House. They made modern jazz happen in Boston, but jazz is a living thing and as one generation makes its mark, another is lining up right behind it. So it was in Boston in the early 1960s.

Boston was still producing musicians of note in the late fifties, next-generation players who were raised on bebop and preparing to lead jazz into its post-bop future. They looked to Sam Rivers and Jaki Byard for inspiration, and among them were Ken McIntyre, Chick Corea, Hal Galper, and Tony Williams.

Ken McIntyre played many instruments, but he was primarily known in Boston for his work on flute and alto saxophone. He was born in Boston in 1931, and after a hitch in the army, began studying at the Boston Conservatory in 1954. He earned both a bachelor's and master's degree in music composition, completing his degree work in 1959. His best-known Boston group was a 1960 quartet with trombonist John Mancebo Lewis, bassist Larry Richardson, and drummer Bill Grant. While still in Boston he took part in two recordings for Prestige New Jazz in spring 1960, *Looking Ahead* with Eric Dolphy, and *Stone Blues*, with his own group of Lewis, pianist Dizzy Sal, bassist Paul Morrison, and drummer Bobby Ward. He moved to New York in spring 1962.

McIntyre was painted with the same brush as Ornette Coleman and labeled "avant garde," although he disagreed with the categorization. He was not without controversy while still in Boston; Cannonball Adderley singled him out for criticism in a 1961 interview with John McLellan: "Not everybody who comes along can automatically be great, when we had to pay dues for so many years. Why should a guy such as Ken McIntyre come in with no experience, no dues-paying, as far as the guys are concerned, and transcend a Johnny Hodges in acceptability?" Sam Rivers, reflecting years later on McIntyre during his Boston years, said: "We kind of made fun of him, people would see him coming and they'd leave the stand, didn't want to be there when 'rigor mortis' sat in. That's what we called him."

Pianist Armando "Chick" Corea was born in Chelsea, Massachusetts, in 1941, and his trumpet-playing father was taking him along on gigs when Chick was in his early teens. He had his own trio while still in high school with drummer Tony Williams, who was even younger, and bassist Don Alias, who as a college freshman was the old man of the outfit. Corea entered Columbia University in 1959 but dropped out after a few months, tried the Juilliard School and wasn't happy there either, and came back to Boston for a time, working in Al Natale's band at the Mayfair, among others. Then he went on the road in the 1960s, working across the broad jazz spectrum, from Billy May to Mongo Santamaria to Sarah Vaughan to Miles Davis. He started his own groups Circle and then Return to Forever. Corea became a jazz polyglot, moving between free playing, fusion, and acoustic jazz with equal skill.

Pianist Hal Galper, born in Salem, Massachusetts in 1938, attended Berklee for two years, finishing in 1957. He completed many of the rites of passage of the young musicians in those years, playing at Izzy Ort's and in the strip joints, and studying with Madame Chaloff for three years. He led a quintet in 1957 that included the Boston tenor saxophonist Rocky Boyd and bassist Benny Wilson, and he replaced Ray Santisi in Herb Pomeroy's band in 1961. At that time he also worked in the Monday night band at the Stable with Sam Rivers and Gene DiStasio. It wasn't his first experience with Rivers; in 1959–1963 he was a member of Sam's renowned quartet with bassist Phil Morrison and drummer Tony Williams. He could look forward to long stints with Chet Baker and Phil Woods, and as a leader of his own groups.

Tony Williams, who was born in 1945, was playing with Rivers and Galper before he was old enough to get a driver's license. When he was 12, his father, saxophonist Tillman Williams, took him to jam sessions, and he studied for a time with Alan Dawson. He was called a prodigy from early on. He had been with Rivers and Galper for almost three years when he sat in with Jackie McLean at Connolly's, and in a matter of months was with McLean in New York. Williams was 17 when he went with Miles Davis in 1963, and stayed for six history-making years, some of them with Sam Rivers and others with

Chick Corea. In a town known for turning out good drummers in these 25 years—Joe Booker, Bobby Donaldson, Bey Perry, Joe MacDonald, Bill Grant, Roy Haynes, Clarence Johnston, Floogie Williams, Jimmy Zitano, Jake Hanna, Alan Dawson, Bobby Ward—Tony Williams might have been the best of them all, and the jazz world was shocked by his death following routine surgery in 1997. He was only 51.

* * *

The scene cooled but never went cold because so many of the participants remained active, and more people arrived every year. But something ended, something more than just a decade on the calendar. What started back with Charlie Mariano's solo on "Autumn in New York" reached a turning point in the early 1960s. That generation had grown up. They were now in their thirties, and many were in the jazz groove where they would reside for the rest of their careers. Though Byard, Rivers, and Mariano would continue as major innovators, many others settled into the mainstream. It would fall to Hal Galper, Ken McIntyre, Chick Corea, Tony Williams, and others to write the next chapter of the Boston jazz story. As the sound of swing had yielded to the sound of modern jazz, so too would the sound of modern jazz yield to new sounds in the post-bop years. When the Stable came down in 1962, it marked another changing of the guard.

Gloomy opinions abounded on the future of jazz. Jazz was dying, said some, laid low by rock and roll, a surplus of musicians, too many concerts, the emerging avant garde, the transformation of jazz from entertainment to art form, television, the predictability of its established stars, spiraling salaries, the 1960 Newport riot, musicians exhibiting contemptuous behavior on the bandstand or delivering perfunctory performances, critics writing drivel, record companies failing to promote their artists. Jazz took some shots, to be sure, but none of them was a knockout punch. Instead jazz changed with the times, although the jazz world of the 1960s resembled nothing that came before it.

Boston jazz—all jazz—had entered a new decade. There would be new faces, new places, and a whole new scene to make.

Appendix: Snapshots of a City

Perhaps some of this book's readers are new to Boston or to its history during these years. For these readers, a bit of context is in order, and this appendix serves as a quick introduction to the city and its people between the late 1930s and the early 1960s. Think of these few pages as snapshots or postcards of Boston at mid-century, offering glimpses of the city and some of the things that shaped its environment, musical and otherwise.

Hard Times for the City on the Hill

Well into the 1950s, Boston was a worn-out city, in the midst of a prolonged decline interrupted only by the economic boomlet of the war years. The city's economy was starving from lack of investment. Its location in a corner of the country made its access to the growing national market more difficult, and meanwhile the roads and rails were crumbling, the port was decaying, and the building stock was old and obsolete. Nobody was building or investing in anything.[1]

Manufacturing employment peaked in Massachusetts during the war years, and then began an inexorable decline. Backbone industries such as textiles and leather goods abandoned the region entirely, while the manufacture of durable goods declined steadily as the postwar shift to the south gained momentum. The postwar years were a time of high taxes, falling property values, and steady job loss.

The relationship between the business community, the domain of the Yankee establishment, and city hall, the clubhouse of James Michael Curley and his supporters, was rancorous.

Boston, for all intents and purposes, was a city with no future, a backwater.

The turnaround began in 1949, when Boston voters ousted Curley by electing John Hynes mayor. Hynes took the first steps in building what became known as the "New Boston" by changing the city's zoning and tax policies, restoring a working relationship with the city's business and financial communities, and creating the Boston Redevelopment Agency. Hynes remained in office until 1960, and it was during the administration of his successor, John Collins, that much of his work bore fruit.

Collins quickened the pace of rebuilding Boston, tapping into federal dollars to fund a period of extensive urban renewal (or "urban removal," depending on your viewpoint) that transformed the physical city. Between 1954 and 1962, the Central Artery opened to traffic; the South End's New York streets area and the entire West End were razed and redeveloped; the Callahan Tunnel opened; and construction started on the Turnpike Extension, the Prudential Center, and Government Center. Most of these projects took a fearsome human toll as neighborhoods disappeared with little thought given to the residents being displaced. The West End in particular became a textbook case of a mismanaged redevelopment project. Still, it was a massive change over an eight-year period.

The city's demographics changed over the 20 years as well. Boston's 1940 population was about 771,000, and it reached its peak in 1950, at about 801,000 thousand. Population fell dramatically in the 1950s, to about 697,000 in 1960. Young adults in particular left Boston in droves for the suburbs in nearby Middlesex and Norfolk counties. That's where the "New Boston" jobs were going, too, in the growing defense, aerospace, and electronics industries locating along the Route 128 ring. The automobile, new highways, and cheap land made suburbanization possible. The population shift represented another enormous change in a short time.[2]

Culturally, Boston was a tribal city, with well-defined Irish, Italian, and Jewish neighborhoods, where the proper Bostonians of Beacon Hill and the Back Bay were separated by mere blocks from the working class melting pots of the West and South Ends. The black population, so important to the jazz story in Boston, resided mainly in the South End and adjoining Roxbury.

Boston's black community was small (three percent of the city's population in the 1940 census, five percent in 1950, and nine percent in 1960) but intellectually robust and significant to our story. They did not join the 1950s exodus from the city. In fact, the opposite was true, as there was an influx of blacks moving in from southern states. Blocked by discriminatory housing practices, blacks remained concentrated in the city, moving across Roxbury and into Dorchester. That's where things stood in 1960, with the worst of the housing story—the redlining, the blockbusting, the violence—still to come.

Jazz, Race, and Boston at Mid-Century

The relationship between blacks and whites in Boston in the middle of the last century merits a book of its own, but here we're looking only at a snapshot.

Boston at mid-century was not a town known for tolerance. Inequality was a fact of life in Boston, but it wasn't a highly visible inequality because Boston was an overwhelmingly white city that marginalized its small black population. The levers of power—in politics, business and finance, the unions, the media—were in white hands. It was easy for white Boston to ignore the minorities because they posed no threat. Nor did the mainstream media feel the need to cover them. The black community had no voice in city decisionmaking, and that was a ticking time bomb all through these years.

Blacks and whites did not mix to any great degree, and when they did, it sometimes had consequences; Boston was one of those places where a mere conversation between a man and a woman of different races could provoke a policeman's interference. It was a time of double standards, when even the American Federation of Musicians sanctioned official segregation with its two-local policy.

Things were a bit more congenial in the jazz spots. Such places were located in commercial districts, for example along the busy thoroughfares of Massachusetts Avenue or Huntington Avenue, where whatever mixing was likely to happen would occur. From the first days of this story, there were jazz clubs downtown in the Theatre District on Tremont Street, and uptown in the South End along Massachusetts Avenue.

Until 1947, all jazz spots were white owned, even places like the Little Dixie that were situated in predominantly black neighborhoods. The entertainers were black. This was an obvious example of a grievance noted time and again by the black community: black musicians made the jazz, and white businessmen made the money. Jazz was an African-American cultural contribution, and African-American musicians were responsible for every advance in the music, yet history shows that it was white business interests that profited from it.

In 1947, Joseph Walcott broke the white owner/black performer model when he opened Wally's Paradise, the first licensed nightclub owned by an African-American in Boston, on Mass Ave in the South End. Fittingly, it was a jazz club. The Pioneer Social Club, the after-hours gathering spot for the jazz crowd in these years, was a black-owned private club. John McIlvaine opened and operated several clubs in the 1950s and 1960s. These remained the exceptions to the rule. The other nightclubs synonymous with Boston jazz in the late 1940s and 1950s—the Savoy, the Hi-Hat, Storyville, the Stable—were white-owned. It went beyond just owning clubs though. White businessmen had ready access to capital and black businessmen did not, making it hard to start any kind of small business. That Tom Wilson was able to form Transition Records in 1954 is a testament to his determination.

The doors of the late 1930s jazz clubs—the Royal Palms and Little Dixie uptown, Southland and the Club Congo downtown—were open to anyone who could afford the price of a drink. As might be expected, there were more whites in the downtown clubs and more blacks uptown. Even in those white-owned uptown clubs, there was some racial pressure; Elliott Freeman in the *Afro-American* described a typical incident in September 1937 involving a popular singer: "Clyde Jones went haywire when one of the proprietors at the Royal Palms, where he is employed, wanted him to segregate sepia patrons. The boy refused to do so and quit on the spot, only to be begged by his boss to remain."[3]

The Savoy, the premiere Boston jazz room of the 1940s, always drew a mixed crowd. So did the Ken Club, the Checker Cafe, and the other jazz rooms. A few of the downtown clubs did have some blemishes on their records; the Tic Toc, a fashionable wartime club in the Theatre District, and the Rio Casino, a block away, did have some trouble during the war and just after it. In the Rio's case, a 1946 fracas involving Billy Eckstine's band was a serious incident, ignored by the Boston papers. Anyone wanting to read about it or other incidents had to turn to the black press, for example Boston's *Chronicle* or the *Afro-American*, the Baltimore paper that published several pages of New England news in each issue.

Places that did not book jazz, such as the Bay Village nightclubs and the Back Bay hotels, were a different story. The Bay Village clubs were all white: musicians, employees, customers. Of the 492 people who perished in the Cocoanut Grove fire in 1942, the only nonwhite fatality was the man who shined shoes. The hotels told a similar story. Boston did not have Jim Crow laws on the books, but there were places that were off-limits to blacks for all practical purposes, starting with hotels. Recalled George Wein: "The hotels...they had no official policy on not admitting blacks as guests, they just managed not to take them. But I do remember meeting musicians at downtown hotels in 1947, '48, at places like the Avery. They weren't the best hotels, but blacks could go there."[4]

The Back Bay hotels took longer. The Bostonian was the only Back Bay hotel with an open guest policy, and some of the road bands stayed there. Because of the problems at the hotels, black musicians generally stayed in rooming houses, because they were both friendly and reasonable—musicians paid room and board out of their own pockets.

Jazz moved into Copley Square in the 1950s, and the doors of Storyville, the Stable, and the 5 O'Clock Club were open to all. But just because the door was open didn't mean people walked through it. Herb Pomeroy said of the peak years that: "In the mid to late 1950s there were ten clubs. Five in Copley Square and five around the Mass Ave/Columbus Ave. corner. Copley Square was the white area and Mass Ave was the black area. The audiences didn't overlap as much as one would have hoped for."[5]

This brings us to the bands on the bandstand. The bandstands were the least restrictive place in the music business, and blacks and whites had been playing together for decades. Integrated bands in Boston in the 1940s were uncommon but not rare. Sabby Lewis employed saxophonist Jerry Heffron, his first important arranger, from 1938 to 1944, and there were others in later years, including trumpeter Leon Merian and saxophonist George Perry. Frankie Newton and Sherman Freeman also had integrated bands, and of course, everyone sat in at the jam sessions.

The trend accelerated in Boston in the 1950s, as it did in all the northern cities. Herb Pomeroy's 1950s big band simply could not have succeeded without the contributions of Jaki Byard, Joe Gordon, Lennie Johnson, and John Neves. In the peak years at mid-decade, Jay Migliori's group at the Downbeat club included three blacks and two whites. Serge Chaloff's sextet included two blacks and four whites. Al Vega's best trio was his 1958 group with Alan Dawson. The house bands at Storyville and the Hi-Hat were integrated more often than not, and the decade ended with Hal Galper as a founding member of the Sam Rivers Quartet.

It's not surprising to see that it was the musicians themselves who were the most fair-minded.

Perhaps it is too simplistic to suggest that places of jazz interest, such as the Savoy, had more open policies when it came to who could work and who could listen, and places of less interest, like the hotels and nightclubs with floor shows, were more restrictive. Hip places had room for everybody. It's one of the things that made them hip.

It was not idyllic by any means, but jazz did its part to improve the climate. Blacks and whites played together in the best bands in Boston, and blacks and whites listened to them together, even if not as many as Pomeroy and others would have liked. At its best, jazz exemplified how common interest and purpose could weaken social prohibitions. No matter how bad it was on the streets, it was always better in the jazz venues. The music did more to bring people together than political posturing ever did. Jazz wasn't *the* answer, but it was *an* answer.

Blue Laws and Bureaucrats

In the forties and fifties, the Sunday blue laws and the Boston Licensing Board were the wet blankets used to smother the fire of Boston nightlife. "Banned in Boston" was the catch phrase that exemplified the public morality inherited from the dour New England Protestants who founded the Watch and Ward Society in an earlier time, and brought to contemporary standards by the conservative Irish Catholics of the Curley era. The city censor was the one who did the banning, and the censor patrolled the clubs and theaters looking for displays of immorality in word, dress, or deed. (Boston finally retired the office of the censor in 1982.)

The censor's office dictated what people could do on the Day of Rest, and "rest" commenced promptly at midnight on Saturday. Everything shut down at twelve. No exceptions. Other nights, closing time, or more correctly, stop serving time, was 1:00 a.m. Places could stay open and serve food, but the entertainers stopped performing and the bartenders stopped pouring at 1:00, except on Saturday, which should have been the busiest night of the week.

Dancing was banned outright on Sunday, so anyone wanting to dance that day joined the other heathens at Revere Beach or Nantasket. A promoter could stage a concert on Sunday in Boston, and almost anything could be classified as a concert as long as people stayed off the dance floor until 12:01 a.m. Monday. Charlie Shribman, at the Roseland-State Ballroom, knew how to work this, especially on the nights before a Monday holiday. Shribman would advertise a concert starting at 10:00 on Sunday night, with dancing commencing at midnight and going until 4:00. He called them "dawn dances."

Of course, everyone making a buck on musical entertainment thought this was a farce, and did what they could to change it. Ballroom operators and the musicians' union would gather their troops for an annual assault on the blue laws. Skirmishes began in earnest in 1949. They were defeated that year, and every year, until 1962, when Sunday dancing was finally permitted in commercial establishments.[6]

The blue laws had something to say about drinking on Sunday, too. A club's patrons could buy a drink on Sunday beginning in 1935, but they couldn't consume it standing at the bar. On Sunday, only table service was permitted. They worked around this at the Stable by pushing small tables up against the bar, and having the bartender reach across it to set the drink on the customer's table, at which said customer just happened to be standing. Sunday bar service was finally permitted in 1963. Cocktail waitresses were sad to see the change, because they made better money the old way.[7]

The Boston Licensing Board was something else entirely, an artifact of an earlier era that confounds the concept of home rule. Unlike other cities and towns in the Commonwealth, the members of the BLB were appointed by the governor, not the mayor of Boston. This dates from 1906, when the Yankees in the Statehouse decided that the Irish Catholics then on the ascent in Boston couldn't manage their own affairs, so the Commonwealth retained authority over law enforcement and public morality in the city. In 1962, the power to appoint the police commissioner was returned to the mayor of Boston, but the governor still appoints members of the BLB.

Every kind of license, be it for a restaurant, nightclub, dance hall, package store, pinball machine, pool hall, or bowling alley was granted by the BLB. It was also an agency swirling in controversy. "This board is in nobody's pocket," fumed chairwoman Mary E. Driscoll in 1952, in refuting charges of influence peddling in a permit case for a South End liquor store.[8]

Mary E. Driscoll, first appointed to the BLB in 1924 after lengthy stretches as a parole officer and public health official, spent 32 years on the Boston Licensing Board. There she confronted vice, real and imagined, in every corner of Boston overseen by the licensing bureaucracy. She was named chairwoman in 1938. Driscoll had political power, and she was feared.

A pious Catholic, Driscoll battled bar owners, burlesque, booze, bookies, and B-girls relentlessly. She outlawed the wearing of pants or shorts by waitresses in 1942, shut down clubs where female impersonators performed in 1949, orchestrated a highly public campaign to close nightclub "vice dens" in 1952, and blocked the appearance of transsexual Christine Jorgensen at the Latin Quarter in 1954 by suspending the club's license. Jazz clubs had their share of run-ins, generally for operating after hours, or for admitting minors and serving them drinks. Such charges usually led to fines or even license suspensions (more serious charges, like solicitation, were police matters). Nobody, but nobody, wanted to be on the wrong side of Driscoll's Licensing Board.[9]

Driscoll resigned from the BLB in late 1956, at the age of 76. She died about a year later, and in a tribute to the longtime commissioner, the Boston Retail Liquor Dealers Association's member stores closed during the hour of her funeral.

The Cost of a Night Out

It didn't cost so much to go out in the 1940s and 1950s because the talent didn't cost a small fortune. There were no cover/no minimum places, including the Hi-Hat, the 5 O'Clock, and all the places on the buckets of blood circuit, like Ort's and the Knickerbocker. Worth noting is that the 5 O'Clock presented the Miles Davis Quintet with John Coltrane without cover or minimum charges. How did they *do* that? Some places, like the Savoy and the Stable, skipped the cover but had minimum charge. The Latin Quarter in 1953 presented Frank Sinatra with no cover…and how did they do *that?* Even when there were cover charges, they don't seem exorbitant. In 1952, for example, the Storyville cover charge for Ella Fitzgerald and a first-rate band was $1.25, equivalent to just under $11.00 in 2012.[10]

In 1938, The Roseland-State Ballroom charged 65 cents ($10.45 in 2012) to see Artie Shaw's band with Billie Holiday. In 1940, a dollar (about $16 in

2012) bought a ticket at the State to a battle between the orchestras of Count Basie and Benny Carter.

Concert tickets did not seem overpriced. At Symphony Hall in 1949, $1.80 or $3.00 (about $17.00 and $28.50) would buy a seat for the Woody Herman's Second Herd and the King Cole Trio. Tickets for the Birdland Stars of 1955 show (Basie, Sarah Vaughan, George Shearing, Stan Getz, Erroll Garner, Lester Young) ranged from $2.50 to $3.85 ($21.00 to $32.50). A reserved seat at the Boston Jazz Festival in August 1959 cost between $2.65 and $4.85 per day ($21 to $38), but it was cheaper if you bought a ticket for all three days.

We should mention the taxing authorities, because they, too, had a hand in the amount of life in nightlife. Most daunting to the club owners was the federal cabaret tax, a sales tax imposed on establishments staging most kinds of public performance for profit, and it applied to all receipts, be they for admission, food and drink, or merchandise. It was a substantial tax. It was ten percent when first levied in 1917, and raised to 20 percent in 1944. Of course, there were wrinkles. Live music and dancing were taxed, unless the music was strictly instrumental. So if a band played quietly during the dinner hour, no tax. A singer added? Taxed. If the same band with no singer played for dancing after 9:00? Taxed. Confusing, yes, and also harmful to employment. Customers didn't notice that extra 20 percent when they were making money during the war, but in the belt-tightening years afterward they did, and they spent less. With fewer dollars rolling in, clubowners hired fewer musicians or went to weekends-only entertainment policies. Held in this light, the cabaret tax gets some of the blame for the postwar collapse of the big bands.

The cabaret tax was lowered to ten percent in 1960 and repealed in 1965.

Getting the News

Without a doubt, during these years Boston was a newspaper town. Oh, there was radio and then television, but if you wanted to know what was happening in Boston, or anywhere else for that matter, you picked up a paper. You want 24-hour news coverage? The *Daily Record* published five editions a day.

The competition was intense, with four daily papers in the morning and three in the afternoon, in multiple editions, and four papers on Sunday. Each paper had its own personality and readership, and the advertisers made their media buys accordingly. The nightclubs advertised in the *Daily Record*, the Hearst tabloid, as well as in its afternoon sibling, the *American*. Monday was the big day. A typical Monday in the early and mid 1950s featured about three pages of ads. The *Record* also employed the columnist most associated with Boston nightlife, George C. Clarke (more on George shortly).

The *Post* was the paper of choice for the dance crowd. It ran a complete calendar, and all the ballrooms and dance halls advertised there until they, and then the *Post* itself, went out of business (it shut down in October 1956).

Neither the *Herald* nor its afternoon sibling the *Traveler* were big entertainment papers, although two of Boston's jazz columnists wrote for them—George Frazier in the *Herald* in 1942, and John McLellan in the *Traveler* from 1957 to 1961—and George Wein penned a late-fifties weekly column for the *Sunday Herald*.

Left behind in these years was the *Globe*, which generally ignored popular culture until the 1960s.

Then there were the community papers. Every ethnic group and neighborhood had at least one weekly paper, making it easy to read the news in Italian or see what was on sale in Roslindale, but only a few paid attention to jazz. The *Chronicle*, serving the African-American community, covered nightlife in Boston in the writing of Vin Haynes from 1953 to 1960. The *East Boston Times* ran Ray Barron's "Melody and Harmony" column in the late 1940s. Not to be forgotten are the college papers, where many jazz writers got their starts.

Of all the writers covering "entertainment" and "nightlife" in the Boston papers, only one outside the jazz sphere merits a mention. George C. Clarke of Hearst chain's *Daily Record* came to Boston in 1937 from New York, where he had been City Editor at the *Daily Mirror*. He began writing his "Around Boston" (its short-lived original title was "Man About Boston") column the next year. He did so every day, in the *Record* and the *Sunday Advertiser*, for 23 years. Clarke was to Boston what Irv Kupcinet was to Chicago or Earl Wilson was to New York.

On balance, Clarke was a friend of jazz, if not well-rounded one. He enjoyed "Harlemania" and publicized any show or venue that reminded him of New York's Cotton Club. He wrote for a show presented by the Schillinger House in 1951 on one of his favorite subjects, *The Roarin' Twenties*. If Clarke liked you, he helped you, and he was an ardent fan of Sabby Lewis (he was the Clarke behind that band's 1948 recording, "Clark's Idea"), Teddi King ("a doll, an ever loving doll"), and Toshiko Akiyoshi, "the bright chrysanthemum of jazz." He didn't like modern jazz but he liked jazz makers such as Dizzy Gillespie because they were good copy.

Clarke was primarily a show-biz guy, and he traveled in the nightclub and theater circles, and if jazz intersected with that, all the better. He had connections and a daily forum, and he landed the exclusive interviews with the likes of Irving Berlin, Billy Eckstine, and George Shearing. Storyville became a favorite haunt, and George Wein a favorite source, and Clarke wrote column after column on Storyville performers and happenings. Clarke was seen less frequently at the Hi-Hat, where it took the opening of a major star like Sarah Vaughan to get him in the place. Otherwise, he was a stranger on Columbus Avenue. Over the years, though, at a time when columnists wielded significant influence, Clarke's promotion helped the jazz cause.

Clarke retired from the *Record* when it merged with its afternoon sibling in 1961 to create the *Record American*. He died in Florida in 1965.

The AM Radio Dial

In Boston in the late 1940s and the 1950s, most of the jazz on the radio was broadcast by independent AM stations, some on the air only during the daylight hours. Here's a look at the radio dial and jazz deejays in the days before conglomerates and public broadcasting.

WHDH 850 kHz	John McLellan, Norm Nathan, Fred B. Cole, remotes from Storyville; jazz programming phased out 1967.
WBMS 1090 kHz	Symphony Sid, Sabby Lewis, Ken Malden; September 1957 call letters changed to WILD; jazz programming phased out in early 1960s.
WCOP 1150 kHz	Symphony Sid, remotes from the Hi-Hat, Bob Martin, Bill Marlowe; went Top 40 spring 1956.
WVDA 1260 kHz	Bob Martin, Ken Malden, Sherm Feller, Bill Buchanan, George Wein, Speed Anderson; December 1957 call letters changed to WEZE and station moved to light pop.
WMEX 1510 kHz	Nat Hentoff, remotes from the Savoy and Storyville, Symphony Sid; went Top 40 fall 1957.
WVOM 1600 kHz	Eddy Petty, Ray Barron, Bill Marlowe, Art Tacker, Milt Kay; remotes from Wally's Paradise and Showtime; May 1956 call letters changed to WBOS and station dropped jazz programming.

Notes

Preface

1 Lars Bjorn with Jim Gallert, *Before Motown: A History of Jazz in Detroit 1920–1960* (Ann Arbor, MI: The University of Michigan Press, 2001); Frank Driggs and Chuck Haddix, *Kansas City Jazz: From Ragtime to Bebop—A History* (New York: Oxford University Press, 2005); Clora Bryant et al., *Central Avenue Sounds: Jazz in Los Angeles* (Berkeley, CA: University of California Press, 1999); William Howland Kenney, *Chicago Jazz: A Cultural History, 1904–1930* (New York: Oxford University Press, 1993); Barbara J. Kukla, *Swing City: Newark Nightlife, 1926–50* (Philadelphia: Temple University Press, 1991).

Introduction

1 Quoted by George Frazier in "Sweet and Low-Down," *Boston Herald*, Mar 5, 1942.

Chapter 1. Before the War

1 *Boston Post*, "Baby 1937 Gets Wild Welcome," Jan 1, 1937.

2 George Frazier, "Boston Remains as Dull and Stupid as Ever," *Down Beat* Feb 1937, 2.

3 George Frazier on the rampage in *Down Beat*: "Plays in tune" and "horrible girl singers" from "Boston Remains as Dull and Stupid as Ever," February, 1937, 8; and Newman, Izen, and Alpert were skewered in "Absolutely Nothing in Boston Spots," Jan 1, 1941, 4.

4 George Frazier, "Beantown Needs a Jimmy Petrillo," *Down Beat* Nov 1939, 5.

5 George Frazier, "Has Scant Respect for Boston Irish," *Down Beat* June 1937, 2.

6 Pat Harris, "All Schools Dig Bobby Hackett." *Down Beat*, Feb 9, 1951, 2.

7 Some accounts of this group include a bassist, Roger Mallencourt, or Malencourt. The first such account was written by George Frazier in 1936, so perhaps the bassist only worked with the band for a short time. Hackett told the Theatrical Club story on the record several times, and did not mention a bassist. To throw a little more fuel on the fire, there was a bassist around Boston in the late 1930s named Roger Melancook, and perhaps he's our man.

8 George Frazier, "Amazing Trumpeter Has Bix' Tone and Taste," *Down Beat*, Jul 1936, 3.

9 Waller's *Hot from Harlem Revue* was at the RKO Boston Theatre Nov 6–10, 1936.

10 James Higgins, "All That Jazz," *Boston Magazine*, Apr 1986, 131.

11 George Clarke, "Around Boston," *Boston Daily Record* Nov 9, 1951.

12 *Boston Post*, "Scant Garb in Yule Skit Draws Ire," Jan 4, 1939.

13 F. W. Lord, "Boston" (news), *Metronome*, Mar 1937, 43.

14 *Boston Post*, "Showdown on Clubs Due Today," Feb 27, 1937; "10 More Clubs Under Fire," Mar 3, 1937; "Police Name 100 Places to Close," Mar 4, 1937.

15 Dan Kochakian, "Say Hello to Highland Diggs," *Whiskey, Women, And...* No. 17, Spring 1988, 6.

16 Dean Earl interview with Ralph Rosen, Berklee College of Music, 1998.

17 Dan Kochakian, "Say Hello to Highland Diggs," *Whiskey, Women, And...* No. 17, Spring 1988, 6–7.

18 An advertisement for Cappy's nightclub in the *Boston Daily Record*, Mar 11, 1940, identifies Sunshine Sammy Davis, a point George Clarke would sometimes bring up in later years, e.g., "Around Boston," Feb 3, 1961. Dan Kochakian quotes Charlie Cox as saying the underaged Davis was often passed off as a midget so he could work; "Charlie Cox," *Whiskey, Women, And...* No. 15, Dec 1985, 44.

19 Dan Kochakian, "Say Hello to Highland Diggs," *Whiskey, Women, And...* No. 17, Spring 1988, 7.

Chapter 2. Big Band Boston

1 The *Down Beat* review of Ward's band appeared George Frazier's "Boston Remains as Dull and Stupid as Ever," February 1937, 2. The *Metronome* review appeared in George Simon's "Dance Band Reviews: Frankie Ward," Jan 1938, 19.

2 Lloyd Trotman telephone interview, Dec 17, 2003.

3 Highland Jazz, "Getting to Know You" (Alan Dawson interview), The Highland Jazz *Jazz Report*, Winter 1990, 4.

4 Al Natale interview, March 1, 2004.

5 William Buchanan, "Musical Memories of Glenn Miller," *Boston Globe*, Dec 12, 1984.

6 Max Kaminsky, *My Life in Jazz* (New York: Harper & Row, 1963), 64.

7 Levaggi is incorrectly identified as "Lavargi" by both Dizzy Gillespie and Max Kaminsky in their autobiographies and as "Lavaggi" in numerous sources. Levaggi details drawn from George C. Clarke's "Around Boston" column in the *Boston Daily Record*, Nov. 9, 1951.

8 Lillian Johnson, "Strictly Jive," *Afro-American* New England edition, Mar 26, 1938.

9 Fred B. Cole, introducing Duke Ellington at the Ritz Carlton Hotel July 26, 1939, and included on the compact disc *The Duke in Boston*, Jazz Unlimited JUCD 2022, 1993.

10 Ibid.

11 George T. Simon, *Glenn Miller & His Orchestra* (New York: Thomas Y. Crowell Company, 1974), 88.

12 Ibid, 104.

13 Artie Shaw, *The Trouble with Cinderella* (New York: Da Capo Press, 1979, originally published 1952), 311.

14 Don Stratton, letter to author, Aug 16, 2010.

Chapter 3. Charlie Shribman and the Roseland-State Ballroom

1 Simon Shribman's name has appeared as "Sy," "Si," and "Cy." I use "Cy" because he did, for example when signing contracts for Shribman Orchestras. It's also the spelling used by his friend, author George T. Simon.

2 Duke Ellington quoted by George Frazier in "Sweet and Low-Down," *Boston Herald*, Mar 5, 1942.

3 Duke Ellington, "The Art Is in the Cooking," *Down Beat* Jun 7, 1962, 15.

4 Albert Murray, *Good Morning Blues: the Autobiography of Count Basie* (New York: Random House, 1985), 183–184.

5 Richard Milne, "Whatever Became of the Great Mal Hallett?" *Boston Post*, Apr 17, 1932.

6 Phip Young, "Duke Slated for Concert at Harvard," *Down Beat*, Apr 1, 1943, 12. The article does not provide the date, but a likely one is Mar 12, 1943, when Duke played a one-nighter.

7 Malcolm X, *The Autobiography of Malcolm X* (New York: Grove Press, Inc. paperback edition, 1966, originally published 1965), 51.

8 Paul Vignoli interview, Oct 13, 2004.

9 George T. Simon, *Glenn Miller & His Orchestra* (New York: Thomas Y. Crowell Company, 1974), 148.

10 Ibid, 146–147.

11 *Time*, "Music: Darwin and the Mambo," Sep 6, 1954. http://www.time.com/time/magazine/article/0,9171,820098,00.htm.

12 *Providence Journal*, "Taunton Dance with Negro Band Is Canceled," Sep 3, 1960.

Chapter 4. Swinging the Home Front

1 Cornelius Dalton, "Boston's Wartime Passing Show Changes in Eyes of Ticket Girl," *Boston Herald*, Jul 2, 1942, and "War Brings Scollay Square Back to Life as Business There Is Tripled," *Boston Herald*, Jul 8, 1942.

2 George Frazier, "Sweet and Low-Down," *Boston Herald*, Mar 19, 1942.

3 George Frazier, "Sweet and Low-Down," *Boston Herald*, Jun 25, 1942.

4 "I hate you bitterly" and "dine with Hitler" from "Sweet and Low-Down," Aug 2, 1942. "Small time person" from "Sweet and Low-Down," Sep 6, 1942.

5 George Frazier, "Sweet and Low-Down: Bunny Berigan Is Dead at Age of 33," *Boston Herald*, Jun 3, 1942.

6 Lloyd Trotman telephone interview, Dec 17, 2003.

7 George Frazier, "Sweet and Low-Down," *Boston Herald*, May 20 and 24, 1942.

8 George Frazier, "Sweet and Low-Down," *Boston Herald*, May 31, 1942.

9   George Frazier, "Sweet and Low-Down," *Boston Herald*, June 5, 1942.

10 Al Vega interview, Jul 16 2004.

11 George Frazier, "Sweet and Low-Down," *Boston Herald*, May 31, 1942.

12 Too many Perrys! It doesn't stop with brothers Ray, Bey, and Joe. In the Checker picture is tenor man George Perry, longtime Bostonian who worked with Sam Donahue, Sabby Lewis and Jimmy Dorsey. Drummer Charlie Perry worked with Goodman and Kenton and was based on the North Shore. Ronnie Perry was a well-traveled swing era tenor saxophonist who saw duty with Ben Pollack, Artie Shaw, Woody Herman and Mel Powell. Ernie Perry was yet another tenor player who toured with Ray McKinley, was a regular at the Savoy in the postwar years, and was known in Boston through work at the Hi-Hat and Connolly's in the Fifties.

13 Lloyd Trotman telephone interview, Dec 17, 2003.

14 James Vaznis, "William Sebastian Lewis, 79; Was Jazz Musician, Disc Jockey," *Boston Globe*, Jul 11, 1994.

15 George Frazier, "Sweet and Low-Down," *Boston Herald*, Apr 17, 1942.

16 Dan Kochakian, "Sabby Lewis: The Boston Legend," in *Whiskey, Women, and...* 15, December 1985, 31.

17 George Frazier, "Sweet and Low-Down," *Boston Herald*, Jul 23, 1942.

18 George Frazier, "Sweet and Low-Down," *Boston Herald*, Jan 28, 1942.

19 Frank Stacy, "No Love Like First Love, Not if It's Sabby's Crew Jumping at the Savoy," *Down Beat* Apr 1, 1943, 14.

20 Sally Sears, "Disaster May Cost U.S. Half Million Dollars," *Down Beat* Dec 15, 1942, 28.

21 Frank Stacy, "No Love Like First Love, Not if It's Sabby's Crew Jumping at the Savoy," *Down Beat* Apr 1, 1943, 14.

22 Phip Young, "Boston Savoy Opens Again," *Down Beat*, Aug 1, 1943, 23.

23 Charles Miller, "Swing," *Harvard Crimson,* Mar 1, 1941; http://www.thecrimson.com/article/1941/3/1/swing-plast-week-when-i-mentioned/.

24 Events surrounding the Taylor case were reported by Elliott Freeman, "The Whirling Hub," *Afro-American*, Jun 12, 1943, and the *Boston Chronicle*, "Board Hears Of Tic Toc Jim Crow," Jul 3, 1943, 1, 8; and "License Board Rebukes Tic Toc," Aug 7, 1943, 1, 8. Sabby Lewis turning down the Tic Toc job was reported by Elliott Freeman, "The Whirling Hub," *Afro-American*, Aug 28, 1943, 21.

25 Tic Toc advertisement, *Boston Daily Record*, Oct 4, 1944.

Chapter 5. A Late Forties Interlude

1   "got" (Bill Gottlieb), "Eckstine, Band, Lose Job After Brawl in Boston," Jan 15, 1947, 4. Hentoff reported the incident in the first issue of his *Counterpoint* newsletter, Jan 1947.

2   *Boston Chronicle*, "New Zanzibar to Open April 16," Apr 10, 1948, 5; and "Peeves Fail to Close Nightclub," Apr 24, 1948, 8.

3 *Boston Chronicle* "Discrimination at Ritz Plaza," Jun 11, 1949, 1–2; "Hal McIntyre Refuses to Play Ritz Plaza," Jul 2, 1949, 1, 8; "Picketing of Ritz Plaza Ends with Victory," Aug 20, 1949, 1.

4 Paul Vignoli interview, Oct 13, 2004.

5 George Clarke, "Around Boston," *Boston Daily Record,* Feb 16, 1948.

6 George Clarke, "Around Boston," *Boston Daily Record,* Oct 26, 1955.

7 George Frazier, "Sweet and Low-Down, *Boston Herald,* Aug 4, 1942.

8 Al Ehrenfried, letter to the author, Jan 10, 2010.

9 Nat Hentoff, *Counterpoint,* issue 8, August 1947.

10 Nat Hentoff, *Counterpoint,* issue 1, Jan 1947.

11 Nat Hentoff, *Counterpoint,* issue 12, Dec 1947.

12 Nat Hentoff, *Counterpoint,* issue 6, Jun 1947.

13 Nat Hentoff, *Counterpoint,* issue 12, Dec 1947.

14 Ibid. Congressman John Rankin of Mississippi was a white supremacist and red-baiting member of HUAC. Senator Allen Ellender of Louisiana was a strict segregationist.

15 Bill Coss, "Jazz in Boston," *Metronome,* Dec 1951, 33.

16 Nat Hentoff, "Two Boston Jazz Clubs Stay Open for Summer," *Down Beat,* Aug 10, 1951, 7.

17 David X. Young, Liner notes for *Nat Pierce Orchestra 1948-1950,* Zim Records Zim-1005, 1977.

18 Don Hayes, "A New Frances Wayne at Jump Town Makes Critic Blow His Top," *Down Beat,* Nov 5, 1947, 4.

19 Not only were Burns and Chaloff at Newton High then, but so were George Wein, saxophonist Hal McKusick, and saxophonist Roz Cron, the first white woman to join the International Sweethearts of Rhythm, the all-girl big band of the 1940s.

20 Dave Chapman telephone conversation, Oct 2005; Alice Ross Groves in a forwarded email, Oct 25, 2005.

Chapter 6. Dixieland Revival

1 George Clarke, "Around Boston," *Boston Daily Record,* Nov 10, 1945.

2 Jazz Society monthly newsletter, June 1945.

3 Ibid.

4 Provided by the U.S. inflation calculator at http://www.bls.gov/data/inflation_calculator.htm, one of many such sites.

5 Simon quote from *Metronome,* May 1936. "True to his record" from *Down Beat,* May 15, 1942. "At present he is thinking" from *Down Beat,* Dec 1, 1943.

6 Max Kaminsky with V.E. Hughes, *My Life in Jazz* (New York: Harper & Row, 1963), 165.

7 Ibid.

8   Ted Chandler, "Maxie's," Cape Cod Jazz Society *Jazz Notes*, Sep–Oct 1977, 22.

9   Ibid, 23.

10 Bill Coss, "Jazz in Boston," *Metronome*, Dec 1951, 15.

11 Ray Barron interview, Feb 4, 2004.

12 Leroy "Sam" Parkins telephone interview, Mar 18, 2008. Parkins was known as Leroy when he worked in Boston, but later chose to be known as Sam.

13 Ray Barron, "Dixie Tops in Boston," *Down Beat*, May 4, 1951, 3.

Chapter 7. Reading, Writing, and Rhythm Physics

Much of the Berklee material is based on Ed Hazell's *Berklee: the First Fifty Years*, and the program notes from the "Montage of Modern Music," April 28, 1957. New England Conservatory material is taken from annual course catalogs and the *Neume* yearbooks; also an interview with Sam Marcus, Apr 12, 2004.

1   Down Beat, "McHugh's View: Live with the Nation's Youth," *Down Beat*, Apr 14, 1960, 13.

2   Ed Hazell, *Berklee: the First Fifty Years* (Boston: Berklee Press Productions, 1995); Bruce McPherson and James Klein, *Measure by Measure: A History of New England Conservatory from 1867* (Boston: The Trustees of New England Conservatory of Music, 1995).

3   Sam Marcus interview, Apr 12, 2004. Additional information on the School of Contemporary Music taken from their 1948–49 course catalog.

4   Ray Barron, *Pick up the Beat and Swing*. Boston: Emerging Press Ltd., 1993, 220.

5   Ray Barron, "Boston Niteries Open Doors to Jazz, Bopsters," *Down Beat*, Jun 16, 1948, 12.

6   George Simon, "Schillinger House," *Metronome*, May 1949, 18, 26–27.

7   *Down Beat* record reviews, *Jazz in the Classroom Volume 1*, Jun 26, 1958, 24; *Volume 2*, May 28, 1959, 31; *Volume 3*, Oct 15, 1959, 40.

8   Program notes, "A Montage of Modern Music," the annual concert presented by the students of the Berklee School of Music, Apr 28, 1957.

9   George Forsythe, "Jazz Internationale at Berklee," *Down Beat*, Dec 25, 1958, 10.

10 Sam Rivers quoted in *Rat Race Blues*, Noal Cohen and Michael Fitzgerald (Berkeley, CA: Berkeley Hill Books, 2002), 60.

Chapter 8. Scuffling

1   Greg Lalas, "Sultan of Strings," *Boston Magazine*, Oct 2001, 91.

2   Joe Ciavardone telephone interview, May 21, 2004.

3   Don Stratton interview, Jul 20, 2005.

4   George Wein, *Myself Among Others: A Life in Music* (New York: Da Capo Press, 2003), 24.

5   Bill Buchanan, "Izzy Ort, Grand Old Man of Boston's Club Owners," *Boston Evening Globe*, Oct 14, 1975.

6   Izzy Ort, "I Wuz Thinkin'" advertisement, *Boston Daily Record*, Sep 4, 1950.

7   Izzy Ort, "I Wuz Thinkin'" advertisement, *Boston Daily Record*, Jan 2, 1956.

8   George Clarke, "Around Boston," *Boston Daily Record*, Apr 10, 1958.

9   The Quincy Jones quote is from Mark Small, "The Best Is Yet to Come," *Berklee Today*, Spring 1995, 13; the Leon Merian quote from his book, *The Man Behind the Horn* (Bradenton, FL: Diem Publishing Company, 2000), 32; and the Nat Hentoff quote from his book, *Boston Boy: Growing up with Jazz and Other Rebellious Passions* (New York: Alfred A. Knopf, 1986), 209.

10   Sam Rivers telephone interview, Dec 19, 2005.

11   Herb Pomeroy interview, May 20, 2004.

12   Don Stratton interview, Jul 20, 2005.

13   Sam Rivers telephone interview, Dec 19, 2005.

14   Paul Vignoli interview, Oct 13, 2004.

15   Leon Merian, *The Man Behind the Horn* (Bradenton, FL: Diem Publishing Company, 2000), 32–33.

16   *Boston Daily Record*, "Board Hits Rum-Saturated Spot," May 15, 1954.

17   Ray Santisi interview, May 10, 2004.

18   *Boston Daily Record*, "Judge Calls Cafe Area Blood Zone," Apr 28, 1951.

Chapter 9. The Jazz Corner of Boston

1   George Wein interview Oct 6, 2010; Myra McAdoo interview Jul 24, 2004.

2   Eddie Logan interview Aug 18, 2005.

3   *Boston Chronicle* Apr 26, 1941.

4   George Frazier, "Sweet and Low-Down," *Boston Herald*, Mar 5, 1942.

5   Ron Gill interview, Jul 1, 2004.

6   George Clarke, "Around Boston," *Boston Daily Record*, Jan 6, 1959.

7   Ray Barron, "Owner Blinks at Receipts of 100-Seat Boston Nitery," *Down Beat*, Sep 8, 1948, 7.

8   Crystal Joy Albert telephone interview Oct 15, 2008.

9   Elynor Walcott interview Nov 15, 2008.

10   Sam Rivers telephone interview Dec 19, 2005.

11   Off limits story: "25 Gay Spots Warned: Mop Up on Vice," *Boston Daily Record*, May 3, 1957. Buchanan quote from "They danced on the roof of the Ritz," *Boston Globe* Calendar section Mar 20, 1975, 4. Sarkis information from his obituary in the *Boston Globe* Jun 8, 1991.

12   *Boston Chronicle*, "Pickets Smash Cafe Jimcrow." Oct 8, 1949, 1.

13   William Buchanan, "The Pioneer Club: An Obituary." *Boston Globe Sunday Magazine*, Sep 14, 1974, 15.

14   *Boston Chronicle*, "Court Says Bob Russell Not Guilty," Nov 20, 1948, 1.

15 The dates represent best guesses. Ellington was at the Bradford Hotel on February 24, 1960 and Armstrong sat in with him there. Armstrong was in the area to play at the Surf in Nantasket on the 27th. Mabel Simms said Holiday only sang once at the Pioneer while Simms worked there, that being just before Simms left in 1955. Holiday was in Boston at the Hi-Hat Jun 6–12, 1955, and at Storyville Oct 24–30, 1955.

16 Leon Merian telephone interview Nov 8, 2004.

17 Elsa Hart interview Apr 25, 2004.

18 Boston Landmarks Commission, Environment Department, City of Boston. "Report on the Potential Designation of Connolly's Bar, 1184 Tremont Street, Roxbury, Massachusetts." July 1997, 4.

19 John McLellan, "The Jazz Scene: Emmett Berry Plays Trumpet in Stand with Tyler Trio," *Boston Traveler*, Oct 25, 1960.

20 John McLellan, "The Jazz Scene: Charlie, Boy, You Sent Me," *Boston Traveler*, Nov 1, 1960.

21 Mentioned by Burrell on his web site: http://www.daveburrell.com/interview.pdf.

22 Mae Arnette interview Mar 31, 2006.

23 Al Vega interview Jul 16, 2004.

Chapter 10. Paradise

1 Yawu Miller, "Historic Jazz Club Recognized by City," *Bay State Banner*, May 1, 1997, 3.

2 Ray Barron, "Tyler Boosts Boston's Boppers to Paradise," *Down Beat*, Nov 3, 1948, 15.

3 Eddie Logan interview, Aug 18, 2005.

4 Ibid.

5 Hiawatha Lockhart interview, May 10, 2008.

6 Elynor Walcott interview, Nov 15, 2008.

7 Ibid.

8 Yawu Miller, "Historic Jazz Club Recognized by City," *Bay State Banner*, May 1, 1997, 3.

Chapter 11. Sabby Lewis, Jimmy Tyler, and the Last Days of Swing

1 The Sabby Lewis Restaurant advertised steadily until mid May 1948 and then stopped. A better known restaurant called Chicken Lane later moved into this location.

2 George Clarke, "Around Boston," *Boston Daily Record*, Mar 25, 1949. The title of the third tune on Mercury 8134 is "Clark's Idea," no "e." Most sources list this session as having taken place in New York.

3 George Clarke, "Around Boston," *Boston Daily Record*, Dec 7, 1949.

4 Eddy Petty, "Eddie Petty's Musical Moments," *Boston Chronicle*, Dec 10, 1949, 5.

5 George Clarke, "Around Boston," *Boston Daily Record*, Dec 13, 1949.

6 Hiawatha Lockhart interview, May 10, 2008.

7 Maurie Orodenker, Review of Sabby Lewis band at the Club Harlem, Atlantic City, July 2, 1949. *The Billboard*, Jul 16, 1949, 23, 49.

8 Ray Perry, another Lewis regular, fit the same mold, and his last job before his untimely death in November 1950 was with Illinois Jacquet. It was on the recommendation of either Tyler or Perry that Bill Dorsey left the Lewis band in 1948 to tour with Jacquet. Coincidentally, when Perry left the Lewis band in 1946 for a stint with Jacquet, his replacement was Jimmy Tyler. When Tyler left the Lewis band in 1948, his replacement was Ray Perry.

9 *Down Beat*, Nov 2, 1951, noted that Tyler was billed as the "wild man of the tenor saxophone" when the orchestra played a New York night club engagement in October.

10 John McLellan, "The Jazz Scene: Teddy Wilson Strikes a Note About Pianists," *Boston Traveler*, Apr 4, 1961.

Chapter 12. Big Bands, New Sounds: Nat Pierce and Jimmie Martin

1 Mert Goodspeed interview, Dec 29, 2004.

2 Sam Rivers telephone interview, Dec 19, 2005.

3 Joining Clinton in 1949 were Pierce, saxophonist Sebastian Giacco, trombonist Mert Goodspeed, guitarist Steve Hester, drummer Joe MacDonald, trumpeter Gait Preddy, and bassist Frank Vaccaro. See Jack Egan, "New Sound Clinton Band a Hit," *Down Beat*, Dec 15, 1948, 16.

4 Nat Hentoff, "Is Boston's Nat Pierce Ork Music's Biggest Paradox?" *Down Beat*, Nov 16, 1951, 2.

5 Mert Goodspeed interview, Dec 29, 2004.

6 Don Stratton interview, Jul 2, 2005.

7 Bill Coss, Review of Charlie Mariano Octet, "Sheba" and "Babylon," Motif 004, *Metronome*, May 1950, 43.

8 Don Stratton interview, Oct 7, 2005.

9 Eddy Petty, "Eddy Petty's Musical Moments," *Boston Chronicle*, May 13, 1950, 5.

10 Les Tompkins, "The Nat Pierce Story," *Crescendo*, May 1966, 17.

11 Nat Hentoff, "Nat Pierce, Boston 88er, Joins Woody," *Down Beat*, Oct 19, 1951, 2.

12 Mert Goodspeed interview, Dec 29, 2004.

13 Almost all biographical material has Byard working with Bostic in 1949–1950, but my research indicates that's too late. He's in Boston from 1948 on, working with Jimmie Martin, and in 1950 with Jimmy Tyler.

14 Hiawatha Lockhart interview, May 10, 2008.

15 Eddie Logan interview, Aug 10, 2005.

16 Sam Rivers telephone interview, Dec 19, 2005.

17 Eddie Logan interview, Aug 10, 2005.

18 Hiawatha Lockhart interview, May 10, 2008.

19 "Edna" was written by Sabby Lewis and Jerry Heffron and was named after a waitress at the Savoy. The Lewis band recorded it in 1946 on Continental 6030.

20 Tom Blair, "Musician's Ball Goes Dizzy," *Boston Chronicle*, Apr 16, 1949, 5, 7. I've changed the order of the last three paragraphs for the sake of readability; the last paragraph here was actually the third-last paragraph in the original article.

21 Hiawatha Lockhart interview, May 10, 2008.

22 Askey lost to Ralph Burns, who won the Oscar for best score for Bob Fosse's *Cabaret*. Those Boston jazzmen of the 1940s cast long shadows!

23 Hiawatha Lockhart interview, May 10, 2008.

Chapter 13. The Hi-Hat: America's Smartest Barbecue

1 Ray Barron, *Pick Up the Beat and Swing* (Boston: Emerging Press, Ltd., 1993), 127–128 describes Rhodes's decision to change his music policy and clientele.

2 Al Vega interview, Jul 16, 2004.

3 Hiawatha Lockhart interview, May 10, 2008.

4 Dan Kochakian, "Say Hello to Highland Diggs," *Whiskey, Women, and...* No. 17, Spring 1988, 8.

5 Don Stratton, letter to the author, Aug 16, 2010.

6 Al Vega interview, July 16, 2004.

7 Nat Hentoff, "National Recognition Due for Pianist Al Vega?" *Down Beat*, Nov 16, 1951, 3.

8 The *Boston Herald's* EXTRA! on March 10 was not part of a story. It was a one-inch header inserted at press time between the masthead and lead story's headline, with a few paragraphs of the late-breaking news. The actual news story was published that afternoon in the *Boston Traveler*, "Fire Destroys Hub Night Club," Mar 10, 1959.

9 Herb Pomeroy interview, May 20, 2004.

Chapter 14. The Melody Lounge Gang

1 Sam Parkins telephone interview, Mar 18, 2008.

2 Nat Hentoff, "Charlie Mariano Cuts Sides for Prestige," *Down Beat*, Jan 25, 1952, 12.

3 Nat Hentoff, liner notes for Sam Rivers's *Fuchsia Swing Song*, Blue Note 90413, 1964.

4 Dan Morgenstern, "Ready, Willing, and Able: Jaki Byard," *Down Beat*, Oct 21, 1965, 19.

5 Ibid, 18.

6   Ira Gitler, liner notes for *The New Sounds from Boston*, Prestige 130, 1951.

7   Nat Hentoff, review of *Charlie Mariano*, Imperial 1M-3006 and *The Modern Saxaphone (sic) Stylings of Charlie Mariano*, 1M-3007, *Down Beat*, Jan 27, 1954, 11.

8   Valerie Wilmer, "Joe Gordon," *Jazz Journal*, Sep 1960, 5.

9   Nat Hentoff, review of *Introducing Joe Gordon*, EmArcy MG26046, *Down Beat*, Apr 6, 1955, 13; Bill Coss review, *Metronome*, May 1955, 34.

10 John S. Wilson, review of *Lookin' Good* by Joe Gordon, Contemporary 3597, *Down Beat*, Jan 18, 1962, 32.

11 John Tynan, "Caught in the Act: Joe Gordon," *Down Beat*, Oct 24, 1963, 35; John Tynan, "The Final Hours of Joe Gordon," *Down Beat*, Jan 30, 1964, 13, 33.

12 Don Nelson, "A Pick-Me-Up Called Gordon," *New York Daily News*, Apr 3, 1960.

13 Tom Herrick, review of Woody Herman's "The Goof and I," Columbia 38369, *Down Beat*, Jan 28, 1949, 14; Mike Levin, review of Serge Chaloff and the Herdsmen's "Chickasaw" and "Bopscotch," Futurama 3003, *Down Beat*, Jul 29, 1949, 14.

14 Bill Coss, review of Serge Chaloff's *Boston Blow-Up!*, Capitol T6510, *Metronome*, Oct 1955, 30.

15 Teddy Charles, review of *The Fable of Mabel*, Storyville LP-317, *Metronome*, Apr 1955, 32.

16 *Down Beat* review of *Trio: Russ Freeman/Richard Twardzik*, Pacific Jazz LP-1212, Jun 27, 1956, 25. Freeman's comment is from the album's liner notes. The Bill Coss review in *Metronome*, Aug 1956, 26, called the record "heart-breaking" because of the loss it represented.

17 Sam Parkins, "Dick Twardzik," 2006. Initially available at http://www.myspace.com/samparkinsakaleroyparkins and accessed there Jan 8, 2008; Parkins died in November 2009 and the site may be inactive.

18 George Clarke, "Around Boston," *Boston Daily Record*, Nov 12, 1955.

19 Dan Morgenstern, "Ready, Willing, and Able: Jaki Byard," *Down Beat*, Oct 21, 1965, 19.

20 Dick Wetmore, interview with Judy Wallace for Simmons College oral history project. Recorded May 26, 1995 at Brewster, MA.

21 Sam Parkins telephone interview, Mar 18, 2008.

22 Dick Wetmore, Judy Wallace interview.

23 Dom Cerulli, "Toshiko: Japan's First Gift to U.S. Jazz," *Down Beat*, Mar 21 1956, 13.

24 John Tynan, Review of *Toshiko Mariano Quartet*, Candid 8012, *Down Beat*, Jun 22, 1961, 34.

25 Marian McPartland, "Focus on Toshiko and Charlie Mariano," *Down Beat*, Oct. 26, 1961, 18.

Chapter 15. Stablemates

1 Nat Hentoff, "Jazz Workshop Gets Under Way in Boston," *Down Beat* Aug 26, 1953, 19.

2 Ray Santisi interview, Jan 4, 2005.

3 Herb Pomeroy interview, May 20, 2004.

4 Ray Santisi interview, Jan 4, 2005.

5 *The Tech*, "Jass in a Stable," May 8, 1959, 2.

6 George Wein telephone interview, Oct 6, 2010.

7 Ray Santisi interview, Jan 4, 2005.

8 Al Vega interview, Jul 16, 2004.

9 Ernie Santosuosso, "Jazz's Gentle Giant Who on the Giant Violin," *Boston Globe*, Oct 11, 1981.

10 Herbie Mann, "The Musicians' Corner," review of *Jazz in a Stable*, Transition TRLP-1, *Metronome*, Feb 1956, 27. Mann was a guest record reviewer that month.

11 Bruce Reeves, "Warm Jazz In Dark Rooms," *Harvard Crimson*, Nov 5, 1955; http://www.thecrimson.com/article/1955/11/5/warm-jazz-in-dark-rooms-pmost/.

12 Herb Pomeroy interview, May 20, 2004.

13 Ibid.

14 John McLellan, "The Jazz Scene: Rock 'n' Roll Makes Newport Festival a Carnival," *Boston Traveler*, Jul 7, 1958.

15 Herb Pomeroy interview, May 20, 2004.

16 Dom Cerulli, review of *Life Is a Many Splendored Gig*, Roulette R-52001, *Down Beat*, Mar 20, 1958, 32–33; review of *Band in Boston*, United Artists UAL: 4015, *Down Beat*, Apr 16, 1959, 31.

17 Manny Wise interview, Nov 20, 2004.

18 Herb Pomeroy interview, May 20, 2004.

19 Elsa Hart interview, Apr 25, 2004.

20 Dan Morgenstern interview, Apr 1, 2005.

21 Sam Rivers telephone interview, Dec 19, 2005.

22 Ibid.

23 John McLellan, "The Jazz Scene: An Accolade to Sam Rivers," *Boston Traveler*, Dec 20, 1960.

24 Dick Johnson interview, Jan 11, 2006.

25 John McLellan, "The Jazz Scene: Pomeroy Album Out; Soloists Given Credit," *Boston Traveler*, Jan 30, 1958.

Chapter 16. Dynamo

1 George Wein, *Myself Among Others: A Life in Music* (New York, Da Capo Press, 2003), 115.

2 George Clarke, "Around Boston," *Boston Daily Record*, Oct 23, 1950.

3 George Clarke, "Around Boston," *Boston Daily Record*, Dec 6, 1950.

4 Nat Hentoff, "Counterpoint," *Down Beat*, Jul 1, 1953, 8.

5 John McLellan, "The Jazz Scene: Local Scene Grows Cloudy," *Boston Traveler* Feb 25, 1960.

6 John McLellan, "The Jazz Scene: Storyville May Be Shut Down," *Boston Traveler*, Apr 14, 1960.

7 M.J. Arlen, "George Wein: Jazz by the Sea," *Holiday*, Jul 1966, 94.

8 "Rabelaisian" appeared in George Clarke's "Around Boston," *Boston Daily Record*, Nov 5, 1954. "Gilded outrages" appeared in Bill Coss's "Dateline USA" column in *Metronome*, June 1955, 5–6. "One bitch of a singer" is from the liner notes for *Lee Wiley Sings Rodgers and Hart*, Storyville LP 312, 1954. These were also published in Charles Fountain's Frazier biography, *Another Man's Poison* (Chester, CT: Globe Pequot Press, 1984), 138.

9 Cecil Steen founded another record company, Pilgrim, and recorded Boston rock groups. Steen became embroiled in the payola scandals at the end of the decade and in April 1960 signed a consent order with the Federal Trade Commission agreeing to stop making payments to television and radio disc jockeys as inducement to play his records. He admitted paying out thousands of dollars to Boston deejays. "I was buying promotion," he said. Boston payola received a thorough going-over in the Feb 22, 1960 issue of *The Billboard* and it is worth noting that no Boston jazz deejays were implicated.

10 Nat Hentoff, "Teddy King Rated Best Singer Ever to Come Out of Boston," *Down Beat*, Jan 11, 1952, 3.

11 Barry Ulanov, review of *Miss Teddi King*, Storyville STLP 314, *Metronome*, Jan 1955, 23–24; George Simon reviews the record in the same issue on 29.

12 John McLellan, "The Jazz Scene: New Teddi King, Now in Hub, Is 'Miss Wonderful." *Boston Traveler*, Dec 12, 1957.

13 George Wein telephone interview Oct 6, 2010.

14 George Wein, *Myself Among Others: A Life in Music* (New York, Da Capo Press, 2003), 133–144 provides detail on Newport 1954. "World series" quote from the program notes for the Boston Jazz Festival of 1959, also a Wein production.

15 George Wein, "Dixieland in Today's Jazz," *Jazz Today*, Jan 1957, 18.

Chapter 17. Stories From the Fifties

1 Al Vega interview, Jul 16, 2004.

2 Manny Wise interview, Nov 20, 2004.

3 Sam Parkins, "The Near-Knifing of Don Asher," 2006. Initially available at http://www.myspace.com/samparkinsakaleroyparkins and accessed there Jan 8, 2008; Parkins died in November 2009 and the site may be inactive.

4 *Down Beat's* Aug 25, 1948 review of Tremaine's "The Things You Left in My Heart" (Signature 15218) observed that "Judy's mother was apparently frightened by an early Helen O'Connell record. She apes, as no one has ever

done very accurately, the former Dorsey vocalist's mannerism of sliding into her notes." The *Beat* gave the record a one-star review.

5   Manny Wise interview, Nov 20, 2004. *Metronome* in August of 1955, 11, listed the personnel as: Bob Golden, Bob Carr, Will Kaslick, trombone; Art Richards, reeds; Joe DeWeese, bass; Tony Procopio (Parker) piano; Wise, drums.

6   George Clarke, "Around Boston," *Boston Daily Record*, Jan 22, 1953; Nat Hentoff, "Sinatra in Deejay Stint," *Down Beat's* Records and Hi-Fi insert, Mar 11, 1953, 11-S. Insert has a dandy cover photo of Sinatra at the WORL microphone.

7   George Clarke, "Latin Quarter Closing Came as a Surprise," *Boston Daily Record*, May 24, 1955.

8   *Harvard Crimson*, "Student-Owned Recording Company Announces Releasing of First Disc," Nov 2, 1955. Also see Calvin Hicks, "Jazz in Stable Marks Advance of Transitions, Inc.," *Boston Chronicle*, Dec 24, 1955, 8. The Boston-born Hicks, who was still in high school when he wrote the Transition article, went on to a distinguished career as an educator and journalist.

9   Nat Hentoff, review of Johnny Windhurst's *Jazz on Columbus Avenue*, Transition LP J-2, *Down Beat*, Jul 25, 1956, 26.

10 For details on Wilson's life and career, see Eric Olsen, "The Amazing Tom Wilson," http://blogcritics.org/music/article/the-amazing-tom-wilson/, Oct 23, 2003. Accessed Jan 8, 2007.

11 Details on the Teenage Jazz Club taken from Dom Cerulli, "Boston Teen-Age Jazz Club Now at 700," *Down Beat*, Nov 14, 1956, and from Stephani Saltman email April 22, 2010.

12 The details on the club's first meeting taken from "Teen-Age Jazz Club," in *Metronome*, Jun 1955, 8.

Chapter 18. Telling It

1   Elinor J. Brecher, "Ken Malden, Longtime WQAM Sportscaster" (obituary), *Miami Herald*, May 8, 2009.

2   Ron Della Chiesa interview, Jan 12, 2004; "purest jazz jockey" from Bill Coss, "Jazz in Boston," *Metronome*, Apr 1956, 22.

3   John McLellan, "The Jazz Scene: Dixieland Back in Cellar Room," *Boston Traveler*, Oct 10, 1957.

4   John McLellan, "The Jazz Scene: Rushing Sparks Swinging Band," *Boston Traveler*, Jul 9, 1959.

5   John McLellan, "The Jazz Scene: Pomeroy Band Roaring Back," *Boston Traveler*, Jul 21, 1960.

6   John McLellan, "The Jazz Scene: Some Good Events Headed for Boston," *Boston Traveler*, Oct 11, 1960.

7   John McLellan, "The Jazz Scene: Pomeroy Band Roaring Back," *Boston Traveler*, Jul 21, 1960.

8 John McLellan, "The Jazz Scene: New Musical Name Needed," *Boston Traveler*, Sep 5, 1957.

9 John McLellan, "The Jazz Scene: Vocal Group Really Swings," *Boston Traveler*, Oct 14, 1958.

10 John McLellan, "The Jazz Scene: An Accolade to Sam Rivers," *Boston Traveler*, Dec 20, 1960.

11 Bill Coss, "Jazz Innovations: Father Norman O'Connor," *Metronome*, June 1955, 25.

12 "My feeling is" from Sidney Fields, "Devotion and Disks," *New York Daily News*, Mar 10, 1965; "Common ground" from Dom Cerulli, "Father O'Connor" (Part 2), *Down Beat* Nov 28, 1957, 48. Also see Helen Dance, "Has Jazz a Place in the Church?" *Saturday Review*, Jul 15, 1967, 46–47.

13 Sidney Fields, "Devotion and Disks," *New York Daily News*, Mar 10, 1965.

14 Bill Coss, "Jazz on the Air," *Down Beat*, Dec 7, 1961, 26.

15 John McLellan telephone interview, Sep 29, 2005.

Chapter 19. Into the Great Outdoors

1 John McLellan, "The Jazz Scene: Want Voice in Festival," *Boston Traveler*, Jul 15, 1958.

2 John McLellan, "The Jazz Scene: Rock 'n' Roll Makes Newport Festival a Carnival," *Boston Traveler*, Jul 7, 1958.

3 John McLellan, "The Jazz Scene: Monk, Basie, Ballet, Ellington Standouts at Newport Festival," *Boston Traveler*, Jul 6, 1959.

4 John McLellan, "The Jazz Scene: Activity Is Picking Up," *Boston Traveler*, Jun 21, 1960.

5 Press release sent under the name of festival director Diggory Venn, and quoted in "Half-Baked Beans" in *Metronome's* Aug 1955 issue. That article also notes the Local 9 decision and the Benzaquin quote attributed to the *Boston Globe*. Benzaquin's "review" was published in the June 14, 1955 *Globe*, "How 'Cool' Can You Get?"

6 Robert Taylor (as "RST"), "Jazz Concert," *Boston Herald*, Jun 14, 1955.

7 Three *Boston Herald* stories follow the Hughes controversy: Michael C. Jensen, "Festival Poet Faces Pickets," Jun 19, 1961; "Extra Police for Hughes at Festival," Jun 20, 1961; "20,000 Crowd Jazz Night," Jun 21, 1961. The latter two articles are uncredited.

8 *Boston Globe*, "Jazz Sends Even Swans in Garden," Jul 3, 1962.

9 Harvey Siders, "Aged Dixieland Combo Rejuvenates Festival," *Boston Globe*, Jul 6, 1963.

10 "Attack by Martians" from "Music News: First 22,000 Are the Hardest," *Down Beat*, Oct 17, 1957, 9. *Daily Evening Item*, "Jazz Lovers to Throng Manning Bowl Tonight," Aug 23, 1957; "Dizzy Gets Festival Off to Cool Start Before 7,000," Aug 24, 1957; Ernie Rosenthal, "Downbeat of Rain Fails to Dampen

Jazz Festival," *Daily Evening Item*, Aug 26, 1957. Vin Haynes, "Jazz Festival in Final Night Shift Draws Well," *Boston Chronicle*, Sep 7, 1957, 4, 8.

11 John McLellan, "The Jazz Scene: Gillespie Night Real Dizzy," *Boston Traveler*, Dec 10, 1957.

12 "Although they had" from Forsythe's comments in the Music News summary, *Down Beat*, Sep 17, 1959, 9. "Jazz festivals are" and the first-night review from Fr. Norman J. O'Connor, "That Good Old Music," *Boston Globe*, Aug 22, 1959. His wrap-up was in "Festival Fans Dig Duke Through Dusk and Dew," *Boston Globe*, Aug 24, 1959. John McLellan's festival report is in "The Jazz Scene: 20,000 Acclaim Boston's First Jazz Festival," *Boston Traveler*, Aug 24, 1959.

13 "More cops than beatniks" from Robert V. Leary, "Beer Ban Cans Trouble, Jazz Stirs Wakefield," *Boston Globe*, Aug 27, 1960. "Too much and too little" from Richard L. Hurt, "Raw-Edge Jazz Sorely Missed at Wakefield," *Boston Globe*, Aug. 28, 1960. The riot-prevention preparations are described in Hurt's "Wakefield Took Massive Precautions Against Riot at Jazz Festival There," *Boston Globe*, Aug. 28, 1960. And the music? Paul E. Hirshon, "Ellington, Dinah Stir Jazz Fans," *Boston Globe*, Aug. 29, 1960. One wonders, why no reports by the *Globe's* jazz columnist, Fr. Norman O'Connor?

14 John McLellan, "The Jazz Scene: 1960 Proves Disastrous Year for Prestige," *Boston Traveler*, Jan 5, 1961.

Chapter 20. Looking Forward, Looking Back

1 *Boston Daily Record*, "Hub Will Shut 100 Cafes, 52 Liquor Stores," May 21, 1958.

2 Al Vega interview, Jul 16, 2004.

3 The McLellan quote was from "The Jazz Scene: Cannonball Talks About Freedom," *Boston Traveler*, Feb 21, 1961. The Sam Rivers quote was from a telephone interview, Dec 19, 2005.

Appendix. Snapshots of a City

1 You won't find much about jazz music in them, but Thomas H. O'Connor's *Building a New Boston: Politics and Urban Renewal 1950 to 1970* (Boston: Northeastern University Press, 1993) and Lawrence Kennedy's *Planning the City Upon a Hill: Boston Since 1630* (Amherst, MA: The University of Massachusetts Press, 1992) describe Boston's dilemma and how it was resolved.

2 Population figures from the U.S. Census Bureau, http://www.census.gov/population/www/documentation/twps0027/twps0027.html and http://www.census.gov/population/www/documentation/twps0076/twps0076.html.

3 Elliott Freeman, "The Whirling Hub," *Afro-American*, Oct 16, 1937.

4 George Wein telephone interview, Oct 6, 2010.

5 Herb Pomeroy quoted in *Rat Race Blues: the Musical Life of Gigi Gryce*, Noal Cohen and Michael Fitzgerald (Berkeley, CA: Berkeley Hills Books, 2002) 57.

6 *Down Beat*, "Mass. Ops Seek Sunday Dancing Permits," Apr 22, 1949, 3;
   Boston Globe, "Censor Urges Hub Permit Sunday Dancing," Oct 8, 1962.

7 Herbert S. Hadad, "No Rush to Stand at Bars Sunday, "*Boston Globe*, Jul 1,
   1963.

8 *Boston Daily Record*, "Dever Help for Liquor Site Denied," Nov 7, 1952.

9 *Boston Herald*, "Slacks, Trousers, and Shorts Banned for Boston Waitresses,"
   Mar 6, 1942; *Boston Daily Record*, "Cute Girl Impersonators Get E. Boston
   Cafe in Jam,_" Mar 22, 1949; the war on nightclub vice was covered in daily
   stories in the *Record* between Jan 1 and Jan 9, 1952; *L'Affaire Christine* was
   covered in daily stories in the *Record* between Jan 28 and Feb 9, 1954; the
   Record reported suspended licenses for Showtime and Eddie Levine's in "Ban
   Liquor at 3 Spots," Apr 9, 1955.

10 Ticket prices for the various events were taken from newspaper advertisements,
   then calculated in 2010 dollars using the inflation calculator provided by the
   U.S.Department of Labor's Bureau of Labor Statistics at http://www.bls.gov/
   data/inflation_calculator.htm. The most outrageous cover charge must be the
   one levied by the Flamingo Room in 1938, and reported by George Clarke in
   "Around Boston," *Boston Daily Record*, Nov 9, 1951. The $5 charge was equal
   to about $80 in 2012, and for this you got Guy Lombardo! By contrast, the
   charge for Chick Webb was $2, or about $32.

Bibliography

This is both bibliography and suggested reading list for Boston jazz at mid-century. All the works pertain to the people and places mentioned in the text, but not all are directly cited in the Notes.

There is no way to adequately represent the Boston writings of George Frazier, Nat Hentoff, and John McLellan in this bibliography. Frazier wrote more than 180 "Sweet and Low-Down" columns in the *Boston Herald* between January and October of 1942, Hentoff wrote twelve issues of his *Counterpoint* newsletter in 1947, and McLellan wrote nearly 400 "Jazz Scene" columns in the *Boston Traveler* between September 1957 and September 1961. These could comprise an entire bibliography on their own, so rather than include them here, I instead suggest that the dozens of citations listed in the Notes be used as a reasonable starting point for their Boston writings.

Arlen, M.J. "George Wein: Jazz by the Sea." *Holiday*, Jul 1966, 91-96.

Attleberry, Phil. "Jack Lesberg Interview." *Cadence*, Oct 1998, 10-19.

Balliett, Whitney. "American Singers: Teddi King, Mary Mayo, Barbara Lea." In *American Singers*. New York: Oxford University Press, 1979.

Barron, Ray. *Pick up the Beat and Swing*. Boston: Emerging Press Ltd., 1993.

Blumenthal, Bob. "Boston Blow Up: A Scene Expands." *Village Voice*, Aug 25, 1987, 13-14.

———. "A Citizen of Jazz Comes Back Home to Boston" (Charlie Mariano). *Boston Globe*, May 14, 2000.

Blumenthal, Bob and Robert E. Sunenblick. Liner notes, *Charlie Parker, Boston 1952*. Uptown Records UPCD 27.42, 1996.

Borgman, George A. "Boston's Grand Old Man of Jazz" (Sabby Lewis). *Mississippi Rag*, Aug 1994, 1-8.

Bouchard, Fred. "Alan Dawson: Teaching the Traps, Gigging with the Greatest." *Down Beat*, Nov 1980, 22-24, 64.

Bourne, Kay. "Reed man Rivers recalls roots in Boston, stories of slaves." *Bay State Banner*, Dec 19, 1996, 13.

Brown, Anthony. The Smithsonian Institution Jazz Oral History Program interview with Roy Haynes. http://www.smithsonianjazz.org/oral_histories/pdf/Haynes.pdf. May 15, 1994. Accessed Sep 12, 2010.

Buchanan, William. "The Pioneer Club: An Obituary." *Boston Globe Sunday*

Magazine, Sep 14, 1974, 12-16.

——, "They Danced on the Roof of the Ritz." *Boston Globe* Calendar section, Mar 20, 1975.

Burns, Jim. "Serge Chaloff." *Jazz Journal*, Mar 1968, 14-16.

Cerulli, Dom. "Boston Teen-Age Jazz Club Now At 700." *Down Beat*, Nov 14, 1956, 51.

——. "Father O'Connor." *Down Beat*, Nov 14, 1957, 15-16 (part 1) and Nov 28, 1957, 18, 49-51 (part 2).

——. "Toshiko: Japan's First Gift to U.S. Jazz." *Down Beat*, Mar 21, 1956, 18.

Chambers, Jack. *Bouncin' with Bartok: The Incomplete Works of Richard Twardzik*. Toronto: Mercury Press, 2008.

Chandler, Ted. "Maxie's." Cape Code Jazz Society *Jazz Notes*, Sep-Oct 1977, 20-23.

Cohen, Noal and Michael Fitzgerald. *Rat Race Blues: the Musical Life of Gigi Gryce*. Berkeley, CA: Berkeley Hills Books, 2002.

Coss, Bill. "Jazz in Boston." *Metronome*, Dec 1951, 15, 33.

——. "Jazz Innovations: Father Norman O'Connor." *Metronome*, Jun 1955, 25.

——. "Teen-age Jazz Club." *Metronome*, Jun 1955, 8.

Coss, Bill. "Jazz in Boston." *Metronome*, Apr 1956, 9-21, 40. Lead story in issue which also included Paul Coss, "Records in Transition," 9,11; Nick Dean, "John Neves: Boston Bassist," 21; Burt Korall, "Mariano," 22; Nick Dean, "Toshiko Akiyoshi," 23.

Coss, Paul D. "Boston: Back Bay Shuffle" (Serge Chaloff). *Metronome*, Jun 1955, 9-10.

——. "Boston: Jazz in a Stable" *Metronome*, May 1955, 13-14.

——. "Boston: London Broil with a Latin Beat Tops Frolic's Menu" (Manny Wise). *Metronome*, Aug 1955, 9.

DeMichael, Don. "Tony Williams." *Down Beat*, Mar 25, 1965, 19, 36-37.

Earl, Dean. Interview with Ralph Rosen for Berklee College oral history project. Recorded Aug 21, 1998. The Stan Getz Media Center and Library, Berklee College of Music, Boston MA.

Ephland, John. "Tony Williams: Still, the Rhythm Magician." *Down Beat*, May 1989, 20-23.

Feather, Leonard. *The New Edition of the Encyclopedia of Jazz*. New York: Horizon Press, 1960.

Frazier, George. "Amazing Trumpeter Has Bix' Tone and Taste." *Down Beat*, Jul 1936.

——. "Boston Remains as Dull and Stupid as Ever." *Down Beat*, Feb 1937, 2, 8.

Gardner, Mark. "Alan Dawson." *Jazz Journal*, Apr 1971, 2-5.

Goldblatt, Burt. *Newport Jazz Festival: The Illustrated History.* New York: The Dial Press, 1977.

Gonzalez, Fernando. "Wally's: Making History Since 1947." *Boston Globe,* Jun 12, 1988.

———. "Where Have All the Jazz Clubs Gone" (Part 2) *Boston Globe,* Jul 5, 1987.

Gottlieb, Bill (as "got"). "Eckstine, Band, Lose Job After Brawl in Boston." *Down Beat,* Jan 15, 1947, 4.

Harris, Pat. "All Schools Dig Bobby Hackett." *Down Beat,* Feb 9, 1951, 1-2, 18.

Hazell, Ed. *Berklee: The First Fifty Years.* Boston: Berklee Press Publications, 1995.

Hentoff, Nat. *Boston Boy: Growing up with Jazz and Other Rebellious Passions.* New York: Alfred A. Knopf, 1986.

———. "Circling the Squares." *Down Beat,* Oct 22, 1952, 7, 18.

———. "Counterpoint" (Storyville). *Down Beat,* Jul 1, 1953, 8.

———. "Is Boston's Nat Pierce Ork Music's Biggest Paradox?" *Down Beat,* Nov 16, 1951, 16.

———. "Jazz Workshop Gets Under Way in Boston," *Down Beat,* Aug 26, 1953, 19.

———. "Self-Promotion: It Pays" *Down Beat,* May 30, 1957, 15.

———. "Serge Seeks Action Again After Two Years in Boston." *Down Beat,* Dec 14 1951, 3,5.

———. "The Shape of Jazz That Was," *Boston Magazine,* Oct 2001, 85-90, 175-177.

———. "Teddi King Rated Best Singer Ever to Come Out of Boston." *Down Beat,* Jan 11, 1952, 3.

Higgins, James. "All That Jazz." *Boston Magazine,* Apr 1986, 128-131, 182-185.

Himmelstein, David A. Liner notes for *Out Front!* by Jaki Byard, Prestige 7397, Jun 1965.

Hoenish, Thomas. The Charlie Mariano Tribute Site at http://www.charliemarianotribute.de/home.html. Ongoing.

Jackson, Eric. "Riff Tide." *Boston Magazine,* Oct 2001, 89, 180.

Jarvis, Malcolm, with Paul D. Nichols. *The Other Malcolm–"Shorty" Jarvis.* Jefferson NC: McFarland & Company, 2001.

Kaminsky, Max, with V.E. Hughes. *My Life in Jazz.* New York: Harper & Row, 1963.

Kathan, Scott. "Hy Life" (Hy Lockhart). *Stuff Magazine,* Feb 2000, 12-14.

Kennedy, Dan. "Jazz Was Their Beat." *Northeastern University Magazine,* Sep 1996, 44–48.

Kernfeld, Barry, ed. *The New Grove Dictionary of Jazz, Second Edition.* New York: Grove's Dictionaries, Inc., 2002.

Kochakian, Dan. "Bey Perry." *Whiskey, Women, And...* No. 15, Dec 1985, 48-55.

——. "Charlie Cox." *Whiskey, Women, And...* No. 15, Dec 1985, 44-46.

——. "Ernie Trotman." *Whiskey, Women, And...* No. 18/19, Fall 1989, 22-29.

——. "The Jones Brothers." *Whiskey, Women, And...* No. 15, Dec 1985, 36-43.

——. "Let It Roll with Hopeton Johnson." *Whiskey, Women, And...* No. 16, Spring 1987, 47-53.

——. "Lloyd Trotman." *Whiskey, Women, And...* No. 18/19, Fall 1989, 4-17.

——. "Mabel Robinson Simms." *Whiskey, Women, And...* No. 18/19, Fall 1989, 63-65.

——. "Sabby Lewis, the Boston Legend." *Whiskey, Women, And...* No. 15, Dec 1985, 28-35.

——. "Through the Years with Preston Sandiford." *Whiskey, Women, And...* No. 15, Dec 1985, 6-11.

——. "Tom Kennedy." *Blues & Rhythm* No. 165, 2001, 10-13.

Kochakian, Dan and Highland Diggs. "Say Hello to Highland Diggs." *Whiskey, Women, And...* No. 17, Spring 1988, 4-11.

Lees, Gene. "Ralph Burns." *Jazzletter*, Apr 2002, 1-8.

Mantler, J. Robert. "Red Beans Boston Style: Wilber Band Knocks Out New England Cats." *The Record Changer*, May 1949, 6-7.

Matthews, Paul B. "Jimmy Woode Interview" (Part 1). *Cadence*, Aug 1997, 10-19.

McKinnon, George E. "Live Jazz? It's Dying Here, Man!" *Boston Globe*, Jan 22, 1962.

McPartland, Marian. "Focus on Toshiko and Charlie Mariano." *Down Beat*, Oct 26, 1961, 18-19.

——. "Just Swinging: Jake Hanna." *Down Beat*, Oct 10, 1963, 16-17.

Merian, Leon, with Bill Bridges. *The Man Behind the Horn*. Bradenton, FL: Diem Publishing Company, 2000.

Morgenstern, Dan "The Poll Winner as Teacher: Alan Dawson." *Down Beat*, Sep 22, 1966, 27-29.

——. "Ready, Willing, and Able: Jaki Byard." *Down Beat*, Oct 21, 1965, 18-19, 38.

Napoleon, Art. "Bunker Hill, Baked Beans and Braff." *Jazz Journal*, Feb 1968, 4-6.

O'Connor, Fr. Norman J. Liner notes for *Now in Vogue* by Teddi King. Storyville Records STLP 903, 1956.

Olsen, Eric. "The Amazing Tom Wilson." http://blogcritics.org/music/article/the-amazing-tom-wilson, Oct 23, 2003. Accessed Jan 8, 2007.

Palmer, Bob. "Sam Rivers: An Artist on an Empty Stage." *Down Beat*, Feb 13, 1975, 12-13, 33.

Santosuosso, Ernie. "Alan Dawson Likes to Play the Drums." *Boston Globe*, Apr 17, 1985.

——. "An All-Star Band of Massachusetts-Born Jazz Musicians." *Boston Globe*, May

19, 1985.

———. "Where Have All the Jazz Clubs Gone" (Part 1). *Boston Globe*, Jul 5, 1987.

———. "Jazz's Gentle Giant Who on the Giant Violin" (John Neves). *Boston Globe*, Oct 11, 1981.

Selchow, Manfred. *Ding! Ding! A biodiscography of Vic Dickenson*. Lübbecke, Germany: Uhle & Kleimann, 1998.

Simosko, Vladimir. *Serge Chaloff, A Musical Biography and Discography*. Lanham, MD: The Scarecrow Press, 1998.

———. Notes and discography for *The Complete Serge Chaloff Sessions*, Mosaic 147, Mosaic Records Inc., 1993.

Stacy, Frank. "No Love Like First Love, Not if It's Sabby's Crew Jumping at the Savoy." *Down Beat*, Apr 1, 1943, 14.

Sulkin, K. C. "Herb Pomeroy." *Down Beat*, Oct 20, 1977, 32-34.

Sunenblick, Robert. Liner notes for *Serge Chaloff – Boston 1950*. Uptown Records UPCD 27.38, 1994.

Tompkins, Les. "The Nat Pierce Story." *Crescendo*, May 1966, 16-17, 34; Jun 1966, 35.

Tynan, John. "The Final Hours of Joe Gordon." *Down Beat*, Jan 30 1964, 13, 33.

Vacca, Richard. "Charlie Mariano and the Birth of Boston Bop." JazzBoston, http://www.jazzboston.org/scene/history-mariano.asp. Jul 2009. Accessed Jul 26, 2009.

———. "Dick Johnson: Never on the Ragged Edge." JazzBoston, http://www.jazzboston.org/scene/history-djohnson.asp. Feb 2010. Accessed Mar 1, 2010.

Van Trikt, Ludwig. "Hal Galper Interview." *Cadence*, Oct-Dec 2007, 18-42.

Vandermark, Stu. "Alan Dawson Interview." *Cadence*, Dec 1983, 5-11, 19.

———. "Jaki Byard Interview." *Cadence*, Mar 1985, 5-9, and Apr 1985, 12-16.

Wein, George. "Dixieland in Today's Jazz." *Jazz Today*, Jan 1957, 18-19, 29, 40.

Wein, George, with Nate Chinen. *Myself Among Others: A Life in Music*. New York: Da Capo Press, 2003.

Welding, Pete. "Portrait of Paul" (Gonsalves). *Down Beat*, Feb 28, 1963, 18-19.

Wetmore, Dick. Interview with Judy Wallace for Simmons College oral history project. Recorded May 26, 1995 at Brewster, MA. The College Archives, Simmons College, Boston MA.

Wilmer, Valerie. "Joe Gordon." *Jazz Journal*, Sep 1960, 4-6.

Wilson, John S. "Can't Type Sabby Lewis; Plays Bit of Everything." *Down Beat*, Jun 3, 1949, 3.

Young, David X. Liner notes for *Nat Pierce Orchestra 1948-1950*, Zim Records Zim-1005, 1977.

The Boston Jazz Chronicles Discography

This is a personal selection of recordings released by Boston musicians active during the years 1946-1962, listed in roughly chronological order.

Recordings go in and out of print constantly, and even the best list goes out of date overnight. For that reason I provide only information about a recording's original release, which is more than enough for an online search.

The 78 Era

Sabby Lewis. *Boston Bounce* (Phoenix Jazz LP 9, 1975) includes some of Sabby's better sides from Crystal-Tone and Continental, including "Minor Mania," "Bottoms Up," "Edna," and the title track. His Mercury, Trison, and ABC-Paramount sides have never been reissued. "Clark's Idea" (Mercury 8134, 1949) and "Blues for All" (Trison TR-688, ca 1951-1952), are favorites.

Fat Man Robinson. Robinson recorded for Motif, Decca, and Regent. "Lavender Coffin," (Motif M2001, 1949), "Sophronia Jones" (Regent 1005, 1949), and "My Bucket's Got a Hole in It" (Decca 48125, 1950) show Robinson at both of his speeds—fast and faster.

Jimmy Tyler. Like Sabby Lewis, Tyler did not record an album under his own name during these years, but between 1952 and 1957, he recorded a series of singles on the Federal label. "Tip Lightly" (12067), "Little Jim" (12080), "Stardust" (12234), and "Pink Clouds" (12275) are representative jazz numbers.

Nat Pierce. Most of the surviving recordings by the Pierce Orchestra or his smaller Boston groups were released on a pair of LPs, *Nat Pierce Orchestra 1948-1950* (Zim Records ZM-1005, 1977) and *The Boston Bust-Out* (Hep 13, about the same time). Hep also released *Boston Bust-Out* as a CD in 1995. One 78 of interest not included on either recording is of Crystal-Tone 524 by Nat Pierce and His Septet, "Pad 458" / "Gale Boogie," from 1949.

Jimmie Martin's Boston Beboppers. I reserve a spot on this list for Martin's band, which recorded "Second Balcony Jump" for Motif in 1949. I've never seen the record, much less heard it, nor have I seen a review of it. But I'm told by people who should know that it exists, so I'll keep looking. And you should look too, because as far as I'm concerned, it's the Holy Grail of Boston jazz.

Nine forgotten ones from the 78 era:

- The Jones Brothers, masters of sophisticated swing: "Ain't She Pretty," Majestic 1038A, 1946.

- Brad Gowans and His New York Nine, "Singin' the Blues" / "Jazz Me Blues," RCA Victor 20-3230, 1946. Jack Lesberg on bass, paired with Dave Tough—his last date.

- Bobby Hackett, "Pennies From Heaven" / "Rose of the Rio Grande," Motif M005, 1949; originally released in 1945 on the Melrose label.

- Paul Clement Trio, "After You've Gone," Crystal-Tone 513, 1949. Dig Lou Magnano's vibes solo!

- Pat Rainey with Clarence Jackson, "Gotta Love You 'Til I Die," Gold Medal GM949, 1949.

- Clarence Jackson, "Poor Butterfly," Crystal-Tone 517, 1949.

- Don Alessi, "The World Is Waiting for the Sunrise," Popular P2-B, 1950, shows a strong Les Paul influence.

- Al Vega Trio, "Cheek to Cheek" / "Makin' Whoopee," Prestige New Jazz 864, 1951.

- Leon Merian, "Turkish Delight," Mood M151, ca. 1952. Just Leon's horn and bongos!

The LP Era

Al Vega. Vega knew drummers. *The Al Vega Trio* (Prestige PRLP 152, 1953) featured Jimmy Zitano, while *All by Al* (Cupid CULP 500, 1958) starred Alan Dawson. The bassists were Jack Lawlor and Alex Cirin.

Charlie Mariano. These records comprise the best surviving statements from the early days of Boston bop. *The New Sounds from Boston,* (Prestige PRLP 130, 1952); *Charlie Mariano's Boston All Stars* (Prestige PRLP 153, 1953), *Charlie Mariano with His Jazz Group* (Imperial IMP3006, 1953), and *The Modern Saxaphone Stylings of Charlie Mariano* (Imperial IMP3007, 1953) mark the progress of the young musicians who found work at the Hi-Hat and Melody Lounge. All have been released on CD.

Dick Wetmore Quartet. Collectors prize *Dick Wetmore* (Bethlehem BCP 1035, 1954 or 1955), which features the compositions of Bob Zieff. Wetmore plays violin exclusively on this recording.

Boots Mussulli. *Kenton Presents Boots Mussulli* (Capitol T6506, 1954) was Mussulli's only date as a leader, as well as Ray Santisi's recording debut.

Dick Twardzik. We have one side of one LP (Russ Freeman has the other) to luxuriate in the genius of Dick Twardzik. *Trio* (Pacific Jazz PJ-1212, 1955) showcases the original voice lost far too soon.

Vic Dickenson. As house trombonist at Storyville Records, Dickenson played on a dozen sessions, from Sidney Bechet's *Jazz at Storyville* (Storyville STLP 301, 1954), the label's first recording, through his own *Vic's Boston Story* (Storyville STLP 920, 1957), its last. *Boston Story* was one of Vic's personal favorites.

Joe Gordon. Nat Hentoff liked Gordon's "comet-like imagination," but what I like about *Introducing Joe Gordon* (EmArcy MG26046, 1955) and his later *Lookin' Good* (Contemporary S7597, 1961) is the intensity Gordon always brought to his playing.

The Stable Quintet. *Jazz in a Stable* (Transition TRLP 1, 1955) did not identify a group leader. It could have been Pomeroy, or Haroutunian, or Santisi, or Neves, or Zitano. Pick your own leader. Or not. Just listen to "Moten Swing" and you won't care about leaders at all.

Teddi King. Teddi King released three LPs on Storyville and four on RCA. Jazz listeners generally prefer the Storyvilles. My picks are *Miss Teddi King* (Storyville STLP 314) and *Now in Vogue* (STLP 903), both from 1955. My choice among the RCAs is *A Girl and Her Songs* (RCA LPM-1454, 1957).

Serge Chaloff. The two great Chaloff LPs, *Boston Blow Up!* (Capitol T6516, 1955) and *Blue Serge* (Capitol T742, 1956) should be on every short list.

Various Artists. *Jazz In Transition* (Transition TRLP 30, 1956), the label's sampler LP, includes the only known recordings of the Dave Coleman Sextet with Dick Wetmore and the Jay Migliori Quintet with Tommy Ball.

Toshiko Akiyoshi. Akiyoshi was finding her own voice when she made *The Toshiko Trio* (STLP 912, 1956) and *Toshiko, Her Trio, Her Quartet* (STLP 918, 1957) for Storyville, with Paul Chambers, Roy Haynes, and Boots Mussulli among others.

Charlene Bartley. My favorite of the Boston pop/jazz singers of the 1950; on *Weekend of a Private Secretary* (RCA Victor LPM-1478, 1957) Bartley is backed by Tito Puente's orchestra and Don Alessi's guitar.

Tom Kennedy. The leader of the Fabulous Four made one Earl Bostic-influenced record, *On His Way* (Golden Crest CR-3011, 1957).

Jimmy Woode. Recorded when he was with the Ellington Orchestra, *The Colorful Strings of Jimmy Woode* (Argo LP 630, 1957) featured Clark Terry as well as another Bostonian, Paul Gonsalves.

The Herb Pomeroy Orchestra. The Stablemates chapter outlines why I think this was Boston's most important band in the fifties, and *Life Is a Many Splendored Gig* (Roulette R52001, 1958) is my preferred recording, with Jaki Byard's arrangements and one of the more powerful brass sections on the planet. *Band in Boston* (United Artists UAL 4015, 1959) marked Pomeroy's band as a writer's band, with Bob Freedman and Neil Bridge featured. *The Band and I* with Irene Kral (United Artists UAL 4016, 1959) pairs a band that never used a singer with a very good one; if this band had liked backing singers, they could have worked for years in Las Vegas.

Crystal Joy. Joy forsakes the piano on *The Fabulous Crystal Joy* (Hanover M8002, 1959) to concentrate on singing, and she does it quite well, despite some weak material. Don Elliott and Hank Jones lead the band.

Don Alessi. Although it's basically a pop record, *Guitar Spectacular* (Tiffany TR2020, 1960) features the nimble Alessi on a set of south-of-the-border tunes.

Bill Berry Quartet. Pianist Bob Freedman's arranging shines on *Jazz and Swinging Percussion* (Directional Sound DS5002, 1961). This recording includes my absolute favorite version of "Old Devil Moon."

Toshiko-Mariano Quartet. Toshiko and Charlie married in 1959 and made *The Toshiko-Mariano Quartet* (Candid CM8012, 1961), which showed them at a critical time, moving away from their bebop roots.

Jaki Byard. Byard did not release a record of his own while living in Boston, but he made two for Prestige New Jazz that still fit into our time period. *Here's Jaki* (New Jazz NJLP 8256, 1961) and *Hi-Fly* (New Jazz NJLP 8273, 1962) showcase the inventive Byard in a pair of trio settings.

Roland Alexander. *Pleasure Bent* (Prestige New Jazz 8267, 1961) is a hard bop date straight out of the Jazz Messengers playbook.

Rocky Boyd. Another hard bop statement, *Ease It* (Jazztime JT001, 1961) is often credited to trumpeter Kenny Dorham rather than the date's leader, the more obscure Boston-born tenor saxophonist Boyd.

Joe Bucci. Organist Joe Bucci and drummer Joe Riddick made *Wild About Basie (*Capitol LP ST1840, 1962) in the Hammond sound's glory years.

Index

CPSIA information can be obtained at www.ICGtesting.com
Printed in the USA
BVOW071846220413

318814BV00002B/19/P